A ...
of Two Halves

Stephen Kelly is the author of a number of books on football and politics, including a biography of Kenny Dalglish. Born on Merseyside, he was educated at Ruskin College, Oxford and the London School of Economics where he studied Soviet history and politics. He later became a political journalist with *Tribune* before joining Granada Television in 1978 where he worked on such programmes as *What the Papers Say*, *World in Action* and *Union World*. Stephen Kelly is now a freelance television producer and writer and is also Teaching Fellow in Media at the University of Huddersfield.

A Game
of Two Halves

Edited by
STEPHEN F. KELLY

Mandarin

For
Judith, Nicolas and Emma

A Mandarin Paperback
A GAME OF TWO HALVES

Originally published in Great Britain 1992
by the Kingswood Press
as *The Kingswood Book of Football*
First published in this form 1993
by Mandarin Paperbacks
an imprint of Reed Consumer Books Ltd
Michelin House, 81 Fulham Road, London SW3 6RB
and Auckland, Melbourne, Singapore and Toronto

Reprinted 1993, 1994 (twice)

Copyright © 1992 The Kingswood Press
Introduction © 1992 Stephen F. Kelly
The author has asserted his moral rights

A CIP catalogue record for this title
is available from the British Library
ISBN 0 7493 1596 2

Printed and bound in Great Britain
by Cox & Wyman Ltd, Reading, Berks

Contents

Part 3 – The Teams

Part 4 – The Players

Part 5 – The Managers

Part 6 – The Fans

Part 7 – The Anguish

Part 8 – The Verse

Acknowledgements

This book was born out of a pre-kick-off discussion with Sandy Ross, then a producer with Granada Television, one Saturday afternoon at Anfield some half a dozen years ago. We were bemoaning the lack of decent writing on football, yet within ten minutes we had already reeled off twenty or so books and articles we fondly remembered. 'Somebody should put all these together in an anthology,' suggested Sandy.

My thanks, then, must go first to Sandy Ross for inspiring the idea, and second to Tony Pocock of the Kingswood Press for his enthusiasm and faith in the project. But most of all my appreciation must go to the many writers and publishers who have kindly given their permission for their writing to be included in my anthology. I should also like to thank the various libraries who have searched so diligently for books on my behalf. And special words of gratitude are due to Tim Bamford for allowing me to browse through his library and borrow from it; to Anthony Rowe Jones for unearthing various books and keeping me endlessly supplied with articles and good meals; to Sue Fisher for her drawings; and to my agent, John Pawsey, for his relentless efforts on my behalf. Finally, especial thanks are due to my wife Judith as well as to Nicholas and Emma who have had to wade through newspapers, books and piles of photocopied articles in my study to get to see me. I trust it was worth it.

Stephen F. Kelly

Introduction

It was George Pimlott who once claimed that the quality of sports writing was inversely proportionate to the size of the ball. Tell that to the Americans! It's a neat notion but, alas, not altogether accurate. If it were, all those books on golf would long ago have edged cricket off the shelf.

Think of fine sportswriting and you automatically plump for cricket – and not without good reason. Books on cricket far outweigh those on any other sport and have attracted some of the finest prose. But why? Perhaps the sedentary nature of the game lends itself to considered words: no rush or panic to put pen to paper. Let the words slowly mature in the mind, roll around the tongue with plenty of time to reflect, rejig or rephrase. Football, on the other hand, is a ninety-minute rush, little time to think or deliberate. It's all over in a flash with maybe half an hour to file that report as you sit in a dreary stand in the back streets of Hartlepool, the wind ripping in from the North Sea, all the lights, bar one, switched off to save the electricity bill.

Boxing, too, is just as hastily compiled with reports filed often directly over the telephone from the ringside. More than one editor has been handed his copy on blood-splattered paper. Yet boxing, like football, has produced some unrivalled prose: think of Mailer, Jack London, McIlvanney, Leibling and Joyce Carol Oates.

The truth is that there is just as much good writing about soccer as about any other sport. Perhaps you have to search harder or maybe it is not quite so evident these days. Certainly there are fewer outlets as more and more papers succumb to sensationalism and write in clichés about the private lives of personalities. And to a large extent the television revolution has ousted the written word from our lives. You only have to visit a high street bookshop to compare the ever increasing number of soccer videos with the declining stacks of football books. However, in spite of television and the tabloids, and the burgeoning shelves of soccer videos, a new generation of soccer writers is striking back. The fanzines, though they may not always contain the finest prose, are surely a reflection of the legions of soccer fans hungry for words.

If television is so powerful, how can a sportswriter hope to compete? How do you attempt to describe that oh-so-casually rolled ball from Pelé to Carlos Alberto in the 1970 World Cup final for Brazil's fourth goal? Or that boyish grin spreading across Kenny Dalglish's face after he had scored the goal at Stamford Bridge that won the first leg of Liverpool's double? Those are true challenges for the wordsmith and the purpose of this anthology is to show that those challenges have been met many times over. There is an abundance of fine writing about football, lucid and uplifting, and with the writers' images often just as strong as those on television.

There are ideologists who have tried to place soccer in a wider forum. Albert Camus, once better known as a goalkeeper, was as erudite when it came to football as he was when he outlined his philosophy of existentialism. 'All that I know most surely about morality and the obligations of man, I owe to sport,' he once wrote; and George Orwell's essay on sport and nationalism is as pertinent today as it was in post-war Europe. He called it 'war minus the shooting'.

In these pages you will find many other writers eloquently reversing the notion that football writing is somehow second-best. This anthology is a celebration of glorious players and outstanding moments. Who could surpass Geoffrey Green on John Charles, Maurice Edelston on the idiosyncratic Len Shackleton or David Miller on the 'Matthews Final'? And like other sports, football, too, has its humour of which there is a fair smattering in this book – Michael Parkinson on Skinner Normanton, Tony Hancock on a possible pools jackpot. The politicians are also represented: oddly all have been Labour MPs, perhaps adding fuel to the theory that sport is class based, soccer to the left, cricket to the right. Whatever, no one, but no one, has ever captured the romance and drama of the FA Cup third round quite like J. P. W. Mallalieu, the one-time Huddersfield MP, with the rain sleeting down across Leeds Road on a bitterly cold January day. And how gratifying to see that fine essayist Michael Foot turning his weighty attentions away from Nye Bevan, Hazlitt and Dean Swift to his other love, Sammy Black of Plymouth Argyle.

But just as football has its highs, so it has its lows, where the drama is not confined solely to the field of play. Who cannot help but feel the pain as H. E. Bates describes the nation's sadness the day Manchester

United died; or the cruel injury to Pelé in the 1966 World Cup? And of course the appalling horror of Hillsborough and Heysel?

Sadly, there was simply not room to include pieces about all the players and teams and the great matches which have distinguished the game over the years. But I hope this selection will not only demonstrate the plenitude of good writing about the sport but will also convey something of the history of a glorious game which has grown out of the fabric of British society to become a world obsession.

Manchester   Stephen F. Kelly
May 1992

PART 1

The Game

The Town Hero

ARNOLD BENNETT

The walls of Bursley called attention, by small blue and red posters
(blue and red being the historic colours of the Bursley Football Club),
to a public meeting, which was to be held in the Town Hall, under
the presidency of the mayor, to consider what steps could be taken to
secure the future of the Bursley Football Club.

There were two 'great' football clubs in the five Towns – Knype,
one of the oldest clubs in England, and Bursley. Both were in the
league, though Knype was in the first division while Bursley was only
in the second. Both were, in fact, limited companies, engaged as much
in the pursuit of dividends as in the practice of the one ancient and
glorious sport which appeals to the reason and the heart of England.
(Neither ever paid a dividend.) Both employed professionals, who, by
a strange chance, were nearly all born in Scotland; and both also
employed trainers who, before an important match, took the teams
off to a hydropathic establishment far, far distant from any public
house. (This was called 'training'.) Now, whereas the Knype Club was
struggling along fairly well, the Bursley Club had come to the end of
its resources. The great football public had practically deserted it. The
explanation, of course, was that Bursley had been losing too many
matches. The great football public had no use for anything but victories. It would treat its players like gods – so long as they won. But
when they happened to lose, the great football public simply sulked.
It did not kick a man that was down; it merely ignored him, well
knowing that the man could not get up without help. It cared nothing
whatever for fidelity, municipal patriotism, fair play, the chances of
war, or dividends on capital. If it could see victories it would pay
sixpence, but it would not pay sixpence to assist at defeats.

Still, when at a special general meeting of the Bursley Football
Club Limited, held at the registered office, the Coffee House, Bursley,
Councillor Barlow JP, Chairman of the Company since the creation
of the League, announced that the Directors had reluctantly come to
the conclusion that they could not conscientiously embark on the

dangerous risks of the approaching season, and that it was the intention of the Directors to wind up the club, in default of adequate public interest – when Bursley read this in the *Signal*, the town was certainly shocked. Was the famous club, then, to disappear for ever, and the football ground to be sold in plots, and the grandstand for firewood? The shock was so severe that the death of Alderman Bloor (none the less a mighty figure in Bursley) had passed as a minor event.

At length a gentleman rose at the back of the hall.

'I don't pretend to be an expert on football,' said he, 'though I think it's a great game, but I should like to say a few words as to this question of new blood.'

The audience craned its neck.

'Will Councillor Machin kindly step up to the platform?' the mayor suggested.

And up Denry stepped.

The thought in every mind was: 'What's he going to do? What's he got up his sleeve – this time?'

'Three cheers for Machin!' people chanted gaily.

'Order!' said the mayor.

Denry faced the audience. He was now accustomed to audiences. He said:

'If I'm not mistaken, one of the greatest modern footballers is a native of this town.'

And scores of voices yelled: 'Ay! Callear! Callear! Greatest centre-forward in England!'

'Yes,' said Denry. 'Callear is the man I mean. Callear left the district, unfortunately for the district, at the age of nineteen for Liverpool. And it was not until after he left that his astounding abilities were perceived. It isn't too much to say that he made the fortune of Liverpool City. And I believe it is the fact that he scored more goals in three seasons than any other player has ever done in the league. Then, York County, which was in a tight place last year, bought him from Liverpool for a high price, and, as all the world knows, Callear had his leg broken in the first match he played for his new club. That just happened to be the ruin of the York club, which is now quite suddenly in bankruptcy (which happily we are not), and which is disposing of its players. Gentlemen, I say that Callear ought to come back to his native town. He is fitter than he ever was, and his proper place is in his native town.'

Loud cheers.

'As captain and centre-forward of the club of the Mother of the

Five Towns, he would be an immense acquisition and attraction, and he would lead us to victory.'

Renewed cheers.

'And how,' demanded Councillor Barlow, jumping up angrily, 'are we to get him back to his precious native town? Councillor Machin admits that he is not an expert on football. It will probably be news to him that Aston Villa have offered £700 to York for the transfer of Callear and Blackburn Rovers have offered £750, and they're fighting it out between 'em. Any gentleman wishing to put down £800 to buy Callear for Bursley?' he sneered. 'I don't mind telling you that steam-engines and the King himself couldn't get Callear into our club.'

'Quite finished?' Denry inquired, still standing. Laughter, over-topped by Councillor Barlow's snort as he sat down.

Denry lifted his voice.

'Mr Callear, will you be good enough to step forward and let us all have a look at you?'

The effect of these apparently simple words surpassed any effect previously obtained by the most complex flights of oratory in that hall. A young, blushing, clumsy, long-limbed, small-bodied giant stumbled along the central aisle and climbed the steps to the platform, where Denry pointed him to a seat. He was recognised by all the true votaries of the game. And everybody said to everybody, 'By Gosh! It's him, right enough. It's Callear!' And a vast astonishment and expectation of good fortune filled the hall. Applause burst forth, and though no one knew what the appearance of Callear signified, the applause continued and waxed.

'Good old Callear!' The hoarse shouts succeeded each other. 'Good old Machin!'

'Anyhow,' said Denry, when the storm was stilled, 'we've got him here, without either steam-engines or His Majesty. Will the Directors of the club accept him?'

'And what about the transfer?' Councillor Barlow demanded.

'Would you accept him and try another season if you could get him free?' Denry retorted.

Councillor Barlow always knew his mind, and was never afraid to let other people share that knowledge.

'Yes,' he said.

'Then I will see that you have the transfer free.'

'But what about York?'

'I have settled with York provisionally,' said Denry. 'That is my affair.

I have returned from York today. Leave all that to me. This town has had many benefactors far more important than myself. But I shall be able to claim this originality: I'm the first to make a present of a live man to the town. Gentleman – Mr Mayor – I venture to call for three cheers for the greatest centre-forward in England, our fellow-townsman.'

The scene, as the *Signal* said, was unique.

And at the Sports Club and the other clubs afterwards, men said to each other: 'No one but him would have thought of bringing Callear over specially and showing him on the platform . . . That's cost him above twopence, that has!'

Two days later a letter appeared in the *Signal* (signed 'Fiat Justitia'), suggesting that Denry, as some reward for his public spirit, ought to be the next mayor of Bursley, in place of Alderman Bloor, deceased. The letter urged that he would make an admirable mayor, the sort of mayor the old town wanted in order to wake it up. And also it pointed out that Denry would be the youngest mayor that Bursley had ever had, and probably the youngest mayor in England that year. The sentiment in the last idea appealed to the town. The town decided that it would positively *like* to have the youngest mayor in England that year. The *Signal* printed dozens of letters on the subject. When the council met, more informally than formally, to choose a chief magistrate in place of the dead alderman, several councillors urged that what Bursley wanted was a young and *popular* mayor. And, in fine, Councillor Barlow was shelved for a year. On the choice being published the entire town said: 'Now we *shall* have a mayorality – and don't you forget it!'

And Denry said to Nellie: 'You'll be mayoress to the youngest mayor, etc., my child. And it's cost me, including hotel and travelling expenses, eight hundred and eleven pounds six and sevenpence.'

from THE CARD *1909*

Playing for Ireland

DANNY BLANCHFLOWER

Last Saturday I trooped victoriously off the field at Wolverhampton, had a quick bath, made a fond farewell to my Tottenham colleagues, and dashed to catch the boat train to Belfast.

It seemed unbelievable to have beaten the Wolves so convincingly on their own ground. On the boat that night I read some of the English papers, and swayed with the glowing tributes: 'Stupendous Spurs' . . . 'Sensational Spurs'. I got carried away to thinking that the least I could expect on arrival at Belfast next morning was a ticker-tape welcome.

It wasn't quite like that. A constant sheet of rain started falling as the boat docked. A little boat steward sprinted up to and past me, stuck his head out of a door, had a squint at the weather and said out loud, addressing nobody in particular, 'Well that's the end of summer'. I looked at the watch on which I had just put back the hour, and marvelled at the precision of his observation.

I went out to the little town of Larne to see my folks; thinking that at least they would have something to say about my soccer feats. But they were full of admiration for some local hero and his devious ways of outwitting the hire purchase companies and local electricity board. . . .

A man of obscure means, he had gone off to Ballymena with his family in his brand new car to see some relatives. There the hire purchase agent had caught up with him, and left the family stranded in the street of Ballymena without the car.

Regardless of his luck, he had charmed some unsuspecting dealer in Ballymena – a notoriously hard place to do business – and had arrived home in Larne that same evening with a different new car. Only to find that his electricity had been cut off. A man of undoubted talents, he had immediately gone to the damned box and, undaunted, connected back the supply.

I began to feel inferior, and got to thinking that perhaps Wolverhampton were nothing and that Tottenham's record-breaking stuff wasn't really so stupendous. Next morning, Monday, I bought all the daily papers to reassure myself. There wasn't a mention of Tottenham. The sports pages were regionalised and full of local stuff. Glenavon had been fined £50 for something and one of their officials had resigned. There was little news about the Northern Ireland team meeting next day to prepare for England.

That afternoon I met a man in Belfast who recognised me. He approached with an aggressive glint in his eye, and I was sure he was going to say something bitter about Spurs. He stuck out his hand. 'Come over to get ready for them?' he said and marched away like he had put me in my proper place.

I mustered with the rest of the Irish team early on Tuesday morning. That little oak of a man, Wilbur Cush, was missing, so were Alfie McMichael and Willie Cunningham. Some of the others had new suits, new styles and stories. They seemed like different people from the ones I had shared glory with over the recent years. But after a few days going through old routines, suffering their partnership at golf, and talking over old times, I began to believe in them once more.

Our training headquarters is at Port Stewart, a north Irish coast resort with golden sands and a timeless air. You can hear the sad, sweet melody of Irish harps in the air and, in the twilight, you can see the 'littlefolk' running about their mischievous business. A few days up here and you can believe anything. The locals charm you with their conviction, the magnitude they can give to things that before have seemed so trivial.

The football talk is about Ireland . . . those gods who have carried the reputation of Ireland to the very pinnacle of the soccer world, those very fellows I met on Tuesday morning and, in a moment's ignorance, probably brought about by the shallow success of eleven wins in a row for Tottenham, somehow doubted.

Right now London doesn't exist for me, and I have not heard of Tottenham.

It is common knowledge that Brazil won the 1958 World Cup. Here you would think that nobody else had played in it but Ireland. In the last thirty years of competition, Ireland have beaten England once, in 1957, at Wembley. The rest of the matches have been *moral* defeats for England. Games in which England have scored as many as ten goals were quickly dismissed by our selectors picking an entirely new team next time out – and somehow proving that England had really scored ten goals against somebody else.

It's been wonderful listening to it all. I feel really confident now about playing England. The rest of the Irish boys feel the same. England haven't got a chance.

As you read this you should know the score. If England have managed to score more goals than us again, take no notice. They have just suffered another moral defeat. And the boys over here will be talking all the more about that game at Wembley in 1957.

from the OBSERVER *1960*

Down in the Dug-out

MICHAEL CALVIN

As they walked slowly, attempting to recognise friends in the stands towering above them, all Woking's players could see was a forest of hands applauding. Goodison Park was theirs, and they didn't want to leave.

When you have changed in dressing-rooms with leaking water pipes, played in front of crowds of less than 150, and been denied the luxury of a professional career, the acclaim of thousands is something to savour. The memory must last a lifetime.

Tim Read, the teenage bank clerk who is serving his goalkeeping apprenticeship in the Vauxhall Opel league, decided he required a memento of the afternoon that justified all the trite, traditional words about the romance of the FA Cup. He raced with unashamed eagerness to swap jerseys with Neville Southall, the boyhood hero who had been his opposite number. 'I don't care if I have to pay for the one I gave him,' he said, pulling the green shirt over his head. 'This is mine, all mine. Brilliant.'

Kevin Ratcliffe, Everton's captain was standing nearby on the touchline, shivering as he waited to offer his congratulations. 'Great this, isn't it?' he said as he watched Woking's slow lap of honour. 'This is what it's all about. Where are they playing next?'

He smiled when informed that Woking would resume normal service at their Kingfield ground tomorrow in a Surrey Demolition and Excavation Cup-tie against Walton and Hersham. It was a reminder of another world.

The worries that had preyed on Geoff Chapple's mind on Friday night, during his four-hour drive to Woking's Southport base, were unnecessary. He knew, as he collected a scarf thrown from the terraces, his team had been the ambassadors he had hoped for.

Success can be as corrosive as failure when it is unexpected. Mr Chapple was concerned about the mercenary instincts of certain players and had been frequently at odds with Fred Callaghan, his coach, during the build-up.

The two men represent different strands of footballing life. Mr Chapple has no experience of the somewhat cynical world of professional football and his ambition is to become chairman of Woking, whom he has managed for six years. He sees beyond the win-and-loss column on a league table. Even minutes before the kick-off of the biggest game of his life he was saying: 'There are more important things than a football match. We've not handled things all that well, to be honest, and certain people have had ideas beyond their station.'

For Mr Callaghan, the former Brentford manager, this was the main chance, the great opportunity to remind chairmen of Football League clubs that he was ready, and able, immediately to abandon his job as a London taxi driver.

On Saturday afternoon their players had been given an inkling of what they were to confront at Goodison. They were introduced to the crowd at Anfield before Liverpool's game against Brighton; the Kop chanted their names and offered Everton ritual abuse in their honour.

They enjoyed the novelty of signing autographs and later in the evening sipped their beer contentedly. They began to be reminded of reality at the team meeting which followed their steak and chips.

'Don't freeze,' implored Mr Chapple. 'But remember this is gonna be one of the biggest things in your lives. It means I've got the easiest job of my career.'

Having kept to an 11 p.m. curfew, grateful that *Match of the Day* kept minds off the diversion of the hotel disco, they claimed to have slept well. But, yesterday morning, captain Adie Cowler and room-mate Bradley Pratt radiated tension.

'This is like waking up on the day of your execution,' mused Pratt over breakfast. Mr Chapple named the team on Southport beach, the players huddled around him in a small, silent semi-circle.

Mr Callaghan was worried that nerves would afflict his young goal-keeper but, once at Goodison Park, he was sidetracked by his sudden celebrity status. 'Forget football,' he said. 'I think I'll become a film star.'

Surprisingly enough, Woking's management team maintained that relaxed approach. The nearest they came to impassioned protest was when they discovered they could barely see the far side of the pitch from the dug-out.

'Get in close. Bite in hard,' were Mr Callaghan's final words before kick-off. However, the part-timers had already determined to do themselves justice.

'They're not overawed are they?' mused Mr Chapple midway through the first half. Mr Callaghan continued to offer comment and criticism at ear-splitting volume, barely taking a breath.

'Sit down, Fred, sit down,' pleaded Mr Chapple who, like the rest of us, had to lean forward on his hands and knees whenever Everton attacked the goal behind which Woking's new found supporters were congregated.

Mr Callaghan railed, to no one in particular, that 'the fitness factor is going to be the difference'. Colin Lippiat, Woking's assistant manager, was more impressed by Everton's technique on the ball.

'They hit the ball well, these pros, don't they?' he reflected. 'So they should, on £2,000 a week,' answered substitute Andy Russell.

Pratt was evidently enjoying himself. 'Why is everyone getting so worked up?' he asked when he came to the visitors' dug-out for a tie-up early in the second half. 'Have a laugh.'

No one felt inclined to take up his offer when Kevin Sheedy scored the decisive goal. The silence lasted for fully thirty seconds.

'We're losing it in midfield,' complained Mr Chapple as Mr Callaghan raged on in his inimitable fashion. 'Biggo's got his blinkers on,' he said after an unsuccessful attempt to bawl advice at the ineffective Mark Biggins.

When Mark Franks was substituted eight minutes from time, he complained: 'Why me? I could have won us the game.'

That disappointment did not last long. The final whistle brought the realisation that, despite losing, they had been a credit to themselves. When, eventually, they returned to the dressing-room, Pratt and Biggins, the subject of Mr Callaghan's wrath, exchanged glances.

'Come on,' they said in unison, 'let's get back out there again.' And with that they were off, to milk the applause just one more time.

from the DAILY TELEGRAPH *January 1991*

Football in Algiers

ALBERT CAMUS

Yes, I played for several years at the University of Algiers. It seems to me like yesterday. But when, in 1940, I put on my boots again, I realised that it was not yesterday. Before the end of the first half, my tongue was hanging out like those *kabyles* dogs that one comes across at two o'clock in the afternoon, at Tizi-Ouzou. It was a long while ago, then, from 1928 onwards, I believe. I made my début with Montpensier sports club. God knows why, since I lived at Belcourt, and the Belcourt-Mustapha team is Gallia-Sports. But I had a friend, a shaggy fellow, who swam in the port with me and played water polo for Montpensier. That's how one's life is determined. Montpensier often played at the Manoeuvre Grounds, for no apparent reason. The ground was bumpier than the shin of a visiting centre-forward at the Alenda Stadium, Oran. I quickly learned that the ball never came to you where you expected it. This helped me in life, above all in the metropolis, where people are not always wholly straightforward. But after a year of bumps and Montpensier, they made me ashamed of myself at the lycée: a 'university man' ought to play for Algiers University, RUA. At this period, the shaggy fellow had gone out of my life. We hadn't quarrelled, it was merely that he now went swimming at Padovani, where the water was not pure. Nor, frankly, were his motives. Personally, I found his motive charming, but she danced badly, which seemed to me insupportable in a woman. It's the man, is it not, who should tread on the toes? The shaggy fellow and I had merely promised to see each other again. But years have gone by. Much later, I frequented the Padovani restaurant (for pure motives) but the shaggy fellow had married his paralytic, who must have forbidden him to bathe, as is the usual practice.

Where was I? Yes, RUA. I was very pleased, the important thing for me being to play. I fretted with impatience from Sunday to Thursday, for training day, and from Thursday to Sunday, match day. So I joined the university men. And there I was, goalkeeper of the junior team. Yes, it all seemed quite easy. But I didn't know that I had just established a bond which would endure for years, embracing every stadium in the Department, and which would never come to an end. I did not know then that twenty years after, in the streets of Paris or even Buenos Aires (yes, it happened to me) the words RUA spoken by a friend I met would make my heart beat again as foolishly as could be. And since I am giving away secrets, I can admit that in Paris, for instance, I go to watch the matches of the Racing Club de Paris, whom I have made my favourites solely because they wear the same jerseys as RUA, blue and white hoops. I must say, too, that Racing has some of the same eccentricities as RUA. It plays 'scientifically', as we say, and scientifically loses matches it should win. It seems that this has changed (so they write to me from Algiers) so far at least as RUA are concerned. It needed to change – but not too much. After all, that was why I loved my team so much, not only for the joy of victory, so wonderful when it is combined with the weariness that follows exertion, but also for the stupid desire to cry on evenings when we had lost.

At full-back I had the Big Fellow – I mean Raymond Couard. He had a tough time of it, if I remember correctly. We used to play hard. Students, their fathers' sons, don't spare themselves. Poor us, in every sense, a good half of us mown down like corn! We had to face up to it. And we had to play 'sportingly', because that was the golden rule of the RUA, and 'strongly', because, when all is said and done, a man is a man. Difficult compromise! This cannot have changed, I am sure. The hardest team was Olympic Hussein Dey. The stadium is beside the cemetery. They made us realise, without mercy, that there was direct access. As for me, poor goalkeeper, they went for my body. Without Roger, I would have suffered. There was Boufarik, too, that great big centre-forward (among ourselves we called him Watermelon) who always came down with all his weight, right on my kidneys, without counting the cost – shin-massage with football boots, shirt pulled back by the hand, knees in the distinguished parts, sandwiches against the post . . . in brief, a scourge. And every time, Watermelon apologised with a 'Sorry, son,' and a Franciscan smile.

I shall stop. I have already exceeded the limits set for me. And then, I am softening. There was good even in Watermelon. Besides, let us be frank, we paid him back. But without cheating, as this was the way we were taught. And at this point, I no longer want to go on jesting. For, after many years in which the world has afforded me many experiences, what I most surely know in the long run about morality and the obligations of men, I owe to sport; I learned it with the RUA. That, in short, is why the RUA cannot die. Let us preserve it. Let us preserve this great and good image of our youth. It will keep watch over yours, as well.

from FRANCE FOOTBALL *1957*

Dressing-room Talk

HUNTER DAVIES

An official appeared and told Bill that the teams were to come out five minutes before the kick-off. The match was to begin at eight-thirty. It was now ten past eight. The room was getting quieter. The time for jokes was over, if you could call them jokes. It had been self-conscious noise and chatter, an outlet for their nerves.

Joe Kinnear was doing exercises on his own in a corner. Outside, inspecting the pitch, he'd been shivering. An evening chill had descended, but he was obviously nervous.

Martin Peters asked Bill if he knew the referee. Bill said he was an East German but he'd forgotten the name, which was unlike Bill Nicholson. Martin thought he might be the same East German ref they'd had in the World Cup. Bill said he didn't think so.

None of the players had programmes. In an English dressing-room the players are always amply supplied with free programmes. I had got one at the hotel from a French journalist. It was a simple four-page, folded-over programme, full of adverts. Leslie Yates, a freelance journalist who writes the Spurs programmes, had come specially to Nantes so that his sixteen-page Spurs programme would be full of information about the Nantes players and club. I handed the Nantes programme to Bill. No, it wasn't a ref he knew.

Martin Peters went into the shower room with a ball and started banging it back and forward against the walls. Eddie Baily moved on from Perryman's thighs to rubbing Gilzean's chest. Johnny Wallis was strapping up ankles. Mike England was putting a new strip of elasto-plast on a cut on his forehead. Phil Beal and Mullery were rubbing vaseline on their faces – to stop the sweat going into their eyes during the match. Bill Nicholson went out of the room again. He told Eddie to lock it and let no one in. He'd knock three times to get back. The room was hot and fetid with embrocation. It was more of a crowded concrete cavern than a dressing-room, with no direct light and no ventilation, just a couple of small holes in one corner of the ceiling.

Bill came back, almost bursting the door down in his rage, swearing and cursing. 'They've changed their bloody strip. They told me last week they'd play in yellow. They always play in yellow. That's why they're called the bloody canaries.'

The players tried to look equally concerned and serious. A few joined in the curses, pleased to have something to vent their anger on, an outside body they could all have a go at. Mullery asked why they'd changed their minds.

'For the bloody French TV,' said Nicholson. 'The TV want them to play in green.'

Everyone groaned even louder this time, all cursing TV, saying you should never do anything for those TV cunts. I couldn't see what all the fuss was about. As Spurs were going to play in white, their normal colour, it could make no difference if Nantes played in green as opposed to their normal yellow.

'Have you brought any others,' said Nicholson to Johnny Wallis. 'Pat will have to get changed.'

Pat was out at the lavatory. I'd forgotten he always plays in a green jumper. Someone shouted down the corridor for him. When he came back, he was already wearing green. He looked annoyed, when he heard what had happened. Roger handed him a red shirt, to try it on, but Pat said it was OK. He went to his corner and searched around till he found a yellow shirt. He said that would do. Bill went to wash his hands.

Everyone calmed down again, the curses dying out as the talking stopped once again and only the stamping of boots could be heard and the stretching of arms and legs in last-minute exercises. Eddie Baily called out the time – fifteen minutes to go. There was a knock at the door and the referee came in, very quickly, catching everyone by surprise. He tapped Pat on the shoulder and pointed to his boots. Pat turned them over to be inspected. He moved on as Pat was holding up his boots, going round the room so quickly that he hardly seemed to look at more than one pair of boots. Bill tried to grab him as he came round the room and was going out of the door.

'They've changed their shirts,' began Bill. 'It means our goalie is now in yellow, will that be . . .'

But the ref had gone, pushing straight past Nicholson, ignoring him. Bill made a face when he'd gone. The players whistled. 'Not much of an inspection that,' said someone.

'East German, eh,' said Eddie. 'I wonder if he was a POW in the . . .' But he tailed off in mid-sentence, unable to think of a suitable insult.

Bill went to the middle of the room and began addressing his players. They sat silently, each of them taut and gleaming, ready for action. Bill had his head bowed and was moving his hands and arms nervously, walking back and forwards, talking loudly and urgently. There was a feeling of embarrassment, as if the players felt worried on his behalf. They were already completely keyed up. Their minds were on the match. There was only three minutes to go. Nothing he could say now could make much difference, not at this late stage.

'The last time we played in France,' began Bill, 'I know you all remember it. You know what happened. I don't have to go over it. We thought we'd have it easy. But we didn't, did we. I don't want a repeat of that. I want you to go hard, but keep your feet down. Even one foot off the ground and you'll be for it. Don't give that referee any excuses.'

The last time in France had been four years ago at Lyons. Olympique Lyonnais had beaten Spurs 1–0 and went on to knock them out of Europe. That was the night that Mullery was sent off, a night not to remember.

Bill went over a few more points, then finished suddenly. It was as if all he'd been doing was nervously clearing his throat, thinking aloud. His mind was seething with details but he knew that it was too late. He stood in silence, the players watching.

'Now no arguing with the ref either,' said Mullery, taking over the silence, becoming keen and captain-like, clapping his hands, moving forward so everyone could see him. 'We've got to go very hard for the first ten minutes. Don't let them get settled. *Hard* all the time. OK lads.'

They were sitting with their heads bowed. A couple of the reserves exchanged looks as Mullery spoke, quickly, and then looked away. All five reserves were in bulky blue canvas track suits – Roger Morgan, Collins, Daines, Ray Evans and John Pratt. They looked like convicts in a work party.

'One minute to go,' said Eddie Baily. Nobody spoke. It was now like a death cell. As if they were all going out to an execution.

'If you beat this lot,' said Eddie, 'you'll be in the last sixteen. Then after that you'll be in the last sixty-four.'

He was trying to reduce the tension, but as always they were ignoring Eddie's jokes.

'Right, bayonets on,' shouted Eddie as a whistle went in the corridor. 'Over the top. Let's have you!'

They all stood up, stamping their feet. Bill had been busily tidying up the already tidy room as Eddie had been joking. He suddenly beamed and looked expansive and benevolent. As usual, he patted them on the back and wished each one by name the best of luck. Then he went to the shower room where he washed his hands yet again and put on his jacket. He helped Eddie to lock the dressing-room door and then followed the players into the tunnel where they were waiting, lined up, just below the entrance. There was a roar as both teams went out together and a blaze of fireworks lit up the night sky.

from THE GLORY GAME *1972*

A Footballer's Lot

HUNTER DAVIES

I started the season with the idea that being a footballer must be a good life. How lovely to be a hero. How wrong I was.

Footballers are worth every penny they can get. When it comes to the crunch, every player, however big a star, is disposable, as we have seen. There's an old joke in football about the manager of a fourth division club, pushing out his humble team for a cup match against a big first division club. 'Go out there lads and do your best,' he exhorts them. 'So I can get enough money to replace you.'

Footballers are the game's fodder, human sacrifices that are thrown without sentiment or apologies into the battlefield. The pressures only cause concern if they impair their powers. Physical injuries, like groin strains, have got to be endured. If they get too bad, out you go. Eddie Baily's continual stream of wartime metaphors made me think of the First World War trenches, with the generals sending out miles of bodies, straight into the graveyards.

It's been interesting to see how the players react to all the pressures. They experience in extremis many of the pressures of the world today. Every occupation has its rat race, but football is one of the few where the race can end every week. From the minute they become full-time footballers at fifteen they're being tested, week in and week out. *No one* at any time is ever secure.

It's been interesting to see their group rituals, at home and at the club. Being accepted, being part of the gang, doing the right thing, being smart but not flash, is very important to them all. When you belong, you really belong. When you're out, you become a pariah.

I don't know how Mullery or Joe Kinnear or Tony Want or Ray Evans survived the season without a nervous breakdown. I don't know how Ralph Coates didn't go back on sleeping pills or come out in strange lumps the way he'd done at Burnley. Footballers are chosen for their character, as we've been told a hundred times, so perhaps the weakest are weeded out from the beginning. It's not just the best footballers who survive but the ones with the strongest nervous systems.

Yet who would be a manager? They have complete power over their charges, but when it really matters they're helpless. Most players do forget, once they're out there playing, but a manager has few releases, few safety valves. Their agony is constant.

The public of course see it as a glamorous life. They're not interested in the fact that it's been a hard season. Only in the trophies. Clubs these days are always going on about the number of matches, but the public don't really care. I didn't either, not until I put in ten thousand hard miles, dragging round Europe. Altogether, Spurs spent five weeks of last season just hanging round strange hotels. My metabolism never got used to it. Putting in two days suspended in limbo in an Italian hotel was bad enough, but having to play before seventy thousand screaming Italians at the end of it would have turned me into a jibbering wreck.

The public don't make allowances, naturally enough. They don't see all the tensions behind the scenes. Like the manager and his board, they want success, not excuses.

The glamour is there, on the outside anyway. The heroes are idolised. The fans thrill to their skills, there is big money to be earned. But inside the club, a player is only as good as his last game. Inside the club, they lead regimented lives, completely at the power of a manager who can ordain their every movement and trained by ex-players whose own playing lives were light years away from the conditions of today. Internally, they're despised more often than admired, criticised for being soft, accused of being spoiled.

At the same time, the old timers feel sorry for today's players' apparent lack of enjoyment. I've no doubt the dressing-room at Spurs is little different from any other big club. Joe Mercer of Manchester City says he often gets the feeling that his players are going off to Vietnam, not to play a game of football.

But each and every player comes willingly to the scaffold, pushing and fighting to be at the front. They know the rules and the pitfalls. They know they'll be sacrificed without a moment's hesitation. They know the physical strains, the disciplined life they'll have to lead and the arthritic middle age that lies ahead. To a man, they haven't the slightest regret. They're almost childlike in their gratitude for what football's done for them.

The alternative for most of them would have been the factory floor or the building site. Thanks to football, they're special.

'I'm glad the end didn't come for me last season,' says Alan Mullery. 'I wouldn't have liked to have gone out like that. In the end I was able to withdraw from the England party. They didn't chuck me out. I've been very very lucky. I've had thirteen good years. I've had all the good times. I've seen the world. I'd have been nobody, but for football.'

from THE GLORY GAME *1972*

More Than Just a Game

PETE DAVIES

I asked Jon Smith, at the end of a long interview, whether there was anything else he'd like to tell me. In PR terms, you could say the answer scored a goal at both ends.

'I'll tell you what might be fun for you. Why don't you come in and watch us if we get one of the FA Cup final pools. It's a bit of an obscene procedure, really. Well, not obscene – but it's a money-grabbing exercise. Unlike the England players' pool, which I can justify from here to kingdom come – but the Cup final pools, the players get to Wembley and they say, right, we've got three weeks. We're hot property. So it's wham bam, thank you ma'am, earn as much as you can. Then go out and spend it . . . that's good fun.

'And the only other thing I'd like to say is that a lot – not a lot, a percentage – a percentage of what we do with the England team, it goes back to good causes, like leukaemia research. A reasonable percentage. And then the players outside of that, they do an awful lot more themselves. It's never recognised, no one asks it to be – but look at Steve McMahon, after Hillsborough. He talked a kid out of a coma; he sat with him for four hours, and talked him out of a coma. And it's hard . . . McMahon's a tough nut, but he just broke down. And no one ever writes about that.'

At Anfield a few days later, McMahon said, yes, he'd done that. He said, 'We still go out with the families. They come up to my house, we go to theirs, we go out of an evening for a meal together – so I've kept in touch with them. Because I think it's important – and they're nice people. It's not as if . . . I'm not doing it because I feel as though I have to. I'm doing it because I want to – and because they're nice people.'

I liked Steve McMahon – he didn't have an ounce of bullshit about him. When I asked him where confidence came from, he looked at me like I was a complete idiot.

'From winning games.'

And he said about his job, 'Obviously we're lucky people. Since I was a kid, the only thing I ever wanted to do was play football. For me to play football, and make a good living at it – it's a bit special. And now, to be considered for a place at the World Cup . . . it's more than I ever thought of.'

Gary Lineker and Peter Beardsley drove down the M4 to Wembley – one in a Jaguar, the other in a Mercedes – a little like the way they played football together. They went extremely fast, jockeying smoothly back and forth – and everyone else on the road just seemed to melt out of the way.

Footballers have a sense of balance about them, an ease of movement that can make you feel helplessly clumsy. Now it seemed they even drove that way. But when you drive a Jaguar, that probably helps.

It was the eve of the Brazil game; I asked Lineker about all the media fuss and the sponsorship palaver.

He said, 'This is a bit of an exception, to be honest, it's not usually this busy. And anyway it's part and parcel; you tend to get used to it.'

I said they seemed sometimes to answer questions on automatic.

'Yeah, but you get asked the same things, time and time again. So you get to the stage where you don't repeat basically the same answer, but exactly the same answer. I've definitely thought, I've said this before – particularly about the World Cup. People ask, who d'you fancy? So you say you fancy everybody, you try to be polite about everybody – and that must have been asked me by forty different people, from forty different countries. So it becomes a routine. But it's the TV you have to get right – because invariably if it's press, they'll put it in their own words anyway.'

So did it bother him?

'Gets a bit boring sometimes. We had training yesterday, medical tests, signed two hundred balls, did fourteen different interviews . . . without being rude, you do try and cut them down a little bit. Because you've got other things to do. Yesterday afternoon, say, I had to see a girl I'd written to a couple of times, she's got leukaemia, and I had tea with her – she's very ill, the bone marrow transplant didn't take . . . that's the other side of things. Hopefully, in this particular case, she'll be OK, she'll get through it.

'A few weeks ago I went to see a little kid in hospital, he'd had a couple of heart operations, and he was going in for another one – and they said he was a big fan, it might cheer him up. So I went to see him before the operation. He seemed a really nice little kid – he was only about seven and he was dead enthusiastic, good-looking kid as well. I said I'd come back after the operation, so I did – and things hadn't gone too well, he was on a life support thing, and he was . . . he came round a little bit, sort of saw me, squeezed my hand. I said I'd come back later, when he came out of that. I went back a week later, and he was still in there. Then a couple of days later I got a call to say he'd died. Things like that, it's upsetting. You feel for the parents.

'But a lot of players do their fair share. Because if you can't be bothered to do that sort of thing for people, when you're so lucky yourself . . .'

Earlier in the season, Trevor Francis at QPR had fined one of his players £1,200 for going to his wife's bedside for the delivery of their child, rather than turning up for a match.

Bobby Robson didn't think too much of that – what use was the player to you anyhow, if his mind wasn't on it? Four years earlier, Francis had complained in the papers that Robson had betrayed him when he took Beardsley to Mexico instead of Francis.

Robson said, with some satisfaction, 'He's learning about management now, isn't he? He just got the sack.'

And the player – Martin Allen – said, 'The manager told me football
is my life. Go and tell that to my cousin Paul, whose son had a brain
tumour. That is life – not ninety minutes on a Saturday afternoon.'

from ALL PLAYED OUT *1990*

Boys in the Park

TERENCE DELANEY

If you love the game, you must pause to watch the small boys – in
parks and playgrounds, or in the back streets of cities. In England,
under grey sky, on scarred grass or damp asphalt, it is a vigorous,
buffeting game with hard shots, theatrical, headlong saves, hard
tackles, and shoulder charges. The players surge about, calling for
passes, shouting protests or instructions; they are flushed and animated, they fall and scramble up again and, from time to time, one
bends to dab carefully a grazed knee.

In Italy, perhaps in a quiet square in Milan, or on the hard sand of
a Mediterranean beach, you lean back in the shade to watch the boys.
It is quieter. If there are about half-a-dozen boys, they stand in a wide
ring; the lighter ball is in the air a good deal, bounced on the instep,
on the knee or on the head; it rolls or bounces, spinning from one to
another; they leap to reach it, topple back for overhead kicks but they
do not interfere with each other much. While one has it, the others
wait or, if impatient, call for their turn. Their legs are bare and their
shoes are light and they move consciously, knowing you are watching.

Climate, temperament, history – all these contribute to style, which
is an aspect of character, individual or national.

from the OFFICIAL FOOTBALL ASSOCIATION YEARBOOK *1963*

Footballers at War

PETER DOHERTY

When the prime minister announced that we were at war on that sunny September morning in 1939, most people realised that the whole fabric of their lives would probably be changed – and changed violently. For professional footballers, the cleavage was a harsh one; contracts were automatically torn up, and for those players who had families to support and no savings to fall back on, the immediate prospect was grave. It was a grim lesson for the professionals, and one that some of us took to heart very seriously. Without a scrap of consideration or sentiment, our means of livelihood were simply jettisoned, and we were left to find fresh ones as best we could.

Obviously, the first thing to do was to find a job. The football moguls had decided that the game, with its value as a morale-stiffener, was to go on. But the 30s. a match which players were to receive was not much use to men with families; when the emergency plans were drawn up, that point must have been studiously overlooked.

I applied to Leyland Motors and Vickers Armstrong, Manchester, for work, but without success. Then a friend in Scotland offered me a job at Greenock, and I accepted. My conscience was perfectly clear. As my contract had been broken, I considered myself a free agent, and perfectly at liberty to find work where I chose. Football was clearly a secondary consideration, and my family responsibilities were my main concern. I would no longer be available for City, and I informed the club to this effect.

Mr Smith, the City chairman, was not quite so sympathetic as he had been when I signed. During the interval in my next game at Maine Road, he called me on one side.

'I have been informed by Mr Wild that you are going to Scotland,' he said. 'Is that true?'

I replied that it was.

'I don't want you to be under any misapprehension,' he went on, 'but you won't play any football in Scotland.'

Because I couldn't turn out for City, I was to be barred from playing with a Scottish club on free Saturday afternoons! We seemed to be getting all the kicks and none of the ha'pence, and I told the chairman so. Tempers became frayed, and the argument was only cut short when the game restarted.

Afterwards, Mr Smith sent for me again. I had been with City for three and a half seasons, he pointed out, and would shortly be due for a benefit. He urged me, in the light of this fact, to reconsider my decision. For a long time we discussed the matter from every possible angle, and at last I agreed to stay, telephoning my friend in Greenock to tell him that I would not be taking up the job.

I had to have work of some sort, however, and Mr Walter Smith, a City director, very kindly found me a job as a chauffeur. My boss was Mr Russell, a big Manchester business man, who treated me exceptionally well. But my heart wasn't in the job, and I was far from happy. After only a day or so I apologised to my employer for what seemed to be ingratitude, and gave it up. With several Blackpool players, I went to the ordnance factory at Risley, near Warrington, and found work there.

I was still playing for City, but was feeling far from settled, and early in 1940 I decided to volunteer for the RAF, rather than wait to be called up. The future was hopelessly insecure, and there seemed to be little point in hanging on in a civilian job until my age-group came along. Most of the boys were joining up, and special efforts were being made at that time to recruit professional footballers as physical training instructors.

With hundreds of other ex-civilians, I was kitted-out at Uxbridge, and in bright, unspoilt blue, we lined up in column of route to march to the station, where we were to entrain for Morecambe. With white, bulging kitbags perched uncertainly on our shoulders, we set off, a shuffling, rather awe-stricken crowd of rookies. Halfway to the station, I threw the column into complete disarray; my kitbag dropped, and as I groped in the roadway for it I was very nearly trampled to death by scores of heavy new boots!

At Morecambe we were marched and drilled for weeks, until gradually we began to bear some slight resemblance to trained airmen. I was very slow in picking it all up, though. Rushing to join the squad at arms drill one day, I found myself approaching an officer with a rifle in my hand, and not the faintest recollection of how to salute with arms! Panic seized me, and I tried to sidle past unobserved. But a voice charged with a mixture of rage and authority hauled me back, and I was given the first 'dressing-down' of my Service career.

The PT course, for which I returned to Uxbridge, lasted five weeks, and to anyone except a trained gymnast they were five weeks of intense and often agonising physical effort. There were many other footballers on the course, including Ted Drake and Kirchen of Arsenal, Barkas and Bray of Manchester City, and Sam Bartram of Charlton Athletic, and the managers and officials of southern clubs were prowling round the school continually, on the look-out for guest players. I played two or three games with Brentford before the joyful day when the course ended, and we passed out as qualified instructors. It was grand to renew acquaintanceship with Mr Curtis, the Brentford manager, and silvery-haired Bob Kane, that grand old man of football, who has trained the team for years, and who looks after the players like a father.

More courses in musketry and gas followed at Wilmslow, and then I was posted to Skegness to take up physical training duties with recruits. I turned out for City whenever possible, but being stationed on the east coast made travelling very difficult, and it was often impossible for me to get over to Lancashire. I played several games with Lincoln City, and then had a short and very happy association with Grimsby Town.

Grimsby is a grand club. There's a thoroughly contented playing-staff at Blundell Park, and men who have seen long service there, such as Hodgson, Vincent, Tweedy and Betmead, will tell you that a considerate, helpful management is the chief reason. The chairman, Mr Pearce, the directors, and Mr Billy Spencer, the manager, are always ready to show a sympathetic interest in a player's personal problems, as well as his football ability; and very few men who once settle down at Blundell Park are eager to leave. The name of Grimsby Town FC is respected amongst footballers throughout the country, and deservedly so. It is a fine club, and worthy of better support from the Grimsby public.

I still managed to make occasional appearances for City, and one week I wired Mr Wild to say I had an unexpected short leave, and would be available on the Saturday, requesting him to send instructions to my Blackpool home. When I arrived there, I found a letter from the manager informing me that the team had been selected, and that Malam had been chosen as inside-left. I could understand this, of course, as Malam was available every week, and I was not. What annoyed me was the fact that after a long, overnight journey, made with the specific intention of playing, no assistance was given to me in the matter of expenses. It was a thoughtless omission, and one that rankled in my mind for a long time. I kept Mr Wild's letter, and to this day it has a place amongst my soccer mementoes.

It might be thought that incidents such as this are small and petty, and not worth worrying about. The reverse is true. When they happen often, a player's loyalty to his club is sapped. Considerate treatment very rarely fails to make a man contented, whether he is a footballer or a bank clerk; but a succession of seemingly trivial annoyances can cause him to nurse a grievance and look round for a change.

As I had a free weekend, I went along to Bloomfield Road to watch Blackpool play Liverpool. Berry Nieuwenhuys, Liverpool's South African winger, who now holds a golfing appointment in the Union, had a chat with me before the game, and a few minutes later Mr George Kay, the Liverpool manager, came along to ask me if I would play. I agreed, and turned out for Liverpool; but I learnt afterwards that George Ainsley, the Leeds United forward, had been standing by to play, and had been left out of the team at the last moment on my account. It was an unfortunate misunderstanding, and I sincerely regretted it. During the war, I was often asked to play for clubs at short notice, and sometimes it was impossible to ascertain whether I was keeping another man out.

Many teams carried so many guests during those hectic years that they were hardly recognisable. Clubs within reasonable distance of camps and Service depots usually invited players who were stationed there to turn out for them, and the club programmes often made strange reading. At one time I made five or six appearances for different league clubs in the space of little over a week!

The guesting system sometimes caused friction between clubs and players, and it was mainly responsible for relations between Manchester City and myself becoming strained once again. I was frequently asked by the press for a statement on the matter, and I usually replied by laying the blame on the war, and the way in which it had changed people's lives; and to the hundreds of City fans who were perplexed over the whole business, and who wrote to me asking for facts, I gave a similar reply. Fuller explanations, of course, were impossible at the time.

The root of the trouble at this stage was my objection to being ordered to play for certain clubs. Whilst at Skegness, I was posted to the Midlands on a course, and on the Saturday following my arrival, I fulfilled a promise I had made to Dave Mason, one of the staff instructors, and played for Walsall. Percy Dickie of Blackburn Rovers and Ivor Powell of Queen's Park Rangers were also on the course, and they, too, played for the third division club. West Bromwich Albion, however, had been in touch with City, asking for permission to include me in their team (without, of course, consulting me), and I eventually received instructions from Maine Road to turn out for them. I wired back, telling City of my promise to Walsall, and asking them to reconsider their decision. The reply, however, merely underlined their original instructions, and I had, therefore, to play for West Brom.

I was annoyed at City's uncompromising attitude. Once again, in spite of the fact that all contracts had been cancelled, I was receiving orders as if I were a full-time player getting a normal weekly wage. I hadn't the slightest objection to playing for West Brom., and I told Mr Everiss, the secretary, so. But I did think I should have some say in the matter of the clubs for whom I played.

It wasn't always easy to get a game at all. Every City player who guested for another club had to be insured by that club according to the value set upon him by City. In my case, the insurance was fairly high, and many clubs were reluctant to pay it. The choice was therefore limited, and offers of games were sometimes very scarce indeed. I was naturally keen to play whenever the opportunity arose; but I resented dictation from my club. In view of the scrapped contracts, I didn't consider it justified.

from SPOTLIGHT ON FOOTBALL *1947*

Team Fun

EAMON DUNPHY

Today we went to Chadwell Heath, West Ham's training ground, to play them. Chadwell Heath is grey and unwelcoming. It was a cold day, shades of Carlisle in winter. West Ham are talked about as a coming team. Last season they finished seventh in the first division. Some people expect them to challenge seriously for honours this year.

It should be a good test for us – a mock battle with serious undertones. We weren't going scalp hunting, there was no desire to kick people, but we would be tight, disciplined. After all there were only four days to go.

There was a small group looking on. Mostly reserves and injured players, including Pop Robson and John McDowell. Bobby Moore is conspicuous by his absence. Which provides us with a real talking point. He is the dominant figure at West Ham: captain of the club, and of England. Where is he today? It turns out that he has gone to Crystal Palace Sports Centre to compete in a TV-sponsored pentathlon against Jackie Stewart, Tony Jacklin, Barry John and other leading sportsmen. We are amazed, and yet how typical of West Ham it seems. Here they are four days before the start of the season, their big season, going into a crucial practice game without their leading player. Staggering that he should choose to be absent, crazy that Ron Greenwood should allow it.

It wouldn't happen at many clubs. Certainly not at Leeds or Liverpool. But here it was almost predictable, a confirmation of all the suspicions one had felt about the club.

They have always had talented players. Aristocratic, some say, yet in spite of an occasional flourish on special days, they have never had the commitments necessary to win a league title.

To be sure, they have had some of the aristocrats' qualities: indolence, an unwillingness to sweat, a reluctance to soil their hands.

In a way they were con-men. Like all good con artists they had a certain style. Their play had a smooth, slick quality; it was seductive. Aficionados often purred at the sight of the Hammers, and denounced football for denying the game's prizes to the purists they saw in West Ham.

It was true they had talent, but so did Leeds and Liverpool. They are the real contenders, the true aristocrats. What West Ham lack are values. When the challenge came, their lack of integrity left them at the mercy of the better-prepared, the people who worked at the game.

To Millwall, today's game had meaning. It soon became clear that to West Ham it was a joke. They strolled around, stockings down around their ankles, disdainful. The 'in' thing that afternoon was the curved pass with the outside of the foot. No simple straightforward pass would soil their boots. For a moment I questioned our attitude. Were we taking it too seriously?

Some of their players too seemed inhibited. Patsy Holland, Ted MacDougall, Billy Bonds. Good, honest and talented pros. Bonds played in the back four, because of Moore's absence. I wondered what he thought. Poor Ted MacDougall looked really fed up. He shrugged his shoulders a lot. How could he possibly justify his huge transfer fee among this lot? Of course they would say that he wasn't sophisticated enough for the Hammers. He couldn't do pretty tricks with the ball, or curved passes with the outside of his boot.

We beat them easily, but there was little satisfaction in doing so. Towards the end of the game Lawrie ran alongside the touchline, urging us on. 'Come on, Eamon, son, keep it going, keep going.'

'It's difficult, Lawrie,' I yelled back, 'when you can't stop laughing.'

Afterwards Ron Greenwood stuck his head into the dressing-room. 'All the best for the season, lads,' he said. 'I hope you come up and we stay up.'

I felt he was only half joking. I felt sorry for him.

from ONLY A GAME *1974*

Out of the East

JOHN FAIRGRIEVE

It has long been accepted, by men of perception, that those who follow such clubs as Hearts, Partick Thistle and Queen's Park are of a special breed. It is easy, after all, to follow the likes of Celtic and Rangers, who have a distasteful habit of winning things just about every year. It is also easy to support the smaller outfits, which never do win anything, and are not expected to do so; in this, geography is usually the deciding factor.

But while I can, in all honesty, speak with no great authority as to what constitutes a Partick or Queen's supporter, there are very few around able to give me any lessons so far as Hearts are concerned.

Heredity matters. So does environment, naturally. Then there is a long apprenticeship, during which one goes through the fire. Hearts always have great expectations, which, with crushing inevitability, fall in ruins, usually just before or just after the New Year.

Occasionally, very occasionally, a cup or a title does come to Tyne-castle, and belief is temporarily suspended. When they were scoring all those goals in the late 1950s, we celebrated well enough, but, some-how, deep down, there was this strange disappointment. It was as if we feared Hearts might become mere pot-hunters, like the people at Ibrox and Parkhead. Soon enough, however, everything returned to normal, and we were able to relax.

Yet had we not gone through that ordeal of apprenticeship in the art of supporting a great club and a team barely above average, we could not have survived. A civilised philosophy has to be developed in that time. Many fall by the wayside. Some even go to Easter Road, and if, suitably ashamed, they come creeping back later to their accustomed spot, are forgiven but not forgotten. They have not failed: nor have they passed, with flying colours. They are flawed. We do not ostracise them, as I have said, for we are kindly men, but we remember.

There were three reasons why I became a Hearts fan . . . and why I achieved a pass mark that can only be described as triumphant. One was my maternal grandfather, one was my father, and the other was Tommy Walker. Since I first saw Tommy play, I think it must have been in 1938, it has been cautiously suggested to me, now and again, that maybe he wasn't the best inside-forward of them all, and that's when my mind closes. I listen courteously, then change the subject, which is not worthy of intelligent discussion. I take my legends seriously and, anyway, that was a legend with plenty of basis in truth.

When he was appointed manager of Hearts in the middle 1950s, the club reached its pinnacle. We had our share of the goodies, then let others take their turn with good grace. But on 28 September 1966, Hearts sacked Tommy Walker. That was a bad day.

I was in Glasgow at the time, and saw the teasing placard for an evening newspaper. 'Tommy Walker shock', it said. The words I wrote that evening were full of rage and sorrow. My refuge was the thought that those who had done such a thing were mere stewards, and rotten ones, at that. They had no right to be where they were, no right at all. Who the hell did they think they were?

Tommy Walker telephoned, and said thanks, but he wouldn't say a word of criticism about the board. I thought about that, too, and realised that this was the last, and cruellest exam of the apprenticeship.

He is on the board himself now but, of course, even before he was recalled, I was back in the fold. Indeed I had never left, not truly. Well, you don't, do you?

from WE'LL SUPPORT YOU EVERMORE *1976*

Hancock's Finest Half Hour

RAY GALTON and ALAN SIMPSON

It is Saturday evening and TONY HANCOCK and SID JAMES are sweating on the possibility of TONY scooping the pools. TONY has seven draws on his coupon and his fortunes depend on a late kick-off fixture at Stamford Bridge between Chelsea and East Cheam.

TONY: What's the time?

SID: Ten past five.

TONY: Oh this is impossible. It's dark outside. They can't play in this. They won't be able to see where they're going. They'll have to have little lamps strapped to their heads ... that's no way to play a game. How are they expected to head a ball like that?

SID: They play under floodlights, you great twit.

TONY: That's unreliable for a start. Get a fuse for a couple of minutes ... wallop, ten goals. The goalie hasn't got a chance. Who's in goal for East Cheam, anyway? (SID *refers to the paper.*)

SID: Um ... Chalky White.

TONY: Chalky White. Oh well, we've had it. We won't get a draw with him between the sticks. Biggest score in history. Ninety minutes of kick-offs and goals. He's useless, that man. He stands there leaning up against the goalpost measuring himself. He can't see what he's doing, that's his trouble. Not only can't he see them coming – he has a job finding them once they're in. Wandering about the back of the net poking around here and there ... he kicked his hat out twice last week. Who else have they got out?

SID: Mel Pritchard centre-forward.

TONY: Mel Pritchard. There's a fine example of athletic prowess for you. Runs out on to the field and he's out of breath. I saw him play his first match. He kicked off and had to have a cartilage operation. Chelsea will murder that lot.

SID: What did you put them down for a draw for?

TONY: Because they're match number three, my brother-in-law's birthday. Mel Pritchard, what a load of old rubbish. I suppose he'll be playing in slippers again; his corns'll be playing him up.

SID: What do you know about it, going on there as if you're an expert.

TONY: Oh come now, Sidney, if anybody is entitled to air his opinions on football it's me. The experience I've had. Playing for years I was . . . you talk to me. Schoolboy International, 1936 . . . Mr Magic, the Wizard of Dribble. Lovely pair of feet I had . . . both pointing in opposite directions . . . nobody knew which way I was going. I would have been playing still but I had to give it up.

SID: What, did you get injured?

TONY: No, no. It was when they did away with the long shorts . . . we had to show our knees, well I wasn't having that . . . fifty thousand people laughing their heads off . . . it wasn't worth twenty quid a week. Did I ever tell you about the highlight of my career?

SID: No, but you're going to, aren't you?

TONY: Picture the scene . . . Wembley Stadium, 1939 . . . packed to capacity . . . Duke of Rutland in the box, the cup in front of him . . . the bloke in the white suit, up on the rostrum bawling his lungs out . . . Land of Hope and Glory'. Then we appeared. Ninety thousand throats roaring a welcome, ninety thousand pairs of eyes all on me . . . will he do it again . . . will he get another hat-trick in the first five minutes? Will he score from the halfway line with a double back flip overhead scissors kick facing the wrong way? We kicked off then, with the hope of all the crowd pinned on me . . . tragedy struck. I went up to a high centre and headed the goalkeeper into the back of the net. Out cold I was. I was carried off in a deathly hush . . . stunned silence. Concussion, multiple bruises, cauliflower earhole and a fractured bracket. They were lost without me, ten minutes to go one-nil down. Their main hope lying on a stretcher surrounded by doctors. I came to. One-nil down they said, I don't know what came over me, but I remember fighting my way through the crowd and then there I was standing on the touchline surrounded by fourteen unconscious St John Ambulance men, three doctors and a copper. My country, that's all I kept saying, I must not let my country down. Oh, call it outdated patriotism if you like, but that's the way I'm built. The referee signalled me on, I swallowed a couple of aspirins and limped on to the field, clutching the bloodsoaked sponge to the sixteen stitches on the back of my head. We started to attack and the crowd shouted as one man . . . 'Give it to Hancock'. The ball was cleared high in the air and I caught it on my forehead, balanced it there, tilted my head back and with my nose holding it into position, I was off. Past one man, past two men, past three men, forty-five yards, the ball never touched my head, they thought I was holding the lace in my mouth . . . my speed was incredible, the wind had caught my shorts and I couldn't stop, into the penalty area, feinted past the back, round the outside of the half-back, sidestepped the goalie, dropped the ball on to my foot and wallop, broke the back of the net . . . a brilliant goal . . .

SID: (*Enthusiastic*) One–all.

TONY: Two–nil. I'd forgotten they changed ends at half-time.

SID: And that was your last game?

TONY: Yes. The rest of the team came up, walloped the life out of me, walked off and left me. I was still lying there when the dog racing started in the evening. Still that's the way it goes. What's the time?

SID: Quarter past five.

TONY: Oh I can't wait that long . . . a fortune within my grasp . . . not knowing . . .

SID: Well, let's go down and see the game then.

TONY: Of course . . . what a good idea . . . it'll be just like old times . . . Chelsea . . . I only ever played at Chelsea once, it was ten minutes to go, we were two–nil down, I was hobbling on the right-wing with a broken ankle waiting my chance, when the ball . . .

SID: Are you coming or not?

TONY: Oh all right then.

They go to the door and leave with TONY *still chatting, following* SID.

TONY: I was only going to say that the ball came to me and I trapped it with my good ankle and set off on a mazy dribble that took me half way down the field, we were playing the W formation at the time . . .

FADE *after they've gone out of the door.*

from HANCOCK'S HALF HOUR *1959*

The Bakehouse and Barnsley

BRIAN GLOVER

'You're dropped. Not my decision, tell your dad. Now off you go. Don't forget to tell him. Your dad. Nothing to do with me. Right, you two, hands out! Straight out!' I must have still been standing there. 'Off you go!'

Even out in the corridor I could hear the swish swish of the cane followed by the two involuntary yelps. Then hear him bark out again, 'Other hand! Straight out!' Then again. Swish, yelp! Swish, yelp! I kept thinking, I wish it was the cane that I'd been sent for rather than to be given the news that I'd been dropped from Barnsley Boys. You get over the cane, no bother, but I'd never get over being dropped from Barnsley Boys. I was right, it was 1949, and it still rankles.

In the same year Barnsley Boys defeated Derby Boys in the final of the English Schools Trophy. It was a two-legged affair; we licked 'em 3–1 at Oakwell, and 27,000 witnessed it, then got stuffed 0–1 in the second leg at the Baseball Ground, and 21,000 saw that. Barnsley Boys were, without doubt, the best schoolboy team in the land, and as a reward Barnsley FC had signed on the team, *en bloc*, except for the centre-forward who signed for Wednesday in dubious circumstances. Skullduggery was mooted, and not without foundation – an eye-witness had seen a brand new gas cooker being carried into their house from a big van with a Sheffield address on its rear doors.

I'd played in the semi-final against Swansea Boys at Vetch Field. We beat 'em by the only goal of the game, and clinched our place in the final. I played well. Followed instructions. The coach had said: 'That lad there, him in short trousers, see him? He's only thirteen, but he can play, name's Allchurch. Got a brother called Ivor who's a pro; don't let him out of your sight. If necessary, you know what to do.' I'd been in long trousers for two years; I was all over him like a big dog, and I didn't have to resort to sticking in the clog.

Then out of the blue I'm summoned back to my old junior school and delivered this bombshell. We lived down Lundwood, an overspill housing estate just outside Barnsley, but by this time I was a big lad, and going to the grammar school up in town. I was somebody down Lundwood, I went to school on a bus. The reason I'd been summoned back to my old juniors was because the headmaster was on the Barnsley Boys selection committee, and they must have thought it would soften the blow if it came from someone who'd seen me grow up; even got me through the eleven-plus. There was also the consideration that my old junior school headmaster knew my dad, and knew his reputation.

My dad was a wrestler. He wrestled as the Red Devil, and I've often wondered what the neighbours thought when they saw the red, balaclava-like masks bouncing on my mam's washing line on Monday mornings. Even before that he'd been a boxer. He had spent his entire working life in the ring trading blows. He'd well over a hundred fights in the 1920s and early 1930s, and two wonderful cauliflower ears to prove that a lot of the punches hadn't missed. It was an era in boxing when there was little or no medical supervision, and although I didn't realise it at the time my dad had had far too many fights and taken far too many punches. As my mam always used to say, 'Your dad just flies off the handle', which was why my old headmaster was so keen to disassociate himself from the decision to drop me.

That my dad was a wrestler was, I suppose, the real reason I followed in his footsteps and spent twenty years of my life bouncing around the pro-wrestling circuit, but being dropped by Barnsley Boys also had a lot to do with my subsequent choice of career. Football boots were very nearly the tools of my trade, not wrestling boots.

I'd been summoned up to my old junior school from out of our back yard. Why I wasn't at school I don't remember, but I wasn't, because I do remember my mam came out into the yard to tell me that Mr Sykes wanted to see me up at the juniors, and that was unusual. My mam usually just stood at the door and screeched my name, and I usually ignored it until the inevitable, 'I'll tell your dad!'. I didn't ignore that. For her to come and fetch me out of the yard she must have known something was afoot.

from SATURDAY BOYS *1990*

Jetlag in Rio

GEOFFREY GREEN

The first I saw of Rio was its airport runway on which the torrent of raindrops were bouncing like sorbo balls. No diamond city below; no Maracana – just a grey sheet over everything and plenty of nothing. The fates were unkind.

Having duly contacted the England party at their hotel and, the storm passed, having lunched with them on a balcony in the sunshine as a beautiful rainbow bridged the width of the bay, the need for sleep at last began to press after the long journey round the clock. 'The coach leaves for the ground sharp at 6 o'clock,' said the boys, 'so if you want a lift, don't be late. We can't afford to wait because of the expected traffic jams.'

'Wake me at half past 5, without fail, Room 504,' I instructed the hall porter, and headed for bed. Then, in a trice, sweet oblivion took over. When at last I awoke with a start the room was in pitch darkness. Night had fallen. Something had gone wrong and every nerve-end suddenly began to jangle like the alarm call I had obviously failed to answer. Switching on the bedside lamp, my watch told the time. It was 8 p.m. Kick-off hour. Here I had come thousands of miles to do a job and fulfil a personal dream, and I was AWOL.

Panic struck. In a strange city for the first time, with only an odd word of the language, and God knows how far from the scene of action the whole hideous realisation of my position struck home. Blindly I flew out of the hotel and within minutes was lucky enough to pick up a stray taxi. 'Maracana. Football, Pelé!' I stammered hopefully. 'Pelé' was quite enough. The driver nodded with a smile and off we set. It was a fevered, nightmare journey. The taxi radio crackled loud and violently. Clearly it was the broadcast from the stadium as recognisable names struck the air amidst a babbling waterfall of words – 'Pelé, Julinho, Gylmar, Greaves, Moore, Charlton . . .' What was the score, I wondered, as the great dome of floodlights from the stadium at last drew closer and closer.

Finally we were there: 8.45. Already half-time! Where was the entrance to the press enclosure amidst all this towering fortress? Blindly I ran round and round one of the tiered galleries inside the stadium, like a rabbit caught in the headlights of a car. Looking through one entrance after another, at last I spied batteries of television cameras. That was it. The press enclosure was through the next gangway and a moment later there were the faces of my colleagues. Often, by the end of a long season, some of us no doubt get tired of the sight of one another. But not at that moment. Never was their presence more welcome.

Gliding as nonchalantly and unconcerned as possible into a vacant seat I enquired what the half-time score was. 'Half-time?' they croaked with one weary voice. 'The flaming match hasn't even started yet and we've been sitting here for two hours. Go back to Paris, you bloody old Green. Is this one of your funny tricks to catch up on your own sleep?' Almost at that same moment a deep roar broke from the assembled company, some 150,000 in number, ranged around that remarkable enclosure. And there, out of the tunnel emerged, side by side, the yellow shirts of Brazil and the white of England.

I had made it in time, after all. One part of the dream at last was fulfilled. As Mortensen had said so long ago in Turin, you need a bit of luck now and then, in life.

from GREAT MOMENTS IN SPORT *1972*

Prison Without Bars

WILLIS HALL

'Is that Willis Hall?' asked the voice on the other end of the line.

'It is.'

My caller identified himself. He was an actor I had worked with and whose features would be instantly recognisable to the regular TV viewer.

'Is it true,' he continued, 'that you're connected with a Sunday celebrity soccer side which turns out for charity and that sort of malarky?'

'Well, yes' – but it was only partly true. I was involved with a Sunday side which boasted a couple of showbiz players on its books and which had been known to fit in the occasional charity fixture. But, when the chips were down, we much preferred the anonymity of playing against north London pub teams. It was not that we were opposed to supporting worthy causes – but we enjoyed the free-and-easy pint-and-a-pie camaraderie of the ale house far more than the marquee-housed genteel finger buffet respectability that went hand in hand with charity football. Besides, I have long held the belief that playing football for football's sake is one of the worthiest causes on God's earth.

In addition to the showbiz celebs, we numbered several ex-league footballers on our books. A quartet of old Fulham players (Johnny Haynes, Jimmy Hill, Bill Dodgin and Tom Wilson) turned out regularly, Dave Sexton, then manager at Chelsea, played his share of games, and (whisper it gently) a couple of pro players still in the game would enjoy a clandestine match with us, unbeknown to their managers. Also included occasionally on the teamsheet were a couple of National

Hunt jockeys; a pro boxer; two bookmakers and, infrequently, a Marseilles restaurateur – a brick-built karsey of a man who made a formidable full-back.

In short we were a catholic bunch of chaps united by a common love of soccer. Our captain, mentor and enthusiastic organiser was an ex-Fulham and ex-Watford goalkeeper, the late Dave Underwood, a kindly, rugged but gentle man. When we had formed the team on a drunken spree Dave came up with a suggestion for a teamstrip that pleased everyone.

' 'Ang about!' he had said, his cockney voice breaking in on the fierce debate ranging across the pub table. 'We'll play in Argentina's colours.'

'Why Argentina?' asked several puzzled founder members.

'Listen to this,' he advised them. 'Blue and white vertical stripes, black shorts . . .' he paused, keeping us all on tenterhooks, and then added: '. . . and dove-grey stockings.' The dove-grey stockings won us over.

We called ourselves Gerry's XI after a Soho theatrical drinking club, and in the faint hope that the establishment would grant honorary membership to all our players. That did not come to pass, but Gerry's Club, at least, did grant us the right to pin our fixtures and teamsheets on its noticeboard.

And thus, to come full circle, had the actor who telephoned me come to learn of our existence.

'What can I do for you?' I asked him. 'Are you looking for a game?'

'Well, sort of . . .'

He was playing it very cagey but, eventually, he explained his problem. He had a brother who was doing time in Ford Open Prison. The brother was allowed two visits a month (I think), but had a long list of both friends and relatives anxious to see him. Because of his brother's busy social visiting calendar, the actor's turn at the visiting pass did not come round all that regularly. It had reached the actor's ears that Gerry's XI played the Ford Open Nick XI, on occasion. The actor's brother was a regular in the prison team. If we could arrange a run out in our team, a brotherly reunion would be effected, over and above prison visiting regulations.

It was, it seemed to me, a reasonable enough request. Also it was true that Gerry's XI had made the odd journey down to the south coast and played friendlies against the prison team. They were among our most enjoyable fixtures. Ford Open Nick were a hospitable lot.

Their team was made up of both screws and cons. They were fitter than us by far – they had a couple of physical training instructors playing up front, both of them dead keen fitness fanatics. But we considered ourselves a more skilful side and, anyway, could look to our Marseilles restaurateur to contain the pair of PTI strikers.

I told my actor caller that I could not promise anything, but that I would see what could be done. As it happened, things turned out quite nicely for all concerned. The prison team had got themselves into the semi-finals of some competition and were delighted at the prospect of a warm-up friendly – particularly against Gerry's XI with its goodly sprinkling of ex-pro players who would provide worthwhile opposition without aggro. (We didn't tell them we might be playing the Marseilles full-back.)

The fixture fitted in nicely with our plans too. A coach trip to the seaside was always welcome. The post-match hospitality at Ford, though simple fare (meat-paste sandwiches, biscuits, prison fruit cake, metal jugs of tea), was abundant. And although pints of beer were not forthcoming inside the wire mesh fence, there were ample welcoming hostelries on the road back to London. Plus the fact that we had a new player who was in need of a run-out before being thrust into the hurly burly of Sunday morning north London pub soccer.

The author and playwright, Bill Naughton, a chum of mine, had put in his formal request to join our ranks. At that time, Bill was playing regularly in Hyde Park in the makeshift spontaneous soccer matches that took place on most weekday afternoons. The teams were mostly made up of Italian and Spanish waiters taking a break between luncheon and dinner duties. Soccer boots were obligatory but, those apart, it was a case of play as you are. The occasional soup-spotted dinner jacket was to be observed doing duty as a goalpost. Bill was wont to take his boots along, knotted around his neck, and hang about on a touchline looking hungry for football.

It was enthusiasm such as that for which Gerry's XI was always on the lookout. Our only slight concern was that Bill Naughton was several years on the wrong side of fifty and it was wondered whether he had the stamina for a full ninety minutes of football. The Ford Open Nick fixture would provide us with the opportunity to put that to the test.

Thus it was, then, that our team coach set out from central London for the south coast early-ish one late summer morning in the 1960s. A pre-match light lunch had been booked in Brighton: fillet steak and toast – the footballer's food of that day. It was back in the good old times, remember, before the dieticians took over with their pre-match dishes of boiled chicken. It is rarely referred to these days, but England won the World Cup on fillet steaks and toast.

After lunch, with the half-digested steaks sitting comfortably inside our stomachs, we reboarded the coach and set out on the final leg of the journey. Our guest actor, around whom this story is loosely spun, had declined our offer of lunch in Brighton and had suggested instead that we pick him up several miles outside the prison.

As the coach trundled along a lonely coastal road, we suddenly saw him up ahead, a solitary figure leaning, in an actorish sort of way, on a fence close by a fringe of trees. He waved at us, cheerfully, as the coach drew up and then instead of clambering on board, turned and gestured towards the trees. To our surprise, a dozen or so ladies stepped out of the woodland and crossed towards where the coach was parked. They all carried bulging carrier bags in both hands. It was an entirely unexpected happening and I got down from the coach to challenge the actor as to their identities. They were, he told me, girlfriends or wives of prison inmates. The actor's brother, it seemed, was not the only convict in need of an unscheduled visit.

'I thought that we could smuggle them into the nick as our team's wives and girlfriends,' the actor explained, diffidently. I looked across at the knot of ladies and they returned my dubious glance with cheery smiles.

'What are in the carrier bags?' I asked the actor.

'Oh, just a few nibbles. For a bit of a snack after the game.'

He had spoken with a fine, professional sense of understatement. The carrier bags, it turned out, were bulging with all manner of good things: a half dozen cold roast chickens; bowls of potato salad; fresh crusty rolls thick with butter; lots of lettuce; tomatoes – food sufficient for a feast.

'Are you allowed to take all that food into the prison?' I asked him, unsurely.

The actor shrugged. 'Not exactly,' he told me. 'But I thought that we might smuggle that in as well – at the bottom of the team hamper, underneath the strip.'

It was at this point I noticed that he, too, was carrying a carrier bag. The contents clinked ominously.

'What have you got in there?' I said.

'Just these,' he told me, lifting out two litre-sized wine bottles, both of which contained a yellowish liquid.

'Isn't that going just a titch too far,' I asked him, 'taking booze into the nick?'

'Oh, it isn't drink,' he explained. 'It's vinaigrette dressing.'

'Vinaigrette dressing?'

'Every Sunday afternoon, the cons get salad for tea. With the salad they get salad cream. My brother can't stand salad cream. Mum's made him up two bottles of his favourite vinaigrette dressing. There's enough here to keep him going until he gets out.'

Correct me if you know better, but it's my belief that Gerry's XI are the only football team to have smuggled two litres of vinaigrette dressing into one of Her Majesty's prisons. We got the rest in through the gates too, without any difficulty at all: prisoners' wives and girl-friends, roast chickens, all the trimmings.

We changed, with the opposing team, in the prison gymnasium. I seem to remember that they played in Manchester United's colours. They cast many an envious glance at our Argentinian strip – particu-larly the dove-grey stockings. As we trotted out onto the pitch, a ragged cheer went up from the touchlines which were deep with cons. Bill Naughton, who was running alongside me, suddenly snatched at a sharp intake of breath.

'What's up, Bill?' I asked him, with some concern, wondering if, perhaps, the sprint from the changing-room to the pitch had been too much for the over fifty-year-old? Nothing of the kind.

'Look!' he replied, pointing down at one of the goalmouths and with wonder in his voice. 'The goal posts have got nets!'

He went on to tell me that although he had played football all his life, from his schoolboy days in Lancashire to his Hyde Park continen-tal waiters' encounters, he had only rarely played with real goal posts and he had never ever played with goal posts that had nets. He was about to fulfil a lifetime's ambition.

I don't know whether it was the goal nets or the dove grey stockings that motivated Bill that afternoon, but he played out of his skin. He roved along the right wing for all of the ninety minutes, an inspired grey-haired dynamo of a man in his mid-fifties. The spectators took him to their hearts. 'Naughton! Naughton!' went up from the make-shift terraces.

Oh, but I enjoyed that afternoon. And if the game was good the post-match shindig was magic. It took place in the prison gymnasium and was attended by all the players, the match officials, and the ladies who had infiltrated onto our coach. There were groaning tables laden with cold roast chicken, potato salad, lettuce, tomatoes, meat-paste sandwiches, biscuits, prison fruit cake and huge metal jugs brimming with steaming tea. It deserves to be stated, too, that the vinaigrette dressing was out of this world.

I can't remember whether our side won or lost. The most important thing about that fixture was that the result was entirely unimportant. It was an afternoon of rare soccer enjoyment – and only soccer provides such afternoons. I rang Jimmy Hill the other day to ask him if he remembered the result.

'You played in that Gerry's XI game at Ford,' I put to him, 'when we smuggled in the women and the grub.'

There was a short pause at the other end before he spoke. 'No, Willis, I missed out on that one. I've often heard about it though. Haynsey played and Bill Dodgin and Tom Wilson. It is still talked about. I wish I had been there.'

Well, I was there, and it will be with me always. Oddly enough, Bill Naughton never played for Gerry's XI again. I think that the goal nets coupled with the dove-grey stockings had provided him with the ultimate soccer experience and to have attempted to repeat it would have been gilding the lily.

from SATURDAY BOYS *1990*

The Hard Men

WILLIS HALL

SCENE TWENTY. FOOTBALL DRESSING-ROOM. DAY.
A Saturday afternoon atmosphere – just prior to the start of a match. The players are already changed into their football strip and are making final adjustments to their kit: fastening their bootlaces; putting on shin-guards; soft-soaping their stockings; rubbing Vaseline on their eyebrows; and performing all the many other tasks plus the occasional idiosyncrasies that footballers are wont to perform. JOCK, *the groundsman, bustles about the dressing-room, handing out cups of tea to the players.* MICHAEL, *the track-suited trainer, has one of the players on the treatment bench and is examin-*

ing an old injury. The SUBSTITUTE *is changing the studs on a player's boots. And through all this hustle and bustle,* EDDIE RITCHIE, *team manager, paces the dressing-room in his overcoat, tense but calm.*

EDDIE: Come along, chaps, speed it up!

There is a knock at the door.

EDDIE: Jock – have a look who that is? I'll have nobody in here not personally connected with the squad.

JOCK *crosses and opens the door a couple of inches. With him, we see the* REFEREE, *changed and ready and requesting permission to enter the dressing room.*

REFEREE: Is it all right if I . . . er . . . ?

JOCK: I'll have to ask him, sorry.

JOCK *closes the door on the* REFEREE *and turns back into the dressing-room.*

JOCK: Mr Ritchie?

EDDIE *is engaged in whispered conversation with a player and is piqued at the interruption.*

EDDIE: You heard what I said, Jock, I don't speak in a foreign tongue!

JOCK: (*Anxiously*) I've told him 'no', only it's the referee wants to come in.

EDDIE *waves his hand, testily, indicating that the official should be allowed instant entry.* JOCK *opens the door again.*

JOCK: He says it is all right, mate. You can come in.

REFEREE: Many thanks.

The REFEREE *enters and stands just inside the door, hesitant.*

EDDIE *flashes him an ingratiating smile.*

EDDIE: Good afternoon, Mister Match Official!

REFEREE: 'afternoon! 'afternoon, lads!

And he receives a dozen or so surly grunts in reply.

EDDIE: And to what are we indebted the pleasure of?

REFEREE: I was wondering, is it all right if I use your loo – your – er – lavatory?

EDDIE *extends his hands towards the shower room and lavatories with old-world courtesy.*

EDDIE: By all means – be my guest.

REFEREE: (*Unnecessarily*) Only mine's blocked up.

EDDIE: Mr Referee, sir?

REFEREE: Sir?

EDDIE: I wonder if you might oblige me with your official time?
REFEREE: (*A glance at his watch*) Certainly. It – is – two thirty-eight and forty seconds precisely.
EDDIE: I'm extremely in your debt.

The REFEREE *goes into the lavatories, shutting the door.*

EDDIE: Right, chaps, settle down, let's have a word, if you *don't* mind, lads, cut the cackle, can I have a bit of HUSH – QUIET!!

He has their attention, or at least he has the attention of everybody except the SUBSTITUTE *who is still struggling with a pair of pliers and the studs on the player's boots.*

EDDIE: That does go for you too, Eddison! You might only be the substitute, lad, and please God I don't have to throw you to the lions today – but don't chance your bloody arm!

He has everybody's attention.

EDDIE: Right. Fifteen minutes to kick-off. I'm not talking tactics. I've done all the tactic-talking I'm going to do. I'm just having a word. When you're out there – you're on your own. I can't get out on that park and do it for you. What has to be done out there, you do it yourselves. (*He taps his forehead*) I can put it in here for you – I've done that. (*He thumps his chest*) I can give you lots of this – I've done that. But when you get out on that park today . . . Listen, *you* know the side you're playing today. Camels. Donkeys. Kickers. So when they start kicking, I want you to kick them back. (*He displays a clenched fist*) Lots of this. Put yourselves about. Because all I have to say to you lads is, I want you to go out there and kick those dirty bastards off the park!

His vicious expression changes to one of beaming serenity as the REFEREE *re-enters on his way back from the lavatories.*

EDDIE: Everything to your satisfaction, Ref?
REFEREE: Many thanks.
EDDIE: My pleasure! Any time!

The REFEREE *has crossed the dressing-room and now pauses at the door.*

REFEREE: Thanks again.
EDDIE: Feel free! And may the best team win, eh?

The REFEREE *goes out and, immediately,* EDDIE's *face is again contorted with anger.*

EDDIE: And don't start to worry about what that bloody fairy thinks, because I know him of old and he couldn't control a public shit-house, let alone a football match! So. You all know what I want?

Murmurs of agreement.

EDDIE: And you're going to go out on that park and give me what I want?

More murmurs of agreement.

EDDIE: I've made myself quite clear?

Still more murmurs of agreement.

EDDIE: Good! But just to recapitulate. (*Again the clenched fist*) Bags of this. It's the big one out there today. Survival of the fittest – and the losers are for the chop. Us or them, and it's up to us to see that we're the ones that stop up in this league. Because they're not going out there to do us any favours! Good luck. Now, ten minutes – get your stretches started, lads.

The players begin, individually, to do their muscle-toning exercises. EDDIE *turns to* MICHAEL, *the trainer, who is still tending to the injured player on the treatment bench.*

EDDIE: Well?

MICHAEL: He'll last for ninety minutes.

EDDIE: Well done. (*To the player*) Good lad. Get yourself ready – quick!

EDDIE *turns and addresses the team.*

EDDIE: Get out there, chaps – (*He throws a frenzied fist in the air*) – and bleedin' give 'em one for me! Straight off – let them see who's boss!

from A SONG AT TWILIGHT *1973*

Religion

CLIFFORD HANLEY

My perverseness was justified as wisdom and knowledge oozed into me later. I hadn't realised then that Celtic, set up as a charity-raising organisation to give hot soup to deadbeats, was Roman Catholic but not stubborn about it. They didn't scruple to play Proddy-dogs, or Muslims if available, and this created its own legends, which may even be true.

One is the tale of a Protestant newly signed for Celtic who came into the dressing-room at half-time with his veins bulging and his nostrils white because a Rangers fan kept barracking him as a dirty Fenian swine. Jimmy McGrory, or maybe Patsy Gallacher, soothed the fellow down by saying, 'They call me that all the time.' 'That's all right for you – you *are* a Fenian swine!'

Another is the story, certainly untrue but all the better for it, about the day when Celtic trounced Rangers on New Year's Day, and John Lawrence excused the defeat by pointing out to Bob Kelly that the Celts had two Protestants in the team. 'Aye, but you've got eleven,' said Kelly.

True, true. Rangers always has eleven Protestants, or at least non-Catholics, on the field, and no crucifix ever darkens Ibrox's doors. At times, they do very well, in football terms, with this line-up, and they too have their legendary names which burn into the brain of even an apathetic child. Meiklejohn and Wee Blue Devil Morton, and Torry Gillick and Willie Thornton and Willie Waddell and Big Geordie Young, who is also an okay guy and runs a very nice pub, and McPhail and Baxter and the rest. At times they have done very badly, and the fans really feel it.

Oh my brethren, do they feel it! Not being an afficionado, nor yet an encyclopaedia, I will not try to recall the team or the year, but I do know that when I worked on the *Daily Record*, I knew a sports writer who was fairly pro-Rangers (what I mean is that he got his eyes dyed blue for his birthday) and the great 'Gers were beaten seven to one by some obscure set of upstarts. I actually tried *to josh him* about it, and he strode past me with unseeing eyes and blood squirting out of *his* ears. And that was a month after the game.

I also gained the suspicion that he didn't like Roman Catholics, because when I was getting married he exhorted me to have fifteen kids as part of the crusade to outnumber the bastards. I told him I was a Buddhist, and he said that was fine, as long as I wasn't a Fenian Buddhist.

So that was what it was all about, really. It wasn't two football teams, it was two living symbols of that cleft in Glasgow's consciousness, the grand canyon separating Prod from Pape.

Maybe that's all right. I wouldn't want everybody in Glasgow, or even in Shettleston, to think the same way or believe the same things. There is much to be said for and against the Roman Church, and much to be said for and against John Knox and John Calvin – or King Billy. One thing to be said for King Billy, or William of Orange to the historians, is that he didn't give a tinker's damn. He was generous to monasteries and convents, and the Pope couldn't have been more pleased when he won the Battle of the Boyne because the Pope had gone off the Stuart dynasty as well.

Never mind, no staunch Proddy is going to swallow that. Notice the adjective. In Glasgow, a Protestant is staunch, a Catholic is bitter.

Was it possible, is it possible, that the existence of Rangers and Celtic provides a fairly harmless outlet, a safety valve, for pent-up hostilities that would blow the lid off otherwise? Or is it that they create a venturi tube, a forced draught, to embers that would otherwise die a natural death?

I don't know, and only a fool could be sure. With the moralistic surface of my mind, I sternly deplore the whole thing. Football should be football and religion should be religion and ne'er the twain should meet. But since I'm sceptical about my moralistic postures, I wonder if that needle is essential to provoke men to great deeds. Since we are by nature evil and violent, maybe we need a bit of football that gives our hostility a wee holiday by adding the fire of sectarian ferocity.

You will not get me anywhere near a Rangers–Celtic game, because I would feel too much of an alien and somebody might say a rude word to me or accidentally stand in my teeth. But while I sometimes make the pilgrimage to Firhill to relish the gentle melancholy of yet another disaster, and enjoy the wittiest patter and the best pies in the football game, I know that there's another, bigger, fiercer, more terrible, more poetic kind of football, and as the pendulum swings, it's the football people get from Rangers or Celtic.

I grew up between them, and whether I like it or not, Rangers and Celtic have helped to make me what I am, and make Glasgow what it is.

Thoreau, in one of his presumptuous moments, proclaimed, 'I accept the universe.' And Thomas Carlyle riposted, 'Egad, he's got to!'

Well, I accept Rangers and Celtic. Because egad, I've got to.

from WE'LL SUPPORT YOU EVERMORE *1976*

A Yorkshire Boyhood

ROY HATTERSLEY

In most of those years, the Saturday of the football semi-final was the point at which my cricket bag was pulled from under the bed. One of the semi-finals was almost invariably played at Hillsborough, a match which became the highlight of the Sheffield football purists' year. For the partisan, no game could compare with a confrontation in which one of the local favourites took part. What I wanted to see was Sheffield Wednesday winning. But once a year I looked forward to the more relaxed pleasure of Derby County versus Manchester United or Newcastle against Wolves. Indeed, like my father, I was so keen on enjoying an uncommitted ninety minutes that I rose at half-past six on the Sunday when the tickets were sold. By seven we were in the queue, waiting with anxious calm for noon and the moment when the sale actually started. By one o'clock we had reached a turn-stile and were about to take possession of the two tickets which each frozen enthusiast was allowed. By half-past one we were back home, having missed *Family Favourites* and the *Billy Cotton Band Show*, but the proud possessors of the ability to take our place on Spion Kop on the next Saturday.

I could of course have gone on my own to buy the two tickets that my father and I needed. The extra tickets which we always bought were less of a boon than a burden. We never even thought of selling them at a profit, and there was always much embarrassed confusion about who should buy them at face value. Indeed, there were times when – for all their scarcity – we were almost left with the valuable property on our hands. We bought them because the offer seemed too good to refuse, and the idea of queuing all those hours and then taking only half the number of tickets we were offered seemed self-evidently ridiculous. Of course, one of us could have stayed in bed whilst the other made the early morning expedition. But football was for my father and me a joint enterprise. We stood on Spion Kop, eating our Mintoes together. And together we queued for the tickets.

On the day of the big game we took our places on the red shale terraces two hours before the time of the kick-off. We always stood in front of one of the steel barriers on which less experienced spectators leaned their elbows. With the Spion Kop crowd packed so tight that it was impossible to take a handkerchief out of a topcoat pocket there was a special danger in standing there behind the goal. At every sudden shot and calculated corner, twenty thousand necks craned forward and twenty thousand chests pressed, with increasing force, against twenty thousand backs. For many of the spectators, the result was a cumulative pressure that lurched them down half a dozen steps, packing sections of the crowd more tightly than seemed possible and lifting grown men off their feet with an irresistible and infuriating force. But anyone wise enough to find a place *in front* of a barrier was protected from the human avalanche. So we arrived at the ground two hours before the teams ran out onto the pitch. Queuing combined with waiting for the kick-off lasted four times as long as the match itself. But the game was always worth it, and there were diversions to help us pass the time.

There was, of course, the local Steelworks Band, playing martial music in a wholly unmilitary way – which was entirely consistent with their wholly unmilitary appearance. And there was the crowd itself – Blackpool fans walking with an orange-ribboned duck along the touchline; wandering Wolverhamptonites passing a black-and-white coffin over their heads in preparation for the slaughter of Newcastle United, and the whole panoply and pageant of coloured hats and supporters club songs. And that was all before the match began.

After the first whistle blew, there were Stan Mortensen of Blackpool and Billy Wright of Wolves, and for two marvellous consecutive years the magpies of Newcastle who won at Hillsborough and went on to win the Cup – Jackie Milburn, Bobby Mitchell, Joe Harvey and the Robledo brothers from South America. It was a short walk home, but our feet always dragged with the sad anticlimax that swallows up the football fan at twenty minutes to five.

from A YORKSHIRE BOYHOOD *1983*

Get Stuck In!

ROY HATTERSLEY

Football began for me on a sunlit autumn afternoon in 1944 when Sheffield Wednesday were at home to Nottingham Forest in the wartime Northern League. Nottingham was my father's town and Forest his team, so off we went to Hillsborough, me filled with hope and him full of nostalgia. Sheffield Wednesday have been my team ever since.

On their ground I experienced all the emotions that the football supporter might enjoy and must endure. Standing on their terraces, I roared my partisan passions. Sitting in the stands I properly suppressed the baser expressions of joy in victory and the cruder manifestations of defiance in defeat. Huddled behind Wednesday's goal I waited for the announcement that every schoolboy expects, but knows will never come. 'Goodfellow' (or Morton or McIntosh – the fantasy survived a whole generation of goalkeepers) 'has been taken ill. Will Roy Hattersley come to the players' entrance at once and bring his boots and jersey with him?' High up on Spion Kop, I learned and sang the Wednesday song:

> Roll along Sheffield Wednesday, roll along,
> Put the ball in the net where it belongs,
> When Jackie Robinson gets the ball,
> Then it's sure to be a goal,
> Roll along Sheffield Wednesday, roll along.

The lyric lacked both the literary invention and the tribal significance that scholars have discovered in the football songs of the 1970s. It did not even possess the graceful parody of Sheffield United's 'Wonderful, wonderful Jimmy Hagan . . .' But it was my song, pure blue and white. I sang away the Saturday afternoons through mouthfuls of Nuttalls' Mintoes and listened to stories of great golden days between the wars.

The late Forties were the boom years of English football. England was still unbeaten at home by any foreign team. 'Full Internationals' were the footballers who had competed in the Home Championship, not the players who had frolicked through ninety friendly minutes with Brazil or Argentina. The World Cup was beneath us and we were on top of the world. The European Club competition was yet to begin and the fans (their enthusuasm for real competitive football built up by years of wartime abstinence) flocked to experience the delights of cup and league. At Hillsborough we queued from six until noon to buy a ticket for the semi-final. But when we actually witnessed the great event, it was never a Yorkshire club which won and took the glory road to Wembley. The triumphs belonged to Lancashire and London, the Midlands and the north-east.

It had not always been like that. In the Twenties and Thirties, when Arsenal was making history by giving its ageing players monkey glands, Yorkshire was quietly dominating cup and league. Huddersfield won the Championship three seasons running and came a close second for the next two years. Sheffield Wednesday won the league (once by a margin of ten clear points) in successive seasons and then came third four times in a row. Sheffield United brought the Cup home to Bramall Lane in 1925, the middle of a decade of absolute Yorkshire domination, when the names which schoolboys conjured with were Stevenson, Capstick, Gillespie, Needham, Blenkinsop, Leach, Marsden and Seed.

In a game which thrives on innovation, the supremacy of Sheffield and Huddersfield could not last. The final fling (putting aside the dying fall of Wembley defeats in 1936 and 1938) was Sheffield Wednesday's Cup in Silver Jubilee year. I was wheeled down to Middlewood Road to see the victorious team come home: eleven heroes on top of an open bus, not wearing the double-breasted blazers and sharp suits of post-war idols, but dressed in the thick shirts and heavy square-toed boots which they wore on every winter Saturday afternoon.

At least, that is how I imagine it. I was two at the time. Strapped in my push-chair, I enjoyed a less than perfect view of the triumphant homecoming. But of one thing I am certain. The victorious captain holding the cup aloft for all but the smallest and most restricted spectator to see, was Ron Starling. I know because we talked about it in his paper shop during the dismal football days of the 1950s. We bought our papers there to ensure that, during an adolescence in which I was denied no advantage, I should handle a *Manchester Guardian* handed to me by a man who had held the FA Cup.

It was nearly forty years before a Yorkshire club brought home the cup again. Between the end of the war and Leeds United's great epoch, Yorkshire supporters had to be content with teams which won no honours, the occasional international who lost his place as soon as he won his cap, the potential star who shot into a new firmament the moment that news of his sparkle and shine penetrated the light years between Yorkshire and football's higher galaxies, and the faded glory of great names who added a touch of retrospective distinction to teams in the third and second divisions.

For Doncaster Rovers to have the ageing Peter Doherty on their playing staff was probably the greatest achievement in the club's history. Horatio Carter's silver hair and long shorts never really suited the greyhound-track-encircled pitch at Boothferry Road. But no one like him has played for Hull City before or since. Only in the far north-east, at Ayresome Park, were regular contemporary internationals on view in Yorkshire. Hardwick – immaculate in appearance as well as style – was permanent left back for Middlesbrough and England. Wilf Mannion, his club colleague, was only left out of the national team when injury or the inability of the selectors to recognise true genius denied him his rightful place. But for ten years after Hardwick and Mannion had gone, Yorkshire internationals either faded and were dropped, or prospered and passed on to more successful clubs.

Barnsley became a human clearing house for footballers on their way from exotic and unlikely places to football fame and fortune. The Robledo brothers called in between Chile and Newcastle in Cup year. The Blanchflowers of Belfast passed through en route to London and Manchester. Some Yorkshire clubs discovered local prodigies and sold their talents to stay solvent. Len Shackleton won his first England cap at Bradford and moved to Sunderland to join Jackie Robinson, late of Sheffield Wednesday. Others scouted the country for incipient heroes, found and developed them and cashed in their investment. So Alex Forbes blossomed for Sheffield United, but bore fruit for Arsenal. No sooner had Yorkshire schoolboys begun to identify with their heroes, copy their mannerisms and aspire to their achievements than the great men moved on and took their glory with them.

The Yorkshire schoolboys had no real cause for complaint. The football supporter's loyalty has to be to a name and a ground not to a team. The club players on whose success his Saturday evening happiness depends are the best that transfer fees and bonuses can buy.

They are mercenaries, fighting for money and love of battle, with no permanent allegiance to any standard, who rally round today's flag because that is what they are paid to do. Although Wednesday was my local team, I never thought of it as part of my local heritage. There was nothing especially Yorkshire about the football they played – no special Yorkshire style, tradition, grace or virtue that distinguished it from football played across the Pennines or south of the Humber. It took twenty years of unswerving support to discover that a real Yorkshire pulse throbbed at least through the two Sheffield teams. The heartbeat could – and still can – be recorded, in the directors' box.

Football directors are nobody's friends except when there are Cup-final tickets to give away, but they represent continuity whether the club fails or flourishes in a way that transient players and insecure managers cannot. They spring from the local soil, take root and often became impossible to dislodge even when the sap no longer rises and the leaves are brown and withered. They are the team's spirit, its tradition, its continuity.

At Bramall Lane and Hillsborough, continuity is so well preserved that the door marked 'Directors Only' is the entrance to a football time machine which rolls the world back fifty years. Of course, physically, both grounds have seen mighty changes. At Hillsborough the great World Cup stand is a memorial to the years when Sheffield Wednesday sank from the first to the third division. At Bramall Lane, the Yorkshire Cricket Club have been evicted and United have built across where the wicket used to be, where the bombs fell in 1940 and where the Hallamshire Battalion mustered in 1914. And on the improved and expanded grounds a new generation of players call their shirts 'strip', the pitch 'the park' and talk apparently knowledgeably about 'purposive running' and 'peripheral vision'. All that is new. But when the directors meet on match days the spirit has not changed since the Twenties.

It is a place where men understand their relative station in life and women accept that they are different. Directors themselves and guests of special distinction stir tea and drink whisky in protected seclusion. Other visitors eat and drink identical victuals but consume them separately because, in a hierarchical world, that is the natural order of things. Ladies – whatever their rank, class, achievement or eminence – are automatically excluded from the first order of football society, with only one exception. A lady Lord Mayor becomes, as far as both Wednesday and United are concerned, a man whenever she wears her chain of office. Other ladies are treated with complicated courtesy and meticulous respect. They are given particularly thick rugs to protect them from the cold and extraordinarily thin sandwiches to spare them the pork pie and cold sausages. The idea that the fur-coated ladies of Sheffield football are inferior to anyone in the world has never passed through their hatted heads. But they would no more expect to drink with their husbands at half-time than they would aspire to sit with them during the match.

For a man who spent his boyhood on Spion Kop, an invitation to sit in the Wednesday directors' box was like a Royal Command. I already knew the 'Royal Family'. Eric Taylor – football's longest serving manager' – was our neighbour. We admired his durability and his canniness. For years he painted his house in blue and white stripes. In bad years after the war (and there were many), dissident fans would be told about the loyalty of his decorations and would instantly accept that a man of such obvious devotion was indispensable to the club. It was Mrs Taylor who suggested that a young Scot – recently arrived from Edinburgh and making ends meet as Sheffield Wednesday's doctor might find the cure for my bronchitis that had already eluded a succession of GPs. Twenty years later he was introducing the Queen to Cup finalists at Wembley: Sir Andrew Stephen, chairman of the Football Association.

But nodding to neighbours and coughing for doctors was one thing. Meeting them in their glory as the men behind the team, behind almost every other team in the second division, was quite another. We did not come straight from the wet and weather-beaten terraces. On the day I tried to put my umbrella up behind Manchester United's goal my father and I agreed that he was too old and I was too decadent for the concrete steps. Indeed, the Mancunians, whose view I obscured, made much the same point, though in different language. So we bought tickets for the extremity of the old stand and squinted from our seats over the corner flag. But we were still unprepared for the padded seats and the heated footrests of the first four rows at the centre line.

We gave up Nuttalls' Mintoes. We learned to stroll nonchalantly into the ground at five to three rather than rush at the turnstile at quarter past two. We sat prim and proper and boasted to each other that we had watched Wednesday from every part of the ground. But I never felt confident in the exalted company until the late Sixties. Then, with Yorkshire two hundred miles and five years behind me, I followed the club and its directors on their visit to London grounds and relaxed in all the friendly familiarity of exiles in an alien land.

In January 1974 I arrived at Stamford Bridge, a hanger-on with the Sheffield Wednesday visitors. I was late for my rendezvous. A minute before the kick-off I stood blinking at the back of the directors' box, adjusting my eyes to the light and deciding where to sit. On my left was carefully cut hair, brushing the back of corduroy suits and touching the velvet collars of cavalry coats. On the right were heads cropped as close as boil-scars would allow. I recognised the men with graces but with few airs, men of property, who had no intention of flaunting or wasting what they had earned. I had no doubt which side I was on.

At the end of the match we all went to drink together – not just the victorious and vanquished directors linked in a moment of mock modesty and bogus sportsmanship, but wives and daughters, joining men with serious business to discuss and serious results from other grounds to ponder. Chelsea beat Wednesday 3–2. But as we say in Yorkshire (after we have lost), 'Some things are more important than winning'.

from GOODBYE TO YORKSHIRE *1976*

Black or Something?

DAVE HILL

There is piss-taking and parody in most dressing-rooms – no other form of communication is permitted. But Liverpool always have been seen as that bit different. The pressure to conform carries everyone before it. 'They're very funny, the Liverpool players,' says one who experienced them at close quarters for years. 'They have a very dry sense of humour. When people join, they may not have it but within a couple of months they will find they have *got* to have it. Nothing is taken seriously. They just have to take the piss out of everything and everybody and that's the way they are. Everton have got a sense of humour, but it's not the same. If you go up to Bellefield [Everton's training ground] after they've finished and they're having lunch, everyone's very quiet. But you go to Liverpool and they're all just taking the piss out of each other. Anyone just walking in would rather be with the Everton players, 'cos they're far more like . . . human beings – people you would want to talk to. But there's just something at Liverpool. It's very tight. When you're new you have to cope with it, and when you do, you're there for ever. But I think that's very hard, because it comes over a period of time and you need a lot of patience. But John Barnes fitted in as if he had been there the season before. Normally, it takes about a week, where they'll all sit alone and have their lunch. They'll say a few things, but they won't actually get right into the team. But John did.'

People were very conscious that Barnes was stepping across the threshold of a white football culture, and not just at Liverpool. Everton's players had lots of 'jokes' to offer. One Liverpool fan, a luminary of the amateur leagues with contacts at both clubs, recalls his first visit to Bellefield after Barnes had been signed. A number of Everton players went out of their way to rib him about it. The word 'nigger' was casually used.

At Liverpool, Barnes had his strategy worked out. On his first day at the training ground he sat at a bench with a couple of his new team-mates. Cups of tea were put before the two established players. Barnes looked up at the woman who brought them. He said: 'What am I, black or something?' Everyone fell about.

from OUT OF HIS SKIN *1989*

Superstitions

JIMMY HILL

One unforgettable superstition which has its more tragic side concerns the late Jeff Hall of England and Birmingham City. While on tour in the West Indies with the FA team in 1955, we were playing at Sabina Park, Kingston, Jamaica. The day before the match Jeff had given his boots to the club cobbler to change his studs. When we arrived at the ground for the match this little function had been forgotten and the cobbler proceeded to make the alterations as quickly as he could. Unfortunately, when the time came for us to walk out on to the field, with the Governor, massed bands, police, and a great reception committee waiting for us, the boots were still not quite finished and one of them was returned before the other – I think it was the left boot. Now Jeff always had a superstition that when changing he should put his right boot on first and, unfortunately, only the wrong boot was available at the time. For quite a time we couldn't get him to put the wrong boot on first. With the officials getting frantic and things becoming difficult, we finally managed to persuade him to put his left boot on and, just when we thought we were never going to get the match started, the right boot arrived. He put it on and hurried to join us in the procession. The match started and, at the outset, a long ball was kicked and bounced about fifteen yards in front of Jeff between himself and the outside-left. Jeff leapt to head the ball. Unfortunately, he didn't quite make contact with it, because the left winger headed him under the jaw, cut his chin and laid him out. He had to go off and have six stitches in the chin and took no further part in the match: the one time he forsook his particular superstition, he didn't make contact with the ball from start to finish of the game! Call that coincidence if you like, but what would you have done in Jeff's place in future matches?

from STRIKING FOR SOCCER *1963*

Where the Cup Begins

BRIAN JAMES

With the flourish of a conjurer performing a tired routine, the portly gentleman pulled two small numbered balls from a velvet bag and offered them on view: 'Number two versus number three,' intoned an official at his elbow . . . 'Hinckley versus Tividale.' Later, in a ground floor room at 16 Lancaster Gate. London (the headquarters of the Football Association), someone pointed at a pink-topped drawing pin on a three-foot square wall map of Britain. 'There you are,' he said, 'that's Tividale.'

With a good road map and fair eyesight you can trace where Tividale FC live in about half an hour. It's a dot on the west side of the A4123, which used to be the main road from Birmingham to Wolverhampton. With a few back numbers of Rothmans Football Yearbook you can trace the pedigree of their best players in a morning's diligent search – an asterisk shows which league club discarded them with a free transfer.

But Tividale Football Club is neither a numbered ball nor a coloured pin on a map: nor is it a map reference or a footnote in an annual. It is a community of people who conceived, built and now maintain a football club in the West Midland League. Most of them were at the club on August 31 1976, a Tuesday, and the final practice night before their match in the Preliminary Qualifying Round, the start of the 1976–77 FA Cup competition.

The ground is half way up a hill. On three sides it is bounded by neat homes, on the fourth it opens out into a panoramic view of the Midlands industrial sprawl. The ground's one entrance lies at the end of a row of new houses, identified with the sign Tividale Social Club.

There is no pub on this side of the estate, so the social club is packed seven nights a week and there is a two-year waiting list for membership. It is the bar takings and pools competitions which keep the football club solvent. The ground of first division West Bromwich Albion is only fifteen minutes away by car; Walsall's Fellows Park is as near in the other direction; and there is a handful of other non-league clubs in the area. The possibility of any of these rival clubs having a stunning run of success doesn't worry Tividale anywhere near as much as the prospect of a brewery opening another pub in their territory.

Being a football club effectively independent of football gives Tividale a marvellously relaxed attitude to life, a fact that became apparent with the introductory telephone call: 'Hello, this is Tividale FC. You're going to write about us? That's smashing! You want to come up and meet our lads? Fine, no problem. What night do we train? Well, what night can you get here?' Wembley, with its players' 'perks' pool, its carefully rationed access for the media, its corps of commissionaires sourly insulating those in the game from their audience, seems a million miles into the future.

from JOURNEY TO WEMBLEY *1977*

The Trial

RICHARD JOBSON

Football held a great symbol of what a young Catholic could achieve in this country. Its name was Celtic. Born from the benevolence of the Irish Christian brothers in 1888, in the East End of Glasgow, and using the motif of an Irish shamrock, Celtic were an identity for a lost generation of Irish migrant workers. The feeling that great events could happen in that poor underdeveloped area, with a team who played heart before money and fun before religion has never stopped. The insurmountable dilemmas which have dogged the club's history have only strengthened the world's most loyal and critical support. When the team are doing well, they walk on water and when they are struggling suddenly everybody's an expert and the manager should be replaced with the man from the Bovril stall.

I first witnessed the hoops on their home territory of Celtic Park, or Paradise, when I was five years old. I remember nothing. But for a boy who faced the banality and claustrophobia of a housing estate, the epic, near cinematic glory the club reached in their endeavours to please me and my mates made a Saturday afternoon the equivalent of a trip to Mecca or a snog with Ursula Andress. I grew up in their most glorious period: the first British club to win the European Cup and nine successive league titles. When they attacked it was like Saracen horsemen humiliating clumsy Crusaders. When we played Rangers we were the Infidel and they the Puritan. We were believers, they were just greedy.

I heard things on the football chatline. Half-time talk of girls, and fighting, drinking and life without work caught my ear in the jungle section of Celtic Park. An orgasm wasn't an Israeli orange after all, and the Labour Party were trying to make things better, said the Big Man to the Wee Man; my ears took it all in. Watching Celtic made me want to play football, but never for them; for I knew I just would never be good enough.

From as far back as I remember I have kicked a ball. Even when it was with just a collection of old rags tied together, it became a big match. It took the importance of the international stage. The cameras were there, there was the build-up, the team talk, and the tactics, which were always, Attack! Attack! Attack!

There were lots of goals. Nobody considered being the defender of the realm. Oh no. It was up and on toward glory. A glory which would bring the television cameras and the legendary Archie Macpherson (rumoured to be a Hun, but actually a very influential media man).

'Well Dick, what do you remember about the goal?'

'Well Archie, Sean slipped it through to Des, who saw Paddy free on the right, who thumped it across to me in the middle. Unfortunately our goalie was off his line and I nodded it past him.'

Learning how to deal with the media was tremendously important to fourteen-year-old boys. Already terms such as 'the lads', 'the boss' and 'one game at a time', had infiltrated our conversation. Potential hooliganism, which was inherent in all at my school, was not to be touched. Scandals could rock a career at an early stage. One report in the local paper would mean the end of those cold Saturday morning rituals which brought such joy to the neighbourhood. A representative of his school, and future international player, could not be a thieving, spray-painting, glass-breaking, street-fighting man like the rest of his family and friends. He had to be bigger than that.

It was an escape. A way out of misery. Though these serious notes were never thought of at the time. The game just helped give a sense of responsibility to potential criminals. It also opened the door to an organised camaraderie.

'Ya f****** eedjit,' boomed Murdo, the team captain. This was ironic seeing as he played on one foot that was not connected to his brain. Murdo was fourteen years old, 6 ft and could drink more Scotsmac and Irnbru than any consenting adult I had ever witnessed. This item of aplomb was one he was very proud of. Someone had once written on a steamed up window in the changing room: 'Murdo is Murder'. That questioned his integrity and ability. He didn't like that. But he didn't trouble himself by asking who had written this slanderous note. No, that wasn't his style. His course of action was much bigger: after a late night practice session he beat up the whole team.

The man was, at heart, a gentle soul, who liked the company of pigeons, ferrets, and fishing rods. He was an earth man, a troglodyte, a basic Neanderthal who couldn't accept that two times two equalled four – it was unfair because it gave him no advantage. Simple but sometimes effective, especially during Cup games, like all men he only really became violent when his manhood came into question. And nobody in their right mind would question the big man. He came from a family of fourteen. The mother was dead. The father was a drunk.

His remark to me had not gone unnoticed by my family. My brother, also big and always angry, replied, 'That's great, coming from you, *le grand merde*'. Even the referee stopped for a moment. Was that Gaelic, Norse or French? This comment had thrown the players into confusion.

I noted the high-collared scout writing something into his wee black book. Could you imagine what the pages of that book had witnessed – Charlie George, George Graham, Super Mac and now, Big Jobbo. At this moment he was probably recording his impressions of the cultural fluidity of the Jobson family. Yes, the man was no fool. He must have understood why I had thumped the ball off the park. What dignity. Putting the ball out of play when I could have carried it up the field on a counterattack.

From my cock-eye, which I had learned to use to my advantage, I saw our coach trying to get the referee's attention with the aim of making a substitution. The boss had decided to bring on a fresh pair of legs to help the lads up front. Our right-back was having a nightmare, poor kid, he could probably do with a break. To be substituted was the ultimate humiliation for a player at this level. I had even heard of a player being substituted when there wasn't a player to replace him. Ten men, it would seem, could do a better job than eleven. That slow walk off the park to your team's changing-room and the shock of being removed is followed by instantaneous hate for the coach, the team, and football itself. Why me? is always the question banging away like toothache. A substitution could be the final spark in a bad year at school. Suicide beckoned as even bad exam results were overshadowed. It was an event. A major one. The legs suddenly didn't work as you trudged, head down, to that faraway place, the dressing-room. The broken soul dragging his legs like the saddest of men, Captain Ahab. Oh, what misery can be caused by a rash decision.

The boss caught the attention of the referee, who turned to me and said, 'It's you, go on, hurry up. Piss off!'

The man had made a mistake. No, surely not me. It couldn't be. Not today. Why me? It all came upon me like a freak thunderstorm. Everything went black, interrupted only by an occasional flash and rumble. Noise and light came from primal motions deep down in my throat. I became a rabid dog. My eyes tried to suppress the tears now falling in disgrace. I hated football, therefore I hated life. This cataclysmic error had uprooted my world and deadened the planet.

Humiliation was then overtaken by inspired thoughts of how to end it all. A nearby cliff, car fumes, a whisky-run away. That's it. I'd run away to London. But first I had to walk past the boss, my replacement and, oh no, I had forgotten about him, the scout. Against great despair, bad times, humiliation, sadness or broken hearts, somehow dignity can rear its proud head. A wind of change can put those shoulders back, head up and eyes ahead, allowing no man to take the last grains of spirit away from you.

For a second I was about to copy Kevin Keegan's act for Liverpool in the Charity Shield match against Leeds United. Sent off with Billy Bremner, he removed his shirt and threw it at the bench. That gesture summed up his feelings toward the misappropriation of justice. The red shirt in the dust: a symbol of the individual's subjugation by a media-influenced decision which said he needed and deserved his comeuppance. But Keegan deserved to have himself and his perm dragged through the Wembley mud. His 'Yes Brian, well, thanks Brian' attitude off the pitch had overshadowed his actual playing ability. This was the time when television had started to dominate the sport. A player's character could be distorted by a clever question from the interviewer like: 'Were you upset when they scored?' Or, 'Do you want to win the Cup?' That really probed, Brian.

Media technique was not and still isn't used by the big clubs. The players have been left to themselves. Warm lager, nob jokes and reading the *Beano* remain the mainstays of the professional footballer. Talking to the camera was left to the more adventurous types like Ian St John or Mick Channon.

' 'Ere I thought they were goot first 'alf'n' n'so goot secon'.' 'The boys were brilliant. Great. Really brilliant, Ah think.' Lowbrow reporting is attractive to the British public. It guarantees you don't have to worry about anything. It takes responsibility away from the reader; participation ends when you buy a paper or watch the box. It ends there. Sit back and just soak it up.

The shirt was off my back. Instead of throwing it at the coach I placed it with great magnificence on the kit bag. I went up to the boss and said straight to his face, 'Stick yir team up yir arse.'

The heavens opened, sunlight fell on my head. Angels roared

approval. On this note of pride I headed toward the dressing-room. I observed I was being followed by the scout. He had witnessed this miscarriage of justice and obviously wanted to add a few points of his own like 'You were the best man on the park', or, 'How soon could you pack? You're going south.' Or even, 'You are the new Ron Yeats'. He approached me. My heart pounded. He tapped me on the shoulder. I turned. He said: 'Richard Jobson? I am arresting you on suspicion . . .'

from SATURDAY BOYS *1990*

The Soccer War

RYSZARD KAPUSCINSKI

Luis Suarez said there was going to be a war, and I believed whatever Luis said. We were staying together in Mexico. Luis was giving me a lesson on Latin America: what it is and how to understand it. He could foresee many events. In his time he had predicted the fall of Goulart in Brazil, the fall of Bosch in the Dominican Republic and of Perez Jimenez in Venezuela. Long before the return of Perón, he believed that the old *caudillo* would again become president of Argentina; he foretold the sudden death of the Haitian dictator François Duvalier at a time when everybody said Papa Doc had many years left. Luis knew how to pick his way through Latin politics, in which amateurs like me got bogged down and blundered helplessly with each step.

This time Luis announced his belief that there would be a war after putting down the newspaper in which he had read a report on the soccer match between the Honduran and Salvadoran national teams. The two countries were playing for the right to take part in the 1970 World Cup in Mexico. The first match was held on Sunday 8 June 1969, in the Honduran capital, Tegucigalpa.

Nobody in the world paid any attention.

The Salvadoran team arrived in Tegucigalpa on Saturday and spent a sleepless night in their hotel. The team could not sleep because they were the target of psychological warfare waged by the Honduran fans. A swarm of people encircled the hotel. The crowd threw stones at the windows and beat sheets of tin and empty barrels with sticks. They set off one string of firecrackers after another. They leaned on the horns of cars parked in front of the hotel. The fans whistled, screamed and sent up hostile chants. This went on all night. The idea was that a sleepy, edgy, exhausted team would be bound to lose. In Latin America these are common practices.

The next day Honduras defeated the sleepless El Salvador squad 1–0.

Eighteen-year-old Amelia Bolanios was sitting in front of the television in San Salvador when the Honduran striker Roberto Cardona scored the winning goal in the final minute. She got up and ran to the desk which contained her father's pistol in a drawer. She then shot herself in the heart. 'The young girl could not bear to see her fatherland brought to its knees,' wrote the Salvadoran newspaper *El Nacional* the next day. The whole capital took part in the televised funeral of Amelia Bolanios. An army honour guard marched with a flag at the head of the procession. The president of the republic and his ministers walked behind the flag-draped coffin. Behind the government came the Salvadoran soccer XI who, booed, laughed at, and spat on at the Tegucigalpa airport, had returned to El Salvador on a special flight that morning.

But the return match of the tie took place in San Salvador, in the beautifully named Flor Blanca stadium, a week later. This time it was the Honduran team that spent a sleepless night. The screaming fans broke all the windows in the hotel and threw rotten eggs, dead rats and stinking rags inside. The players were taken to the match in armoured cars of the 1st Salvadoran Mechanised Division, which saved them from revenge and bloodshed at the hands of the mob that lined the route, holding up portraits of the national heroine Amelia Bolanios.

The army surrounded the ground. On the pitch stood a cordon of soldiers from a crack regiment of the Guardia Nacional, armed with sub-machineguns. During the playing of the Honduran national anthem the crowd roared and whistled. Next, instead of the Honduran flag – which had been burnt before the eyes of the spectators, driving them mad with joy – the hosts ran a dirty, tattered dishrag up the flagpole. Under such conditions the players from Tegucigalpa did not, understandably, have their minds on the game. They had their minds on getting out alive. 'We're awfully lucky that we lost,' said the visiting coach, Mario Griffin, with relief.

El Salvador prevailed, 3–0.

The armoured cars carried the Honduran team straight from the playing field to the airport. A worse fate awaited the visiting fans. Kicked and beaten, they fled towards the border. Two died. Scores landed in hospital. One hundred and fifty of the visitors' cars were burnt. The frontier between the two states was closed a few hours later.

Luis read about all of this in the newspaper and said that there was going to be a war. He had been a reporter for a long time and he knew his beat.

In Latin America, he said, the border between soccer and politics is vague. There is a long list of governments that have fallen or been overthrown after the defeat of the national team. Players on the losing team are denounced in the press as traitors. When Brazil won the World Cup in Mexico, an exiled Brazilian colleague of mine was heartbroken: 'The military right wing,' he said, 'can be assured of at least five more years of peaceful rule.' On the way to the title, Brazil beat England. In an article with the headline 'Jesus Defends Brazil', the Rio do Janeiro paper *Jornal dos Sportes* explained the victory thus: 'Whenever the ball flew towards our goal and a score seemed inevitable, Jesus reached his foot out of the clouds and cleared the ball.' Drawings accompanied the article, illustrating the supernatural intervention.

from THE SOCCER WAR *1990*

Putting The Boot In

DAN KAVANAGH

The Piggeries end were in good voice, but the rest of the crowd was subdued. A hot spring sun made the football seem unreal, and time went quickly. Two corners, a free-kick and a couple of throw-ins, it seemed, and the referee was already blowing his whistle for half-time. Nil–nil. No good at all to Athletic. No sign, either, of what they could do about it. Brendan had been a bit subdued; neat, but subdued. Duffy wondered what Melvyn Prosser was thinking. Forty-five minutes from . . . from what? From the sound of Charlie Magrudo's bulldozers?

Athletic were playing towards the Layton Road end in the second half; though most of the action was taking place in the clogged midfield. Slowly, it seemed, Preston were beginning to batten Athletic down. They won a couple of free-kicks in dangerous positions, and then a corner. Everyone went deep into the Athletic half except for Brendan, the big Preston centre-back, and the Preston keeper. The corner was an outswinger, the Athletic keeper committed himself too early, and was dragged further and further out of his goal in pursuit of the ball. To everyone's relief he caught it, somewhere near the penalty spot. Three strides and he was at the edge of his area and giving the ball a hoofing drop-kick. Chase that one, you buggers, he seemed to say, and eighteen players did. Two, however, had a good thirty yards start on them. Or rather, suddenly, just one: Brendan. The big Preston defender had tripped, somehow – did anyone see what happened? – and was lying on his back near the centre-circle. Brendan was sprinting alone towards the Preston goal, his head cocked as he watched the ball descend towards him. The keeper, seeing his centre-back on the ground, came out fast. Bring him down, Duffy found himself whispering; and he was talking to the keeper, not Brendan. Both players went up in a flail of arms; both players came down in a flail of legs; the ball, quietly, bounced over their falling bodies and continued its unimpeded progress until it settled in the back of the Preston net. One–nil.

No one knew where to run. Half the Athletic team ran to their keeper; half to Brendan. Most of the Preston team besieged the referee, claiming offside, a foul on the centre-back or a foul on the goalkeeper, according to their temperament. A few went over to the linesman and expressed doubts about his eyesight, parentage and sexual habits when alone. A couple bent over the prostrate keeper, who was feigning injury quite well and worrying about next season's first-team squad. One–nil.

Preston, not surprisingly, seemed to resent the goal, and attacked with an additional muscularity. Brendan, for his part, found himself on the end of some close attention from the big centre-back who had earlier mysteriously lost his footing. There would be bruises to count on the Sunday morning. But Athletic weren't eager to throw away their sudden gift. They scrambled, they hoofed, they scrapped, they battled; they were not above getting a touch physical themselves; and their keeper, spurred on by his first goal ever in league football, saved them twice with full-length sprawls. Suddenly, it was all over. One–nil. Athletic were safe.

Ten members of the Athletic team ran towards Jimmy Lister's dug-out. There was hugging and shouting, and a few tears were shed, before they all turned to the main stand for acclaim. But the attention of the main stand was temporarily elsewhere. They were watching Brendan Domingo. So was Duffy, and he was a lot closer.

When the final whistle blew, Brendan had stopped where he was. He offered his hand to the Preston centre-back, who refused it, and carefully took out his earplugs. Then he began trotting very deliberately towards the Layton Road end. On his way he passed the Preston keeper and offered his hand, and was refused again. Slowly, he walked round behind the net until he faced the phalanx of yobbs. Duffy wondered what Brendan was going to do next, but he clearly had it all planned out. He began clapping the yobbos, as if thanking them for their kind advice in telling him to go back to the jungle. The yobbos were puzzled by this; but they were less puzzled by Brendan's next gesture. He turned his back to the Layton Road end, bent and lowered his shorts. The two white straps of his jock seemed to emphasise the blackness of his bum. He stayed like this for some five seconds, then pulled up his shorts, turned round, and started clapping the Layton Road enders again. Slowly, tauntingly. Duffy thought Brendan was extremely brave, even if there were a few coppers around.

Then, suddenly, Brendan was felled. He clutched the top of his head and keeled over heavily. The coppers, who had been looking on almost as puzzled as the yobbos, took this as their cue and waded into the terracing. The rest of the Athletic team, who had only caught the end of Brendan's performance, were already rushing over. The fans in the main stand started booing the yobbs at the Layton Road end. Must have been a coin, or a brick or something. The physio came running across and bent over Brendan. The police were vigorously bidding an end-of-season farewell to the yobbos. The main stand carried on booing, until, after a couple of minutes, Brendan got slowly to his feet; then they started cheering. While Jimmy Lister and the ten other players began a lap of honour, Brendan, his arm round the physio's shoulder, made his way groggily to the tunnel. Everyone knew exactly what had happened. Everyone except Duffy, that is.

from PUTTING THE BOOT IN *1985*

As Others See Us

DAVID LACEY

Scottish contacts in that RAF team enabled me to see my first England–Scotland match at Wembley. The game, in 1963, should have been one of the greatest in the long history of fixtures between the countries. The English attack contained Greaves, Smith, Douglas and Charlton; Scotland had a half-back line of Mackay, Ure and Baxter, with White, St John and Law in front of them.

I remember well the sickening, almost selfish feeling of disappointment when, after only six minutes, Smith and Eric Caldow collided. The Tottenham centre-forward returned eventually but the Scottish captain, and surely one of their most cultured defenders since the war, had broken both bones in his left leg. An easy win for England? Not a bit of it. Jim Baxter and Dave Mackay attacked gloriously for Scotland who won 2–1.

Perhaps it is necessary, at a distance of more than a decade, to check the details of Baxter's two goals and the fact that the second was a penalty after Henderson had been tripped. What will never fade is the picture of Baxter dispossessing Armfield and shooting past Banks in the space of a couple of heart beats. It was a good day to be standing at the predominantly Scottish end of Wembley Stadium. Everybody was thoroughly happy, considerably inebriated, and generally well behaved. One fan spent the entire game perched on the edge of a step at an angle of 45 degrees, a feat which he could not have achieved had he been sober.

Several years later it was sad to see Baxter plodding heavily about the field with Sunderland and Nottingham Forest. The 'Slim Jim' who had orchestrated that Wembley game had now taken to wearing his shirt outside his shorts to lessen the effect of a thickening midriff but if his pace had gone he would, from time to time, sway away from an opponent and deliver a perfect pass to the other side of the field.

I first became professionally involved with Scotland in 1965, being detailed to cover their fateful World Cup qualifying match against Poland at Hampden. Coming from Sussex, where there was a tendency to regard anyone who did not have a front garden as under-privileged, it was hard to believe how the tenements in Glasgow could have been allowed to exist. With each subsequent visit to the city another horror seems to have been removed although there is still much to offend the eye, and not all of it through age.

Hampden itself, grey and grubby, can surely never alter. It must be the only ground in the world which, apart from the grass, looks much the same in colour as in black and white. That night Scotland were led out by a lone piper and, of course, the wave of sound which greeted the players momentarily numbed the senses. It was one thing to read about the Roar, quite another to experience it first hand.

What a pity Scotland blew it against the Poles. Piped on, whistled off, they lost the best chance they will ever have of winning a World Cup, unless that is, FIFA ever decide to hold a tournament on Scottish soil. Denis Law, it is said, spent the afternoon of the final playing golf. He could well have been leading Scotland's attack against England at Wembley that day if Liberda and Sadek of Poland had not been given two late goals.

Being London based, it is easy to get a disproportionate view of the game in Scotland. While it is clear that the majority of clubs exist on gates some way below those in England the enthusiasm of the Scottish, or should one say the Glasgow crowds, for the important fixtures is rarely equalled for intensity further south.

One of the most dramatic moments encountered in my experience as a soccer writer came in 1969 when Celtic played Benfica at Parkhead in the European Cup. For an hour before the start paradise had echoed to its songs of praise and the main talking point of the day was the future of Tommy Gemmell, who had been off form and was not seeing eye to eye with the club. Within two minutes of the start Celtic were awarded a free kick a yard from the penalty area. Auld and two colleagues stood over the ball like Macbeth's witches; a tap sideways, a firmer, longer square pass and there was Gemmell thundering in on the opposite side to score with a glorious shot into the top far corner. Gemmell raced eighty yards back up the touchline, saluting the ecstatic crowd. In one delicious moment all his problems had been solved . . . or so it seemed at the time.

The other, quieter side of the Scottish game was glimpsed at Aberdeen in 1971 when, after a Scottish side revitalised by Tommy Docherty had beaten Belgium in a European Championship match at

Pittodrie, it seemed worthwhile to stay in that impressive city for a few days to watch the local side play East Fife.

Martin Buchan, Willie Young and Joe Harper were all playing for Aberdeen then and the side sauntered to a five-goal victory looking rather bored with the proceedings, which were half-paced for the most part. This explained the difficulty which some Scottish players have had in adapting themselves to the greater speed at which most of the football in the English first division is played. A number of outstanding forwards – Law, Gilzean and, most recently, Dalglish among them – have found little trouble making the transition but for some defenders the process has been hard. Gordon McQueen, now one of the best centre-halves in the English league, looked slow and awkward when he first came into the Leeds side, and Young's ponderous performances for Arsenal are beginning to earn him the sympathy that some crowds reserve for those who will never fail for want of trying.

Where Scotland has caught up and passed England is in the midfield positions. Whereas the English have yet to replace Ball, Bell, Mullery, Peters and Charlton with players of comparable talent, it must be a long time since a Scottish manager has had such an abundance of quality in the creative positions. Billy Bremner was one of the best midfield players in the 1974 World Cup finals in West Germany but Scotland surely have a much broader base in Masson, Hartford, Rioch and, if they choose to play him there, Macari.

All of course are Anglos and Rioch might have been wearing a white shirt had England been quicker to appreciate what he had to offer. But even Rioch, Aldershot-born with a Home Counties accent, appears to be infected by the demands of Hampden for success.

Of all the Scots playing in the English league Lou Macari is consistently the most delightful to watch. The weight and angle of his passes save so much time and create so much extra space for Manchester United that in the end one is tempted to take the little man's accurancy for granted. Yet it is impossible to tire of seeing him chip the ball on the run without breaking stride, usually hitting the pass with the outside of his left foot so that it spins gently past the defence into the path of a colleague.

Are there any more Macaris in Scotland, or Massons, Hartfords, Grays and Jordans, not to mention Mackays, Whites, Gilzeans, Bremners and Laws? Much though the steady stream south is appreciated by English audiences it is worrying to hear of the decline in attendances even starting to affect the Old Firm. Sad, too, to see Celtic signing Fulham reserves so soon after selling Dalglish to Liverpool.

In England there are frequent demands for a creation of a super league, that is a Premier Division of a dozen or so clubs who would play fewer matches, leaving more time to concentrate on improving skills and greater opportunities for the national squad to train together. This has never had much chance of gaining substantial support among the clubs and will have even less if the Scottish league's reorganisation into smaller divisions proves to be a false hope.

Where Scotland can still give a lead is in the continuing introduction of foreign players into the domestic game. Only Rangers and Celtic could afford to pay the wages demanded by Europe's better players and then the state of the currency and the prevailing tax system would stop most of them. But even the occasional Scandinavian cap brings a little of the Continental European's concept of soccer to a team.

Perhaps only an Englishman could suggest that the Scots sign Swedes and Icelandics to replace the talents swallowed up by English clubs. But if the results in the European competitions are any guide the overall standard in the Scottish league is not what it was, however excellent the form of the national side may be.

from WHEN WILL WE SEE YOUR LIKE AGAIN? *1977*

Leaving the Lira

DENIS LAW

It was some time before I got around to examining possible reasons for my being sent off the field by my own coach. Even today it has got me puzzled, though a friend 'on the inside' told me he had no doubt that I had been framed.

'You mustn't blame Santos, for he was only obeying orders from his superiors,' this chap said. 'Believe me, some of the club officials were absolutely determined to get rid of you, and to get Del Sol in your place. This wasn't as easy as it might appear, since you remained so popular with Torino supporters, so a way had to be found to discredit you in front of them.' Could this be the truth of it? Certainly I had no quarrel with Santos. As a coach you could hardly say Santos was Herreira, Hidegkuti, and Winterbottom rolled into one. He was just Santos rolled into one. But he was quite a decent fellow – a pleasant Argentinian who, like everyone else on the payroll, was simply a tool of the directors.

Incredible though it may seem to British fans, such plotting and intrigue are quite common in Italian football, and everyone except the victim seems to get a great deal of pleasure out of dramatic situations of this kind.

For the next fourteen days I was confined to the flat. I had been banned from the ground, and hardly anyone would speak to me. Joe and Gigi brought me morsels of information.

Then I was instructed to travel to Lausanne, not to play there for Torino in a Friendship Cup-tie, but to meet Mr Busby with a view to my transfer to Manchester United.

You can imagine with what joy I undertook that journey. Though I wasn't invited to the talk between Mr Busby and the Torino president which took place in an hotel room, I was waiting eagerly outside when the Manchester United manager broke the news: 'It's going to be all right, Denis. Everything is more or less fixed.'

You can guess I wanted to hop on a Manchester-bound plane right away, but first there had to be a board meeting to approve the terms. After watching the Friendship Cup-tie in company with Mr Busby I was told to return to Turin with the rest of the team.

Well, I thought, at least it isn't going to be a long-drawn-out affair like that of Jimmy Greaves. And it wasn't. But the news from the Torino board meeting came as a severe shock. It was that Signor Fillipone had sold my contract to Juventus for £160,000.

'Since when,' I wanted to know, 'can a footballer be sold like a piece of meat without having any say in the matter himself?'

'In Italian football,' officials assured me, 'a player under contract must do as he is told, and go where he is sent. The sale of your contract to Juventus is perfectly legal.'

Legal it may have been, since I signed all kinds of papers for the Italian league that I was unable to understand. But I had no more intention of going to Juventus than of going to the moon. The only place I was going was home, as I told Signor Agnelli at the meeting, and I lost no more time in argument.

Back at the flat it took only a few minutes to pack a bag and to telephone Giuseppe, a friend who owned a taxi. Joe Baker was away from home with the rest of the team, so I scribbled him a quick note. Then I stepped into the taxi and we made the seventy-five-minute journey to Milan as if Stirling Moss was on our tail. Fortunately I knew some people at Milan airport and they fixed me up with a seat on a plane. Before anyone knew I had gone I was in London, getting fixed up on another plane which would take me home to Aberdeen.

Originally, I had intended to be away for only three or four days to get away from it all and to discuss events with my family. Naturally Mum and Dad were worried by the reports they had received and wanted to hear all about the situation from me at first hand. Then I would have returned to sort things out. But, according to the news, Torino still insisted that I had been sold to Juventus, so I realised it would be pointless to go back only to engage in further argument. If necessary I would have gone back to play for Torino, but for no other team. They knew where I stood, and where to find me when they were ready to talk sense. So I stayed at home, and let things work out for themselves.

The club president sent a telegram demanding my return. I must remember to answer it sometime.

I filled in the next few weeks playing golf and enjoying the company of my family and friends again. As a long-standing member of the Professional Footballers' Association I sought advice from Cliff Lloyd, the secretary. Cliff promised that the players would give me all the help I needed to resist being sold to Juventus against my wishes.

'We've never had to contend with anything like this before,' he told me. 'If Torino were to have their way it would be sheer slavery.'

Weeks passed, and all that happened was that I slightly improved my disgracefully high golf handicap. Then at last I got a message from Gigi Peronace to meet him at Edinburgh airport.

He told me at once that he had authority to sell me to Manchester United. I was, of course, delighted. It meant a victory for me, and, above all, for common sense. Italian league soccer and I no longer had anything to offer each other, that was obvious.

When I actually signed on for Manchester United, the club I had always wanted, it was like signing a peace treaty after a long hard battle. And as one might expect, most of the participants in that battle bore scars.

from LIVING FOR KICKS *1963*

The World Cup Final 1970

HUGH McILVANNEY and ARTHUR HOPCRAFT

There is a beautiful self-contained quality about a World Cup final. All the other matches, whatever their own vivid excitements, can only nourish the expectations of that last collision. Earlier days offer sudden death but this is the only one that offers instant immortality. Now the thousand background noises of the competition, the politicking, the training camp gossip, the accusations and insinuations, the boasts and hardluck stories, are stilled by the imminence of a pure climax. The thousand complex pressures that shape a World Cup have squeezed out all irrelevance and left the single thrilling reality of a game of football. That process of simplification is not always fair but its drama is to do with irrevocability rather than justice. No matter how many start out, in the final only two can play, and only one can win.

To those of us whose childhood and adolescence left us permanently impregnated with the mythology of football, it is inevitably a moving occasion. Sprinting through the rain to the bare, hard-seated buses that were to take us from the Maria Isabel Hotel to the Aztec Stadium on the morning of Sunday 21 June, we had that heightened sense of anticipation that invests every trivial preliminary with a tremor of pleasure. Every joke seemed funnier, every face friendlier. You could say that our behaviour was childish or you could say that we were reaching normally to the prospect of one of the last great communal rituals available to our society. You can say what you like. We were just glad to be going to the World Cup final.

The rain thinned and the exhaust fumes thickened as the bus hurried in a series of lunges through traffic that was even more raucously lively than usual. Brazilians, with vast flags streaming behind tall poles thrust from their car windows, weaved hazardously between lanes, seeking Italian victims for their banter. The Italians, for their part, were a minority but not a meek one. Disembarking in a gentle smirr at the Aztec, we were happy to let them get on with it. We could not lose. And yet it would be dishonest to claim total objectivity. Seeing the Brazilians come to this last obstacle was like watching Arkle gallop into the last fence of a steeplechase. A bad fall, even an ungraceful stumble, would be a painful blow to anyone who loved the sport. No one would begrudge Italy victory so long as they beat Brazil at their best. Indeed, if they rose above the highest standards of Pelé and Gérson and Tostão and the rest, the world would be obliged to acclaim them great champions, a team fully deserving to keep the Jules Rimet Trophy as their own property. What no neutral wanted, however, was to see Brazil undersell themselves. It can happen to the finest teams: the brutal anticlimax of an unworthy performance in the final. We suspected that it would not happen to Brazil, that their thinking players, and above all Pelé, would not let it happen. We had flown up with them from Guadalajara and been impressed by their deep calm. Most of the damaging tension had been drained out of them by the defeat of Uruguay. They would obviously be nervous now as the kick-off approached but theirs would be an alert, stimulated edginess, uncomplicated by neurotic apprehensions. At the technical level they admitted that they would have been far more concerned if set to face England, whose zonal marking presented much greater problems than the man-for-man covering of Italy. But no opposition would have frightened them. They believe Brazilian football is made for World Cup finals and could not wait to prove the point.

from WORLD CUP 70 *1970*

Covering Celtic

JOHN MACKENZIE

Show me a football writer who has covered a game in Lisbon, and I'll show you a guy with ulcers. They do have a telephone system in Portugal, but I have never been convinced that the instrument sitting in front of me on a ledge in the press-box is connected to anywhere else in the world. And somehow in this city where contact with Glasgow becomes a matter for prayer and crossed fingers, there is always drama that should be pouring back over the hot line. Celtic's most famous occasion, the European Cup final against Inter Milan, was comparatively straightforward, because it kicked off in late afternoon and there was time to spare, all of it needed. The telephone that cost the *Daily*

Express £30 to install has still to ring, but there was telex as a stand-by.

But night games in the Portuguese capital start usually around ten o'clock, and few of the men charged with the responsibility of keeping the Scottish public informed will forget the night Celtic played Benfica, with a comfortable three-goal lead to defend. It was a nostalgic return, staying in the Palaccio Hotel again, the Estoril HQ for the historic final a year or two earlier. I got off to a bad start, in bed with a chill after risking a dip in an allegedly heated swimming pool, in the month of November. When Jock Stein, with some camp followers, visited my bedroom carrying a huge bunch of flowers borrowed from the lounge, and singing 'Nearer my God to Thee' it did nothing to help my recovery.

But I made it to the match and often wished I hadn't. Eusebio and Graca scored before half-time to put Celtic on a tightrope, and there was a miracle . . . the phones were working. Political intervention somewhere along the line had guaranteed uninterrupted service for the duration of the match. Celtic fought a rearguard action throughout the second half, but two minutes into injury time Diamintino pushed the ball over the line. In the press-box, nobody knew whether the referee's whistle had signalled a goal or the end of the game. Were Celtic through or not? There was no way of knowing until the teams came back out to play an extra half hour. It was then the writers realised that every phone in the press-box was dead. Service had been guaranteed for the duration of the game and nobody in the international exchange had ever heard of extra time.

Fingernails were nibbled down to the knuckle, and faces got whiter and whiter as the thirty minutes dragged on, with no further score. And the phones were still dead while the drama continued in the referee's room below the stand. It was a toss-up.

Billy McNeill, Jock Stein, Coluna and Otto Gloria, the Benfica boss, gathered round the referee. In those days there was no question of replays, or penalty-kick deciders. The referee explained that he would toss the coin twice. The first toss would decide who had the right to call first in the toss that really mattered. He asked if everyone understood. Jock Stein said he did, but it was the first thing the referee had done all night that he understood. Billy McNeill won the first toss. Next time up, the coin hit the floor, rolled against the referee's boot, and then round in a full circle before falling over. And it fell the right way for Celtic. To complicate the issue for the writers who were still trying frantically to contact Glasgow, a roar from the crowd seemed to indicate that Benfica had won. The phones started working again just in time to get the facts across, but a few writers cut their life expectancy by a year or two that night.

from WE'LL SUPPORT YOU EVERMORE *1976*

Huddersfield in the Rain

J. P. W. MALLALIEU

On Saturday 6 January, it rained in Huddersfield. It rained like anything. It rained all morning. When I looked from my bedroom window I could hardly see across the road for the rain. I should have been drenched on my way to the office if a friend had not given me a lift; and I should have been drenched again if at any time before 1.30 p.m. I had been able to leave my desk. So you can imagine what happened to Tottenham Hotspur's supporters who had travelled through the night by special train and reached Huddersfield at breakfast time. They got drenched again after breakfast as they moved unhappily from doorway to doorway. They got drenched a third time as they trudged to Leeds Road and waited for the gates to open.

The second fact is mist. If there had been no rain I'd still have had some difficulty in seeing across the road. For the mist, which hung thickly on the high surrounding moors, trailed dark wisps down the hillside into the main streets of the town itself. So the rain-soaked supporters of Tottenham, suffering already in body, had in addition the dulling fear in their minds that all this journeying might prove in vain, that the match, in fact, would be postponed. This fear increased after midday, when the force of the rain diminished and allowed the wet, clinging mist to press down from the hills in bulk.

On normal days the walk from town to Leeds Road is one of the greatest pleasures of my football Saturday. I leave the main street where people are sauntering purposelessly, and, in a side street, I join a trickle of men and women who are walking intently. In this trickle I emerge on the old Beast Market and that great slum-cleared waste below Southgate. On to this open space I see other trickles emerging from other side streets and converging on the far corner by the gas works. If the wind is right, you get the smell from the gas works, and maybe from the sewerage works as well; but it's not the smell that makes you hurry. You hurry for excitement, excitement which feeds on itself as the trickles converge into a stream and the stream converges into a flood, a flood of blue and white scarves, of clattering feet and, even on the brightest day, of precautionary mackintoshes (for in Huddersfield, during the football season, you never know). On this walk I have no care. The two points seem there for the taking and the world is young, and when the match is the third round of the Cup and the favours and rattles are out for the first time, the world is not only young but gay as well.

But there was no walk for me this third round. I was kept so late at the office that it seemed I might miss the kick-off; so I took a taxi. And there were no floods, nor streams, nor even trickles of men and women. Those who were eager enough to brave the day at all had long since reached the ground, and from the streaming windows of the taxi I could see only a few stragglers swirling through the mist.

The ground itself was appalling. Water trickled off the crown to the surrounding running-track or lay in wide pools. How could anyone play football on such a quagmire? And if they did play, how would anyone see? The terraces on the far side loomed faintly through the mist, and outside the ground behind one of the goals a ghostly mill peered for a moment warily and then withdrew. The world, it seemed, had closed in around this watery, silent space. The water, the mist and the space remained throughout the afternoon, but not the silence.

from SPORTING DAYS *1955*

The Third Round of the Cup

J. P. W. MALLALIEU

Yet it began so well . . .

When I fed the rabbits, the sun was as high as it can go in January, and the frost on the lawn was melting. The whole morning seemed to glisten. So it should; for this was the shiniest morning in the football calendar, the third-round-of-the-Cup morning, when the big clubs come in for the first time and those little clubs which have insinuated themselves through earlier rounds think they are going to knock the Brylcreem off their betters.

What a morning this always is! The earlier rounds are important, no doubt, to those who habitually engage in them. But no one else bothers. We just notice when, say, Blyth Spartans and Tranmere Rovers fail to reach a decision at their first meeting; fail to reach a decision, after extra time, at their second meeting; and have, in all, to play 300 minutes before they can tell which of the two is to be slaughtered in the third round. The other results cause about as much stir as a maiden over in a Test match with India.

But the third round is real. You get the clash of the great, like Newcastle and Aston Villa. You get the minor local derbies like Brentford and Queen's Park Rangers. Above all you get the babies against the giants, like Scunthorpe against the Spurs or Workington against Liverpool – and presumably Tranmere Rovers were playing somebody too. How we all hope that these babies will repeat the fairy story – and well they may if they are playing on their own ground. These baby teams sometimes have baby grounds which cramp the giants; and on these baby grounds there are sometimes baby hillocks and baby valleys which upset billiard-table players from the first division. How everyone laughs when one of the giants comes a cropper, when Arsenal falls to Walsall or Sunderland gets stuck at Yeovil. That's all part of the Cup. Anything can happen. So the morning of the third round glistened, even when, as so often happens, you can't see a yard in front of you for fog.

There was no fog for *this* third round. The warmth of the sun had made even rabbits lazy. At any rate, they had not bothered to burrow into my lawn. After feeding them, I sat in the sun and wondered idly which team I would back that afternoon. Usually I pick North v. South, but I couldn't decide which was which from Brentford (of Brentford) v. Queen's Park Rangers (of Shepherd's Bush). I should have to get these two sorted for me by Mercator himself. I plumped for the Rangers, only because their manager, Dave Magnall, used to play for Huddersfield, and because their inside-right, Conway Smith, not only played for Huddersfield himself, but is the son of the late Billy Smith who for twenty years almost was Huddersfield.

Leaving my rabbits to the sun, I set off by car for Griffin Park. Most English football grounds are so hidden by terraced, redbrick houses that you would think the game was some sort of sin, to be kept from the notice of the police and the churches. But on a Cup-tie day there's no disguising them. Those three mounted policemen trotting up the street – I'll bet they are not defending the Brentford gas works; and those newspaper bills, tied round lamp posts, advertising all the sport – they're not *always* showing in back streets; nor, I am sure, are those elderly men with walking sticks, who wait hopefully at corners and beckon cars. These are the pointers to a football ground which even Dr Watson could not have missed, and if you follow them, as I did, around midday, you will find the little queues, rubbing their noses against closed gates, which are the final proof without which Holmes never closed his mind.

Little queues? I was surprised myself. But the older I get, the more I become like Dr Watson. So I drew no sensible conclusion. After circling the ground and finding only little queues, I assumed that there would be no difficulty about seeing the match. So I left my car in the care of one of those old men with sticks, and went into The Griffin for a sandwich and a glass of beer. In the pub I discovered that this Cup-tie was 'ticket only'; and I had no ticket.

I appealed to the landlord. No go. The landlord appealed all round the bar. No go. The landlord's son, aged ten, announced that *he* had a ticket but made it clear that that was no go either. Then someone remembered that, twenty minutes ago, the local butcher had had a spare ticket. The landlord rang him up; the ticket was still spare: the landlord's son trotted off to fetch it, and I was in. I was among strangers in The Griffin; but if you are a real football fan and meet other real football fans you are among strangers no more.

I was able to pick my place, on the rails, right behind one of the goals. The empty stands had all the hollowness of a main-line railway station in the early morning, so that the rattles and the shouts of the men who, quite seriously, on this January morning, were selling ice-cream echoed against the corrugated iron roofs. But, hollowness and ice-cream notwithstanding, I felt warm in expectation. I remembered the first time, thirty-two years ago, that I had stood directly behind a goal. Within two minutes of the kick-off my Huddersfield had fired a beautiful, new yellow ball into that goal and had almost blown the net away. I thought cosily of Huddersfield playing an easy match, 190 miles away, playing an easy match which might even at the eleventh hour provide the spark to light them home.

'Ladies and gentlemen, it is exactly sixty minutes to the kick-off.' The echo from the loudspeaker seemed dulled, and I noticed that the ground was beginning to fill. By the time the loudspeaker announced:

'Ladies and gentlemen, the kick-off will be in, approximately, seven minutes. Will people standing on the gangways move away?' there was no echo at all, and, so far as I could see, nowhere for the people on the gangways to move away to. I myself had been edged from the rails, politely but effectively, by four small boys, who unscrupulously used their lack of height to play on my better feelings. However, I could still see, and anyway was spellbound in those magic moments which immediately precede the launching of a Cup-tie.

Yes, the day had begun well.

from SPORTING DAYS *1955*

Sporting Manners

J. P. W. MALLALIEU

One November afternoon, at Old Trafford, Bob Hesford, of Huddersfield Town, received one of the most prolonged ovations ever given to a goalkeeper. The odds against saving a penalty are probably about 10 to 1. Against a dead-ball kicker with the skill of Manchester United's Mitten, they must be much longer. Yet Hesford saved Mitten's shot. Unhappily, one of Huddersfield's backs had moved into the penalty area prematurely. So the referee ordered the kick to be taken again – and bless me if Hesford did not make *another* save. The odds against doing *that* must be in the hundreds; and the 40,000 crowd at Old Trafford went on cheering for minutes.

But it was only after the game that I discovered why some of the crowd, at least, were so enthusiastic. I had said: 'Well, that was nice work!' 'Yes,' said my neighbour, 'you won't often see the like of it. *Hesford's a real gentleman*.' It seemed that before the kick was taken Hesford had carefully cleaned the muddy ball on his jersey and himself placed it on the penalty spot for Mitten. This little courtesy, so rare on professional soccer grounds, had warmed the hearts of the Manchester crowd almost as much as the astonishing feat that followed it.

There are, of course, some soccer players who are just bad tempered. If they are penalised they will kick the ball away petulantly and leave their opponents to fetch it. Any schoolmaster, and some referees, can deal easily with them. But it is true that even the majority of pleasantly

tempered players do not think that courtesy should come into soccer.
If they dribble a ball out of play, they do not fetch it back. Let the
other side do that. If a wing-half is about to throw in from touch and
is told that it is his opponent's ball, he does not hand the ball over.
He throws it on the ground, preferably well out of reach. To most
players that is not rude. It is just common sense. By throwing the ball
out of reach, by leaving an opponent to retrieve a ball, a player gives
himself and his team time to get into position. If he handed the ball
over courteously on the touch-line, his team might be a man short for
vital seconds, since his opponent would certainly not repay courtesy
by waiting until he had got back into play. This practical attitude to
the game is in fact so prevalent that, when I mentioned Bob Hesford's
courtesy to another player, he said: 'Courtesy my foot! Bob knows
it's easier to stop a clean ball than a muddy one.'

I personally have never been able to make up my mind about courtesy, or about the somewhat wider question of 'being sporting' in
games. In mid-week, sitting at home, I like to think that all Huddersfield players behave like perfect gentlemen on the field. But if, on the
following Saturday, one of them gave a goal away by being 'gentle-
manly', I should be very angry. When a team is winning by the odd
goal, and there are only a few minutes to go, it is, I am sure, most
unsporting for their players continually to kick the ball out of play.
Yet if one of my team in such circumstances sportingly opened the
game and thereby let an opponent equalise, he would hear about it
from me at once.

from SPORTING DAYS *1955*

A Yorkshire Derby

J. P. W. MALLALIEU

My train shot from the long Standedge tunnel just as dawn was creeping down Wessendon and lighting Black Hill. I cleared a circle on the
streaming window and peered at the moorland peaks which stretch
away to Woodhead, to the Snake, to Featherbed Moss and to Sheffield. Black Hill was white, and, as the train clattered down the Colne
Valley, I saw that the long grass was stiff and that the usually warm,

soft peat was hard and cold. Thank goodness this is not a rugger match, I said.

At the hotel a sleepy night porter brightened when he saw me. 'You're up for the match, I suppose,' he said. The waiter at breakfast was too busy guessing the score to find the marmalade, constituents who came to see me during the morning with serious personal troubles could yet find time to peer anxiously through my office windows at the snow-laden clouds, and in the café where I had lunch the customers exchanged eager gossip about the teams while the waitresses, who would be tied to their jobs all afternoon, made sarcastic comments about people who wasted their time at football matches.

How different all this was from last season, when Huddersfield seemed full of Rugby League fans, when no one mentioned football except to say that 'Town' was doomed and a few faithful dragged their long faces and leaden feet to Leeds Road only in the confident anticipation of disaster. But now, as we began our walk to the ground, there were bright faces everywhere, shining from the sharp air and from the hope of victory, there were brisk, longstriding feet and there was the humming bubble of excitement. For that afternoon Huddersfield Town, second in the second division, were playing the division leaders, neighbouring Sheffield United; and not a man in the West Riding was indifferent to, not a man in Huddersfield was uncertain of, the result.

We joined the groups of men and women who were trickling down every side street from the shopping centre. We hustled and jostled along, counting the years – twenty-four, if you allow the New Year as one – since Sheffield United had won at Leeds Road, we winked at each other and at last we were in the ground with fifteen minutes to spare and 43,000 fellow-fanatics packed around us. Then we had time again to notice the weighted sky and the sand-covered pitch. We'd be lucky to see good football on a surface like that. We'd be lucky to see anything if that sky gave way.

For a moment expectancy ebbed, for snow clouds and a skating surface were not the only reasons for caution. This was a needle match between two teams who, with more than half a season gone, seem to be fighting it out on their own. It might well decide the championship, and such matches often produce more vigour than science. Moreover, this was a local derby, and you can guess what that may mean. Between Huddersfield and Sheffield there is none of that division of Protestant and Catholic which turns a game between Celtic and Rangers into a religious war. Huddersfield and Sheffield men often speak to each other, and, during the cricket season, will even risk taking their hands out of their pockets in each other's company. But a local derby is a local derby, in which the players can expect more bruises than goals and from which spectators can suffer severe injury to their local pride. When you are beaten at home by a team from far away you at least know that when the last train or coach leaves you will be shot of that team and its supporters for a twelvemonth. But a man from Huddersfield may bump into a man from Sheffield any day of the week and get salt rubbed into the sorer places. So when the red and white of Sheffield appeared beneath the stand and provoked a roar which showed that many men from Sheffield had risked the moorland snow and ice, the appearance beneath the stand of Huddersfield's blue and white provoked an explosion of defiance, plus some cautionary boos for the referee.

For about five minutes the Huddersfield team seemed to be playing on skates. They glided over the ground and round the Sheffield *players*, while the home crowd exulted and a covey of Sheffield supporters near me gabbled to each other darkly in some language of their own. Then one of the skaters was tripped and the home crowd yelled, first at the referee, then at this covey of foreigners, in language that is universal. The Sheffield men looked down their noses and said nothing. Before turning back to the game a home spectator fired a parting shot at them. 'Yon's third division stoof, yon is,' he said. Seconds later, a Sheffield player was tripped and the Sheffield covey rose as one. '*Yon's* third division stoof,' they yelled. 'Ay,' said a Huddersfield man, 'we've learned it from thee.' Then opening his eyes in round surprise, he added: 'Well ah nivver did! Tha' can talk King's English same as oos.'

from SPORTING DAYS *1955*

The Sporting Spirit

GEORGE ORWELL

Now that the brief visit of the Moscow Dynamo football team has come to an end, it is possible to say publicly what many thinking people were saying privately before the Dynamos ever arrived. That is, that sport is an unfailing cause of ill will, and that if such a visit as this had any effect at all on Anglo-Soviet relations, it could only be to make them slightly worse than before.

Even the newspapers have been unable to conceal the fact that at least two of the four matches played led to much bad feeling. At the Arsenal match, I am told by someone who was there, a British and a Russian player came to blows and the crowd booed the referee. The Glasgow match, someone else informs me, was simply a free-for-all from the start. And then there was the controversy, typical of our nationalistic age, about the composition of the Arsenal team. Was it really an all-England team, as claimed by the Russians, or merely a league team, as claimed by the British? And did the Dynamos end their tour abruptly in order to avoid playing an all-England team? As usual, everyone answers these questions according to his political predilections. Not quite everyone, however. I noted with interest, as an instance of the vicious passions that football provokes, that the sporting correspondent of the russophile *News Chronicle* took the anti-Russian line and maintained that Arsenal was *not* an all-England team. No doubt the controversy will continue to echo for years in the footnotes of history books. Meanwhile the result of the Dynamos' tour, in so far as it has had any result, will have been to create fresh animosity on both sides.

And how could it be otherwise? I am always amazed when I hear people saying that sport creates goodwill between the nations, and that if only the common peoples of the world could meet one another at football or cricket, they would have no inclination to meet on the battlefield. Even if one didn't know from concrete examples (the 1936 Olympic Games, for instance) that international sporting contests lead to orgies of hatred, one could deduce it from general principles.

Nearly all the sports practised nowadays are competitive. You play to win, and the game has little meaning unless you do your utmost to win. On the village green, where you pick up sides and no feeling of local patriotism is involved, it is possible to play simply for the fun and exercise: but as soon as the question of prestige arises, as soon as you feel that you and some larger unit will be disgraced if you lose, the most savage combative instincts are aroused. Anyone who has played even in a school football match knows this. At the international level sport is frankly mimic warfare. But the significant thing is not the behaviour of the players but the attitude of the spectators and, behind the spectators, of the nations who work themselves into furies over these absurd contests, and seriously believe – at any rate for short periods – that running, jumping and kicking a ball are tests of national virtue.

Even a leisurely game like cricket, demanding grace rather than strength, can cause much ill will, as we saw in the controversy over body-line bowling and over the rough tactics of the Australian team that visited England in 1921. Football, a game in which everyone gets hurt and every nation has its own style of play which seems unfair to foreigners, is far worse. Worst of all is boxing. One of the most horrible sights in the world is a fight between white and coloured boxers before a mixed audience. But a boxing audience is always disgusting, and the behaviour of the women, in particular, is such that the army, I believe, does not allow them to attend its contests. At any rate, two or three years ago, when Home Guards and regular troops were holding a boxing tournament, I was placed on guard at the door of the hall, with orders to keep the women out.

In England, the obsession with sport is bad enough, but even fiercer passions are aroused in young countries where games-playing and nationalism are both recent developments. In countries like India or Burma, it is necessary at football matches to have strong cordons of police to keep the crowd from invading the field. In Burma, I have seen the supporters of one side break through the police and disable the goalkeeper of the opposing side at a critical moment. The first big football match that was played in Spain about fifteen years ago led to an uncontrollable riot. As soon as strong feelings of rivalry are aroused, the notion of playing the game according to the rules always vanishes. People want to see one side on top and the other side humiliated, and they forget that victory gained through cheating or through the intervention of the crowd is meaningless. Even when the spectators don't intervene physically they try to influence the game by cheering their own side and 'rattling' opposing players with boos and insults. Serious sport has nothing to do with fair play. It is bound up with hatred, jealousy, boastfulness, disregard of all rules and sadistic pleasure in witnessing violence: in other words it is war minus the shooting.

Instead of blah-blahing about the clean, healthy rivalry of the football field and the great part played by the Olympic Games in bringing the nations together, it is more useful to inquire how and why this modern cult of sport arose. Most of the games we now play are of ancient origin, but sport does not seem to have been taken very seriously between Roman times and the nineteenth century. Even in the English public schools the games cult did not start till the later part of the last century. Dr Arnold, generally regarded as the founder of the modern public school, looked on games as simply a waste of time. Then, chiefly in England and the United States, games were built up into a heavily-financed activity, capable of attracting vast crowds and rousing savage passions, and the infection spread from country to country. It is the most violently combative sports, football and boxing, that have spread the widest. There cannot be much doubt that the whole thing is bound up with the rise of nationalism – that is, with the lunatic modern habit of identifying oneself with large power units and seeing everything in terms of competitive prestige. Also, organised games are more likely to flourish in urban communities where the average human being lives a sedentary or at least a confined life, and does not get much opportunity for creative labour. In a rustic community a boy or young man works off a good deal of his surplus energy by walking, swimming, snowballing, climbing trees, riding horses, and by various sports involving cruelty to animals, such as fishing, cock-fighting and ferreting for rats. In a big town one must indulge in group activities if one wants an outlet for one's physical strength or for one's sadistic impulses. Games are taken seriously in London and New York, and they were taken seriously in Rome and Byzantium. In the Middle Ages they were played, and probably played with much physical brutality, but they were not mixed up with politics nor a cause of group hatreds.

If you wanted to add to the vast fund of ill will existing in the world at the moment, you could hardly do it better than by a series of football matches between Jews and Arabs, Germans and Czechs, Indians and British, Russians and Poles, and Italians and Jugoslavs, each match to be watched by a mixed audience of 100,000 spectators. I do not, of course, suggest that sport is one of the main causes of international rivalry; big-scale sport is itself, I think, merely another effect of the causes that have produced nationalism. Still, you do make things worse by sending forth a team of eleven men, labelled as national champions, to do battle against some rival team, and allowing it to be felt on all sides that whichever nation is defeated will 'lose face'.

I hope, therefore, that we shan't follow up the visit of the Dynamos by sending a British team to the USSR. If we must do so, then let us send a second-rate team which is sure to be beaten and cannot be claimed to represent Britain as a whole. There are quite enough real causes of trouble already, and we need not add to them by encouraging young men to kick each other on the shins amid the roars of infuriated spectators.

from TRIBUNE *1945*

His Normal Game

HAROLD PINTER

OLD MAN: Compressed. I thought he was looking compressed, didn't you, Fred?

BARMAN: Depressed. He means depressed.

SEELEY: No wonder. What about that game on Saturday, eh?

KEDGE: You were going to tell me. You haven't told me yet.

BARMAN: What game? Fulham?

SEELEY: No, the firm. Firm's got a team, see? Play on Saturdays.

BARMAN: Who'd you play?

SEELEY: Other firms.

BARMAN: You boys in the team, are you?

KEDGE: Yes, I've been off sick though. I didn't play last week.

BARMAN: Sick, eh? You want to try one of my sausages, don't he, Henry.

OLD MAN: Oh, ay, yes.

KEDGE: What happened with the game, then? (*They move to the bench.*)

SEELEY: Well, when you couldn't play, Gidney moved Albert to left-back.

KEDGE: He's a left-half.

SEELEY: I know he's a left-half. I said to Gidney myself, I said to him, look, why don't you go left-back, Gidney? He said, no, I'm too valuable at centre-half.

KEDGE: He didn't, did he?

SEELEY: Yes. Well, you know who was on the right wing, don't you? Connor.

KEDGE: Who? Tony Connor?

SEELEY: No. You know Connor. What's the matter with you? You've played against Connor yourself.

KEDGE: Oh – whatsisname – Micky Connor.

SEELEY: Yes.

KEDGE: I thought he'd given up the game.

SEELEY: No, what are you talking about? He plays for the printing works, plays outside-right for the printing works.

KEDGE: He's a good ballplayer, that Connor, isn't he?

SEELEY: Look. I said to Albert before the kick-off, Connor's on the right wing, I said, play your normal game. I told him six times before the kick-off.

KEDGE: What's the good of him playing his normal game? He's a left-half, he's not a left-back.

SEELEY: Yes, but he's a defensive left-half, isn't he? That's why I told him to play his normal game. You don't want to worry about Connor, I said, he's a good ballplayer but he's not all that good.

KEDGE: Oh, he's good, though.

SEELEY: No one's denying he's good. But he's not all that good. I mean, he's not tip-top. You know what I mean?

KEDGE: He's fast.

SEELEY: He's fast, but he's not all that fast, is he?

KEDGE: (*doubtfully*): Well, not all that fast . . .

SEELEY: What about Levy? Was Levy fast?

KEDGE: Well, Levy was a sprinter.

SEELEY: He was a dasher, Levy. All he knew was run.

KEDGE: He could move.

SEELEY: Yes, but look how Albert played him! He cut him off, he played him out of the game. And Levy's faster than Connor.

KEDGE: Yes, but he wasn't so clever, though.

SEELEY: Well, what about Foxall?

KEDGE: Who? Lou Foxall?

SEELEY: No, you're talking about Lou Fox, I'm talking about Sandy Foxall.

KEDGE: Oh, the winger.

SEELEY: Sure. He was a very smart ballplayer, Foxall. But what did Albert do? He played his normal game. He let him come. He waited for him. And Connor's not as clever as Foxall.

KEDGE: He's clever though.

SEELEY: Gawd blimey, I know he's clever, but he's not as clever as Foxall, is he?

KEDGE: The trouble is, with Connor, he's fast too, isn't he?
SEELEY: But if Albert would have played his normal game! He played a game foreign to him.
KEDGE: How many'd Connor get?
SEELEY: He made three and scored two.

from A NIGHT OUT *1961*

Bruddersford United

J. B. PRIESTLEY

As he moved slowly down Manchester Road, the press of fellow spectators still thick about him, Mr Oakroyd found himself brooding over the hollow vanities of this life. He felt unusually depressed. His physical condition may have had something to do with it, for he was hot, dusty and tired; there had been a full morning's hard work for him at the mill; he had hurried through his dinner; walked to the ground, and had been on his feet ever since. Manchester Road after a match had never seemed so narrow and airless; a chap could hardly breathe in such a crowd of folk.

And what a match it had been! For once he was sorry he had come. No score at all. Not a single goal on either side. Even a goal against the United would have been something, would have wakened them up a bit.

The first half had been nothing but exasperation, with the United all round the Wanderers' goal but never able to score; centres clean flung away, open goals missed, crazy football. The second half had not been even that, nothing but aimless kicking about on both sides, a kids' game.

During the time that it took him to progress 300 yards down the crowded road, Mr Oakroyd gave himself up to these bitter reflections. A little farther along, where there was more room, he was able to give them tongue, for he jostled an acquaintance, who turned round and recognised him.

'Na Jess!' said the acquaintance, taking an imitation calabash pipe out of his mouth and then winking mysteriously.

'Na Jim!' returned Mr Oakroyd. This 'Na', which must once have been 'Now', is the recognised salutation in Bruddersford, and the fact that it sounds more like a word of caution than a word of greeting is by no means surprising. You have to be careful in Bruddersford.

'Well,' said Jim, falling into step, 'what did you think on 'em?'

'Think on 'em!' Mr Oakroyd made a number of noises with his tongue to show what he thought of them.

'Ah thowt t'United 'a' made rings rahnd'em,' Jim remarked.

'So they owt to 'a' done,' said Mr Oakroyd, with great bitterness. 'And so they would 'a' done if they'd nobbut tried a bit. I've seen 'em better ner this when they've lost. They were better ner his when they lost to Newcastle t'other week, better bi far.'

'Ay, a seet better,' said the other. 'Did you ivver see sick a match! Ah'd as soon go and see 'tschooil lads at it. A shilling fair thrawn away, ah call it.' And for a moment he brooded over his lost shilling. Then, suddenly changing his tone and becoming very aggressive, he went on: 'Yon new centre-forward they've getton – MacDermott, or whativver he calls hissen – he'll nivver be owt, nivver. He were like a great lass on t'job. And what did they pay for him? Wer it two thahsand pahnd?'

'Ay.' Mr Oakroyd made this monosyllable very expressive.

'Two thahsand pahnd. That's abaht a hundred for ivvery goal he missed today. Watson were worth twenty on 'im – ah liked that lad, and if they'd let him alone, he'd 'a' done summat for 'em. And then they go and get this MacDermott and pay two thahsand pahnd for him to kick t'ball ower top!' Jim lit his yellow monster of a pipe and puffed away with an air of great satisfaction. He had obviously found a topic that would carry him comfortably through that evening, in the taproom of *The Hare and Hounds*, the next morning, in the East Bruddersford Working Men's Club and possibly Sunday, Monday and Tuesday nights.

Mr Oakroyd walked on in silence, quickening his pace now that the crowd was not so thick and there was room to move. At the corner of Manchester Road and Shuttle Street, both men halted, for here their paths diverged.

'Ah'll tell tha what it is, Jess,' said his companion, pointing the stem of his pipe and becoming broader in his Yorkshire as he grew more philosophical. 'If t'United has less brass to lake wi', they'd lake better football.' His eyes searched the past for a moment, looking for the team that had less money and had played better football. 'Tha can remember when t'club had nivver set eyes on two thahsand pahnds, when t'job lot wor not worth two thahsand pahnds, pavilion an' all, and what sort o' fooitball did they lake then? We knaw, don't we? They could gi' thee summat worth watching then. Nah, it's all nowt, like t'ale an' baccy they ask so mich for – money fair thrawn away, ah calls it.'

'Well, we mun 'a' wer teas and get ower it. Behave thisen, Jess!' And he turned away, for that final word of caution was only one of Bruddersford's familiar good-byes.

'Ay,' replied Mr Oakroyd dispiritedly. 'So long, Jim!'

from THE GOOD COMPANIONS *1928*

Sunday Morning

JACK ROSENTHAL

The play takes place throughout a Works League Sunday morning football match in Manchester. The REFEREE, *after twelve years of reffing these games (each of which he likens to Custer's Last Stand), has become an idealist in the cause of justice and fair play. (Unlike any of the players or their managers.) At this moment in the play, the* REFEREE *is making his way towards the centre-circle to begin the match between Parker Street Works and the CWS.* SAM *is the elderly manager of the Works team.* BRIAN *is the no-nonsense manager of the CWS. The* REFEREE *is striding towards the circle, looking like – and imagining he is – a World Cup referee.* SAM *slides ingratiatingly up to the* REFEREE *and falls into step.*

SAM: *Morning,* Mr Armisted.
REFEREE: No, thank you.
SAM: I haven't offered you one yet!
REFEREE: Offered me a what?
SAM: Cigarette. I'd no intention of doing.
REFEREE: Good.
SAM: Fancy some chewing gum?
REFEREE: Good morning.

Defeated, SAM *trails off to the touchline.* BRIAN, *the opposing manager, promptly catches up with the* REFEREE.

BRIAN: (*Effusively*) Nice to see you again, Mr Armistead!

REFEREES: (*Striding on*) I've brought my *own* lemon, thank you. And embrocation.

BRIAN: I never said a word! No one offered you a lousy lemon!

REFEREE: (*Stopping dead*) Would you like to go before the League Committee?

BRIAN: Would you like to go to *hell*?

REFEREE: I've been, laddie. That's what I'm doing *here*.

He strides on, leaving BRIAN *behind. The* REFEREE *reaches the centre-spot and blows his whistle sharply to summon the two captains. They trot towards him like two bloodthirsty bull elephants. The Works' captain is* GRAHAM. *The* CWS *captain is* STAN.

REFEREE: (*Amiably*) Morning.

The two captains grunt gracelessly and fix each other with baleful, murderous eyes. The REFEREE *sighs*.

REFEREE: A few pearls of wisdom. From one who knows. (STAN *and* GRAHAM, *who've heard it all before, assume expressions of long-suffering.*) What we're now about to witness is called a football match. Not the beginning of World War Three. Not the destruction of the human race. A football match. In it, each team will attempt to score more goals than the other—

STAN: (*To* GRAHAM) What are *you* staring at?

GRAHAM: Not much.

The REFEREE *watches the exchange with apprehension.*

REFEREE: —and that will be done by kicking the ball in the net – as opposed to kicking other people in the crutch.

STAN: Right.

GRAHAM: Great.

STAN: Thank you.

GRAHAM: Now shall we start – or stand here and *freeze* to death?

REFEREE: If I see a good, clean exhibition of football skill, you won't know I'm here. If, on the other hand—

GRAHAM: Like a bloody tape-recorder . . .

REFEREE: Did you speak?

GRAHAM: No, I was yawning.

REFEREE: . . . If, on the other hand, and acting upon the new Gospel according to Lytham St Annes, there's any foul tackles from behind, swearing at me, shirt pulling, writhing on the ground in apparent childbirth in an attempt to win an Actress of the Year Award – because another player accidentally *looks* at you – then out comes my little book, and in it goes the name. (*Another long-suffering sigh*

from STAN *and* GRAHAM) If it happens *again*, the gentleman in question will be back in the dressing-room so fast his backside'll be a blur.
Arguing with the referee will naturally not be tolerated.

STAN: (*Argumentatively*) Why? Who the hell's arguing?

The REFEREE *looks at him calmly.*

REFEREE: Are you trying to get in the Guinness Book of Records?
The only player to be sent off before the game's even started? (*He
takes a coin from his pocket*) Heads or tails?

GRAHAM: Tails.

The REFEREE *tosses the coin, picks it up and looks at it.*

REFEREE: Heads.

STAN: As we are.

REFEREE: Have you shaken hands yet? (*They stare at him impassively*)
Well, do it now. (*They don't move*) Shake hands ! ! !

*They shake hands as though trying to break each other's fingers; their
faces making no attempt to hide the primeval hatred they're feeling for each
other – and promising each other.*

REFEREE: Thank you. May the best team win.

STAN: Why?

He crosses himself and trots off to join his team-mates. GRAHAM *joins
his. The* REFEREE *sighs and blows his whistle to summon the teams into
position for the kick-off.*

from ANOTHER SUNDAY AND SWEET FA *1972*

The Mind's Eye

MIKE ROWBOTTOM

In a way, playing in a Wembley final is like having a school picture
taken. If your tie is askew on the appointed day, or the spot on your
nose is raging for attention, too bad. That's the way you were; that's
the image that goes on the mantelpiece.

Over the years, a wretched few have come home with pictures they
would prefer to turn to the wall. One thinks of the Sheffield Wednesday defender Gerry Young, stricken on the turf after the blunder
which allowed Derek Temple in for Everton's winner in the 1966 FA
Cup final. Or of Arsenal's Willie Young, infamous in perpetuity for

the trip which denied Paul Allen, bright-eyed and seventeen, a goal for West Ham in 1980.

For others, the indelible nature of the image gives cause for a warm glow. These are the men whose goals, for ever and ever, won a Wembley final. In 1981, when Ricardo Villa's inspired slalom run earned Tottenham the FA Cup, another player earned himself a place in that select company. I speak, as anyone in Bishop's Stortford will know, of Terry Sullivan.

The year Stortford went all the way to Wembley was, lucky for me, the year I started on the local paper. Their progress was an unlikely one. As members of the Isthmian League first division – not even the premier division, mind – they were outside the non-league élite, although they did have the distinction of being the last winners of the old FA Amateur Cup in 1974. Their pursuit of the FA Trophy, the Amateur Cup's successor, began not in the first round, not in the first qualifying round, but in the preliminary round. By the time they fetched up at the twin towers to play Sutton United, they had already played twelve games.

Worthy as well as unlikely winners, then. But what gave their victory its true satisfaction, what made it as full and weighty as a round marble paperweight, was the fact that it should be Sullivan who scored the only goal of the game. Because – well, let's go back a little.

Sullivan was brought up in Mile End, along with ten brothers and sisters, and when he began to show ability on the football pitch it was natural that he should go down the road to train with West Ham. This was 1969. The World Cup-winning trio of Hurst, Moore and Peters was still intact in a side that on its day could beat anybody, even if that day came around much less often than once a week. But any hopes the fourteen-year-old Sullivan might have had of contributing to that cause were shortlived. Like many a talented schoolboy, he found that more than talent was required to succeed as a professional footballer. It didn't help that he was unable to call on parental support, his father having died when he was young and his mother being fully occupied with her large family. While other prospective Hursts and Moores were ferried to and from matches and cheered from the touchline, young Sullivan found himself making the same journey on the bus, alone.

He dropped out, disillusioned. Back at school he took up with the smoking and drinking crowd, and for the next seven years he never kicked a ball. His reacquaintance with the game was a matter of accident rather than design. In time-honoured fashion, he was roped in to play for his brother's Sunday team when they found themselves a man short. It was enough to remind Sullivan of what he had been missing. Soon he was back playing regularly, albeit in the undizzy heights of the Hackney and Leyton League.

But Sullivan, who by now was working as a telephone engineer, was not to be just another promising schoolboy who settled for Sunday football. In the summer of 1980 he was persuaded by three friends from a rival side to join them in pre-season training at Bishop's Stortford. At that time, the club had a lot of players who knew their way around the non-league scene – people like Terry Moore, the goalkeeper who had played for them in the Amateur Cup final before moving on to Enfield, or the sweeper, John Knapman, another ex-Enfield man who had captained the England Youth side in his time. They also had the usual smattering of ex-pros, including Ian Smith, briefly of Spurs before injuries curtailed his chances, and John Radford, one of Arsenal's 'double' winners, who had arrived at the club via West Ham, Blackburn and a position as licensee of The Greyhound pub in nearby Dunmow.

Radford apart, the names meant nothing to Sullivan. At twenty-five, he was effectively starting his career. Even the training sessions came as a novelty to him – he had never worked so hard before in his life. For all that, his initial impact on the club was almost terminally unpromising. In company with a crowd that must have been nigh on forty-strong, I witnessed his first stirrings for the reserves in a pre-season friendly. The score and the opposition have faded from my memory, but the recollection of Sullivan has not.

He was thin and drop-shouldered. His long face, with long prominent nose and deep-set eyes, was framed by unsophisticated swathes of dark hair, centrally parted, and a Christ-like beard. The face of an icon rather than a footballer. When he moved, it was in a shuffling kind of way. As he approached an opponent he bent over the ball, keeping it close to him, using both feet. A drop of his already dropped shoulder and he was by. Why, surely, this was the lost art of dribbling, the arcane practice employed to advantage by Stanley Matthews, jinky Jimmy Johnstone and suchlike?

Indeed it was. But the art was lost on the gathering at Stortford's Rhodes Avenue ground that sweltering Saturday afternoon as our hero ran in barmy circles, beating one man, beating two before whirring out of control like a clockwork toy. You can fail in many ways on an English football field, but woe betide you if you fail trying to be clever. Far safer to be the honest trier, the desperate fetcher of the ball for a throw-in, the anguished clutcher of the head after yet another chance is sliced narrowly wide.

There was none of this as-seen-on-TV, eager-to-pleaseness about Sullivan. But he was a worker. When his jaunts failed to come off, at which point other, more cynical souls might set their hands on their hips and raise their eyes to the heavens, he would beaver back in pursuit of the ball. That, perhaps, helped explain why the Stortford manager, Trevor Harvey, also in his first season with the club, refused to concur with the opinions of the multitude – all right, of the forty-odd – and persisted with his odd winger.

It was not long before Harvey's judgement was vindicated. Sullivan, encouraged to employ his gifts in straight lines rather than circles, became a key figure in a team that was rapidly gaining impetus. By the time they reached Wembley, they were champions of their division. But it was the Trophy which truly tested them.

One of the beauties of all long cup runs is the way in which they draw upon the different talents and characters of a team at different times. Radford began the season short on pace and long on resigned gestures as his team-mates failed to match the standards he had known as a professional. But the prospect of reaching Wembley ten years after he had been there with McLintock, George and Co. gripped him. By the end of the season all that knowledge and experience was being worked to its full on the team's behalf. The old scoring instincts, clearly on the wane at West Ham and Blackburn, perked up. In the first round proper, when Stortford looked like going out after being held to a home draw by Bridgend, his goals won the replay. In the next round it was the turn of Knapman, the sweeper, to respond to the challenge of keeping the momentum going as his colleagues faltered; two goals helped dispose of Dagenham, the Trophy holders, in another replay.

What had begun as a diversion – a crowd of just 219 turned up at Rhodes Avenue to watch Spalding United being beaten 3–1 in the preliminary round – was becoming a tantalising possibility. And it was the thrilling contribution of Sullivan, as much as anything else, which turned that possibility into heart-thumping probability, then glorious certainty.

He scored in the third round, quarter-final, both legs of the semi-final and the final itself, linking himself inextricably to Stortford's cause in the same way that the emergent Alan Taylor had done with West Ham by scoring twice in the quarter-final, semi-final and final in their FA Cup-winning year of 1979. But while Taylor's goals, by and large, were a matter of darts and dabs, Sullivan's were, by and large, exhibits.

Take the third round tie, against Alvechurch. The Midlanders, who had a youthful Alan Smith in their squad, ended the season as Southern League champions. For an hour they ran Stortford all over the park, but neglected to score more than once. It seemed nevertheless an ample margin until the moment Sullivan collected the ball in his habitual lurking place, wide on the right. The hunch. The shuffle. And then he found what he called his little break, his angle of attack. In like a whippet past two defenders, round the keeper, and the ball was thrashing about in the net like a landed pike. That set in train a 3–2 win, and when Worcester City arrived for the quarter-final a crowd of 2,500 saw them beaten 4–0, Sullivan once again starting matters off with another piece of improvisation which left Jim Cumbes, the former West Bromwich Albion 'keeper and Worcestershire cricketer, clutching air.

The first leg of the semi-final against Dartford, played at Watling Street, was a tense and rancorous affair. The home side went a goal up in the first half, but just before the hour Sullivan struck again, moving in from the right after Radford's pass had given him some rare space to have a decent run. This time he seemed to drift past two players before scoring with a low shot from just outside the area.

That earned a draw, and although Sullivan was sent off ten minutes from time after an altercation with the opposing centre-forward, he was eligible for the second leg a week later, which was just as well. Nearly 3,000 people – Stortford's biggest crowd since an FA Cup-tie with Peterborough nine years earlier – turned up. Interested faces loomed in the windows of houses backing onto the unenclosed side of the ground, separated from the hurly-burly by narrow lengths of football-bombarded garden. Sullivan did not let anyone down, other than the visiting supporters. Once again, his was the goal which broke the deadlock, another second half effort, although this time he cut in from the left and shot with his right foot. Dartford equalised, but a penalty nine minutes from time saw Stortford (or the Bishops, as they somehow came to be known in some national Sunday papers) at Wembley.

Ah, Wembley. The sleepy market town of Bishop's Stortford – admittedly less sleepy than in the Amateur Cup days before the M11 had slunk up from London and Stansted Airport, a couple of miles up the road, had become more than a track for US war planes – roused itself like a middle-aged bridegroom, more out of duty than expectation.

I glance through the pre-match supplement that appeared in my paper. Good luck at Wembley, said the garden centre, open seven days a week for all your gardening needs. Congratulations – PLEASE do it again, said the tobacconists. The bookies gave the odds – 6–4 Sutton, 15–8 Bishop's Stortford. Meanwhile the players' keenest supporters – their wives! – posed obediently for the photographer with scarves and banners.

May 16 dawned damply, and the omens favoured Stortford as they took over the 'lucky' north dressing-room that had been used by Spurs for their replayed final two days before.

Sutton, from the division to which Stortford had just earned promotion, were managed by Barrie Williams, the pipe-smoking ex-schoolmaster whose predilection for quoting Shakespeare and Kipling in moments of high emotion tickled the fancy of the media when his side embarked on FA Cup exploits in later years. They had Larry Pritchard who, at thirty-six and with forty-eight England amateur caps, was a towering figure in the non-league game. But they did not, sadly for them, have their leading scorer, Micky Joyce, who was injured.

Both sides had an open, attractive style, but the game had a curiously muffled quality as each absorbed the other's efforts. As the final whistle approached, a pitch made heavy with overnight rain became peopled with cramp sufferers. It was clear that the 22,500 who had come to watch, packed into sections rather than spread around the vastness of the stadium, would have half an hour's extra football to mull over.

One minute remained of normal time when Sullivan seized his moment; or the moment seized him.

David Brame, Stortford's strapping left-back, was one of the fittest men around in the non-league game. As others plodded through the motions, he galloped purposefully up his wing and hoisted a deep cross into the centre of Sutton's defence. John Rains, Sutton's captain and centre-half, did his weary utmost to head the ball away, but he was under pressure. Radford, forcing his heavy legs to a last effort, rose with him, and the ball merely glanced onwards via the defender's head to – well, who else?

One touch nicked him past a desperately backtracking defender; as he approached the angle of the six-yard box, he let fly. Pandemonium. Within nine months, a Sunday footballer had done what all Sunday footballers dream of. In its way, the whole thing was perfect.

Belatedly, Sullivan had arrived. But while he went on to have success with, ironically, Dartford and Dagenham, there would be nothing to match this moment; and he knew it.

After the match, as the players basked in anticipation of beer, boisterousness and, who knows, perhaps even the Bishop's Stortford Town Council reception scheduled for the bleary following morning, Sullivan was not one of those larking around the changing-room. He seemed, if anything, a little dazed.

He has garnered every possible memento of his grand occasion. He has reports in his scrapbook; photographs on his mantelpiece; even the match ball. His one regret is that he has not been able to obtain a video of the goal which, for ever and ever, won a Wembley final. Ah well, Terry, the mind's eye will do.

from MOMENTS OF GREATNESS, TOUCHES OF CLASS *1990*

PART 2

The Matches

The Wembley Wizards

SANDY ANDERSON

Scotland beat England 5–1 in an unforgettable display at Wembley Stadium, March 1928.

Unexpectedness gives piquant flavour to a gift or triumph. Barren of a single success in the international arena this season, and still licking the wounds of a 2–6 League humiliation, Scotland could be pardoned for viewing the Wembley encounter with appropriate modesty. The somewhat timorous demeanour, however, did not possess the players. The reason: eight of the eleven were Anglo-Scots. I will explain. Following the Ibrox debacle, Scottish players in England were placed on the Saxon spit and roasted and basted. In every club drawing room they were teased unmercifully about what Hulme and Dixie Dean had done, and what they would do at Wembley.

The baiting served Scotland well. The eight Anglos knew what awaited them if defeat was their portion – a whole season's malicious chaffing than which nothing is more galling to a lone Scot or two placed among dozens of Englishmen. In order to save their own reputations and the reputations of every other footballer in exile in England, victory had to be won, if possible. Never again, after this English match, should the Anglo-Scot chosen to play for his country be regarded up home as a 'foreigner'. The more home Scots in an international team the better, other things being equal, but if an Anglo is picked because of superior ability, the 'interloper' idea must now be dropped completely. The Anglo has even more to fight for than the home player. The latter is not subjected to shafts of English wit which, if not very subtle to Scottish ears, can always elicit a loud 'Ha, ha' at the expense of poor 'Scotty'.

Scotland scored in six moves without an English foot touching the leather . . . a zigzag advance which ought to go down to posterity as a classic of its kind. M'Mullan, Gibson, James and Gallacher placed Alan Morton in possession. The Ranger lofted the ball in beautifully and Jackson headed cutely down and into the net . . .

Exultant Scots indulged in cat and mouse cantrips. Full revenge was extracted for all the London press forecasts about Scotland's midgets being foredoomed to heavy defeat. From toe to toe the ball sped. The distracted enemy was bewildered, baffled and beaten. One bit of weaving embraced eleven passes and not an Englishman touched the sphere until Dunn closured the movement with a skyhigh shot over the bar . . .

Jackson is gifted with a sublime disposition for the great occasion. His close dribbling, now halting, now accelerating, all with the ball tied to his toe, put Jones in a state of stupor. Only with a lassoo could the Englishman have stopped this Scottish deerfoot. Morton marked his seventh 'go' at the old enemy with touches of his palmiest days. Scraping past Goodall with not the space of a tram ticket between the two men and plunking the ball into goal, the Ranger enjoyed a jubilant time . . .

Gallacher fearlessly rushed the English defence and suffered for his temerity. Dunn played well but with ordinary shooting 'Tim' could have made the score eight goals. Law may develop to the full international standard. Only nineteen years of age, he did not fail in a testing ordeal. Harkness proved himself a goalkeeper worthy of the day. His advances from goal were well timed . . .

What a smashing ball Jackson drove into the roof of the net for his third goal. The whole netting structure shuddered as if an elephant had leaned against it. By accident one of the Scottish players was about to help himself to an interval refreshment of methylated spirits when someone stopped him in time. Alan Morton was half strangled by jubilant Scots at the close of the game. With attendants pulling him one way and his countrymen tugging the other, Alan thought he was going to be distributed as a souvenir.

Jack Harkness secured the ball at the finish. 'It's not April 1st yet and we've been made a damn fool of already,' remarked an Englishman. Scottish excursionists travelling north yesterday were a quiet company. Their voices had conked out after so much singing and shouting.

'It's been a day,' muttered a haggard looking Scot as he boarded the forenoon train at Euston Station yesterday. Of course, if you counted it from seven o'clock Friday night, it certainly was a day. Lyon's corner house was a favourite rallying point for the tartan tourists. They not only made the welkin ring with their choruses. They broke it into wee bits.

from the EVENING NEWS *1928*

North Korea v. Portugal, 1966

JOHN ARLOTT

Three goals down at one stage to North Korea, Portugal, inspired by Eusebio, eventually ran out winners by 5–3 in a 1966 World Cup match at Goodison Park.

North Korea beating Portugal 3–0: Goodison giggled with disbelief. One could feel the waves of incredulity echoing back from the receiving end of every television, radio and telephone cable out of the ground. It sounded like freak: but the three goals had been well made and well taken.

Now Portugal measured up to World Cup stature. Their attacks were urgent, yet free from panic. First Eusebio and then Augusto shot well and hard, only for Li Chan Myung – slim and whippy as a rapier – to curve in the air and make a clean catch.

Eusebio was grafting like three men, but Torres was not winning the ball and Augusto could not 'lose' Ha Jung Won. Only Simoes, switching from left, to centre and to right, was effective. On the half-hour, Eusebio passed to Simoes, moved on, collected the return, jinked along the defensive line, seeking an avenue for his shot and fired it home. In the last minute before half-time. Torres burst through on to Simoes's pass and Shin Yung Kyoo, sturdier than most of his colleagues and a hard, fast back, somewhat in the European mould, tripped him. Eusebio sent the penalty-kick fiercely and steeply beyond Li Chan Myung's spreadeagled leap.

Portugal undoubtedly received some sound counsel during half-time. They started off with firm efficiency and at once began to uncover the basic weakness in the Korean defenders – they are 'suckers' for the man in possession. So Portugal let them chase the ball, parting with it quickly. Yet this was a fine period for the North Koreans. Small but wiry fit and devoted, sharp and quick as needles, they won the ball again and again. If their flaw was fundamental, it had not yet told against them. Then, however, the game was decided by a flash of genius. Again Eusebio sent Simoes cutting down the left and, as the cross came over, hard and low, there was Eusebio lancing in to meet it and crack it home, right-footed, in mid-leap. Level at 3–3: half an hour left.

The ball was hardly in motion again before Eusebio, bent upon absolute decision, was on it again, racing down the left wing, taking on three men, beating them round the outside and cutting in on goal, only to be tripped as he was poised to shoot. This time the impact of the trip slowed and altered his approach to the penalty-kick, but the ball hit the same uncoverable point in the net.

Now Portugal were in command and could play at their own pace: Eusebio could relax. Yet surely the Koreans, like the rest of us, realised that, at need, he would do it again. Just to make the point, immediately after a foray by Pak Doo Ik, Eusebio picked up a loose ball a dozen yards outside the penalty area and with a long swing of that mighty right foot, struck it through the line of defenders so savagely that it burst through Li Chan Myung's hands and bounced leadenly away from his body.

With some few minutes left, and in case of accidents, Portugal scored through their stock move. Eusebio moved down the left and centred high for Torres, by the far post, to nod it precisely back across the goal where Augusto was waiting to head in.

Korea, gamely and with genuine skills, had achieved as much success as they could have hoped. Portugal had shown themselves as sound in temperament as in technique and Eusebio stood in what, until a few days before, had been Pelé's place.

from WORLD CUP 66 *1966*

Walsall's Greatest Day

CLIFF BASTIN

Walsall astonished the world by beating Arsenal 2–0 in the third round of the FA Cup, 1933.

We never liked to play against third-division teams. Such teams, when pitted against the glamorous Arsenal, found themselves in a position of having everything to gain and nothing to lose. Consequently, they would fling themselves into the game with reckless abandon, and, win, lose, or draw, the gashed, bruised legs of the Arsenal players, after the game was over, would bear grim testimony to their misguided enthusiasm. The third-division footballer may not be a soccer artist, but when it comes to a heavy tackle, he ranks with the best.

As was now the Arsenal custom, we went down to Brighton to tune up for the Cup-tie. Whether the opposition was to be Walsall or Aston Villa made no difference to this routine.

At this period, a severe influenza epidemic was sweeping the country, and three of our regular team – Eddie Hapgood, Bob John and Jack Lambert – fell victims to it, shortly before our match was due to be played. Further, Joey Hulme was in the middle of one of those bad periods which come to even the greatest of footballers at one time or another, and, in consequence, Mr Chapman had some team selection problems on his hands.

In an endeavour to solve them, he chose Tommy Black, who had recently joined Arsenal from a Scottish junior team, to replace Eddie Hapgood. Norman Sidey, our reserve centre-half, took over at left-half, from Bob John; while to take over from Lambert and Joey Hulme, Mr Chapman chose, respectively, Charlie Walsh and Billy Warnes. In doing so, he made two of his very rare mistakes.

Warnes, an amateur international who had come to us from the Isthmian League club, Woking, was entirely the wrong kind of player for such a match as we were going to play. Essentially an artistic footballer, robust methods were liable to shake him off his game, and he was very chary of involving himself in a full-blooded tackle.

Charlie Walsh had long been trying to bring Chapman round to his own way of thinking – that he was the best centre-forward on Arsenal's books – so far, without success. In this match, however, Chapman gave him his chance. He missed it, all too emphatically.

Almost as soon as play had started, on the microscopic Walsall ground, it became quite clear to me that all our fears about the tactics our opponents might employ were fully justified. As soon as the ball came out to me on the left wing I was blatantly fouled by the Walsall right-back, who bowled me over without ceremony. No foul was given, however. Throughout the game, the referee was curiously lenient.

Walsall could not have complained had five of their men, at least, been sent off the field in the first quarter of an hour. Arsenal were awarded ten free-kicks in as many minutes after the first whistle. Compared with this apology for a football match, the replayed semi-final against Hull City, three seasons back, had been child's play.

Soon after the kick-off, big Herbie Roberts sustained a cut eye, in a violent aerial collision, and was handicapped accordingly. Do not misinterpret me. I don't want to level an indictment at the Walsall players. They played, a little too vigorously, perhaps, the game which was right in the circumstances. If David had worn heavy armour against Goliath, the Philistine might have lived to a ripe old age! But it was rather disconcerting for Arsenal.

Yet for all Walsall's crude tactics, and for all the difficulties imposed by the tiny pitch, and the proximity of the spectators who sat around it, I still say we should have won. We had quite enough chances to have banged in half a dozen goals. Not one was accepted.

Charlie Walsh was the chief offender. His nervousness was pitiable to behold. On one occasion, during the first half, I crossed the ball right on to his head, with not one Walsall defender standing within yards of him. He misjudged the centre hopelessly and missed the ball completely. It bounced off his shoulder, to be pounced on by a thankful Walsall defence.

Half-time came without any score. The Walsall supporters cheered their team to the echo, as it came off the field. It had held the mighty Arsenal for fully three-quarters of an hour! How this had been done was a matter that did not need to be discussed.

For the second half, Charlie Walsh was switched to inside-right. David Jack took over from him as centre-forward. Perhaps, we thought, this switch would do the trick. We were wrong.

Walsall took the lead after fifteen minutes. Gilbert Allsop, their centre-forward, headed in a corner taken by the outside-right, Lee. The resultant clamour was heard fully two miles away. (This, incidentally, is a fact.)

Far from converting the Walsall players to less vigorous ways, this goal only served to encourage them to further excesses of zeal. Alex James, who was literally knocked off his game, was a particularly bad sufferer. The gravest casualty of the second half was, however, left-half Norman Sidey. Norman – a sound player, but always inclined to be a little slow – was moving in leisurely fashion for a ball which he seemed to have plenty of time to bring under control, when a Walsall player appeared on the scene, and kicked him very scientifically on the knee. Sorry as I was for Norman, I must confess that I had to laugh at his resultant antics. He doubled up with pain, then sank slowly, very slowly, to the ground. If he had collapsed at once, it would not have been in the least amusing. But the sight of Norman sinking to the earth in slow motion brought a ray of humour even into this evil-tasting game. Still, isn't it said that humour is always just a step away from tragedy?

If Arsenal had had plenty of chances in the first half, we could not complain of lack of opportunities in the second. On one particular occasion, we would almost certainly have equalised, had it not been for the presence of one Charles Walsh.

I gave David Jack a head-high centre. It was a golden chance, and I could sense that David was picking his spot in the Walsall net. But just as the ball was about to reach him, who should come thundering up from behind like a runaway tank but . . . Charlie Walsh!

The astonishing leap through the air with which he ended his run deserved a better fate than it actually received. Alas, all Charlie did was to divert the ball away from David Jack, far, far from the Walsall goal. I can remember vividly to this day the look which David Jack gave Charlie.

Walsall ultimately made things sure by converting a penalty. It was, I felt, rather curious that we, and not they, should give away a spot-kick, after the manner in which some of their players had behaved. However, there was no doubt at all that the penalty award against us was thoroughly deserved.

It came as the climax of a long series of duels between one of our defenders and a Walsall forward. Relations between these two had gradually been becoming more and more strained, until it ultimately came to a point at which the question was which of them would be the first to vent his feelings on the other. Unfortunately for us, it was our man. The incident was almost followed by a free fight in the Arsenal penalty area, but eventually wisdom prevailed.

Sheppard, the Walsall inside-right, took the penalty. His hard, low shot gave our goalkeeper, Frank Moss, no possible chance of saving.

As soon as the ball was safely in the back of the net, a factory chimney near the ground suddenly began to belch thick clouds of black smoke, with the result that the pitch was obscured for several minutes. I felt a little amused at the time. I sensed that the chimney was saying to itself: 'Well, we won't let Arsenal score any more goals now, anyway!'

Arsenal didn't. The final whistle blew, with the score Walsall 2

Arsenal 0; and, as the frantically happy crowd chaired the Walsall players from the pitch, newspaper correspondents rushed to the telephones to tell the world of Arsenal's sensational defeat.

We certainly were an unhappy team as we changed slowly and moodily in the dressing-room. It was all the more infuriating because we knew we ought to have won. True, the Walsall players had at times behaved more like steamrollers than footballers. True, Charlie Walsh and Billy Warnes had been misfits. Nevertheless, granting all this, we had still been presented with enough chances to have won.

Never have I seen Herbert Chapman look so miserably unhappy. He made a brave, desperate, but unavailing effort to cheer us all up. 'Never mind, boys,' he said, 'these things do happen.' But we were all inconsolable, and so, for that matter, was he. I think he felt the blow more than any of us. Here was the team which he had come to when it was struggling pathetically at the bottom of the first division; the team which he had made one of the greatest in the history of football, beaten by a fifth-rate side. Napoleon must have felt like that in Russia, a hundred and twenty-one years before.

Of all the players, I think I felt the effects of the defeat most deeply. At twenty years old, I was the youngest of the side, so perhaps this was only natural. On my way home to my lodgings that night in the underground railway, I felt positively suicidal. Visions of the Arsenal goals that might have been rose up before my eyes; hopes that the events of the afternoon had been nothing but an evil nightmare would delude me for a brief moment, only to be banished away by the cold, grim reality.

from CLIFF BASTIN REMEMBERS *1962*

Every Dog Has His Day

DANNY BLANCHFLOWER

The roar of that Spurs v. Manchester United game still rings in my ears. They called that the game of the 1956–57 season, a meeting of the giants, the match of the century. It was certainly a big one and it lived up to its reputation. I could tell you about that one – but perhaps another time. It's much too close; the sweat of it still seems to tingle my brow; and anyway, a game like that deserves the same treatment that good whisky gets. It demands a good distiller and time to mature.

A guy I used to work with could have done it justice. He had the feeling for such a cause. His name was Jimmy Thompson – known locally as 'Bluff', no doubt because of his powers of illusion. His favourite yarn was about a Rangers v. Celtic clash. I heard him tell it about a couple of dozen times, and it got better and better each time. What a picture he painted! There was Ibrox Park split right into two. At one end, horseshoe-style from the half-way line right round to the same mark on the opposite side, was a mass of green and white. The other half, no more, no less, was a human sea of loyal Ranger blue.

That was a great game, even before it started. The atmosphere was there; the feeling was ripe. Those two teams could have stayed put in the dressing-rooms and it wouldn't have made a lot of difference to the game, because many of the crowd undoubtedly remember things that never really happened. But the teams came out and added fuel to the fire.

'Bluff' remembered it all, kick by kick, and he sure did it justice. As he told the story, I could actually see the whole thing take place before my very eyes – which was all the more remarkable because I'd never been to Ibrox Park – and I don't suppose he had either.

However, that story helped me to understand what it is about a game of soccer that appeals to the average fan. It led to the realisation of what makes a football match great. Anything about a game that brings to the surface a sense of contest or challenge is sure to rouse the spectators: it might be the uncertain excitement of goal-mouth scrambles, or the wide-eyed wonder of hard accurate shooting; maybe some complex tactical battle, or the unrestricted antics of crowd-pleasing personalities; perhaps a 'local derby', or the inspired challenge of a 'not-so-under' underdog; or maybe the death-or-glory consequence of a late-round Cup-tie, just a step or two from the big day itself.

It could be a game of goals, where bitter fortune fluctuates until the not-so-bitter end; a match where the big hand of time 'roulette wheels' its way around ninety minutes, and the see-sawing scales of decision balance as equally as they did at the start.

Any of those factors can place a game in the 'good' column. But add them all together, throw in the inconspicuous efficiency of three

alert officials, stage it all before 69,118 units of humanity – a prejudiced mass with no time for honest agents of neutrality – and what
you get must surely be 'great'.

Such a game was the 1956 sixth-round Cup-tie between Spurs and
West Ham at White Hart Lane.

The big day was 3 March, but it all began long before that. It was
after our fifth-round victory at Doncaster that we got to surmising
about our next opponents and by Monday morning (20 February) we
had mutually resolved the possibilities. So we shrugged aside our
relegation worries, finished training with a smile, and humoured away
the time awaiting news of the Cup draw.

The jungle drums sounded in the distance and somebody answered
the trainer's phone. A few mumbled words . . . and then the procla-
mation: 'Tottenham Hotspur v. Blackburn Rovers or West Ham
United.'

At first we wouldn't believe it. It couldn't be? It was some sadistic
joke: because, after all, wasn't that the way we had figured it? So
someone else phoned back – and got the same reply. And then, like
the dropping of a stone in water, the circle of acceptance began to
increase, until all thought of question disappeared. Then came a council of war. It was an indecisive pow-wow, because at the time we were
really playing two teams. We fancied the Rovers to clinch it; but, just
in case, we decided to commission a three-man scouting party to cover
the replay from every conceivable angle.

At noon on Thursday, 23 February, manager Jim Anderson, coach
Bill Nicholson and captain Yours Truly – I was skipper then – dined
in a Manchester hotel which is a popular meeting-place for visiting
teams in that area. Bill and I were tempted to enjoy a heavy lunch,
but played it safe and settled for fish. He was taking on the Rovers
and I was to battle it out with West Ham.

The West Ham party were lunching at the same place and we
managed to poach a lift to Blackburn in the coach they had hired for
the journey. On the way I tried to psychoanalyse the team. It was a
crazy idea. A few of them sat quietly at the front of the bus, as if they
were in church; and all the others were at the back, singing like mad
and acting as if they were coming home from Wembley with the Cup
in their pockets.

My star-gazing activities were interrupted by Bernard Joy, who had
moved up from the back of the coach to join me. He was quite
impressed by the Hammers' enthusiasm and confidence. He thought

they would win, although he admitted that their record up there was not very inspiring.

I told him we were all the way with Blackburn, probably because we wanted it that way. Not that we didn't respect the London club; but we reasoned that the Rovers' style would suit us better. It would be easier that way – and anyone who tells you that he doesn't want it as easy in the Cup as he can get it is kidding either you or himself.

But Joy was right. The West Ham boys won that time and won convincingly. We came away with a more healthy respect for their ability; and a few ideas that we thought might help us defeat them.

A few days later, Saturday, we had a league game at home with Chelsea. Les Bennett, the old Tottenham stalwart who was with West Ham at the time, came along as their 'cloak-and-dagger' man. We had one of those days, thrashing Chelsea 4–0. So the Hammers, Les Bennett and all, moved down to the seaside for the week before the game, to figure it all out.

We carried on with our normal routine, with the exception that we discussed and practised a few ideas which we thought would particularly demoralise our opponents. During the week I appeared on a television programme with the West Ham manager, Ted Fenton, and our 'secret weapon', Tommy Harmer. Ted said he had plans to stop the 'weapon', and a few other things as well, but he was giving no secrets away.

One man who was daily reminded of the approaching ordeal was the Tottenham postman. The mail that week was really heavy. I know, because I got my share. The usual stuff: requests for tickets; a few autographs to sign; plenty of advice on how to beat the Hammers, with diagrams enclosed; good-luck omens; and so forth. But one of those letters was different, as it showed even before I opened it. It was a buff envelope with a half-inch black border inked all the way around. It contained the curse of 'Gipsy Dan': a horrible omen to the effect that we were out of the Cup, because he had cast his terrible spell upon us. I informed the boys. Most of them laughed; but a few smiled like they didn't think it was funny.

And so the days of preparing and wondering slowly lapped away, until the big one came. I got to the ground about noon and even at that early hour I could sense the atmosphere building up. The pitch was in good condition and yielding enough to take a long stud; the boots I wanted to wear that day were properly studded for the occasion.

About 1 p.m. I crossed the High Road to the local café, where a few of the lads and some local characters always meet before home games and parley about topical events. We chatted about – the Cup. Somebody rushed in with a message that Ed Gibbins, the ticket manager, would like to see me in his office back at the ground. When I got over there, Ed introduced me to a young man of medium height, slight build, dark hair and deep brown, mysterious eyes. The stranger said he came from Pakistan.

'That's a long way to travel for a football match,' I mused.

'No,' he explained, 'I now live in London.'

He also added that he was a fervent Spurs' supporter, and sported the proper rosette to prove it. This match he wanted us to win. He was worried about it; but had the right medicine for us, if only we would take it.

Back in his locale, if a team wanted to win something special, they used the old 'black magic'. A young girl of about thirteen years with her hair shrouded would stand outside the dressing-rooms, holding a bowl of water. The captain would drop about eight different coins into the water before leading the team on to the field, and – hey presto, that did it. I told the stranger I would try it, if I could get the 'props'. But where could I get a little 'Goldilocks' to believe such a thing?

'Most mothers hide their children when we play at home,' I smirked, 'but I'll do my best.'

The tale of magic spread and soon a posse of superstitious helpers was searching for a suitable maiden. It was proving a futile business, so I thought of using the helping hand of the law and mentioned our plight to the district chief of police. But he threatened to throw us all in jug, so we abandoned the search, and I beat a hasty retreat to the dressing-room.

This was about an hour before kick-off time; and I was first there as usual. Gradually the others joined me, and soon the place showed signs of the coming struggle: the pile of bandages and cotton-wool began to disappear; the essence of strong liniment choked the air; our ever-busy trainer was more than ever busy; and those pent-up feelings were more than normally pent.

As the moment approached, the preparations assumed the role of panic. The late urgent reminders and instructions; and then that strident buzz – the referee's transmitted signal to take the field.

Off we went – 1. Reynolds, 2. Norman, 3. Hopkins, 4. Blanchflower, 5. Clarke, 6. Marchi, 7. Harmer, 8. Brooks, 9. Duquemin, 10. Smith, 11. Robb. Off we went with the wishes of all Tottenham; with our secret weapon – Tom-thumb Harmer – at outside-right; but without the black magic of the stranger from Pakistan.

Out we went to face all that stood for West Ham: the treason of Les Bennett; the plans of Ted Fenton; the curse of Gipsy Dan; and the eleven boys in claret and blue: Gregory; Bond, Cantwell; Malcolm, Allison, O'Farrell; Hooper, Foan, Dare, Dick and Tucker.

The coin was tossed, the whistle blew, and the game started with a rush. In spite of the fast end-to-end play, the pattern of our opponents' defensive plan began to show. It was as we expected – a simple effective answer to erase any defensive doubts that our secret weapon might cause. The weapon was really playing a deep inside-forward game at outside-right. Hammers' left-half picked him up; while their left-back marked our forward-lying inside-right.

We, of course, had alternative ideas; but the football was so fluid, and the state and fortune of the game so fluctuating that there was little time to develop a tactical affair.

After about ten minutes of fast whirling football the visitors went ahead, to the delight of their many fans – who, local gossip has it, included all the layabouts from Arsenal, Chelsea, Charlton and other quarters of London. It was a just reward for a fine movement; and it was Hooper and Foan, on the right, who did the carving. When Foan reached the edge of our penalty area, in possession, I made a quick impulsive tackle at him. But in the midstream of my movement the ball glided frustratingly past me: he had timed the situation perfectly and executed the pass expertly. With the finish of my forward thrust, I glanced back to note, in despair, Dick crashing the ball past the helpless Reynolds.

Before the anguish had subsided, the same fellow had done the same thing in a similar sort of way. This time it was Hooper rocketing in from the right seeking a better angle for aim. As I anxiously moved to intercept him, for some unaccountable reason – unless it was that gipsy's curse – I slipped. Hooper mistimed his kick and the ball rolled rather anaemically past me straight to the close-at-hand Dick, who had a quick eager slash at it and, although he just didn't hit it sweetly enough, it was travelling fairly fast in the right direction. I followed its flight with reasonable contempt, as I glimpsed Ron Reynolds swaying the right way to deal with it. But that Romany curse made a monkey out of Ron, as the ball cannoned off Harry Clarke's leg, changed direction and finished up in the opposite side of the net.

As we lined up to kick off again, no sign of psychological defeat showed on the faces around me. It was early yet; and we started off as if we were two up instead of two down. Continuous pressure earned us corners galore, so we moved up the big artillery – Harry Clarke and Maurice Norman. In those goal-mouth scrambles they stood out like the twin towers of Wembley.

After five minutes' violent onslaught on the West Ham goal, our efforts finally bore fruit. A corner on the right, and the ball floated into that massed area of frantically active footballers . . . big Clarke got his head to it . . . and then, a kick at it and the ball hit the upright . . . then Bobby Smith hammered back the rebound . . . and then a brilliant one-handed save, but – it wasn't the goalkeeper who made it, and the referee was aware of the infringement. Our secret weapon potted the penalty kick.

It was 2–1; but not for long. The Hammers kicked off, pressed forward and gained a throw-in on their left about thirty yards inside our half. I marked Tucker on the touch-line. O'Farrell threw the ball short to him and he hooked it aimlessly into the middle. My eyes went with it, and at the end of its flight, Reynolds and Dick hung in the air like a couple of executed criminals, and the ball trundled into the net. At the time I thought, 'Boy, all you seem to be doing is looking back and seeing Dick get that pill into the net!'

This last thrust of West Ham's roused us and we got back to business. Another corner on the right, taken by Johnny Brooks . . . and missed by the leaping Bobby Smith and Gregory . . . but George Robb was there to head it hard and fast . . . above the stretching hairs of full-back Bond's head. That made it 3–2, and respectable again.

Then the referee blew the half-time whistle just to show that somebody had control of the situation. We replayed that first half again in the dressing-room, with better result of course, and we came out for the second half thinking we had the advantage. And it showed that way in the run of play.

Although West Ham looked dangerous in breakaways, it was we who did the hammering. Yet, twenty-five minutes of near-continuous pressure and that defence didn't look like yielding. But I had noticed the anxiety in their eyes when the tall Norman and Clarke went up for corners. So I suggested to big Maurice Norman that he might like to go up into the attack for the rest of the game. His eyes lit up and he nodded approval. So off he went to inside-right, with instructions to send Johnny Brooks to wing-half; and I filled in at full-back.

The big fellow's presence seemed to worry that hard-working defence, and in a moment of chaos up there he forced the ball out to George Robb whose first-time cross was flicked in by the joyful Len Duquemin, the equaliser that killed the score and gave life to the future.

But the game's allotted span was fading fast. At the funeral of the dying moments we nearly buried our opponents with a last treacherous thrust, but – it was not to be. The widowing of West Ham and the Cup, that day, would have been unjust. It finished 3–3; and justice was done.

The following Thursday, the same cast appeared in the same play, at a different theatre, to another capacity audience – but it turned out to be a shadowy performance. We got through by 2 goals to 1.

The next morning I received a letter in the post. The writer stated, in no uncertain manner, that we were the dirtiest, luckiest team that he had ever seen. It was also his expert opinion – nay, a definite certainty – that Manchester City would beat us in the semi-final. They did, 1–0. The handwriting was uncommonly like that of Gipsy Dan.

Alas! every dog has his day.

from ASSOCIATION FOOTBALL *1960*

Yeovil, 1949

BRYON BUTLER

The weather was now closing in. Fog was stealing over the ground and from the directors' box, a tall and rather weird wooden structure behind a corner flag, next to the dressing-rooms, it was becoming increasingly difficult to see what was going on at the far end of the pitch. The directors did not help themselves: they were all puffing away on cigars the size of rolling pins – an unaccustomed luxury for the Yeovil directors but in no phase of the game, they had decided, were they going to be outdone by Sunderland. The fog and the clouds of cigar smoke were an interesting combination.

Outside the ground there were hundreds who would have given

their souls for any glimpse of the game. They were still living every second of it, however, because radios in the waiting police cars – volume full up – were relaying the BBC radio commentary of Raymond Glendenning.

Sunderland were playing a town as well as a team and it proved too much for them. Yeovil took the lead again with just a minute left of the first period of extra time. The scorer was Bryant and, living now in Dorset, he is still asked to describe his contribution to history. He tells it like this:

> Len Shackleton gave the ball away because he was dead scared of our right-half Bob Keeton. Bob pushed the ball through to Nick Collins and he moved it on to Ray Wright. A little push forward to me and I ran past their centre-half, got just inside the box and put the ball into the bottom left corner of the Sunderland net. I think what really won the match for us was the way Alec Stock wound us up before the match. He was such a marvellous talker he could have told us black was white and we would have believed him.

Now the minutes seemed to grow and multiply. Sunderland drew again on their bruised pride and their attacks acquired shape and point. Yeovil, for their part, decided this was no time for all the finer things in the game. They were banging the ball forward as if they hated it, towards the Sunderland corner flags or, better still, up into the back row of the stand. They were tactics which hardly suited the first division side and Shackleton, sidling up to Stock, said: 'Don't spoil a good game.' 'A good game!' retorted Stock, 'It's life and death.'

The fog and the tension got thicker together. Two leading referees, Jim Wiltshire, who had controlled the Cup final a couple of years before, and Bill Edwards, were among the crowd and they decided they could not bear to watch any more. They went into Stock's office to suffer alone.

Three minutes from the end the referee, Mr W. F. Smith from Aldershot, blew his whistle for a Sunderland free-kick. The crowd thought it was the final whistle and surged triumphantly onto the pitch. Police and officials cleared them off with mounting desperation.

The free-kick was just outside the Yeovil penalty area and no one was in any doubt that the match was hanging on the slenderest of slender threads. There was now less than a minute left and Stock can still taste the tension:

This was it. We lined up our defensive wall, four others and myself, and waited. 'Blokes', I said, 'if one of you duck you're bound to get the sack, aren't you?' Barney Ramsden, Sunderland's left-back, came up to take the kick – a big fellow with thighs like tree-trunks. I had a vision of the ball carrying me into the back of the net. We braced ourselves but big Barney made a lovely mess of it, his foot seemed to hit the ground and as the ball bounced forward I think most of the Yeovil team made contact with it. There was no messing about. The ball went out of the ground and as far as I know it's still going. We'd done it.

from THE GIANT KILLERS *1982*

The Revie Plan

H. D. DAVIES ('OLD INTERNATIONAL')

Manchester City, inspired by their deep-lying centre-forward Don Revie, beat Birmingham City 3–1 in the 1956 FA Cup final.

There is a story of how Philip of Macedon on one and the same day, realised three ambitions. He himself was proclaimed Supreme Victor in the Olympic Games. One of his generals routed a dangerous enemy in the field. His wife bore him a son. Philip, overwhelmed, is said to have flung himself to his knees and to have prayed Jove to send him at once a little misfortune.

Paul, captain of the Manchester City team which defeated Birmingham City 3–1 in the FA Challenge Cup final here today had a somewhat similar experience. He, too, realised three ambitions. He kept his promise, made in an unhappy hour last year, to lead his team back to Wembley and receive the Cup from the Queen. He added a cup-winner's medal to his own forty-three caps and sundry other trophies. He did his duty to his adopted City of Manchester by adding City's Cup to United's Championship and so completing a brilliant double. But he showed no disposition after the game to kneel down and pray for any more misfortunes. He and his colleagues, had had enough of those, beforehand, and to spare.

Paul's leadership throughout the competition has been based on the conviction that to reach Wembley two years in succession gives to a team an advantage over its opponents equivalent almost to an extra man. Newcomers are more apt to be put off balance by pre-match strain and ballyhoo; by the long-drawn-out formalities; by the sight of the huge bowl lined by 100,000 spectators; by the presence of royal patrons; and by the chafing to begin. Above all, they are apt to think that Wembley's lush green turf is as innocent as it looks. Old hands tell us that the soft spongy surface can turn the legs of the fittest of men into leaden aching limbs at the end of an hour's running; and that the secret of playing there is to learn how to alternate intensive effort with periods of comparative ease.

If such, indeed, were Manchester City's ideas today they worked out admirably. Their forwards set about the Birmingham defence at once before it had time to settle down, and a superb opening goal by Hayes, in the third minute, was at once a tribute to their skill and their timing. Then a great equaliser by Kinsey seemed to restore Birmingham's poise, and for the next half hour it was the turn of the Manchester defenders to take the shock. That they were able to do so and indeed hold out to the end, without conceding another goal, was due first to the matchless skill and reckless daring of Trautmann, and after that to the willingness of Ewing, Paul, and Little, and to a lesser degree Barnes, each to do two men's work in order to lighten the burden of those whose fitness was suspect.

To the general surprise, and to Manchester's relief, Leivers, on whom Birmingham naturally exerted the greatest pressure, got through a tremendous amount of work apparently without discomfort. Not so Johnstone. The little Scot, heavily bandaged, hobbled about, and dodged tackles during the first half in a most painful manner. Many, including the writer and the Birmingham defenders, wrote him off as a complete passenger. We ought to have known better!

Though Manchester City made a great leap forward in the second half, when Dyson and Johnstone scored admirably for them, and were thus encouraged to spread their fine feathers in a manner rarely seen in Cup finals, it should not be forgotten how often the Manchester goal itself appeared to lie at the mercy of the Birmingham forwards. How else shall we explain the prodigies of skill and pluck and dogged effort whereby Ewing and Trautmann, the real heroes of the last tense phase, repulsed desperate attacks?

Twice Trautmann made what appeared to be suicidal dives at the feet of Brown and Murphy; and on the second occasion received for his pains a purely accidental, but none the less frightful blow on the back of the neck or head. This left him reeling and swaying with pain and concussion and how in this state, and with twelve minutes to go, he contrived to make two further saves of the last-ditch variety, even he cannot explain. But he does remember vaguely hearing a large portion of the crowd singing 'For he's a jolly good fellow': a novel way of showing sympathy, anyway, to a man, who, as it later turned out, had a broken neck.

Revie, brought in at the last moment as a substitute for Spurdle, the hapless victim of boils, chose the occasion to give one of the finest performances of his career, and so added another vivid chapter to one of the strangest stories in professional football. His skilful assortment of long and short passes, timed and measured to perfection, probed ceaselessly into the Birmingham defences; while his shrewd positioning in deep midfield enabled him to collect, re-label, and redespatch Trautmann's constructive throws and clearances to his fellow-conspirators lurking up-field.

Johnstone, by his quiet behaviour in the first half, was perhaps conserving his energies for the second. Certainly, when he scored his decisive goal, and again when he beat three men almost in the space of a hearthrug, he seemed to shake off his physical disabilities absolutely. To such purpose that one or two of the more cynically minded accused him of 'putting it on'. If that were so then Sir Laurence Olivier ought to be told about Johnstone. He would be glad to meet a mime of such first-rate quality.

For Birmingham Brown, the sprinter, strove zealously and perhaps a little monotonously, to break through along the left wing. Occasionally he did so, but he rarely found Murphy uncovered for the return pass: and if he tore on himself he met either Ewing charging in to kick the ball or, as once happened, Trautmann diving down to roll the ball from his questing instep.

All in all Manchester City richly deserved their victory. In a game which was pleasantly free from all save minor infringements and, excepting the injury to Trautmann, which no one could help, they had the greater number of exceptionally gifted and experienced artists. What is more, they had been at Wembley twelve months before.

MANCHESTER CITY: Trautmann; Lievers, Little; Barnes, Ewing, Paul; Johnstone, Hayes, Revie, Dyson, Clarke.

BIRMINGHAM CITY: Merrick; Hall, Green; Newman, Smith, Boyd; Astall, Kinsey, Brown, Murphy, Govan.

from the GUARDIAN *1956*

Spurs in Europe

HUNTER DAVIES

A 1–1 draw with AC Milan was enough to send Spurs through to the 1971 UEFA Cup final.

About a mile from the San Siro in Milan all roads were completely blocked, despite the efforts of the police car which was guiding the team coach. All seventy thousand supporters going to the match seemed to be going by car, each with his horn wailing. When the Spurs coach slowed down gangs of youths screamed and spat at the windows, banging so hard that the players took cover, convinced they were going to be broken. 'It'll be bricks on the way back,' said Gilly.

In Italy it's assumed that all British footballers are brutes, concentrating more on the physical side of football than on ball skills, tackling from behind, going in hard, charging the goalkeeper and other nasty tricks. In Britain it's assumed by the man on the terraces that Italian footballers are a bunch of hysterical fairies who throw tantrums, pull shirts, body check and other nasty tricks. It's not surprising, therefore, that Anglo-Italian matches have not got a reputation for their sweetness and light. Many matches have ended in brawls, on and off the pitch. Ralph Coates told the rest of the team about the time he played for Burnley in a match at Florence. They had to be locked in the dressing-room for two hours to stop the crowd lynching them.

The San Siro stadium is built like the Coliseum, with a high oval wall all the way round. We could see the thousands of supporters marching up it like ants on a treadmill, up and up and round and round, carrying their red and black banners and flags, screaming and chanting.

I went out with the team onto the pitch to inspect the turf and immediately ducked for cover. Fire crackers and smoke bombs were let off the minute the crowd caught sight of the Spurs players. I'd never expected them and thought it was gunfire. I made a quick retreat back to the dressing-room, my ears blocked and my head reeling.

The dressing-room was long and enormous, with blue tiles half way up each wall. It seemed to swallow up the seventeen Spurs players as they got themselves undressed – except Gilly who was injured and not playing.

The drive through the dense crowds had taken so long that it was now eight thirty, just three quarters of an hour before kick-off. The players got ready very noisily, showing few signs of nerves or tension. They'd had the usual two days of waiting and hanging around, but for once it had left them relaxed. They'd used an Italian training camp up in the pine woods towards Como, lazing in the lounges, watching films, playing putting.

Joe Kinnear was looking for lavatory paper. Despite all the excellent amenities none had been left out. The substitutes, particularly Terry Naylor and Jimmy Pearce, were making up daft jokes. Eddie Baily was massaging Chivers' legs, telling him how brilliant he was, what a physique, while Chivers groaned, pretending to be annoyed with him.

'You better win this one lads,' said Gilzean, buttoning up a short raincoat he'd borrowed from someone. 'I need the bonus. I've got a wife, two kids and a budgie to keep.'

'And a pub,' shouted someone.

Ten minutes before time Alan Mullery started clapping his hands, trying to make everyone concentrate and in the right mood, but players were still chatting in little groups. Steve Perryman was worrying about his dad. He gave me some tickets and asked me to find him outside. He was coming on a day trip from London for £3.50 (as he works at London airport) but hadn't got a match ticket. I rushed out and found him. I also saw Morris Keston. He and his wife had been staying for several days at one of Italy's poshest hotels beside Lake Como.

Back in the dressing-room Bill started his last-minute rites. John Pratt, in place of Gilly, was going to play his first match since his broken nose. He and Steve were told to keep a tight hold of Rivera and Benetti. Peters wasn't to play his usual midfield role but to move up front and try to take Gilzean's place, linking with Chivers and being ready to flick on free kicks or back head corners.

'You'll be Martin Gilzean tonight,' said Bill as he went over what he wanted him to do. Even Bill was still in surprisingly light-hearted mood. The corner kickers, Steve and Mullery, were told to try short corners when possible. This was Eddie's idea. He'd been to Italy to scout the Milan team and was convinced it would work. Their man marking system wasn't suited to short corners. If a man went out, then it still left Spurs with a two-against-one situation. And if Cyril and Joe were coming up on the flank, that would mean three to one.

Bill then went very serious and said on no account must anyone argue with the referee. 'I want you all to go back ten yards at every free kick. You don't have to rush back, but give the referee no chance to take your name. Everybody hear that? I want no dissent of any sort.'

'Bayonets out, lads,' said Eddie once again. 'England expects every man this evening to do his duty.'

The buzzer went and they shouted the usual encouragements at each other. On the pitch they were met by a roar of fireworks, smoke bombs, streamers and a wall of screams. The noise was deafening but the chants were short and repetitive. There was no singing, just a continual roar of Mee-lan, Mee-lan. They could have been shouting any two syllables, any name you cared to imagine. I thought at first they were shouting Cee-ral. It's probably a help when playing in front of a foreign crowd not to understand a word of their shouts. All the same the noise was the loudest I'd heard all season, at home or abroad.

As usual Eddie kept up his constant screams from the bench, but this time I was half-deaf already. Even Eddie couldn't compete with a seventy thousand crowd.

The first five minutes were very worrying. Milan stormed forward and Spurs' defence looked very shaky, particularly Mike England. There were some wild clearances which might easily have failed. Then Spurs scored a goal, the goal they'd all been hoping for, the vital early goal which Milan dreaded above anything else. Milan's pressure had taken them up field, which gave Cyril his first chance to overlap. He carried on unimpeded almost to their goal line, then pulled the ball back for Chivers to shoot. It was cleared, but only about forty yards to Steve Perryman. He picked it up and moved forward as the defence ran at him, expecting a blockbuster shot as he'd done at Tottenham. Instead he pushed it square to Mullery on his right who shot on the run first time, a brilliant shot, high and curving, scything through the defence and giving the goalkeeper no chance. Only seven minutes had elapsed. The goal was one of those which comes at the perfect psychological moment. And with the scorer being Mullery, the prodigal returned, it was indeed like a story straight out of the *Wizard* or *Hotspur*.

Milan now needed to score three goals to win. Judging by the low scoring standards of Italian football (Milan had scored only thirty goals in twenty-six league games), that was too much to expect.

Spurs steadied themselves after the goal, though it didn't stop Eddie screaming at Mike England for the rest of the first half, especially when he headed the ball against his own crossbar. But the midfield men were giving Milan few chances and the ones they did get were being wasted with bad finishing. Most important of all, Milan had no answer to Spurs' overlapping full-backs. Both Joe and Cyril were making tremendous runs down the wings. When the move did break down, they could be visibly seen to be on the point of collapse as they began their fifty or sixty yard haul, all the way back to the full-back position. But when it worked and they got their final cross into the penalty area, causing panic amongst the Milan defence, then it was all worth it and success gave them the extra energy to rush back.

It was Milan's man-marking system which was at fault. No one was prepared to move out of defence to go and meet Cyril, scared to leave the man they were meant to mark, hoping someone else would do it.

It was 1–0 at half-time. In the Spurs dressing-room no one was smiling or boasting. They all looked intense and purposeful. Bill told them they were doing well but Benetti had to be picked up much quicker. He was their danger man and causing most trouble. Rivera was showing little determination in his finishing and Prati, Milan's leading scorer who'd missed the Tottenham match, was playing out on the wing, not in the centre as Bill had expected, and was getting nowhere. Cyril complained that his leg was sore. Johnny Wallis treated him with a pain-killing spray. 'Just forty-five minutes to go,' said someone as they trooped back on again.

In the second half Eddie turned his invective from Mike England to Martin Chivers when he missed an open goal. He received the ball, alone and unmarked, and only ten yards from goal. He took his time, not rushing the shot, and fired wide. Eddie and Bill both buried their heads in their hands. It might have been offside as the linesman's flag was up, but the referee appeared to let it go and pointed for a goal kick. All the same it was a terrible shot. If Spurs went on to lose Martin would be for it in the dressing-room.

Milan at last managed to score, thanks to Cyril making his only mistake of the game. He lost possession just outside his penalty area and let Bignon through. He was brought down by Philip Beal and Rivera scored from the penalty. Now, for the final twenty minutes of the match, Milan were being urged on by the crowd to score again and force extra time. Spurs were pushed back into their own half for long spells, but they held out and the game ended in a draw, 1–1. Spurs were now in the final, their first European final since 1963.

The crowd went silent, accepting the result without acrimony. Before the end they'd seemed irritated at times by some of Milan's passing movements. Spurs had won fairly and squarely and there could be little argument. It had been a well refereed match, played fairly by both sides. There had been few fouls and only one incident.

In the dressing-room Bill and Eddie were ecstatic, going round praising everyone. Bill said that Cyril had played an excellent game – apart from one mistake. He said Perryman had also been great. In fact everyone had done well. Eddie was personally praising Peters. 'You played a real team game, Martin,' said Eddie, shouting in Peters's ear. 'Do you hear me? Bloody great.' 'I hear you,' said Martin. 'Now I want to hear Bill say the same.'

Most of all, Mullery was being congratulated by everyone for his goal, a goal which had won the tie and got them into the final. 'I've scored a few good goals in my time,' said Mullers. 'But that must be the most valuable ever.'

The only player not joining in the shouting and congratulating was Martin Chivers. He went to his place and sat silent and alone, looking sullen and morose. His natural expression tends to be rather grim, except when he's actually smiling, but this time there was no doubt he was feeling dissatisfied with himself. He knew he'd missed a great chance, one that he normally never misses. He knew that Bill and Eddie were displeased with him, thinking he should have tried harder and done more running. Once again, he had been left on his own up front. Peters had been forced for long spells to go back to midfield. It had been a game which had been won in the middle and on the flanks. The rest of the players left him alone with his thoughts, carefully walking round him.

The referee came in to congratulate Spurs, followed by the manager of Milan, Nereo Rocco. Through an interpreter he too congratulated Spurs on their good game, saying he had no complaints about the result. They were a fine team, worthy winners and he hoped they would do well in the final. Bill was equally profuse in his thanks, congratulating the Milan team. 'I know what it's like to be knocked out of a semi-final,' said Bill. 'It's like the end of the world. But I hope you do well in the league.'

The British press were eventually allowed in. They rushed to Mullery, asking about his goal, then to Cyril Knowles for his view on his great game. The Spurs directors arrived, plus Brian Curtin, the team doctor, Geoffrey Jones, the club secretary, and Bill Stevens, the assistant secretary, all three of whom had flown in that day from London. Mr Broderick of Cooks went into the bathroom to congratulate the players and emerged with his best suit soaked through. They'd shouted him over and then sprayed him with water. Brod, always a goer, stripped off naked and got in the bath with them. They roared when they saw his thin, weedy body. 'I thought Belsen had closed,' said John Pratt.

It took about an hour for the team coach to get clear of San Siro. Spurs were given strong police protection – a police car with a siren at the front followed by five camouflaged jeeps, full of extra policemen – but there were no incidents.

The team were going back to their hotel up in the woods near Lake Como, with no chance of any night life, but they were too excited to be worried by lack of any celebrations to come. Winning was excitement enough. At the hotel, Bill ordered champagne all round for the players, then most of them went straight to bed.

from THE GLORY GAME *1972*

A Missed Penalty

PETE DAVIES

West Germany beat England after a penalty shoot-out in the 1990 World Cup semi-final.

Ninety minutes: 1–1. And who goes to applaud them before the restart? Gazza . . .

Walker saved us with a flying last-gasp tackle off Klinsmann's feet; I had to stand, I couldn't take it sitting down any more. Now Shilton saved us, a reflex reaction to Klinsmann again. It was all Germany, attacking, attacking . . . Klinsmann went clear through yet again – and missed by inches.

At the other end, another razor-sharp pass from Gazza went to Beardsley – who lost it. Bully and Macca were warming up on the track; and then Gazza was booked, for the most innocuous of fouls. He'd gone for the ball – but Berthold made a meal of it, diving and rolling; and the German bench were up in noisy protest, making the foul look worse than it was . . . it was Gazza's second booking, he was out of the next game – and the next game might well be the World Cup final.

He looked mental, torn up, cut to the heart and the knife twisted hard. Lineker was tapping a finger to his temple, warning the bench that Gazza might have lost it – it was the harshest injustice.

> We love you Gascoigne, we do
> We love you Gascoigne, we do
> We love you Gascoigne, we do
> Ohhhh, Gascoigne we love you

He didn't lose it – he threw himself in more fiercely than ever. And Chrissie Waddle hit the post . . . Jesus. You couldn't bear to watch it – and you couldn't tear your eyes from it.

Fifteen minutes left; turn-round time. But the song was still the same.

> There's only one Paul Gascoigne
> Only one Paaw-uuhl Gaaaaa-uh-scoigne

Every piece of me was frozen bar the heart that beat and the hand that wrote.

Brehme crunched Gazza, ugly and hard. The English fans rose in a tumult of outrage. Brehme was booked instantly – and Gazza got up, and shook the German's hand.

He'd been threatening to grow up all this time – but there was the moment, booked himself and heartbroken, that he proved that he'd done so. Six months ago he'd have hit him, and got himself sent off.

So whatever happened here now, England could go home knowing that we had on our hands a player who'd come of age, at twenty-three promising to be one of the world's greatest in the 1990s . . . and from the free kick, Platt put the ball in the net.

Offside, offside . . . it was disallowed. No matter –Beardsley went through two, and came within an ace of releasing Lineker. It was all

England now, forward, forward, finding speed to run and strength to play in their sixth game in twenty-four days, their third extra time in nine days – it was a performance of matchless pride. The fans sounded like they filled the whole stadium.

And we deserved to win this. We'd fought hard, and our hearts were big. Who says they were better than us?

But then, it takes two to make a great game of football – and what I've just written could just as well be written of the Germans.

Shilton saved from Thon; a shot from Brehme went rocketing close over the crossbar; Steven went searing through on a lovely lay-off from Beardsley, and crossed to win a corner; then at the other end, Buchwald hit the post just as Waddle had. So no one deserved to lose here. But after two hours, we'd battled to a standstill – and no one did lose. The score was 1–1 and we had to settle it on a duckshoot instead.

Applause rang out round the whole of the magnificent arena, pure and wholly merited by both sides. In the centre circle, players from both sides shook hands, put arms round each others' shoulders, and exchanged congratulations on the game. Gazza was crying; Robson took time out from organising the penalty takers to console him. And in London, Bryan Robson said from the heart, 'They should take the camera off him.'

In the VIP box Kissinger watched with Agnelli, the latter wearing the fattest kipper tie on earth.

And the keepers went to the goal; the players sat down in the centre circle.

> There's only one Peter Shilton
> Only one Peter Shilton

But he didn't make any saves – though he did go the right way all four times. And thirty million English people watched this game; we all know the cruel way it ended.

The penalty shootout's a heartless piece of ersatz TV drama, irrelevant to the game of football . . . ah well. Lineker, Beardsley, and Platt all scored; Brehme, Matthäus, and Riedle ditto. Then Pearce fired it straight at Illgner, who, diving left, saved with his legs. Beardsley ran to Pearce as he walked back, and Lineker – but what could you say to him? And Thon scored; then Waddle fired his kick over the top; 4–3 to the Germans.

Nightmare. The black pit of loss opened wide . . . and the sound system immediately blared out, 'All English fans are kindly requested to remain in your seats for fifteen minutes. You will then be escorted by security to where your buses are located. All English fans . . .'

1984. I mean, how dare they, *how dare they*? It was staggeringly, brutishly insensitive. And there were people with little flags forming up a silly bloody Ciao on the pitch in some naff Turin closing ceremony . . . a decent period of silence and respect was called for here. And look what we got instead.

Gazza was crying in the big arms of Terry Butcher. And I was crying too; from a tight chest and an aching head, the tears had been threatening since they sang, 'You'll Never Walk Alone'. Robson, putting the bravest imaginable face on it, gulped down his sorrow, and subjected himself to the instant interview. He said, 'This is a cruel situation, but we just have to accept it. We played a big part in the tournament.'

We certainly did, sir. We certainly did.

A Scottish journalist going out, I don't know who he was, saw me crying, staring out blindly over the huge emptying stands. He said, with the softest kindness, 'It's hard for you. It's very hard.'

And it was. Our story was all played out – but how bravely, in the end. How very bravely.

from ALL PLAYED OUT *1990*

You Haven't Lost My Medal, Have You?

TOM FINNEY

Jimmy Hagan, the famous Sheffield United and England inside forward, was once asked: 'What is your greatest sporting thrill?' And like a shot came Hagan's reply: 'Every Saturday when I pick up the ball and go out for a game of soccer.'

I think that was a very sensible answer to a very difficult question. In a footballer's lifetime he plays many games, and each has a special thrill all of its own. When I look back on my own career, the memories come crowding back. The thrill of playing in a wartime Cup final against Arsenal; playing for the Services in the Middle East in the war; the many overseas trips with the England team; the 1954 Cup final when my club, Preston North End, lost in the last two minutes to West Bromwich Albion.

So you see, when someone asks me what is my greatest match, it would have been rather like asking the late Signor Beniamino Gigli which was the best performance he ever gave of *I Pagliacci*.

But there are matches which stand out above the rest. I don't know why, but I always seem to have a good game against Portugal. It is a far cry from Preston to Portugal, but I always seem at home when I am playing there.

For my first game for England at outside-left, I was naturally a little anxious about what might happen. The England team had lost 1–0 in Switzerland and as Portugal had held them to a draw, England weren't given much of a chance. Stan Mortensen was playing his first peace-time game in a full international, and I would say the whole England team was just a little bit keyed up.

The night before the game, Bob Kelly, that great England inside-forward of the 1920s, who played with Burnley, Preston North End and Huddersfield Town, was coaching in Portugal. He rang me up to wish me all the best, and at the same time sounded an ominous warning by saying: 'You'll have to watch this lot, Tom. Take it from me, they are a great side.'

Well, when you hear that sort of comment from a player of Kelly's calibre, you know that he is speaking sound common sense. Even before the game, we had our minor troubles. Portugal wanted to use their smaller ball; we wanted the English type. The continental referee spoke no English, and it was quite amusing to see our captain, George Hardwick, trying to make himself understood.

As a matter of fact, we kicked off with the English type of ball, and in twenty minutes we were leading 4–0. A smaller ball was brought on, but it made no difference. This was a day when Englishmen could feel proud, because we won 10–0 and, although I say it myself, I had quite a day on the left-wing.

In 1950 we played Portugal again, as a warming up for the World Cup series in South America. We won that match 5–3, and I scored four of the goals (two from penalties) from outside-left. Jackie Milburn was our right winger that day.

These were great games in the sun and heat of a foreign land. Were these the greatest games I ever played? I wonder! I find myself now debating about other games in the cold of an English winter. Yes, there was that game at Maine Road when England beat Ireland 9–2.

On that occasion I was playing outside-right, with Stan Mortensen as my inside partner. I think that day we played football to perfection – and yet I didn't score a goal. But it is a game which thrusts itself into the forefront of my memories.

Then there was a match which Preston played in the promotion season of 1949–50. Remember when Preston had that run which brought them fourteen successive victories, and we were unbeaten in twenty-one games? I recall when we went to Brentford that season. Many games were postponed that afternoon, and when we stepped on to the pitch at Griffin Park we were almost lost without trace! It was just a sea of mud, at least four inches-deep. Charlie Wayman, our centre-forward, tried to kick off by sweeping the ball out to the wing. All he managed to do was move it about two yards. That is how bad it was. Yet Preston contrived to play some great football.

I had been dropped from the England team, and was naturally keen to get back for the game against Scotland. I think my performance that day helped me win back my place in the international team.

I scored a goal, and Ken Horton, my inside partner, made it 2–0 before half-time. Just after the interval I beat three men in a run from the half-way line and Preston were three up.

We couldn't lose – or so it seemed! Then a faulty back-pass let Brentford in to score. Now they were surging forward confidently, and our defence was in turmoil. Another Brentford goal and 'Proud' Preston were hanging on grimly at 3–2.

Three times in as many minutes Gooch, our goalkeeper, made miraculous saves to thwart the Brentford chaps. And then, sweet relief! A clearance found me on the half-way line. I set off in a break-away which ended with Ken Horton heading in to make it 4–2. All our goals had come from the right-wing pair. A happy day for me in league football that – and yet, the greatest game I ever played?

No, hardly. Is there no answer to this most vexed question? Ah! Through the mists I see a game. Yes. It was the greatest match in which I ever played. And what a game for any player to remember.

As a boy I had one idol – Alex James. As a boy I had one ambition – to play at Deepdale, which was only five minutes from my home. Deepdale, where my hero Alex James had played so many great games. And in April 1934 my dream came true.

I was twelve years old, just a frail pale boy of 4 ft. 7 in., and weighing less than 5 stone. But my school Deepdale Modern reached the final of the Dawson Cup that year. Don't ask me how we managed it, but we did. And on that April evening of 1934 I trotted out proudly at Deepdale playing inside-left – just like my idol Alex James.

My dad was there. So was my brother Joe. In fact, the Finney family was there in force to see what young Tom could do. I don't recall doing very much, really, except trying to do my best and play like Alex James.

Ten minutes to go, and still no score. The cheers of the 3,000 spectators were just like background music, heard but not appreciated by the warriors. Win . . . we must win . . . but how? And then our right-winger cut in, and slammed the ball towards goal. Up went the goalkeeper's arms to parry the ball out – out to my waiting left foot. I crashed it into the back of the net, just as I hoped Alex James might have done, from three yards' range!

Now the cheers could be heard. Cheers for young Finney, playing his first game at Deepdale. I was chaired off the field and, like all the lads, was much too excited to speak. I had won my first, and only, medal in school soccer.

They let me stay with my grandmother that night. So proudly I went with her, medal earnestly clasped in my hand, hardly daring to let it out of my sight. I was packed off to bed, and my grandmother, like grandmothers all over the world, wanted to take my medal to show it to friends. Fearfully I let her have it, but sleep was not to be mine. I was still wide awake when she returned a long time later. And from an upstairs room a weary but anxious little voice enquired: 'You haven't lost my medal, have you, grandma?'

She hadn't. So young Tom Finney slept peacefully at last. The medal under his pillow as he dreamed of great games to come in the world of soccer.

I didn't know it then, but that schoolboy match was, of course, the greatest game I ever played in.

from ASSOCIATION FOOTBALL *1960*

England v. USA, 1950

BRIAN GLANVILLE and JERRY WEINSTEIN

England's first appearance in the World Cup ended in humiliation, beaten 0–1 by the USA in Belo Horizonte.

The England World Cup team spurned the rudimentary dressing-rooms of the Belo Horizonte stadium, and changed in a nearby hotel, arriving a few minutes before the kick-off, while the Americans, hardier, perhaps, changed at the ground. The day, suitably enough, was heavy with cloud, through which the sun broke, occasional and uncertain. Hundreds of Englishmen from the gold mine were among the crowd, looking forward to a gentle exhibition of the fine arts of the game from their team.

The Americans were apparently of like opinion; their approach to the game can be described only as cavalier. A number of them had stayed up until two o'clock that morning, dancing and drinking – soft drinks. Several of them asked an English journalist, before the match, whether he had brought a cribbage board with him, to keep the score.

England began well enough. Playing in red shirts, because of the clash of colour with the Americans, they hit the post, shot over the bar, and generally seemed to be spending the early minutes adjusting their sights for the ultimate barrage.

It never materialised. The American defence, with Borghi superb in goal, and the half-back line of McIlvenny, Colombo, who played in gloves, and Bahr, performing prodigies, fought tigerishly to keep them out. It was destructive football, some of it open to moral criticism, but it served to keep the American goal intact.

After thirty-seven minutes the incredible occurred: the United States opened the score. There seemed little danger in Bahr's shot from left-half; Williams appeared to have it well covered. But Gaetjens, the Haitian centre-forward, dashed in and deflected the ball out of his reach with his head. There are those who uncharitably said that the ball merely hit Gaetjens, and luckily went home. It is immaterial. The goal stood, and it was enough to decide the game. An English forward-line containing at least three players whose reputations were global failed wretchedly to penetrate America's defence. They kept the ball far too close, and when the chance of a shot arose, they either sent the ball wide or did not shoot at all. Behind them, the wing-halves insisted on holding the ball, instead of moving it about, thus adding to the congestion in midfield.

In the United States forward-line, the clever John Souza, at inside-left, was making far more use of the few balls that came to him. Meanwhile, as the minutes evaporated, the English forwards became first anxious, then desperate. The pitch set their efforts at too precise football at naught; sparsely covered with grass, bumpy underneath, played on only for the third time, it was a travesty of an international ground. Beyond the touch-line, only a few inches' clearance separated the red cinder track, a hazard for the players.

After half-time England moved Bentley to the wing, put Mortensen at centre-forward, and Finney at inside-right. It made no difference; the score remained unchanged, though there was one moment at least when England could claim to be unlucky.

'Wake up, England!' shouted the miners, and England awoke, to the extent of a dash by Mortensen through the middle. He was heavily brought down, and Ramsey, Tottenham's right-back, placed the ball for the free-kick in his careful, compulsive way. His lob was beautifully floated to the far post, where Medley had scored so many goals for Tottenham, and Mullen met it perfectly. The ball passed Borghi, in goal, and seemed to have crossed the line when it was scrambled past the post. The referee, however, awarded a corner-kick, and England's last chance had gone.

At the final whistle hundreds of spectators invaded the little ground, to carry the Americans off the field, while others lit bonfires of newspaper on the concrete terraces: a funeral pyre for English football.

The impossible had happened.

'The Americans,' said Sir Stanley Rous, the secretary of the Football Association, 'were faster, fitter, and better fighters.'

'This,' said Bill Jeffrey, with jubilation, 'is all we wanted to do. This is what we need to make the game go in the States.'

It would be wrong to read too much significance into the match. If it had been played again the following day, no doubt England would have won quite easily. By the football world at large it was treated as a joke; a flippant excrescence on the competition. Walter Winterbottom, the English manager, summed it up, in later years,

'Everybody who saw the game would say that England didn't take their chances, hundreds of them, and when a team doesn't take its chances, it doesn't deserve to win. Our forwards tried too hard. For the first twenty minutes, they were shooting in, then they began to worry; "We must have a goal", they thought. For superiority to show, one must have a good pitch.'

As for the gallant American team, as for the future of the game in the United States, it would be pleasant to say that everything ended happily ever after, that America reached the final Pool, and that barefoot boys with cheek abandoned baseball for soccer all over the country.

Instead, the United States were well beaten, 5–2, in their final match, against Chile, while soccer was obstinately rejected, despite their remarkable success, just as it had been for the past fifty years. It may well be, as many American critics and administrators have alleged, that the real cause has been less rejection than a lack of enterprise among the organisers of the game there. The fact remains that baseball, basketball, and the peculiarly violent pastime of American football still reign unchallenged as the national sports.

from WORLD CUP 58 *1958*

England v. Hungary, 1953

GEOFFREY GREEN

Yesterday by 4 o'clock on a grey winter's afternoon within the bowl of Wembley Stadium the inevitable had happened. To those who had seen the shadows of the recent years creeping closer and closer there was perhaps no real surprise. England at last were beaten by the foreign invader on solid English soil. And it was to a great side from Hungary, the Olympic champions, that the final honour fell. They have won a most precious prize by their rich, overflowing, and to English patriots, unbelievable victory of six goals to three over an England side that was cut to ribbons for most of an astonishing afternoon. Here, indeed, did we attend, all 100,000 of us, the twilight of the gods.

There is no sense in writing that England were a poor side. Everything in this world is comparative. Taken within the framework of British football they were acceptable. This same combination – with the addition of the absent Finney – could probably win against Scotland at Hampden Park next April. But here, on Wembley's velvet turf, they found themselves strangers in a strange world, a world of flitting red spirits, for such did the Hungarians seem as they moved at devastating pace with superb skill and powerful finish in their cherry bright shirts.

One has talked about the new conception of football as developed by the continentals and South Americans. Always the main criticism against the style has been its lack of a final punch near goal. One has thought at times, too, that perhaps the perfection of football was to be found somewhere between the hard hitting, open British method and this other more subtle, probing infiltration.

Yesterday the Hungarians, with perfect team work, demonstrated this midway point to perfection. Theirs was a mixture of exquisite short passing and the long English game. The whole of it was knit by exact ball control and mounted by a speed of movement and surprise of thought that had an English team ground into Wembley's pitch a long way from the end. The Hungarians, in fact, moved the ball swiftly along the ground with delicate flicks or used the long pass in the air. And the point was that they used these variations as they wished, changing the point of attack at remarkable speed. To round it off – this was the real point – they shot with the accuracy and speed of archers. It was Agincourt in reverse.

One has always said that the day the continental learned to shoot would be the moment British football would have to wake up. That moment has come at last. In truth, it has been around the corner for some time, but there can no longer be any doubt. England's sad end on the national stage now proclaims it to the skies.

Outpaced and outmanoeuvred by this intelligent exposition of football, England never were truly in the match. There were odd moments certainly when a fitful hope spurted up, such as when Sewell put us level at one-all at the quarter hour and later during a brave rally that took England to half-time 2–4 down. Yet these were merely the stirrings of a patriot who clung jealously to the past. The cold voice of reason always pressed home the truth.

Indeed from the very first minute the writing loomed large on Wembley's steep and tight-packed banks. Within sixty seconds Hungary took the lead when a quick central thrust by Bozsik, Zakarias, and Hidegkuti left the centre-forward to sell a perfect dummy and lash home, right foot, a swift rising shot to the top corner of Merrick's net. The ball was white and gleaming. It could have been a dove of peace. Rather it was a bird of ill-omen, for from that moment the Hungarians shot ten times to every once of England.

Just before England drew level a sharp move of fascinating beauty, both in conception and execution, between Czibor and Puskas was finished off by Hidegkuti. But the Dutch referee gave the centre-forward offside, which perhaps was charitable as things ended. Yet the English reply when it did come also arrived excitingly, for Johnston, intercepting in his own penalty area, ran forward to send Mortensen through. A quick pass to the left next set Sewell free and that was one all as a low left-foot shot beat Grosics.

But hope was quickly stilled. Within twenty-eight minutes Hungary led 4–1. However disturbing it might have been, it was breathtaking. At the twentieth minute, for instance, Puskas sent Czibor racing down the left and from Kocsis's flick Hidegkuti put Hungary ahead again at close range, the ball hitting Eckersley as he tried a desperate interception. Almost at once Kocsis sent the fast-moving Czibor, who entered the attack time after time down the right flank, past Eckersley. A diagonal ground pass was pulled back by Puskas, evading a tackle in an inside-right position – sheer jugglery, this – and finished off with a fizzing left-foot shot inside the near post: 1–3.

Minutes later a free kick by the progressive Bozsik was diverted by Puskas's heel past the diving Merrick, and England, 4–1 down with the half-hour not yet struck, were an army in retreat and disorder. Certainly some flagging courage was whipped in that rally up to half-time by Matthews and Mortensen, both of whom played their hearts out, crowded as they were, but though it brought a goal it could no more turn back the tide of elusive red shirts than if a fly had settled on the centre circle.

After an acrobatic save by Grosics to a great header by Robb it was Mortensen, dashing away from a throw-in, losing then recovering the ball and calling up some of his dynamic past, who now set Wembley roaring as he sped through like a whippet to shoot England's second goal. But 2–4 down at half-time clearly demanded a miracle in the space left after some of the desperate escapes at Merrick's end that had gone hand in hand with the telling Hungarian thrusts and overall authority.

Within ten minutes of the interval the past was dead and buried for ever. A great rising shot by Bozsik as the ball was caressed back to him on the edge of the penalty area after Merrick had turned Czibor's header on to the post made it 5–2, and moments later Hidegkuti brought his personal contribution to three within a perfect performance as he volleyed home Hungary's sixth goal from a lob by Puskas. It was too much. Though Ramsey said the last word of all for England with a penalty kick when Mortensen was brought down half an hour from the end, the crucial lines had been written and declaimed long since by Hungary in the sunshine of the early afternoon. Ten minutes before the end Grosics, with an injured arm, surrendered his charge to Geller, his substitute, but by now a Hungarian goalkeeper was but a formal requirement.

So was history made. England were beaten at all points, on the ground, in the air, and tactically. Hidegkuti, a centre-forward who played deep in the rear supplying the midfield link to probing and brilliant inside-forwards and fast wingers, not only left Johnston a lonely, detached figure on the edge of England's penalty area but also scored three goals completely to beat the English defensive retreat. But Johnston was not to blame: the whole side was unhinged. The speed, cunning, and shooting power of the Hungarian forwards provided a spectacle not to be forgotten.

Long passes out of defence to five forwards who showed football dressed in new colours was something not seen before in this country. We have our Matthews and our Finney certainly, but they are alone. Taylor and Sewell, hard as they and the whole side now fought to the last drop, were by comparison mere workers with scarcely a shot between them at the side of progressive, dangerous artists who seemed able to adjust themselves at will to any demand. When extreme skill was needed it was there. When some fire and bite entered the battle after half-time it made no difference.

English football can be proud of its past. But it must awake to a new future.

from THE TIMES *1953*

The 1954 World Cup Final

GEOFFREY GREEN

West Germany surprisingly defeated Hungary, the great team of the 1950s. 3–2 in the 1954 World Cup final in Berne.

No one, using pure logic, could have foreseen anything but a Hungarian victory. But in the persistent rain of a day that might have come straight from an English winter a great and simple lesson was taught. Nothing is over until the final whistle, and the only certainty of life is its uncertainty. So Germany became the world champions against all the odds and against all premeditated opinion, except, perhaps that of their excited 20,000-odd supporters who formed perhaps a third – and a vociferous third at that – of the gathering within the Wankdorf Stadium. Thus, amidst surging closing scenes, with the waving of Deutschland banners forming a rich backcloth, the precious golden trophy was presented by Jules Rimet, the father of the competition, to Walter and his gallant team. At their side stood the Hungarians, gallant also and generous in defeat, though understandably dejected that their first loss in four years of football, which included the Olympic prize, should have come at the very moment when their superb prowess seemed about to be crowned. Their deportment, let it be said, at that moment was all that it should have been. It must have been all the more difficult for them to bear, too, for the realisation that they ought to have won must have chilled and prodded them as they stood there at the very end in the slanting rain. Certainly on the run of the play, and on the chances that went spinning away, the victory ought to have been theirs. So easily could they have scored five or six goals in all. At the very last, too, they might have rescued their record that was slipping away, a record that had spanned four triumphant years embracing twenty-eight victories and four draws. For even after Rahn had shot past Grosics for Germany's third and last decisive thrust with only five minutes left, there was Puskas to hit home Toth's diagonal cross from a position fractionally off-side behind Posipal, the right-back. The very last minutes were then unwinding themselves. But the flag of Mr Griffiths, the linesman on Puskas' wing, went up, and so the last drop of succour was dashed from their lips. It seemed a doubtful decision, but angles are often difficult from the stand. Yet it was tragic that so much hung on such a decision.

Germany's was a remarkable performance. They were two goals down before the match was eight minutes old. Again the Hungarians had struck like lightning, as was their fashion. But from what seemed a hopeless position the Germans fought their way back to fame by their tremendous enthusiasm, drive, stamina, strength, and their willpower. They played fast, direct, and intelligent football when they attacked – and they did less of the attacking – with Walter, the persistent schemer who brought Rahn and Schafer into the game down the wings as often as possible. But, if any one man won for himself a crown that day, when the world of football suddenly seemed to shift on its axis, it was Turek, the German goalkeeper. He made four saves that bordered on the miraculous – from Hidegkuti's close volley before half-time from Kocsis's header no more than six yards out; twice from Puskas after the interval when the Hungarian captain had streaked through the defence with no one in the world to challenge him except the goalkeeper; and in the last thirty seconds as he dived full length to keep a blinding shot from Czibor out of his net. By that very last save he kept the prize at his side and consummated a fantastic exhibition.

Turek certainly was the rock on which the Magyar waves finally dashed themselves hopelessly, but he was grandly covered by the whole of a quick-tackling defence, in which Liebrich at centre-half and Eckel and Mai on either side of him were outstanding. They refused to be mesmerised by the Hungarian passing. When it was short they tackled like tigers, quickly, chasing every move and every man with an unflagging energy; when it was the long ball, on which the Hungarians often looked for the decisive breakthrough, there was always Eckel or Mai or the full-back ready to cover the thrust. True these moves outwitted them from time to time, but it was one of those days which comes to every side, and even to the greatest, when things will not always go right. And certainly things did not finally go right for the Hungarians. This was one of those days that was bound to come to them, and it came for them at a sad time. But, in truth, the Hungarians, after that swift start of theirs, struck one as being decoyed into a false sense of security. In fact one felt at times that they were taking things rather too much for granted. There seemed a little bit too much assurance about their play, even an overweening superiority, for which they had to pay, together with all the bad luck that was going, at the last. Technically, too, on this occasion they kept the ball rather closer than in the past, often playing into the quick-tackling feet of a German defence that would never give up.

Puskas, their great man for finishing, started brilliantly, but as the game wore on his influence grew less and less as Eckel slowly got the measure of him. The incisive bite and the finishing power which one had come to expect from this, the greatest football machine in the world, were on this occasion below their peak of perfection. So were the mighty brought down. Out of the beginning few could have expected such an ending. At the sixth minute Bozsik sent Kocsis through with a glorious ground pass; Kocsis, changing direction and veering right to gain position, had a fast cross-shot charged down, but the ball ran loose to the waiting Puskas. He was on it like lightning, and his low left-foot shot to the far corner put Hungary into the lead. Within two minutes another central thrust by the Hungarian inside-forwards saw Kohlmeyer muddle his goalkeeper badly under pressure from Kocsis, and at the height of the muddle the lightning little Czibor, who played the first half rather unhappily out of position on the right-wing, nipped in to flip the ball home into an empty net. Hungary were two up, and one could only conclude one thing.

But that was the last time that the Hungarians were to be happy. If it was a blitzkreig Hungarian start the Germans were not to be put out of their stride. At the tenth minute Morlock stuck out his right foot to divert a cross slash from F. Walter past Grosics to cut the lead, and at the eighteenth minute a fourth goal arrived to set the crowd alight. This time it was again for Germany, when Rahn, for whom fate was keeping a special place, half-volleyed a deep corner kick from the left through the Hungarian defence. Thus it was 2–2. From that moment the tide flowed the more strongly against the defiant German defence, but time after time, by some miracle or other, the Hungarians were held at bay. First there came that save by Turek from Hidegkuti, and then before half-time Hidegkuti hit the foot of a German upright. Within the first twenty minutes of the second half Puskas had his two shots that seemed certain goals parried, and when Turek was beaten there was Kohlmeyer to kick Toth's shot off the line after a brilliant, penetrating move that strung the whole Hungarian forward line together in a poetry of movement. Next Kocsis, always brilliant in the air, headed Czibor's centre against the German crossbar.

The strength of the Germans, seemingly endless, began to grow stronger and course right through the side. It was a psychological reaction against a side that expects to win. As this German strength grew, so F. Walter kept prodding his forward line into swift counter-attack, and once, just before the half-hour, with the Hungarians now clearly worried, Rahn forced Grosics to a terrific diving save under the angle of his left post. A back-header from Kocsis then sent Czibor flashing through the middle, but once more Turek was equal to the demand, hurting himself in the process as he dived at the winger's feet. Now a feeling had begun to grow within one that some sort of drama was being withheld for the finish. And sure enough that drama unfolded itself. The Germans, going strong on a greasy surface, and with the rain and breeze at their back, shook Lorant and his defenders with more than one direct quick-passing move. But it was Bozsik who finally made the critical slip. All through the match he had been inclined to hold on to the ball, caress it, toy with it, and dribble too much for a wing-half; much of his work was of the highest artistry, as he linked with Hidegkuti in midfield. But now he held on once too long. In a trice he was robbed down the left touch-line by the challenging Schäfer, and as F. Walter's cross was headed out the ball came loose to Rahn, who had moved inwards intelligently. With steady aim he shot left-footed like lightning, low from fifteen yards, past Grosics, the Hungarian goalkeeper, who clawed vainly at the air to his right.

So, with only five minutes left, Germany, amidst remarkable scenes, took the lead. But Hungary, showing character, fought to the last inch. In what time was left – and each second must have seemed like eternity to those Germans – there first came that shot by Puskas that found its mark but was disallowed. Then as the hands of the clock had all but reached their goal, Turek made his last dramatic save from Czibor.

It was all over. The cup was presented, and the band played *Deutsch-land Uber Alles*.

from SOCCER IN THE FIFTIES *1974*

Pelé's First Final

GEOFFREY GREEN

Brazil, inspired by the skills of the young Pelé, beat Sweden 5–2 in Stockholm to win the 1958 World Cup.

In the first final between the New and the Old Worlds it was they, the lordly representatives of the New, who brought a lustre, a magical quality that dazzled Sweden. It was a climax that had a 52,000 crowd holding its breath in wonder from start to finish in the Rasunda Stadium – from the moment when Sweden took a swift lead through Liedholm, only to find themselves finally bewildered by a brand of football craft beyond the understanding of many. Here were dark, expressive sportsmen of a distant continent. When the moment of triumph finally was sounded by the whistle, in an excited, demonstrative and kindly way they broke into triumphal circuit of the soft battlefield scarred by rain, brandishing above their heads a huge Swedish flag – a gesture of appreciation for their reception. The stadium stood to them as if it were the host nation who had won, and at the end the King of Sweden posed for photographs with the victors while many of them were openly overcome by their achievement.

After twenty-eight years of effort Brazil were the world champions. To the Briton, perhaps, such scenes might seem far-fetched. But warmth, and an undisguised emotionalism, gushes out of the Brazilians. So it was as Mr Arthur Drewry, president of FIFA, presented the gold statuette to Bellini, Brazil's captain, that he said in echoing terms: 'Here indeed was a match to remember, a clean, sporting struggle between two great teams.' Every word was true. None could disagree with that, for indeed it was a match to remember. Perhaps one of the finest ever played in history came four years earlier in Switzerland when Hungary overcame Uruguay in the semi-final round. This, perhaps, lacked the fire of that other occasion, but for sheer skill it was little behind. The cycles of the game, unfortunately, seldom coincide. If only it were possible to put Puskas and his

Hungarians of 1954 on the field with the Brazil of 1958. But that must be something for one's dreams.

The bones of the performance were these. At the fifth minute Liedholm, completing a slick penetrating move with Bergmark, Borjesson, and Simonsson, beat two men on an old sixpenny piece and shot home low to put Sweden one up. On a slithery green pitch it looked as if the favourites were in for trouble. The Swedes had got in the first blow. But doubt was put to flight summarily as Vavà, at centre-forward, with goals in the ninth minute and then again at the half-hour, put Brazil 2–1 ahead by the interval. After that Pelé and Zagalo made it 4–1, and though Simonsson brought Sweden back to 4–2, the swarthy Pelé, leaping like a black panther, headed Brazil to 5–2 as the last seconds of a breathtaking exposition ran out. Brazil, in fact, proved that they could play in the wet.

Thus Sweden, a fine side by any standards, were finally run into the ground by a brand of footballing dexterity that knew no bounds. Strongly and bravely as the Swedish defenders faced the surging tide – Gustavsson, Bergmark and Borjesson in particular – they were at times left spinning like tops. Gren, especially, Simonsson and Liedholm, too, worked heroically in attack, threading many a subtle central move. But where they were stifled was out on the flanks and that, if nothing else mattered, finally settled their fate. Hamrin and Skoglund, their match winners in the past, were now blanketed by the majestic covering of D. Santos and N. Santos at full-back and Sweden's sharpest fangs were drawn. Not so Brazil. Didi floating about mysteriously in midfield was always the master link, the dynamo setting his attack into swift motion; and besides Didi, with Vavà and Pelé a piercing double central thrust, they had the one man above all others to turn things upside down – Garrincha, at outside-right. Rightly had he been called the Matthews of the New World. As I have said, his methods were the same: the suggestion of the inward move, the body-swerve, the flick past the defender's left side, and the glide to freedom at an unbelievable acceleration. Poor Axbom stuck to him as best he could, but time after time he was left as lonely as a mountain wind. Garrincha, in fact, and the subtle use made of him by Didi in a swiftly changing thread of infiltration, was beyond control and that was that. There lay the most sensitive nerve-centre of the whole battle and so Brazil stretched out and grasped their ambition.

from SOCCER IN THE FIFTIES *1974*

Wolverhampton Wanderers v. Honved

BOB HOLMES

During the 1950s Wolverhampton Wanderers played a series of floodlit friendlies against top-class Continental opposition. The highlight was Wolves' 3–2 victory over Honved.

All that glistered in British football in 1954 were the old gold shirts of Wolverhampton Wanderers. The previous, Coronation, year had seen Everest scaled and cricket's Ashes regained, but at the winter game, which was all that really mattered to millions, England had been humbled 3–6 by Hungary at Wembley. Six months on, the nation's football pride had still not recovered when the Magyars won the return in Budapest 7–1. Salvation came from an unlikely source: the misty flicker of the new floodlights at Molineux. Compared to the searchlight shafts of today, their benign gaze was like that of a Victorian street lamp but it was sufficient to ignite the touch-paper of revival. That and the high-voltage management style of Stanley Cullis.

'Those lights were something special,' recalls Cullis. 'It was as if an electric fuse went all the way round the ground. The atmosphere was unique, and the crowd and the players responded.' Cullis's own fuse was much shorter, but did as much from the dressing-room. No club in England turned it on like Wolves did in the mid-1950s: they were not merely the first with new-fangled illuminations, but they were the pioneers of both the long-ball style and a series of unforgettable friendlies against foreign opposition. All of which they won. 'Of course, there were people who said the friendlies would be a flop,' says Cullis. 'But we invited the finest continental teams: Real Madrid, Moscow Spartak and Dynamo. But Honved is the match I remember most as there was an element of revenge about it. After all, Honved were the Hungarian champions and had six of the national team which had beaten England. The build-up had been perfect. A month before we had won 4–0 against Spartak, which was acclaimed England's greatest post-war soccer victory. I said then that that was the proudest day of my life, as we had struck such a great blow for English football. You know, I did not even bring on a substitute when Eddie Stuart was injured; I was determined to play the game the good old British way. But the Honved night was even better.'

Adding to the occasion was a live telecast to the nation, the cameras whirling just as the second half got under-way and Wolves got into their stride. But the armchair fans had missed a display of artistry at which the 54,998 who squeezed into Molineux could only gasp. Honved took the field throwing flowers to the massed ranks, and the distinctive gabled roof of the Molineux Street stand quivered in anticipation. Wolves stood atop the first division, undisputed masters of England and voracious hunters of the long-ball game. Honved, with Puskas, Kovacs, Kocsis and Czibor, were the princes of the short pass.

'I have never known an atmosphere like it,' says Cullis. 'It was quite extraordinary.' So was the football. Springing like gazelles over the Molineux mud, the Hungarians were soon displaying the ball skills of conjurors. When these were allied to a slickness of pass that had the crowd open-mouthed and the Wolves defence frequently ajar, a repeat of England's drubbings looked likely. After just fourteen minutes of Magyar mastery, it looked a certainty. In the eleventh minute Ron Flowers handled a cross from the left and Kocsis rose majestically to ram home a Puskas free-kick. Three minutes later, after a couple of bold Wolves counterattacks, Bert Williams was again bending disconsolately into the back of his own net and, once again, he had had little or no chance. Koscis this time carved up the committed Wolves defence with a superb through-ball for the dashing Machos to run on to and slot firmly home.

Molineux's misery was only tempered by a sense that this was something very, very special, a kind of football not seen in the ground before or since. The crowd watched transfixed. The television people did the same when they might well have pulled the plug – what kind of humiliation was this to set before the watching nation? Cullis himself might have blown a fuse, but didn't. The pitch was cutting up, the Magyars were losing their razor's edge and, as the first half wore on, Wolves were turning the tide. The crowd could hardly wait for the second half to start.

'Contrary to what was said in many papers,' claims Cullis, 'I did not explode at half-time and there were no shenanigans. In fact, all I told them was to carry on as they were and the goals would come. Even if they didn't, I would be quite satisfied.' He did not have to wait long. Four minutes into the second half, Johnny Hancocks was bundled over by Kovacs and the Welsh referee, Mervyn Griffiths, awarded a penalty. The 5ft 4in Hancocks used his size 2 boot to hammer it past Farago's left hand. The gabled roof swayed as the roar swelled. Honved, too, began to creak, and the old gold shirts were now ablaze.

Urged on by skipper Billy Wright, eager to erase the personal anguish of England's defeats, Wolves were rampant now. Peter Broadbent assumed control of midfield and found a few gaps. Hancocks almost bent the bar with a free-kick, Dennis Wilshaw had a fierce drive tipped past the post, and Flowers, too, was forcing Farago into frantic action. Roared on by 55,000 Black Country throats, Wolves could sense Honved's resolve weakening as the pitch sapped their strength and blunted their skills. The scent of a famous victory in their nostrils, the English leaders went for the kill.

Long balls continued to pound the Hungarian lines, foraging wingers snapped at the retreating full-backs' heels and every loose ball was voraciously gobbled and hoisted toward an overworked Farago. Amid unbearable tension and with just fourteen minutes remaining, Wilshaw escaped the clutches of Bozsik and Lorant to send a pinpoint lob for Swinbourne to head home.

Two minutes later, full-back Bill Shorthouse got in on the act, winning possession on the left, swapping passes with Smith and slipping a ball in towards Wilshaw, whose centre was hooked in by Swinbourne on the volley. Delirium broke out in a few million homes as well as Molineux, and although Honved, their reputation as world champions on the line, were not yet done, Wolves held on.

The *Daily Mirror* wrote of the match: 'It had everything – furious speed, blinding skill, pounding power, superlative goal-keeping, and something more.' England's reputation was restored, and a glorious new chapter was embossed in old gold. On an incandescent night, that iron man, Cullis, was, well, satisfied.

WOLVERHAMPTON WANDERERS: Williams; Stuart, Shorthouse; Slater, Wright, Flowers; Hancocks, Broadbent, Swinbourne, Wilshaw, Smith.
Scorers: Hancocks (pen.), Swinbourne (2).

HONVED: Farago; Palicsko, Kovacs; Bozsik, Lorant, Banyai; Budai, Kocsis, Machos, Puskas, Czibor.
Sub: Tichy (for Machos).
Scorers: Kocsis, Machos.

from THE MATCH OF MY LIFE *1991*

The World Cup Final, 1974

BOB HOLMES

The two teams which dominated international football in the 1970s met fittingly in the 1974 World Cup final in Munich. West Germany beat Holland 2–1 after a memorable contest.

'You are an Englishman,' blurted out Franz Beckenbauer to Jack Taylor. It was the Munich Olympic Stadium in the summer of 1974, and the World Cup final between West Germany and Holland was a minute old. The hosts had yet to touch the ball and the referee, Jack Taylor, who had been an Englishman for forty-four years, had awarded a penalty against them. Taylor knew that Beckenbauer was not being complimentary. 'He was cold, clinical, and he meant that our countries were old enemies,' says the former master butcher from Wolverhampton. 'We are friends now and I respect Franz a lot, but I'll never forget that comment. Not least because it was uncharacteristic. He *was* a gentleman on the field but, obviously, it was not any old game, not any old set of circumstances.'

Indeed, it was not. The classic all-European World Cup final was a bit special. The two nations playing in it were old enemies, too, and there was still no love lost between their footballers or their fans. Munich was a magnificent venue and Holland, certainly, had a magnificent team with one player, Johan Cruyff, among the all-time greats.

England had, of course, failed to qualify for the finals but, through Taylor, were always in with a chance of having a hand in the final. Taylor and Scotland's Bobby Davidson were both candidates for the supreme honour and, as Taylor points out, it is a rather exclusive club. In the history of football, the number of people who have refereed a World Cup final is just fourteen. Taylor was well-respected and fearless, a good communicator whose decisive actions ensured that both players and fans knew exactly where they stood. Not a homer, not a prima donna, not a man to throw cards around like confetti: Taylor was an ideal choice who would not bottle it.

But even Taylor, who can lay convincing claim to having seen everything in football, had never witnessed a start like it. Holland, the favourites and thrilling exponents of total football, surpassed themselves from the kick-off. Before a crowd of 77,833 and some one billion around the globe, they proceeded to string together a move of sixteen passes. At first, the Dutch masters switched the ball about in their own half to derisive whistles from the Bavarian crowd who thought it negative. When it continued, the decibels increased, annoyance being the prevailing sentiment from the screeching klaxons. This was no longer negative, they felt, but a mickey-take. Then the ball was in the German half. Still no home player had got near the thing. Then a lightning thrust, and the ball was deep in home territory. Cruyff was in possession and Berti Vogts was bearing down on the maestro.

'I knew Vogts would mark Cruyff,' says Taylor. 'I'd reffed them enough times.' But it was not Vogts who brought the Dutchman down. He could not get near enough to him to do that. In one coruscating flash of genius, Cruyff was past the lumbering German, and it was Uli Hoeness who sent him tumbling in the penalty area. There was no doubt on the television. There was none on the terraces, either, apart from those who were accustomed to referees of a weaker will. Taylor immediately put them right on that one: without hesitation, he pointed to the spot.

When the shrieks of protest had died down – and after Beckenbauer had had his little chat – Johan Neeskens calmly placed the ball beyond Sepp Maier's reach. One–nil to Holland. The time: ninety seconds. It was the first time a penalty had been converted in a World Cup final, and the first one awarded before one side had touched the ball. It was not, however, the first big decision Taylor had had to take.

'I was just about to kick off, the whistle was in my mouth, both teams were lined up and the world waited,' remembers Taylor. 'Then I remembered the habit of a lifetime and checked for the corner flags. They weren't there! I held the game up while a little man sprinted round the field sticking in the missing flags. It caused great embarrassment to the West German FA, who, like most of the country's organisations, prided themselves on their efficiency. But, in view of what was about to happen, I shall be eternally grateful I held up play. I still have nightmares about the repercussions there might have been over the penalty then. Technically, the match would have been incorrectly started, and who knows what would have happened then?'

Holland continued to stroke the ball around almost arrogantly. But instead of trying to wrap the game up with a second goal, they lapsed into the laid-back habits of the training ground. Gradually the Germans, who were anything but laid-back, got back into the match and, playing with the efficiency that makes Volkswagens start in the morning, they capitalised on the Dutch complacency. In the twenty-sixth minute, they, too, had a penalty. Beckenbauer had slipped them into a higher gear without the Dutch noticing and, when Wolfgang Overath threaded through a lovely ball for Bernd Holzenbeim, the German forward went down under a challenge from Jansen.

Taylor admits: 'There was more of a furore about whether the second was a penalty than the first.' He does not, however, bother to add what he thought about it, except that he was 'on the lookout for wingers who dived.' Suffice to say that Paul Breitner did not miss from the spot. With Bonhof ably supporting Beckenbauer, West Germany continued to press. Then, two minutes before the break, Gerd Muller turned in a Bonhof cross, a typical effort on the turn, for his fourteenth goal of the championship, which surpassed Juste Fontaine's record for France in 1958. Holland were understandably chastened, and Taylor had to deal with Cruyff's demand for greater protection from Vogts as the teams walked off at half-time.

Holland were all over Germany after the interval but were already beginning to rue a first-half miss by Johnny Rep. Cruyff had inveigled his way past Beckenbauer to set up Rep, who hesitated fatally and the chance was lost, Maier diving at his feet to foil him. Maier then stopped a fierce drive from Neeskens. How they could have done with a Muller!

The 'Bomber' almost notched his 69th goal for his country but for a marginal off-side decision – Taylor's mettle was certainly tested – although Holland continued to play the Germans off the park. However, Beckenbauer, performing like an athletic Herbert von Karajan, was just about keeping Cruyff's Rembrandt at bay. A desperate second half unfolded, Taylor remembers, 'with plenty of whistle. A lot happened, but it went very quickly as I was so involved.' The Dutch cause was hardly helped by the injuries to Rensenbrink and Rijsbergen and, as the game wore on, Dutch pressure notwithstanding, most neutrals felt that the Germans would hold out. Their organisation was admirable, but once again one of the great sides left the ultimate arena empty-handed.

Helmut Schoen, the West German manager, said: 'We could have been unsettled by that early penalty, and it was a brave decision by the referee.' Beckenbauer added: 'In a strange way, conceding that early goal worked to our advantage. It brought defeat into focus and, once we had weathered that opening burst, we knew that we had lived with their best efforts.'

WEST GERMANY: Maier; Vogts, Schwarzenbeck, Beckenbauer, Breitner; Bonhof, Hoeness; Overath, Grabowski, Muller, Holzenbeim.
Scorers: Breitner (pen), Muller.
HOLLAND: Jongbloed; Suurbier, Rijsbergen, Haan, Krol; Jansen, van Hanagem, Neeskens; Rep, Cruyff, Rensenbrink.
Substitutes: R. van der Kerkhof (for Rensenbrink), de Jong (for Rijsbergen).
Scorer: Neeskens (pen.).

from THE MATCH OF MY LIFE *1974*

Dreams do come true . . .

ARTHUR HOPCRAFT

Sunderland beat Leeds United 1–0 to win the 1973 FA Cup final.

This hearteningly, unlikely outcome – not since 1931 had a second-division club won the FA Cup – was made possible by some vivid luck, by a dazzling miss in front of an open goal by Lorimer, and by two extraordinary saves from Montgomery, as well as by the admirable diligence of this young Sunderland team.

When Mr Burns blew the final whistle Sunderland's manager, Bob Stokoe, left the bench at a sprint, in track-suit, raincoat and trilby, making immediately for Montgomery to hold him in a crushing embrace. Clearly nobody at Wembley was more aware than Stokoe of the overwhelming importance of his goalkeeper's contribution in the sixty-sixth minute: two reflex reactions by which he turned aside

Cherry's flying header, then immediately finger-tipped Lorimer's shot up against the bar.

The red and white scarves of the massed Sunderland supporters swayed in an ecstatic, deep-throated acclaim as their players hugged one another, and as Don Revie's men sank to their knees in exhaustion and dejection.

Leeds might properly complain that they were denied a penalty which Watson's tripping of Bremner in the eleventh minute of the second half deserved. But Mr Burns was unhesitating in his refusal. Leeds, to their credit, wasted no time in fruitless protest.

'We want Stokoe,' the Sunderland fans chanted for minutes at the end, and the manager was entitled to every ounce of their delirious gratitude.

His side gave him all their heart, and perhaps more skill than they, or he, had any reason to expect on this most challenging of football's big occasions. In contrast there was less of Leeds's huge aggregate of talent than we hoped for. Not until deep into the second half did Revie's team start putting together the accuracy of passing and the impetus which showed how much the better side than Sunderland they really are.

But that is not to say that Sunderland did not deserve this famous victory. They were never less than their best; and in spite of the succession of near-misses around the Sunderland goal in the thrilling closing minutes, it was also necessary for Harvey to make a spectacular save from Halom a matter of seconds from the end.

The game is always going to be remembered for its result. But not much of the first half play will live very long in the memory. The first three minutes were ominous: a violent foul by Pitt on Clarke, then a repetition of the same offence. And there were three successive passes by Hunter and Bremner and Giles, which were remarkable for their massive misdirection. The inevitable, taut nerviness and enough rain on the pitch to produce miniature fountains whenever the players struck the ball hard combined to produce a great deal of error. But after a quarter of an hour there came the first piece of individual enterprise; and, coming from Hunter, it was naturally menacing.

Hunter plunged deeply into the Sunderland penalty area, and managed to get that left leg of his round behind Kerr on the byline to lift the ball improbably towards the near post. Lorimer was there to try a flicked volley, and the ball flew past the back stanchion.

Soon afterwards Horswill struck; Sunderland's first shot, and the ball was deflected past Harvey's right-hand post. Immediately Leeds counterattacked, and there was Clarke spinning to Cherry's excellent pass to the penalty spot. Watson saw the danger in time to stab the ball away on the instant Clarke went for the shot.

Clarke had his name taken shortly after that for tripping Hughes from behind. Briefly it appeared that the game would develop a general violence. Among a series of harsh fouls the most alarming was a wild kick at Tueart's shins by Hunter. But this disagreeable promise was not fulfilled, happily. The game was to be an hour old before the play reached an impressively high standard. But even though Hughes was cautioned ten minutes from the end for a foul on Cherry, there was generally an unusual scrupulousness about the tackling once that unpleasant little flurry of the first half had passed.

The goal, in the thirty-second minute, was handsome. It came, appropriately, from Porterfield, the most stylish of Sunderland's eager forwards. Harvey had been forced to tip a lob from Kerr over his bar, and Hughes placed his corner kick firmly beyond the thick grouping in the penalty area to Halom, all alone on the right of the box. Halom used his body to get the ball down at Porterfield's feet. Then Porterfield flicked the ball up with his left foot and struck hard with his right. Harvey was cleanly beaten.

Now, as Leeds found some of the urgency that had been missing, there grew from Madeley one of those exceptional personal performances which remain bright in the mind. He is naturally a graceful player: the head always held high, the ball hit with an easy accuracy. In the last ten minutes of the first half, and throughout the second, he devoted much of his skill to prompting his forwards – a rare ability in a centre-back. Just before the interval he ran thirty yards with the ball, before placing it exactly at the feet of Clarke well inside the Sunderland penalty area. One felt Clarke ought to have scored here. He is capable of sharper response than he showed. Pitt was allowed time to make ground and stab the ball away for a corner. The first half closed on a dramatic shot from Lorimer's right foot. Montgomery stopped the ball by defending his face with both palms.

Montgomery, in fact, looked frequently insecure, in spite of his several vital saves. He lost the ball just outside the goal area, after stopping a shot from Bremner, and again it was Pitt who cleared. Quickly afterwards there occurred the incident which might have given Leeds their equaliser – Watson's lunge at Bremner's legs as the little Scot hurried into the Sunderland penalty area from the left. There must have been many among the spectators who would have awarded Leeds a penalty for that. Mr Burns adjudged otherwise.

That degree of disappointment is bound to cut deeply into any team's morale. Commendably, Leeds shrugged off the effects quickly. Soon Madeley was again running smoothly at the retreating Sunderland defence. His ground pass was aimed for Lorimer's right foot, and the shot sent the ball scraping along the side netting.

Then came the remarkable melodrama. Jones, in considerable trouble with his back to a cluster of Sunderland defenders on the edge of their penalty area, intelligently played the ball back to Reaney. Carefully, Reaney crossed high for the far post. Thrillingly, Cherry hurled himself forward to meet the ball hard with his head. But Montgomery, with an unlikely flap of one hand, turned the ball away to his left. It dropped straight in front of Lorimer. The man with one of the strongest and most certain shots in football had no obstacle between him and the goal. He showed no sign of fluster. But Montgomery managed to recover position and get his fingers to Lorimer's shot and the ball came down off the underside of the cross-bar.

That was in the sixty-sixth minute, and for the remainder of the game the initiative was almost wholly with Leeds. Bremner joined the attack, and stayed. Eddie Gray, whose form had been disappointing, was replaced by the strong, if rather blunt, Yorath.

The substitute was given a perfect pass by Madeley, sending him running clear on Sunderland's left flank. Yorath's shot seemed to be passing under Montgomery's body, but the goalkeeper snatched the ball back from behind him. A shot from Madeley beat the goalkeeper, but Pitt cleared off the line.

That was Leeds's last assault. Fittingly, and to delight the Sunderland followers, the last shot of the game was Halom's, and Harvey needed all his ability to beat the ball away beside the angle of post and bar.

LEEDS: Harvey; Reaney, Cherry; Bremner, Madeley, Hunter; Lorimer, Clarke, Jones, Giles, Gray.
Sub: Yorath.
SUNDERLAND: Montgomery; Malone, Guthrie; Horswill, Watson, Pitt; Kerr, Hughes, Halom, Porterfield, Tueart.
Sub: Young.
Referee: K. Burns (Stourbridge).

from the OBSERVER *May 1973*

Mannion's Greatest Game

WILF MANNION

The majority of my journalistic friends have told me that my greatest-ever game was for Great Britain against the Rest of Europe at Hampden Park, Glasgow, in May 1947, and some have even gone so far as to name me as the 'man of the match', a tribute which I did not really deserve. It is true that I scored a couple of goals – one from a penalty – and helped to lay on a third, but my own view is that I was a long way from being the hero of that star-studded side. I honestly don't think anybody who played that day could be singled out for such a distinction.

It was team spirit, and nothing else, which gained that very convincing victory. As an inside-forward I was just a useful cog in a well-oiled machine which functioned perfectly from start to finish. It was a pleasure to 'fetch and carry' in a team like that, and it seems to me that I just had to get goals. Anybody else would have done the same.

But that super-international is well down the list when I sit back and recall the match which provided me with my greatest thrill. This took place some months later against Blackpool – 22 November 1947, at Ayresome Park, Middlesbrough, to be exact – and it was a game in which I didn't even get a goal, though goodness knows it was not through lack of trying. As a matter of fact, I hadn't scored for my club since the start of the season, and I was really worried.

For some weeks the critics had been getting at me. They were saying that I had lost my touch; that there was no power in my shooting boots any more, and that Mannion was not the player he used to be. But after that game against Blackpool it would not have mattered had I never scored another goal during my whole life for more than ever that day, it became clear that I could be a 'hero' without having to bang the ball into the net to prove it. For me, there is no doubt about it, this was the greatest game of my career, and apparently something like 40,000 Middlesbrough fans thought so too.

There was a very special reason why, as I stepped on the field that day, I was determined if humanly possible to make it my greatest exhibition. Only a few hours before the match I had become engaged, and Bernadette, the girl I was later to marry, had promised to be there to watch me. It was the first time she had seen a soccer game in her life, and naturally I wanted her to remember it with pride. Since then she has become as much a fanatic as any Tees-side fan, but that is another story.

It was a perfect day for football – dull, with no wind. The ground was just right for a good stud hold, and the conditions all round were what every footballer likes. This is how the teams lined up:

MIDDLESBROUGH: Goodfellow; Robinson (R), Hardwick; Bell, Whitaker, Gordon; Spuhler, McCormack, Fenton, Mannion, Walker (G).

BLACKPOOL: Wallace; Shimwell, Suart; Farrow, Hayward, Johnston; Nelson, Mortensen, McIntosh, McCall, Munro.

It was one big party as far as I was concerned. Before the match I had received a number of congratulatory telegrams, and it seemed my enthusiasm had spread to the rest of the team, who were also out to make it their greatest match as well. The only disappointment for the onlookers was that Stanley Matthews was missing from the Blackpool attack, though it is doubtful if even he could have made much difference to the result. Middlesbrough were in such great form that I'm certain we would have licked any team in the country. Blackpool certainly found us too hot to handle, anyway, though admittedly we were somewhat lucky. The seasiders had just as many chances as we had; the big difference was that we turned them to good account.

Throughout my career I always got a big kick playing against Blackpool, for their style was similar to our own and we could always rely on them turning in an attractive display. This match was no exception. For the full ninety minutes it was brain against brain, with immaculate pattern-weaving movements all the time, first from one team and then the other. It was straight from the textbook all right, and to this day I doubt if Middlesbrough's followers have seen a better game. Certainly I never played in a better one. It was touch and go, at any rate in the first half, which team would eventually come out on top.

Mortensen was at his international best. I can see him now, with that famous daredevil rush of his, dashing in to pick up a loose ball in the first minute. Fortunately for us our full-backs, Robinson and Hardwick, were well matched to cope with the fast-stepping Morty, and for a while we seemed out of danger. But not for long. When

Munro fell over Harry Bell's leg and the referee awarded a free kick, the Blackpool forwards surged in for the kill, yet again our defence held tight, and Goodfellow saved another Mortensen hot-shot.

The best move I remember making in that first half was when I dropped back, dispossessed McCall well in our own half, and immediately sent out a long ball to Walker, who responded with a grand centre. It was just too high for Fenton, but Spuhler dashed in and blinded one from close range, his shot just scraping the bar. As the game progressed I gradually began to feel that nothing could go wrong. Every pass I made was perfect; from every tackle I came away with the ball. It was an encouraging feeling, and it seemed I had a magnet attached to my feet; a pretty powerful one, at that.

Play had been in progress for thirty-five minutes before we scored the first goal, a real beauty from McCormack. He went through on his own, beat two defenders and then slammed the ball past Wallace in a manner which gave the visiting goalkeeper no possible chance. In the second half Blackpool switched Mortensen from inside to centre-forward, hoping to get those goals that so far had not come. But they were no better, for our defence squashed every move that came, and remained in complete command of every situation. Blackpool seemed to lose heart after that, and who could blame them? They were playing perfect football, and might well have netted half a dozen goals against an ordinary side.

But Middlesbrough were more than an ordinary team that day. Although I may be prejudiced, I reckon we were a side of miracle men, every man jack of us. We scored three more goals after the interval, Spuhler, Fenton and McCormack getting the credit. We should have had more, too, but for the brilliance of Wallace in the Blackpool goal, who made many wonderful saves. I thought I had a certainty near the end, when I sent in a sizzling drive from inside the Blackpool penalty area, but again Wallace was equal to the test. I would have loved to have got that goal, for it would have meant the end of a perfect day.

In the last few minutes we bombarded the Blackpool goal with every shot in the book. It was bang, bang, bang all the time, and there was little that Blackpool could do to stop it, though they never gave up trying and stuck to their task most courageously. The crowd were all for chairing me off the field at the end, and apparently made me out to be the real hero of the game. Several newspaper men patted me on the back and said they had never seen me play better. They even likened me to the great stars of the past, which was rather flattering but very pleasing. It was certainly a thrilling moment, and one which I shall never forget.

But, even after all these years, I still say that I could not have played anything like so well if my colleagues hadn't backed me up so well and unselfishly. After all, it is team work that counts most in football, not individual brilliance. That was certainly the case that day.

from ASSOCIATION FOOTBALL *1960*

The 1966 World Cup Final

HUGH McILVANNEY

England beat West Germany 4–2 after extra time to win the 1966 World Cup.

The hammer blow England had received at the end of the hour and a half was almost repeated in the final minute of extra time when Seeler lunged in and narrowly failed to make decisive contact with a headed pass by Held. And that was only the prelude to the climax. Nonchalantly breasting the ball down in front of Banks, Bobby Moore relieved a perilous situation and then moved easily away, beating man after man. Glancing up, he saw Hurst ten yards inside the German half and lifted the pass accurately to him. The referee was already looking at his watch and three England supporters had prematurely invaded the pitch as Hurst collected the ball on his chest. At first he seemed inclined to dawdle-out time. Then abruptly he went pounding through in the inside-left position, unimpeded by the totally spent German defenders, his only obstacle his own impending exhaustion. As Tilkowski prepared to move out Hurst summoned the remnants of his strength, swung his left foot and smashed the ball breathtakingly into the top of the net.

The scene that followed was unforgettable. Stiles and Cohen collapsed in a tearful embrace on the ground, young Ball turned wild cartwheels and Bobby Charlton dropped to his knees, felled by emotion. Within seconds the game was over and the players, ignoring the crippling weariness of a few minutes before, were hugging and laughing and crying with their manager, Alf Ramsey, and the reserves who must go through the rest of their lives with bitter-sweet memories of how it looked from the touchline. 'Ramsey, Ramsey,' the crowd roared and in his moment of vindication it was a tribute that no one could grudge him.

Eventually Moore led his men up to the Royal Box to receive the Jules Rimet trophy from the Queen and the slow, ecstatic lap of honour began. 'Ee-aye-addio, we've won the Cup' sang the crowd, as Moore threw it in a golden arc above his head and caught it again. England had, indeed, won the Cup, won it on their merits, producing more determined aggression and flair than they had shown at any earlier stage of the competition. As hosts, they had closed their World Cup with a glorious bang that obliterated memories of its grey, negative beginnings. In such a triumph there could be no failures (the very essence of Ramsey's England was their team play), but if one had to name outstanding heroes they were Ball, Moore, Hurst and the brothers Charlton, the one exhibiting the greatness we always knew he had, the other attaining heights we never thought he could reach.

The Germans had been magnificent opponents and they deserved their own lap of honour at Wembley and the acclaim that awaited them at home. If they were in the West End of London that Saturday night they would have seen some interesting sights. The area was taken over for one great informal party. Some people said it was another VE night, but perhaps that was not the most tactful analogy. At the Royal Garden Hotel, where the English team were spending the night to unwind, there were visits from Harold Wilson and George Brown, who joined in the singing with the crowds outside. Hundreds of people were still dancing a conga around Charing Cross Station at midnight and nearby, in Trafalgar Square, there was the ritual of leaping into the fountains. For most of the nation, however, it was enough to be bathed in euphoria.

from WORLD CUP 66 *1966*

The Lisbon Lions

HUGH McILVANNEY

Celtic became the first British club to win the European Cup when they beat Inter Milan 2–1 in Lisbon, 1967.

Today Lisbon is almost, but not quite, back in Portuguese hands at the end of the most hysterically exuberant occupation any city has ever known.

Pockets of Celtic supporters are holding out in unlikely corners, noisily defending their own carnival atmosphere against the returning tide of normality, determined to preserve the moment, to make the party go on and on.

They emerge with a sudden flood of Glasgow accents from taxis or cafés, or let their voices carry with it an irresistible aggregate of decibels across hotel lounges. Always, even among the refugees who turn up at the British Embassy bereft of everything but the rumpled clothes they stand in, the talk is of that magical hour-and-a-half under the hot sun on Thursday in the breathtaking, tree-fringed amphitheatre of the national stadium.

At the airport, the impression is of a Dunkirk with happiness. The discomforts of mass evacuation are tolerable when your team have just won the greatest victory yet achieved by a British football club, and completed a clean sweep of the trophies available to them that has never been equalled anywhere in the world.

They even cheered Helenio Herrera and his shattered Inter when the Italians left for Milan yesterday evening. 'Inter, Inter, Inter.' The chant resounded convincingly through the departure lounge, but no one was misled. In that mood, overflowing with conquerors' magnanimity they might have given Scot Symon a round of applause.

Typically, within a minute the same happily dishevelled groups were singing: 'Eee Aye Addio, Herrara's on the Buroo.' The suggestion that the most highly paid manager in Europe is likely to be queueing at the Labour Exchange is rather wild but the comment emphasised that even the least analytical fan had seen through the hectic excitement of a unique performance to the essential meaning of the event.

Mundo Desportivo of Lisbon put it another way: 'It was inevitable. Sooner or later the Inter of Herrera, the Inter of *catenaccio*, of negative football, of marginal victories, had to pay for their refusal to play entertaining football.' The Portuguese rejoiced over the magnificent style in which Celtic had taken retribution on behalf of the entire game.

A few of us condemned Herrera unequivocally two years ago after Inter had won the European Cup at their own San Siro Stadium by defending with neurotic caution to protect a luckily gained one-goal lead against a Benfica side with only nine fit men. But he continued to receive around £30,000 a year for stifling the flair, imagination, boldness and spontaneity that make football what it is. And he was still held in awe by people who felt that the statistics of his record justified the sterility of his methods.

Now, however, nearly everyone appreciates the dangers of his influence. The twelfth European Cup final showed how shabbily his philosophy compares with the dynamically positive thinking of Jock Stein. Before the match Stein told me: 'Inter will play it defensively. That's their way and it's their business. But we feel we have a duty to play the game our way, and our way is to attack.

'Win or lose, we want to make the game worth remembering. Just to be involved in an occasion like this is a tremendous honour and we think it puts an obligation on us. We can be as hard and professional as anybody, but I mean it when I say that we don't just want to win this cup. We want to win it playing good football, to make neutrals glad we've done it, glad to remember how we did it.'

The effects of such thinking, and of Stein's genius for giving it practical expression, were there for all the football world to see on Thursday. Of course, he has wonderful players, a team without a serious weakness and with tremendous strengths in vital positions. But when one had eulogised the exhilarating speed and the bewildering variety of skills that destroyed Inter – the unshakable assurance of Clark, the murderously swift overlapping of the full-backs, the creative energy of Auld in midfield, the endlessly astonishing virtuosity of Johnstone, the intelligent and ceaseless running of Chalmers – even with all this, ultimately the element that impressed most profoundly was the massive heart of this Celtic side.

Nothing symbolised it more vividly than the incredible display of Gemmell. He was almost on his knees with fatigue before scoring that thunderous equaliser in the sixty-third minute but somehow his courage forced him to go on dredging up the strength to continue with the exhausting runs along the left-wing that did more than any other single factor to demoralise Inter.

Gemmell has the same aggressive pride, the same contempt for any thought of defeat, that emanates from Auld. Before the game Auld cut short a discussion about the possible ill-effects of the heat and the firm ground with a blunt declaration that they would lick the Italians in any conditions.

When he had been rescued from the delirious crowd and was walking back to the dressing-rooms after Celtic had overcome all the bad breaks to vindicate his confidence, Auld – naked to the waist except for an Inter shirt knotted round his neck like a scarf – suddenly stopped in his tracks and shouted to Ronnie Simpson, who was walking ahead: 'Hey, Ronnie Simpson! What are we? What are we, son?' He stood there sweating, showing his white teeth between parched lips, flecked with saliva. Then he answered his own question with a belligerent roar. 'We're the greatest. That's what we are. The greatest.' Simpson came running back and they embraced for a full minute.

In the dressing-room, as the other players unashamedly sang their supporters' songs in the showers and drank champagne from the huge cup ('Have you had a bevy out of this?'), Auld leaned forward to Sean Fallon, the trainer, and asked with mock seriousness: 'Would you say I was the best? Was I your best man?'

'They've all got Stein's heart,' said a Glasgow colleague. 'There's a bit of the big man in all of them.'

Certainly the preparation for this final and the winning of it were impregnated with Stein's personality. Whether warning the players against exposing themselves to the sun ('I don't even want you near the windows in your rooms. If there's as much as a freckle on any man's arm he's for home') or joking with reporters beside the hotel swimming-pool in Estoril, his was the all-pervading influence.

Despite the extreme tension he must have felt, he never lost the bantering humour that keeps the morale of his expeditions unfailingly high. The impact of the Celtic invasion on the local Catholic churches was a rewarding theme for him. 'They're getting some gates since we came. The nine o'clock and ten o'clock Masses were all-ticket. They've had to get extra plates. How do they divide the takings here? Is it fifty-fifty or in favour of the home club?'

It was hard work appearing so relaxed and the effort eventually took its toll of Stein when he made a dive for the dressing-rooms a minute before the end of the game, unable to stand any more. When we reached him there, he kept muttering: 'What a performance. What a performance.' It was left to Bill Shankly, the Scottish manager of Liverpool (and the only English club manager present), to supply the summing-up quote. 'John,' Shankly said with the solemnity of a man to whom football is a religion, 'you're immortal.'

from the OBSERVER *May 1967*

The Matthews Final

DAVID MILLER

Blackpool 4 Bolton Wanderers 3: the 1953 FA Cup final.

In the main stand, behind the Royal Box, the Matthews family was close to hysteria. Jack was sitting with his brother, Arthur, his wife, their mother, and the Vallances. When Mortensen made it 3–2, Mrs Vallance had fainted. As Jack recalls, 'Someone drew Jimmy Vallance's attention to this, and Jimmy said, "Oh, bugger it" and just left her, and carried on watching the match. She came round, and when Morty scored again, she fainted a second time.' Jean says: 'At 3–3 we were all crying, and someone offered mother a brandy. Granny was sitting there intent but not saying a thing.'

Ralph Banks, whose mind was in a spin, was busy thinking that it shouldn't have been a foul against Holden when he brought down Mudie. 'I was in the defensive wall, and I think it was Wheeler who changed ends,' he says. According to the referee there was, with the score 3–3, less than a minute of injury time still to go.

Of those agonising last ten minutes, Lofthouse recalls: 'I had no sense of panic, only tiredness. I spent the time just watching Stanley. He stood there, toes turned inwards, looking like a little old man – until he moved. In that final spell, he could do it, and he *knew* he could do it.' As the Blackpool players hurried back to the half-way line, Matthews looked round at his team and clapped his hands, slowly, three times, as if to say 'Come on, time is short now, but it's not over.' Those of us who half an hour ago had supposed Blackpool could never win were now merely thankful that, after this spectacular equalising goal, we and our hero could draw breath and prepare for extra time. Not so.

From the kick-off, Bolton lose possession almost immediately: ship-wrecked men adrift in a leaking life-raft not knowing which way to paddle. Instantly the ball flies once more to Matthews. Now follows one of the most photographed and debated goals in history.

Matthews receives the ball level with the 18-yard line, a few yards to the goal-side of Banks and the centre-half Barrass, but kept on-side by Ball, the right-back, who has moved centrally to cover. Matthews now does what he has done ten thousand times before over the past twenty-one years: pauses, the ball at his feet, in order to compel Banks and Barrass to come to him, which they obligingly do. The usual sway to the left, ball on the right foot, as though to come inside, then in an instant gone past Banks on the outside, now in a position midway between the touch-line and the penalty area line.

Mortensen, as he has done a thousand times, is moving away towards the left-hand side of the penalty area; while Barrass abandons any thought of covering Mortensen, to move across to the right-hand side of the penalty area, in the hope of jockeying Matthews. Perry, meanwhile, is moving in from the left-wing, coming across behind his inside-forward, Mudie, into a central position; Hassall is racing back beside Banks in a vain pursuit of Matthews.

Matthews is cutting in towards the goal area; and is now three or four yards clear of Banks and Hassall. Ball, commendably for a defender trying to react intelligently in such crisis, has raced back and is already on the goal-line, with Hanson crouched anxiously on the near post. Barrass, arms and legs spread in a desperate attempt to smother the tormenting menace now facing him eight yards away, is just inside the edge of the goal area. Mortensen, from a yard outside the goal area, is watching Matthews's approach; and Perry is now in line four yards or so behind Mortensen. Matthews takes a glance upwards, and reads the situation in a flash: a pass pulled back to Mortensen will in all probability be blocked or deflected by Barrass. Matthews's concentration is total, head down over the ball, like a potter moulding his clay.

Now leaning at such an angle only he has mastered over the years, arms spread in perfect balance, he pulls his pass backwards beyond Barrass at an angle of thirty-five to forty degrees. As he does so his left foot, his anchor on the soft turf, slides; and with the ball gone, he slips down on to his left knee. It will be argued later, by those who seek to denigrate his achievement in this moment of glory, that he slipped before he passed, that the slip was contributory to his and Blackpool's moment of fortune. Yet photographs clearly disprove this, for his studs still held at the moment the ball was on its way. I can vouch for the likelihood of his falling in such a position at such an angle on this turf; in almost the same spot eighteen months later, playing on the wing for Cambridge against Oxford, I dislodged a piece of turf, almost the size of a chair seat, with my grounded foot when making an acute centre.

As Matthews falls and Barrass turns, having just failed to intercept the ball, Mortensen checks a yard inside the goal area: the ball is going behind him, too far behind him, almost back towards the penalty spot. Straight to Perry. Holden, Bolton's right-winger, is likewise doing his best in this moment of crisis, and has come back to shadow Perry. But now, having placed himself goal-side of Perry, he has no chance of reaching the pass that is speeding on to Perry's *right* foot. It will also be claimed afterwards that the ball runs almost beyond Perry; that he has to hook it through nearly 180 degrees. This is not so. As it comes to him and he places his left foot in preparation to shoot, he is able to have half an eye on the goal, and at the moment of impact he is almost square on to the goal. The angle between pass and shot is probably sixty degrees. As he meets the ball, there are eight players clustered in and around the goal area: Hanson and Ball, poised on the goal-line like a couple of relay runners waiting for the baton; Mortensen static, and Matthews sitting on the ground watching; Barrass, Banks, Hassall and Holden all vainly moving towards the ball, like men hoping to grasp a rabbit bare-handed.

Perry shoots. Hanson and Ball lunge helplessly on the line as the shot streaks beyond them into the left-hand corner of the net, almost striking the net stanchion. Mortensen wheels away in triumph, Perry throws out his arms in acclaim; while Bolton's defenders stand looking at that ball in the back of the net in utter resignation, their resilience and their spirit finally crushed. The roar that swells up from the stadium, a roar that has been riding a crescendo for the last five minutes, now has an intensity that threatens to shake the girders from their rivets. Blackpool, indeed the nation, celebrates; Matthews, in the most extraordinary of circumstances, has his medal. And Mrs Vallance is in a permanent faint.

The stadium is in pandemonium. People lose hats, scarves,

umbrellas, and probably some of their children, in an ecstasy of celebration. Thousands are in tears, tens of thousands are limp with emotional exhaustion. Such an event could not have been achieved by
design for Coronation Year. As Blackpool wearily go forward to climb
the steps and collect the Cup from the Queen, Johnston dashes over
to Johnny Crosland, Blackpool's twelfth man, to collect his teeth. If
he has to shake hands with the Queen, he wants to be properly dressed.
The Queen is having quite a year, what with Hillary and Tensing
ascending Everest, and Gordon Richards about to win the Derby on
Pinza.

from STANLEY MATTHEWS *1989*

Spurs Go Down Fighting

DAVID MILLER

*Tottenham Hotspur beat Benfica 2–1 in the European Cup semi-final at
White Hart Lane, 1962. But Benfica had won the first leg 3–1 and so
went through to the final on aggregate.*

At the end of a surging drama, which left the nerves trembling, the
throat dry, mighty Tottenham Hotspur, the pride of England, bowed
out of the European Cup to the magnificent champions, Benfica, at
White Hart Lane last night. They went down still fighting, and as
few, surely, could have fought. Never, never was there such a match
in England, or for that matter anywhere, said some who have followed
this great international game round the globe longer than I. And I
could well believe them.

Spurs, if any still need be told, had their chances – and what chances
– to have won; or at least to have forced a play-off. Yet, like many
heroes before them, the slings and arrows over two matches cut too
deep into them, left too great a hill to climb. Luck is the greatest ace
in football, and it was not dealt to Spurs.

Nor could a soul deny that Benfica were deserved winners. Their
technique, agility, anticipation were a match and more for Spurs;
their hearts and lungs as big. The events tumbled over each other, so
desperately, so swiftly, that the whole superlative ninety minutes left

the mind spinning. In the final reckoning two sad defensive errors in Lisbon and three disputed, disallowed goals by Spurs, one last night, were handicaps that finally consumed them. But, oh, the agony as, with strength sapping, they hurled themselves again and again recklessly into attack over the last pulsating half hour. If only they could have drawn level, one sensed the whole majestic edifice of Benfica's skill would crumble; highly excitable, they might then have floundered.

Bill Nicholson, Spurs manager, put his normal side in the field, on the strength of Saturday's FA Cup victory. Who is to say he was wrong? I think, in retrospect, that had Mackay been in attack his dynamic pace and power perhaps would have changed the tide and brought Benfica to the point of panic.

This was a memorable match, and of all the great players on the field more than any it was Mackay's match. At times it seemed he would willingly have played single-handed. No one ever possessed more energy or resilience, more power to come and come again. No one will ever forget his solo efforts in the last quarter of an hour, bringing Pereira to his knees and, with mere seconds to go, hitting the bar.

As the sun dipped behind the stands, giving way to night, the 65,000 were there, wedged in shoulder to shoulder, half an hour before the start. Right to the start the singing accompanying the band, impromptu, was far greater than anything Wembley has known. And once Benfica were into their stride they made north London realise, deftly, mercilessly, just why they are champions. It was all one could do to keep up with the pace of events on paper: Norman, a nervy pass, letting Germano, the centre-half, clean through the middle, a corner; Greaves, an electrifying burst, bringing a crescendo of noise that not Hampden, nor Old Trafford, nor even White Hart Lane had heard before.

What a forward line is Benfica's! What wingers, Augusto and Simoes. These, and the dusky lithe Eusebio were a menace: Augusto, a great dribbler, extending the dapper Henry. Within minutes from one of these runs, Eusebio, with a raking, defiant swing, sent the ball leaping inches over Brown's bar.

Then, fifteen minutes gone, and the first vital blow. Benfica went into a 4–1 lead. Aguas out to Simoes: then the centre-forward went like a greyhound for the return centre, skimming low to the far corner of the goal area, where he slid feet first past Henry to glide the ball in – a lightning, cruel blow. Yet almost immediately Spurs, buoyant, compelled by the dynamic roar, were at the other end and Mackay slashed the ball on to a post via a defender. Benfica's technique was superior, yet Spurs now had it all going for them.

In the twenty-third minute, for the third time in the two matches, Spurs had a seemingly fine goal disallowed. One of White's perfect centres was volleyed on by Smith to Greaves, who scored from close in, though tightly marked. The referee gave a goal, but Benfica players dragged him over to an uncertain linesman who had momentarily flagged – no goal. Not out-done or disheartened, Spurs scored, to make it 4–2 seven minutes from half-time. White, at the second attempt, chipped into the middle, Smith chested the ball down, and let fly an unstoppable shot.

On the stroke of half-time Aguas hit the bar. Such was the impact of this great Portuguese side that while at the start they had been mildly booed, when they reappeared after the interval they were applauded on to the pitch. Within four minutes came the most dramatic turn possible – a penalty for Tottenham. White was fouled by Cruz, and in an overwhelming, awesome hush, Blanchflower, the Spurs captain, prepared to take perhaps the most important kick of his career. Coolly, he sidled up, sent Pereira the wrong way, and put the ball in the corner: 2–1 and 4–3 (to Benfica) on aggregate.

It looked like another penalty for Spurs when Germano cupped it away to stop Medwin's header, but the referee waved play on. Growing desperately tired, Tottenham flung themselves again and again into attack, but the vital goal would not come.

from the DAILY TELEGRAPH *April 1962*

A Black Day for Scotland

DAVID MILLER

England 9 Scotland 3: at Wembley, April 1961

How to be truthful, but not exaggerate? How to speculate on the future, while keeping the present in perspective? It is almost impossible, after a fabulous afternoon in this sunstrewn stadium. England sauntered, serenely confident, through the first half, reducing Scotland to relative, almost embarrassing incompetence, though all the while Scotland kept their chin up. Then two goals, immediately after half-time, gave the game a new face, and with the Scottish forwards darting in and out of an uncertain defence, it seemed, even with the score 4–2, that England were not secure. Then in one of the most rip-roaring sprees imaginable, England proceeded to bang in five goals in ten minutes.

The highest score in a home international this century speaks for itself. What made Scotland collapse as they did, after being in with a chance, is impossible to say. Not since the Hungarians has Wembley seen such majestic, opportunist and unanswerable attack as shown by all five England forwards, bringing their total to an incredible 32 goals in five matches.

At times it seemed there were twenty white shirts scything their way through the reeling Scottish ranks. Yet they were only five: Douglas, Greaves, Smith, Haynes and Charlton. If only they can recapture the wizardy over the next fourteen months, England could once again lead the world. Now for Mexico here on 10 May, and then on to Portugal. It would be so easy, one's pen shaking, uncertain which moments, which superlatives to pull out, not to keep proportions – difficult not to make England a certainty for Chile, let alone Lisbon.

Poor Scotland! They will best remember that quarter of an hour after half time, and stick to this side for their World Cup matches with Eire and Czechoslovakia next month. They cannot now question their need of Law, of Mackay, Wilson and McLeod. It was, I think, fate that they should have been the chopping blocks, not helped by the inexperience of four new caps, and Haffey's erratic goalkeeping. I wonder what Brown, so agile for Spurs and despondent at being ignored once more, would have made of this avalanche? As I expected, too, the full-backs, Caldow and Shearer, buckled in the final reckoning.

Picking up where they left off in November, poised and precise, England in no time had the match in hand. The ball sped from man to man instinctively. Anticipation of each other seemed second nature – as did their successful 4–2–4 formation, so unwisely discarded for the inter-league match. Haynes was always free of Mackay, by ten yards or more. Mackay seemed almost content to let him have his head. Yet here also was Greaves, slipping into Haynes's constructive web, playing his part on the assembly line, but up to finish too.

Haynes's wandering virtually cut Charlton out of the game on the wing, but always Charlton was searching inside, making himself useful, with many subtle flicks and chips. Smith was helped by the yielding turf partly controlling the ball, while Douglas was once again the nimble little man we saw against Russia just over two years ago.

With the ubiquitous Law, Mackay was Scotland's attacking inspiration, though they were able to take advantage of the space provided by Flowers playing his withdrawn role. Quinn seemed inadequate, and once again one wonders what Scotland might have done with White there to link with Mackay, as at White Hart Lane.

More than anything, there was the genius of Greaves. He must not be lost to our national team. His composure is uncanny, his feet lick round the ball like a serpent's tongue, he seems to have eyes at the back of his head, and his judgement of half a chance is almost unfailing. McCann could make little of him. So, with Haynes outshining Law as a midfield general, there was really only one answer.

There had been a dramatic start, Springett missing Mackay's cross after only thirty seconds, but Wilson fell and failed to take advantage. After nine minutes, Greaves put Smith away down the wing, and Robson raced up to crash home the pass back from the line. Law then had Flowers worried for a time, but in the twentieth minute an incomparable pass from Haynes carved Scotland apart, and Greaves curved in from the left to lob over the advancing Haffey, who might have got there sooner.

With twenty-five minutes gone, England were at their best, their passes clicking home with the certainty of a cobbler putting in his nails. Soon it was 3–0, Haynes opening the way and Greaves punishing Haffey's error.

Three minutes after the interval Mackay shot in a free kick from the edge of the area, and quickly Wilson headed home McLeod's corner, Springett at fault. But a saucy free kick by Greaves, with Scotland still preparing a wall, gave Douglas the fourth. Now England took control again, and, with seventeen minutes to go, Smith began the landslide after Greaves had juggled the opening. Quinn made it 5–3, but two imperious shots by Haynes, a lazy, insolent solo by Greaves, and Smith's second came bubbling up like champagne.

from the SUNDAY TELEGRAPH *April 1961*

The World's Greatest Save

JOHN MOYNIHAN

Gordon Banks's wonderful save from Pelé in the 1970 World Cup in Guadalajara was not enough to prevent England losing 0–1.

It came after ten minutes when Jairzinho was sent down the right by Carlos Alberto. Jairzinho's strength took him past Cooper to the byeline and he swept the polka-dot ball, with the ferocity of a trench mortar, over to the far post, way beyond where Labone, Moore and Banks were stationed. And towards the blurred object now hurtled Pelé, leaping over Mullery and heading the ball down towards a layer of black netting and all for one were shouting goal and rising to acclaim the 'King'. What happened next remains indistinct in the memory, a blurred and outrageous flash of movement, a combination of sprawling arms and legs. Banks was suddenly over to the right of goal lying sideways with his left leg thrust out straight, his right leg bent at right angles and his groping right hand scooping the ball up and over the cross-bar. What he had, in fact, done was to reach a ball going at outrageous speed at a point when most other goalkeepers would have not even moved. The ball seemed to tumble over the goal and roll down slowly on the other side of the net with the sudden abatement of an ocean wave after breaking on a rock. One wondered, amid all the commotion, the shouting and screaming, whether Banks had broken his arm and suffered grievous damage; he lay on his back with his shoulders on the grass, his colleagues standing around too nonplussed to yell their praise. The Brazilians took a very quick corner. It was all over before it had begun, like a short Disney cartoon. So let us once again drag Banks back by his ankles and give him a rerun. Jairzinho's rushing centre, Pelé, on top of Mullery, heading fiercely down towards the gaping hole left by Banks guarding the near post, Banks, in an attitude of a praying mantis, after spinning on to a new twig, playing the ball up and away with an extended palm into oblivion.

'Did you see that!' roared Harry turning round at us. His face was sweating profusely, his cowboy hat tilted back off his head, his yellow nicotined fingers trembled with tension – 'By Christ, did you see it?' It was a fatuous remark, but he had to say something to relieve his windpipe. He wanted to convince himself we had seen what he had seen and make sure in his normally placid mind that it was not some figment of the imagination, a confidence trick, a sudden mirage brought on by the unrelenting rays of the sun. To this day I cannot recall how Banks managed to get across goal and touch the ball as it rose off the turf towards the roof of the net.

from FOOTBALL FEVER *1974*

A Merseyside Derby

IVAN SHARPE

In 1962 Everton and Liverpool fought out a 2–2 draw in front of a crowd of 73,000 in the first Merseyside league derby for more than ten years.

This was bedlam – 73,000 people packed into Goodison Park and turned this first Merseyside 'derby' in the league for eleven years into eleven derby days rolled into one. It was the Blue Army versus the Red Army, and to heighten the local excitement the teams came out to the musical accompaniment of the *Z-Cars* theme tune: it was simply pandemonium.

When Furnell, in the Liverpool goal, fumbled the ball in the very first minute so that Vernon, who was challenging him, rolled it into the unguarded net, the whole place exploded. What a send-off! Poor Furnell rolled on the ground in mental agony at his mistake. But the frantic joy of the Blue Army turned into amazement and every kind of noise an angry crowd can let loose when the referee awarded not a goal, but a free-kick for Liverpool near the penalty spot . . .

But the battle roared on. The tension was terrific. Due to the extreme pressure on their nerves, the players developed Cup finalitis, and mistake followed mistake, to the accompaniment of jeers from the opposing army of Blues or Reds. All was wild and woolly. No one drew back, as they say in the dressing-rooms. Everyone bundled in

. . . (Everton scored from a penalty-kick by Vernon; Lewis equalised. Half-time: 1–1. Morrissey of Everton made the score 2–1).

Thus Everton led again but, as in the Manchester derby a week ago, the occasion was to be rounded off by a dramatic finale. In the minute or so of extra time, with boths sides all desperation, A'Court landed the ball in the jaws of Everton's goal, Lewis was there to head it down to earth, and Hunt raised the roof of Goodison Park and all the property for miles around by crashing it into the net.

Perhaps that was a fair result, as it had been anyone's game. But it was not a calculating football match so much as a mad struggle. There were no £50,000 stars. Reputation counted for nothing. It was each man for himself and nearly all came down to one level. Thus Yeats was the longest and highest kicker of the afternoon and Vernon the strongest kicker-out.

What a day! In comparison, the pulsating Manchester derby of a week ago was merely a PSA.

EVERTON: West; Meagan, Thomson; Gabriel, Labone, Harris; Bingham, Stevens, Young, Vernon, Morrissey.
LIVERPOOL: Furnell; Byrne, Moran; Milne, Yeats, Leishman; Callaghan, Hunt, Lewis, Melia, A'Court.

from the SUNDAY TIMES *1962*

Made in England

FRANK SWIFT

In 1948, England beat Italy 4–0 in Turin in one of the great post-war internationals.

It was my first match as captain of England in a full international. It was my greatest match and it was also one of England's greatest matches. No man can ask more than that, and I know that I will never forget the golden sunshine of that Sunday evening in 1948 when England thrashed a great Italian side 4–0 at Turin.

The match had everything. It was the climax of an England tour of the Continent and it came at a time when Italy were thought to have the finest football team in the world. This was the team which afterwards was almost wiped out by a tragic air crash in which nine of the Italian players were killed.

But at that time they had beaten nearly everybody and I was very conscious of the great honour of leading England against them, particularly as it was the first time that England had been captained by a goalkeeper. My selection as captain was naturally criticised. It was felt that as a goalkeeper I would be too remote from the play to encourage and direct my colleagues. But captaincy is not a matter of hand-clapping and shouting. It is a matter of confidence and comradeship in one another and I think that the England team proved it that night.

This confidence and comradeship started in the dressing-room. We knew what we were up against and we changed quietly.

As the players finished lacing their boots, I knew that I ought to say a few words. I had heard Eddie Hapgood, Stan Cullis, Joe Mercer, George Hardwick and Tommy Lawton all say their piece in the dressing-room as captains of England. But as silence fell and the players looked over towards me, I was too full of emotion to say anything. Words just would not come. Then Stanley Matthews got up, walked across and shook my hand.

Quietly, he said, 'I'll give you everything I've got tonight, Frank.' One by one, the other players did the same. It was a wonderful moment.

I walked into that vast Turin stadium feeling on top of the world. Eighty-five thousand people – all seated – were spread in a vast bowl around us. Most of them expected Italy to win. But I knew that we were going to give them the fight of their lives. And we did.

It had rained an hour or two before the kick-off. It wasn't much, but it settled the dust and gave the ball a bit of weight and somehow it made us feel at home.

All our strategy was based on an early goal. Most Continental teams lose heart as soon as they lose the lead and we felt that we would knock these master-men down to life-size if we could score quickly. So we were delighted when we did.

After only four minutes, Stanley Matthews beat left-back Eliani and stroked the ball forward. Stan Mortensen went after it with a burst of speed which in those days had to be seen to be believed. He cut to the right of goal – down to within a yard of the goal-line.

Then, travelling at top speed, he smashed in a shot with the outside of his right foot which twisted past the astonished Italian goalkeeper into the net. It was a goal in a million. Morty originally intended to centre the ball, but he saw the goalkeeper moving away to cover the cross and with almost nothing to shoot at, he had the ball in the net like a flash.

That started it. Far from discouraging the Italians, that goal goaded them into magnificent fury. For twenty minutes, they threw everything at us with bewildering inter-passing and brilliant speed. Shots, overhead kicks, headers and even back-headers flew at me from all directions and once I had to scoop the ball one-handed off the line.

But I was lucky and the England defence in front of me was magnificent. Laurie Scott, Jack Howe and Neil Franklin, Billy Wright and Henry Cockburn – they all played their hearts out. And Wilf Mannion, at inside-left, trod nearly every blade of grass in Turin, covering, covering for all he was worth.

Twice the Italians got the ball into the net but they were offside, and the Spanish referee Pedro Escartin will always have my gratitude for having the courage to say so. Menti shot straight at me from four yards. Then Carapellese twice nearly beat me after baffling four-man movements, first with a shot and, five minutes later, with a brilliant header.

Then the maestro, Stanley Matthews, pushed another short ball through to Mortensen. This one was well inside our own half, but Morty sprinted fifty yards, changing pace to beat that fine centre-half, Parola, before hooking the ball back from the byeline again.

This time, though, Morty didn't shoot. He pulled the ball back into the centre and Tommy Lawton – coming up like a train – blasted it first time into the back of the net. I was glad Tom scored that goal because I think only I knew just what it had cost him in pain to get into that England team.

Tom was my room-mate on the tour and for days before the match he had been in intense pain with kidney trouble. Night after night he lay awake sweating as the attacks came and went. It was doubtful whether he would play, and when he was selected, I was worried in case the pain came stabbing back in the middle of the game. I still don't know whether it did, but I do know that Tom never gave any sign of it. He hit that ball as if he hated it and it never left the ground as it slashed into the right corner of the net.

Italy came right back. A lob from their captain, Mazzola, left Gabetto in the clear but I had come right out and so was able to smother his shot. Then Gabetto beat me with a surprise back-header, but the ball hit the crossbar and I managed to dive on the rebound and hurl it away.

We were still two goals up at half-time and slowly we started to play with power and rhythm. The Italian defence began to get really worried about Matthews and Mortensen and, unconsciously, the game began to drift more and more towards those twin barbs of danger. As soon as it did, Tom Finney exploded into the match from the left wing.

Midway through the second half, Tom sprinted in as a Mannion pass cunningly changed the direction of the attack and hammered in a low left-foot shot for our third goal. A minute later, he scored again. And that broke the Italians' hearts.

For this goal, Finney moved into the centre as Mortensen worked down the left of the field. At just the right moment, Morty slipped the ball across goal. The Italian goalkeeper expected another left-foot snorter past his right hand, but Finney left him helpless with a right-foot cross-shot past his left hand.

As he did so, a little grey-haired man, all alone, slumped disconsolately on the touch-line. It was Signor Pozzo, the Italian team manager, and no one had to tell him that he was already out of a job. He knew.

The rest was all England. They toyed with the tattered Italian defence, and gave a beautiful display of combined attacking football. Poor Bacigalupo, the Italian goalkeeper, had as many shots slung at him in those last twenty minutes as I had in the first. But England were now only playing an exhibition. Goals did not matter any more, and in the end, even the Italian crowd had to cheer.

As the match ended, a wave of applause rolled up into the late evening. The whole 85,000 spectators – including a few delirious British servicemen – stood up, clapping and cheering in a terrific ovation as we walked off the field.

Next day, the biggest shop in the centre of Turin cleared its windows of everything but a giant photograph of the England team. It was larger than life-size and across the top in huge letters ran a simple caption.

It just said, 'Made in England'.

I stood and looked at that for a long, long time.

from ASSOCIATION FOOTBALL *1960*

Dixie Dean's Sixtieth Goal

NICK WALSH

Dixie Dean's record-breaking sixtieth league goal came with a hat-trick against Arsenal at Goodison Park in 1928.

On Saturday afternoon, 5 May 1928, soccer fans from the Merseyside area converged in their thousands on Goodison Park. Ferryboats and trains from across the Mersey plus the special football trams in Liverpool, steamed, purred, and clanged along to convey fans from far and near. The crowds were all imbued with the mystic expectancy of a religious pilgrimage, set on bearing witness to some supernatural vision and bathe in its glory. There was no guarantee the spirit would appear, but the slimmest hope was sufficient attraction. Not to be there if it should happen would condemn devout football souls forever to purgatory, a penance Everton fans were determined not to suffer.

So every able-bodied supporter who could manage to get there *was* there, ready to put up with the thronging, jostling and other attendant inconveniences without complaint. Throughout all the marshalling and travel arrangements, no disturbances occurred, and there was a complete absence of any kind of hooliganism, despite the excitement and tension which the occasion inevitably created. Supporters willed and wished and prayed the miracle would happen. That 'Dixie' would capture those three goals and be credited with the nice round figure of sixty to establish an all-time record. There was no dispute about that, except perhaps among the Arsenal players and supporters.

The ground was packed with more than 60,000 spectators when the teams ran on to the pitch to be welcomed by tumultuous cheering, mostly and especially for the man of the moment. The referee, 'Lol' Harper, of Stourbridge, shook Dean by the hand. However there was another man for whom this match must be regarded as memorable. Charlie Buchan, the Arsenal forward who had graced the English football scene so well for many years, had announced his retirement from the game and this was to be his final appearance. It was perhaps unfortunate that his departure from the soccer stage had to be overshadowed by an event which diverted attention from him and which inevitably had to take prior importance. The crowd enjoyed the electric atmosphere of the occasion and the sense of privilege it conveyed. The red jerseys of Arsenal and the blue of Everton's strip all appeared brighter than usual. The green background of the pitch combined to add a sense of gaiety in contrast to the serious challenge and purpose which the game presented to a deliriously cheerful and expectant multitude.

The Arsenal team was as follows: Paterson; Parker, John; Baker, Butler, Blythe; Hulme, Buchan, Shaw, Brian, Peel. The Everton side was: Davies; Cresswell (captain), O'Donnell; Kelly, Hart. Virr; Critchley, Martin, Dean, Weldon, Troup. The kick-off which the huge crowd of spectators had so patiently waited for was duly approved by the referee, but within minutes Everton hearts sank, ostensibly with all their hopes. Arsenal had scored. Shaw, Arsenal's centre-forward, hit a cannonball shot which would have done credit to Dixie himself. Davies in the Everton goal fumbled the shot and allowed the ball to go through his legs. The early tension and excitement had no doubt affected him and this early reverse did no good either for Everton's or Dean's intentions at that moment of crisis.

The situation demanded immediate retaliation if the game's expectations were to be fulfilled. Dean realised this and right from the restart he was on his way goalwards sweeping through the Arsenal defence to score with a thunderous shot to chalk up Everton's 100th goal of the season. And of course his own fifty-eighth! Only two more wanted! Hearts and hopes were immediately restored to their pre-match elevation in the Everton camp. Dean was determined to reach his target. He was in top form and rampant throughout. Arsenal players, however, were resolved – so far as they were concerned, Dean would not score again.

The score remained at 1–1 until midway through the first half when Dean was unceremoniously bought down in the penalty area by an Arsenal defender. The referee pointed to the penalty spot. The crowd, with feverish excitement, roared 'Give it to Dixie!' and impatiently waited whilst it was being established that the great man would take the kick. Dean took the ball and placed it on the spot. Silence descended over the ground as though every single one of the 60,000 spectators had been temporarily transfixed, that all life had been extinguished by some supernatural force. An eerie silence, breathless yet electric in its intensity, inert like a fuse ready to be ignited. Dean ran up to take the kick. The fuse was burning and suddenly the vast arena exploded with a deafening roar. The ball was in the back of the net. The crowd shouted and screamed, delirious with ecstasy and delight. The miracle was on the horizon. The goal-scoring record had been equalled and now it was surely not beyond Dean to score another goal. But the Gunners were not taking it lying down. They pressed hard during the remainder of the first half and ultimately got their reward. O'Donnell, the Everton full-back, put through his own goal and the teams went into the dressing-room with the score 2–2 at half-time.

The crowd naturally thought the interval was far too long. They sensed somehow the miracle must happen. That elusive goal must come, but a lot of nails would be bitten in the meantime. The second half opened and Arsenal made it obvious that they would do their utmost to prevent Dean scoring that vital goal. A tight rein was kept on Dean throughout. Arsenal frequently adopted the off-side trap. Time was evaporating. There were only eight minutes to go, and still the goal, that diamond goal, did not come. The atmosphere was charged as though an electric current was continually passing at varying force through spectators and players alike. Everton players were concentrating in trying to feed Dean with the essential ball that would give him the goal that everybody (except Arsenal) wanted and prayed for him to get.

The tension reached fever pitch when five minutes from the end Everton were awarded a corner. Alec Troup, the diminutive Scot, placed the ball to take the corner kick. The crowd, tense with bated breath, wondered whether this could be it. Would Dean get that magnificent head of his to the ball? Alec sent over his speciality, a hanging centre and Dean was there. With a perfectly timed leap above the fourteen players in the goalmouth Dixie had nodded it past the Arsenal goalkeeper for his record sixtieth goal. The sound of the roar from the crowd must have reached a thousand decibels. The co-ordinate of voices was like a thunder-clap heard throughout the length and breadth of Merseyside. The crowd was jumping with joy and blessed with what must have been the most ecstatic delight ever bestowed on any sporting gathering in history. Dixie bowed his head modestly. The crescendo of the storm of idolatrous worship echoed around the ground for several minutes. The players of both teams ran to shake Dean by the hand or otherwise show their appreciation of his remarkable achievement. All, that is, except Charlie Buchan, who according to Dean showed no inclination to express any form of congratulation. Dean thought this was simply pique on the part of Buchan because his own farewell to football had been overshadowed by the sixty-goal event.

from DIXIE DEAN *1977*

Burnley Survive, 1987

IAN WOOLDRIDGE

We gathered like predatory undertakers and professional mourners, lured by the death throes of a stricken giant.

Reporters who'd forgotten where Burnley was, spilled out over the press seats which had gathered the dust of disinterest. Some had their obituaries already written.

There was coruscating criticism of the club that became too big for its boots, posthumous debunking of Bob Lord, the small-town butcher who'd built himself a grandiose memorial and there was lyrical lament for one of the twelve founder clubs of English, and thus world, football.

We noted that the sun shone down on the old dying mill town with ironic brilliance. We recalled that for years it had the highest suicide rate in Britain. We looked at the beautifully appointed ground with a pitch barely scarred at the end of the season and agreed how sad it all was.

We'd done our homework, too. Burnley, founded March 1888 as a league club; the smallest town in Britain to sustain a first-division team for years on end; the first club in England to establish a training ground elsewhere to work on brilliant tactical moves; the club which had a crowd of 49,734 for a match in 1914 and a record gate of 54,775 for a cup game against Huddersfield in 1924.

Now, at the end of the 1986–87 season, poverty-stricken on attendances of fewer than 3,000, Burnley were about to fall through the floor of the fourth division. They had to beat Orient and rely on miracles elsewhere. It wasn't going to happen so let's get it over with and catch the 5.47 back to London.

But it was, of course, the day that Burnley made fools of the ghouls.

The script started going wrong when Burnley and Orient came out for the 3 p.m. kick-off and were immediately shooed off again by police. Thousands were still outside the ground clamouring to get in, yell their encouragement and join in the singing of 'You'll Never Walk Alone'.

Burnley would never have been in this plight had they not been abandoned to walk alone several seasons ago but their players were too panic-stricken for cynicism when they finally kicked off in front of 15,781 spectators. They were playing for their own careers, let alone Burnley's survival and the sporting term 'sudden death' takes on new shades of meaning when the last pay cheque is only ninety minutes away.

I shall never quite determine who won that match: the Burnley team or the crowd.

The Burnley team were fuelled by 45 per cent talent – which means they played above themselves – and 180 per cent adrenalin. The crowd, in this recently echoing concrete mausoleum at the foot of a damp Lancashire valley, was as passionate, pro rata, as I have ever heard.

They came from everywhere. Cliff Knights, who left Burnley in 1960 to become a prosperous chartered engineer near Bristol, had driven up that morning with his wife Betty, for what he was convinced would be a wake. John Ratcliffe, who cut his teeth on Burnley football until he went to London University and started teaching geography in Catford, spent £100 simply to go back and stand on the terrace and roar.

There were hundreds in the crowd who were on similar pilgrimages back home, thousands who had actually stirred themselves from TV just down the road now that Armageddon was near.

They were immaculately behaved, as were the visiting Orient fans from London, and I have to report that if I could see matches of such passion and intensity even three times a season I would cease being one of the soccer's missing millions tomorrow.

It was a classic sporting occasion, if not a classic exhibition of football, superbly refereed and ferociously contested by an Orient team themselves in contention for promotion.

The roar that greeted the goal that put Burnley 2–0 ahead was probably heard in Blackpool. The silence that met Orient's goal was such that many couldn't believe it was scored until play restarted in the centre circle.

A draw was no good to Burnley. So began the thirty-five minutes that were to determine whether Burnley died, aged 99 without so much as a formal telegram from the Queen. The spectator immediately in front of me, a local businessman with a tartan scarf wrapped into an extremely expensive mackintosh, had assured me earlier that if Burnley lost the match Burnley, as a town, would die. Hyperbole to the visiting undertakers but in his case a personal understatement.

I thought he was going to have a heart attack every time Orient fired a shot at goal during those leaden minutes to survival. He turned round and almost strangled me when it was over.

Burnley made it at the expense of Lincoln City. The recriminations of lunch-time were forgotten in the tea-time euphoria.

But have the lessons been learned? Did Burnley really deserve to live? Is reprieve merely the prelude to more complacency? And is 'You'll Never Walk Alone' the anthem of ultimate hypocrisy?

The answers, I suppose, are that if you want a league football club locally, go and support it. Burnley did, with only a few minutes of almost a century to spare.

from SPORT IN THE EIGHTIES *1989*

PART 3

The Teams

Reading

JOHN ARLOTT

They were a third-division team when I first saw them, which was, I fancy, in 1923: I remember that the match was against Northampton Town, and that is as far as my memory serves me. Reading, sixteen miles away – in those days a one-and-sixpenny return railway fare – was the nearest club to my home, and a friend of my father's took me to the match: I was nine years old and, as I recall, behaved abominably.

My next match, I can pinpoint exactly: it was played on 2 October, 1926. Reading had just been promoted to the second division – leaving behind them, in the third, Charlton Athletic, Brentford, Queen's Park Rangers, Coventry City and Luton Town. Their opponents on this particular day were Portsmouth, who had been promoted from the third (southern) two years earlier and who were, that same season, to win their way to the first division. They beat Reading – to my great hurt – by two goals to one. A penalty awarded to Portsmouth as a vital moment was taken by Billy Haines – the Portsmouth crowd used to greet him with 'To Be A Farmer's Boy'. He bent down to place the ball, the referee blew his whistle, and Haines, without even straightening up, toe-ended it into the corner of the net while the Reading goalkeeper was still adjusting his cap. I can see that goalkeeper – Duckworth, a Lancashireman – even now, running indignantly out to the referee to protest against the goal: but it stood, and Reading lost.

I remember, too, going after the match, with my autograph album, to the creosoted wooden hut which then housed the dressing-rooms at Elm Park before the present stand and offices were completed just a few weeks later. The first signature in that book, written in a somewhat laboured, boyish hand, was: 'F. Cook' – Portsmouth's Welsh international outside-left. It is fourteen years now since I gave that book to a schoolboy: as I handed it to him, I lifted the cover with my thumb and there it was, all alone on the first page – 'F. Cook' – my first autograph.

The bug had bitten. I was lucky: the Reading side of those days, although it never had a really good record during its five seasons in the second division, held some colourful players. Duckworth, in goal, was a stooping, eager player of incredible courage who would go down at the feet of advancing forwards with great daring. My own particular favourite was Billy McConnell, the Irish international left-back. Tall, rosy-faced, fast, utterly fearless and a terrific kicker, he was of the old school of backs. For four years he was a regular choice for Ireland, refusing one cap – against Scotland – to play for his club, when they were in danger of relegation. A broken leg in 1928 ended the career of the man who was one of the deadliest tacklers of his day.

A few weeks ago, travelling in Wales, I bought a local paper, to find announced the death of Dai Evans, who was a Welsh international left-half in Reading's promotion side. Evans was not a consistent player, neither, I now realise, was he particularly conscientious about his training; but he was a polished player who took the game of football with the natural ease with which it came to him. His transfer to Huddersfield, I always felt, coincided with the start of Reading's slide back to the third division.

The 1926–27 season at Elm Park, however, held no thought of relegation. The small, quick, fiery Hugh Davey, Ireland's centre-forward, and Frank Richardson, the inside-left, a treasure for a third-division side – his socks trailing, fair curls flopping over his face – were eager for goals. Behind them, Alf Messer was a centre-half so dominating that, despite the contemporary Seddon, Hill, and Kean, he came close indeed to England honours. If Evans's transfer marked the beginning of the slide, Messer's move to Tottenham completed it. He was the coolest penalty-kicker I ever saw. He always put the ball about a foot inside the right-hand post at a height of about eighteen inches off the ground: I never saw him fail with a penalty. When Messer left, Tommy Meads, Evans's successor, an immense worker and a fine long-shot, went with him to White Hart Lane and the half-back line, backbone of any side, was gone. But, in 1926–27, Reading were not a selling side.

Their ground was about eighteen miles from my home: it was a cycle ride – a hard one, but a cycle ride – and worth it. Eighteen miles there, eighteen miles back. I can still remember every mile of the route and, given the same circumstances, I would cycle it the same twenty times a year again.

What a season that was – 1926–27. At every opportunity I would see football; I would bury my nose in the football papers which were then so numerous. Alas, that the boy football enthusiast of today has no *Athletic News* which used to appear on Monday morning with a full account of every match in the four English leagues *and* the Scottish first division, with due attention to the amateurs and the Irish competitions, *plus* special articles as well. *The Topical Times, The Sports Budget, Football Favourite*, their names alone bring back their smell and look and feel.

from CONCERNING SOCCER *1950*

Tottenham Hotspur

A. J. AYER

How good is this Spurs side? Are they the team of the century, in merit as well as in achievement? By the very highest standards, they are not a team of stars. Blanchflower is a very great player, at his zenith the best wing-half that I have ever seen, but he is nearing the end of his career. Of the others only Jones, a wing-forward with the speed and swerve of a rugby three-quarter, could clearly command a place in a current world XI. Of course they have good players besides these. Norman is a dominating centre-half. Mackay can play like a tornado. Though White is erratic, his intelligent play at inside-forward has won the team many of its matches; he has the positional sense of a great player. Smith, who is now the England centre-forward, has played better this year than he ever has before. He is a clumsy-looking footballer, and there are periods when nothing will go right for him, but he has more skill than one might think and he rises splendidly to an occasion. In the semi-final as well as in the final of the Cup, and in the critical league match with Sheffield Wednesday, which settled the championship for the Spurs, it was his well-taken goals that turned the scale.

Nevertheless, it is not so much to the individual merits of the players as to their team work that the Spurs owe their extraordinary success. They have kept very nearly the same side for two seasons, and they have in this season been very little disturbed by injuries. The result is that they have achieved a remarkable understanding. In their use of the open space, they resemble the famous Spurs team which won the league Championship ten years ago. But whereas the 1950 XI relied, under Arthur Rowe's management, exclusively on 'push and run', a style which is very beautiful to watch when it is successful but one which makes very heavy demands upon the players' energy, the present team has been able to blend this 'Continental' style with the English long-passing method. One of their most considerable achievements has been their ability to pace a game, to conserve their energy between bouts of pressure: it has repeatedly brought them goals in quick succession. For this they owe much to their manager, Bill Nicholson, who was himself a member of the 1950 team, but still more, I think, to their captain, Danny Blanchflower, whose control of them on the field has always been intelligent and sure. At their best, I think they have been superior to any English team since the war, though the Manchester United side which was broken by the Munich air crash ran them very close. I am not sure that they are better than the great Arsenal sides of the thirties, though it is perhaps in their favour that the game is probably played nowadays at a faster pace.

How will they fare next season in the European Cup? A fast, hard-tackling side like some of the West German teams might throw them out of their rhythm. Against a team of artists like Real Madrid, their own artistry should flourish. I cannot wager that they will beat Real Madrid; but if at any stage they are drawn against them, it should be a wonderful game to watch.

from the NEW STATESMAN *1961*

Hibernian

ALAN BOLD

Going to Easter Road was a blessed release. It was the big world, the place to be. It represented an arena, away from home, where matters of moment were enacted. There was the warm sensation of walking along with Tommy and his dad as part of a big happy crowd. There was buying programmes (and remember that Hibs, at that time, offered the best programme in the country, a really professional job, edited by Magnus Williamson). And there was the scarf. I remember having two scarves; an ordinary woollen one in green and white and a special one made of silk and decorated with a painting of a Hibs player heading a goal.

The silk scarf was for when Hibs played Hearts. Hibs and Hearts were, in our childish minds, symbols of good and evil, twin aspects of life. Apart from winning the League and all that, nothing tasted so sweet as a victory over the folk from Tynecastle. Hearts, with their dull maroon strip and their inferior stadium, seemed perpetually shabby. In Willie Bauld they had – we all knew it in our heart of hearts – a great player but we could not admit that. For me, in particular, Willie Bauld was a bugbear, a name that made me boil with moral indignation. And to make matters worse I was always teased about him. My father's name was Willie Bold so, of course, when that fact became known adults would laugh and say 'Willie Bauld – so yer faither plays fur Herts'. No, I would explain, his name was Bold not Bauld, but that just set me up for more ribbing. It did not cross my mind that it would be a feather in one's cap to have a father like Willie Bauld who had once played for Scotland and who was the idol of half of Edinburgh. He might be a great player – but he played greatly for Hearts. That was the rub.

from WE'LL SUPPORT YOU EVERMORE *1976*

The Red Devils

EAMON DUNPHY

The new champions were called the Red Devils. It was an apt description, for their vivacious roguishness was one of their most attractive qualities. Denis Viollet who scored twenty goals that season brought another distinctly Manchester dimension to the side. Denis was a devil, a rogue, smooth, elegant and sophisticated, as were the Manchester nightclubs he loved to frequent. Denis was a Manchester lad to his marrow. Not for him the coffee-bars or ice-rinks or the innocent cavorting of Sale Locarno. The Cromford Club, perhaps, preferably the velvet promise of the Queens and Continental Clubs where the real action was. He was a loner. Liked by the lads and liking them, but to them he was elusive, mysterious, Town, after the last bus had long since gone. And that's the way he played his football, beautifully balanced, subtle, a gliding, powerful presence, composed and deadly when the opening came. David Pegg was Manchester too, sharp, brazen, young and handsome. A lad.

Devils, yes, powerful ones. Duncan Edwards dominating everything around him, physically, spiritually, a force of extraordinary impact. So hungry for the ball that sometimes, as Jackie Blanchflower recalls, 'he would brush you aside to get possession'. Duncan broke up attacks with ruthless authority, the diffidence of dance-hall and bank-counter transformed into imperious conviction. When a goal was needed, a defeat looming, other spirits beginning to tire, his was the galvanising extra drive that turned the issue in their favour. The others were in awe of him, all except little Eddie Colman, the Salford urchin who wasn't in awe of anyone.

Tommy Taylor scored twenty-five goals that year, leading the forward line with lusty vigour and delicate touch. His pal, Jackie Blanchflower, added another virtue to the whole, poise and intelligence, wry Manchester humour. A team of many talents for a city of many faces, a city made up of outsiders. A city where rogue and priest could sit together with rabbi and inventor, each feeling they belonged as truly as Beckett, Barbirolli and Alex Bird. Cottonopolis. Here the first Catholic church bells rang after the Reformation; here, half-a-mile from Old Trafford, on Stretford Road, the illiterate Polish Jew, Michael Marks, joined Tom Spencer to open their first Penny Bazaar in 1894. Men of many kinds dared to dream.

Matt Busby had dreamed long and quietly. As he sat in the stand watching his 'Red Devils' he experienced something much more profound than professional pride. He thought of Alex James, of the glorious vision of his bleak childhood, the light that first entered his soul beneath the pit-head bing in Old Orbiston. Matt didn't *think* of that so much as sense the old magic of the past surging through his blood. The feeling of fulfilment was chilling.

Matt hadn't expected this so soon. He was pleased and a little frightened. They'd won the Championship by *eleven* points. Their average age was twenty-two.

Busby knew there was more to come. United won the FA Youth Cup for the third year running in 1956. McGuinness, Charlton, Alex Dawson, Mark Pearson and Kenny Morgans played in the side that beat Chesterfield in the final. They looked as good as their predecessors. McGuinness had already made his first-team début. Bobby

Charlton had almost got in at Easter. He looked an unbelievable prospect.

Reflecting on that time, Bobby outlines his fears: 'I was scoring goals and everybody kept saying you'll be in the first team soon. But I looked at them and I thought, "How am I going to get in?" I was an attacking inside or centre-forward. And we had Tommy Taylor, Denis Viollet, Billy Whelan, John Doherty, Colin Webster. I'll never forget the Easter they won the first Championship. I'd been playing well and scoring goals so I thought with three games over Easter somebody's bound to get injured and I'll get my chance. They went to Newcastle on Easter Monday and drew 0–0. I'd played in the reserves at West Brom on the Saturday and scored five or six goals in a 9–1 win. The next Friday I was waiting for the team-sheet to go up, thinking, "This is it," but the Boss kept the same team.'

When Busby, Jimmy Murphy and Bert Whalley assessed their incredible riches that summer the biggest problem they seemed to face was keeping restless players worthy of first-division football happy in the reserves. Almost every position was up for grabs. Thinking about how good this side, which had finished eleven points clear of the rest, might become when the average age was twenty-five, Busby and his staff were left speechless.

from A STRANGE KIND OF GLORY *1991*

Plymouth Argyle

MICHAEL FOOT

His name was Sammy Black, and he played outside-left for Plymouth Argyle. Having been born in Scotland, he naturally qualified for what the sports writers of those days called 'international honours'. But once the Scottish selectors, after a few trials, failed to renew the appointment, I lost interest in such distant, diversionary rites. He was the greatest outside-left of his day, in an age of outside-lefts.

His style was his own; he was deadly and *insouciant*. I have never dared used the word before: I doubt whether I shall ever need to do so again. Indeed it was the discovery that there was a good English usage of it (Sir Walter Scott, according to the Oxford English Dictionary, was one of the first to purloin it from the French) which prompted me to write this piece. So, without more ado, back to insouciant Sammy, the William Wallace of my youth.

His method was mostly to saunter along the touchline, utterly impassive, unprovoked by events on or off the field, oblivious certainly of any catcalls or encouragement from the crowd. The arrangement whereby his black shorts, concealing his white knees, draped that diminutive body all added to the air of calculated unconcern. But when required he would leap into action with electric assurance.

He could hold the ball, beat his man, initiate movements of his own, but all these desirable faculties were quite subordinate to his special exploit, once the enemy penalty area came within range. The point of argument in all the Plymouth pubs was whether he was more lethal with his left foot or his right. The narrower the angle, the more he revelled in the test. Rarely did the cannonball rise more than a few inches above the ground.

He had a few partners in glory, most notably Jack Leslie, one of the first black footballers to make his mark in the English league, a truly cultured, constructive inside-left, and one who could recharge the Sammy Black cannon more smoothly than anyone else. Another was the Welsh left-back captain, Moses Russell, whose head was as bald as Yul Brynner's and who drew rapturous applause from the Feverell end on any wet Saturday when he acquired the first black patch upon that shining, white scalp. A third was another Scot, the goalkeeper Fred Craig, who also, according to one of our favourite Argyle idiosyncrasies, took the penalties, and just occasionally, when Argyle were safely two up, we almost wanted him to miss, just to see him sprint back homewards. But he never did.

Argyle were good; no doubt about that. It was generally conceded that they played better football than any other team in the third division. But somehow they tended to lack the so-called 'killer' instinct, particularly during the critical Easter holiday engagements. Year after year, after excruciating lapses, they finished second (in those far off times, of course, only one team at the top was promoted). So much so that ugly suggestions and suspicions spread throughout the city – one, that the unique but unlucky colours, green and black, should be abandoned; second, that the alien and inexplicable sobriquet 'Argyle' should be abandoned too; and third, and most sinister, that the directors just didn't want promotion: they preferred the big crowds and fat profits afforded by a sure place at the top of the lower league.

This last explanation gained some added credibility one desolate winter afternoon when infallible Fred Craig appeared to let through on purpose a late equaliser for Swansea Town, the dirtiest of all our rivals by any reckoning. ('Robust' was the euphemism preferred by the football reporters, of whose prose I made a deep, linguistic study). To add to the injury, Swansea went up instead. Nothing was spared us. Only Sammy Black was unperturbed. He reminded me of one of my father's Cromwellian generals, who would return from victory as if it were a defeat. What recoveries from desperate plights did we owe Sammy's poise.

Eventually, after no less than six years as runners-up, we did go up ourselves, to join Swansea and Portsmouth and Brentford and a few others who had scrambled there before us, and, lo and behold, we were heading for our rightful place in the providential scheme of things. Was it our first or our second season when we finished fourth? First-division football was there within sight for all Home Park to see. Only the Second World War, it seems now in retrospect, intervened to rob us of our destiny. But even Armageddon and all its worst could not quite efface the imprint which Argyle left on the second-division style of the 1930s.

One casual recollection should be enough to clinch the case. It was Christmas 1935 or 1936 maybe, and I found myself, not quite accidentally, working over the holiday in London alone, and unable to get home to the West Country. Argyle were playing Spurs at White Hart Lane at 11 o'clock on Christmas Day morning.

I was there on the terraces in good time, well placed to see any Argyle goals from the left and to engage in protective argument with any too-aggressive Tottenham supporters, who somehow still fancied their chances of a return to the first division.

I had never been on a London ground before; I knew nothing of cockney chauvinism. I could not help imagining that Tottenham players must be Homeric figures, Olympian Gods; how could we prevail against the tricky footwork of Mercury, Jupiter's resourceful, defensive skills. Yet they were human after all. Argyle won, 2–1, both of ours scored by Sammy Black, one with each foot.

An hour or so later, still alone, I found a restaurant called the Criterion open in Piccadilly Circus. No Christmas turkey before or since ever tasted quite like that one. Never in the realms of human conflict had two away points been so spectacularly or insouciantly garnered by one man.

Previously unpublished

Blackpool

GEOFFREY GREEN

There remain, certainly, many experts who to this day will dispute Matthews's superiority as a winger over Tom Finney, 'the Preston plumber' as he was called. Yet this is an argument that can be carried *ad infinitum* without ever being resolved and I do not intend to open the case, either as prosecuting or defending counsel, at this point. That belongs to another court: perhaps even to the final judgement of the House of Lords.

Let it merely be said that Matthews was the Pied Piper supreme of his day. Held in deep affection by the public at large, he belonged to the nation as a whole. He was Britain's most valuable and treasured export and woe betide any full-back who resorted to cruel, rough, or unethical means to stop him. At once such a player became an enemy of the people: even though he might prove to be the left-back of the home side! Matthews possessed an aura which demanded protection by everyone from everyone. Not that Matthews was not well capable of looking after himself. However, if Matthews remained the number one magnet wherever he appeared, there were others in the Blackpool sides of those years who became, and remained, special favourites. There were two in particular – Stanley Mortensen, one leg of the 'terrible twins, the two Stanleys'; the other, Harry Johnston, the skipper in the middle line, either at right-half as part of a devastating wing triangle partnership with Matthews and Mortensen, or later at centre-half. Upright, cultured, and constructive, he breathed a calm discipline with every gliding step he took. The other two, 'the Stanleys,' might have produced all the fireworks and fired the bullets, but it was Johnston, unobtrusively, who passed the ammunition. These were the three cornerstones on which the Blackpool of those years was founded. And sad to say one of them – Harry Johnston – has now passed on (October 1973), aged only 53.

Blackpool in a way resembled their own illuminated promenade with all its 'razzamatazz' and entertaining side shows. With Matthews and Mortensen around there was always something happening on the field of play, something to excite or astonish. It was all the fun of the fair. Matthews had been signed by Mr Joe Smith, the Blackpool manager, from Stoke City in Glasgow the night of the Great Britain v Rest of Europe match. That was in May 1947. The sum was £11,500, a paltry, miserly figure by present-day standards, but a record for a winger at that time. But Joe Smith, a tough, but kind-hearted, shrewd Lancastrian – who himself had captained Bolton Wanderers to the FA Cup at the first Wembley final of 1923, and again in 1926 – knew the man he wanted to transform his side. Matthews did not fail. The rest caught his tail and like a kite they all sailed over the horizon – suddenly – to find themselves in the Cup finals of 1948, 1951 and 1953.

Till Matthews arrived at Bloomfield Road – leaving behind him a seething indignation in the Potteries that Stoke City had allowed him to leave – Blackpool had never truly hit the national headlines or caught the public imagination. But now all at once, from 1948, a magician's wand was waved over them. Not that Joe Smith ended his search for perfection with the acquisition of Matthews. Splitting his partnership with Mortensen on the right flank and switching the dynamic 'Morty' to centre-forward, Smith searched for the right type of inside forward to feed the 'master'. He found the ideal in little Ernie Taylor, who had helped Newcastle to win the Cup in 1951. By 1952 Taylor was Matthews's partner and provider at Blackpool, a move which was to lead to one of the most dramatic finishes in the whole history of the Cup as the 'Matthews Cup Final' of 1953 was played out to its bizarre climax.

The holiday town, with its lovely sands, with its tower, illuminations, winkle stalls, side shows and pilloried landladies, was at last on the football map.

From SOCCER IN THE FIFTIES *1974*

Newcastle United

GEOFFREY GREEN

Emerging from the second division shortly after the war – a stride or two ahead of Spurs – they suddenly became the Cup-fighting giants of the new age. Though the league Championship continued to elude them – their last title came in 1927 – not so the knock-out tournament which stimulated them like some Mississippi river-boat gambler. Time after time in these 1950s they chanced their arm and it came off. To win the trophy three times in five seasons remains a feat untouched since the earliest days of the competition: 1951, 1952, 1955. It seemed something beyond the range of any club in the modern game, especially since Newcastle at the time were not a truly classy team in the mould of Manchester United, Spurs or Wolves. Yet when it came to the Cup they became touched by some magic. Stardust was in their eyes.

At this period they remained among the front runners of the league for a span of four successive seasons without ever quite threatening to lift the title. Positions of fourth, fifth, fourth, and eighth between 1949 and 1952 made them worthy opponents, especially with men like Joe Harvey and Brennan, the granite Scot, at centre half-back, and the galloping, long-striding Jackie Milburn, England's centre-forward in succession to Lawton, and the elusive Mitchell at outside-left, up in attack. For a spell, too, there was little Ernie Taylor at inside-right, a diminutive, sensitive creator who was soon to add another Cup-winner's medal with Blackpool to the one he had lifted with Newcastle in 1951. The rest, as it were, completed the side as mere makeweight. If that should sound ungracious and hyper-critical let me add that so soon as the bell rang for the cup they came out of their corner like a charger, nostrils dilated, tail and mane flowing in the wind, ready for battle. Some unseen conjuror waved a wand over them.

Newcastle United have earned their place among the top people of the 1950s purely on their performances in the Cup. No club had won the trophy in successive years since Blackburn Rovers in 1890 and 1891, so that when Newcastle pulled it off in 1951 and 1952 it was achieved for the first time in the twentieth century. Little did the country sense what lay ahead in January 1951 when Newcastle set off on their consuming trail with a 4–1 victory in the third round over Bury. Next followed 3–2 over Bolton Wanderers and a threatening 4–2 at the Victoria Ground, Stoke. Then came a shock in the last eight as unconsidered little Bristol Rovers, of the third division, surprised the giant with a goalless draw in the North-east. When young Lochinvar came out in the West to clinch what would have been a sensational victory, Bristol's Eastville Stadium was full to overflowing, with the gates shut over an hour before the kick-off. I was amongst that excited, expectant crowd. The spring sun shone; a prototype Comet aeroplane soared overhead in the blue, a huge white bird. And when Bristol Rovers scored first a spectator in the far distance, trying to watch through field glasses, fell off a railway bridge in his agitation, to end up in hospital. Newcastle, however, had caught their tide and goals by Milburn duly finished off Rovers by 3–1. So to the semi-final where Wolverhampton Wanderers were not to bow easily. A 0–0 draw at Hillsborough, Sheffield, eventually saw Newcastle through by 2–1 at Huddersfield and Wembley was on their plate again after a lapse of almost twenty years.

Blackpool proved to be the final hurdle, but Milburn – 'Awa, Jackie!' went the proud cry from the North-east as the sounds of the Blaydon Races washed over the stadium – put paid to Lancashire with two dazzling goals. The first came as Milburn broke free suddenly from the half-way line. Blackpool appealed for off-side but the centre-forward was fractionally on the right side as he sprinted from the centre circle towards the distant goal with all the hounds of hell in pursuit. Farm, the Blackpool Scottish international goalkeeper, came out to challenge near the edge of the penalty area, but Milburn, perfectly balanced and in control, slid the ball home. It was a delicate back-heel from Taylor and a thundering left-foot shot to the far top corner from some twenty yards which saw Milburn ring down the curtain amidst wild jubilation.

The Newcastle spirit of those days was always uplifted by the approach of the FA Cup. There was a deep *esprit de corps* that was handed on from one year to the next under the direction of the sturdy Stanley Seymour, an all-powerful figure within the club, who had been outside-left in the Newcastle Cup-winning side of 1924. A man amongst his own folk, he exuded all the fiery independence and pride of the cold North-east shores. Seymour was the man who activated Newcastle.

When the time came the following season to hand the trophy back to the Football Association at Lancaster Gate, London, no one at Newcastle United could find the infernal thing. They hunted St James's Park high and low until at last an under-groundsman unearthed it in some out-of-the-way closet, hidden under piles of old newspapers and abandoned brooms, brushes and buckets. Covered in dust and even dented, it had quickly to be sent to a local silversmith for a face-lift before being returned to the right authority. It was as if Newcastle, almost casually, already regarded it as their own property.

From SOCCER IN THE FIFTIES *1974*

St Mirren

WILLIAM HUNTER

The 1959 road to Hampden was, comparatively, a low road – Peebles Rovers (10–0), Motherwell, Dunfermline. Then came Celtic and a most remarkable semi-final. The Celts were having, for them, a lean year. Even so, all conventional wisdom rooted for them. Celtic's tradition and experience of winning would carry the day, the soothsayers insisted. St Mirren were living beyond their dreams.

Only small local voices predicted that, one generation after 1926, it would be Paisley's turn again. Some daft mysticism was bound up in the fond forecast. It had come to be believed that St Mirren would never win the Cup until the tramcars had totally left town. And, lo, all the car lines had, at last, been lifted. At a cost of £400,000 the town treasurer, Neil McMillan, pointed out, forbearing to say, but only just, that Paisley expected back its money's worth.

By half-time St Mirren were three up. Into the second half, impossibly, they made it 4–0. Out of nowhere the Buddies started to sing.

Sing! St Mirren have always had the most hard-to-please – not to say grumpy – supporters of any team in Scotland, except, perhaps, Airdrie. We are not rough or boisterous or bad but, my, are we crabbit. Right from the start in 1877 Paisley boards of directors have received especially wondrous abuse. The modern practice of throwing things on to the pitch may have begun with an irascible butcher who used to sit, this side of apoplexy, in the stand at Love Street, throwing sweetie papers. Cairters' Corner, tucked under the east gable of the stand, was the most noisome stretch of terracing in Scotland, perhaps the world. Local carters, fresh from the stable, gathered there to make the air as blue as the thick plug tobacco they smoked between mouthfuls of advice to their heroes.

Four up, their spiritual descendants suddenly changed the tune. Hampden filled with a great, growing unrehearsed surge of, not song exactly, but happy sound. Before that semi-final afternoon the kids who lined the front of the terracing, whiles, had cheeped out the 'Saints.' Now everybody was giving them laldy. A group of dyers from the thread mills may have activated the choir.

The West of Scotland is a hard place which breeds hardy men – caulkers, cairters, riveters, the men from the foundries and yards. But the hardiest of all may have been the textiles dyers. Theirs was a damp hard darg. Yet some of them developed an apparent difficulty about controlling their face muscles and tear ducts while their lungs worked like bellows. Nobody knew the words, of course. The hell with the words, they got on with the singing:

> Oh, when the Saints go marchin' in,
> Oh, when the Saints go marchin' in.
> Dum, dum-dum, dum dum
> Dee dum-dum,
> When the Saints go marchin' in.

Long before the end, the Celtic lads had furled their banners and crept home. The choir had Hampden to themselves. It was all ours. After that semi, even in this lousy, imperfect world, there was no way the Cup could get away. At the final whistle Davie Lapsley and Jackie Neilson hugged. It was unusual in those days for giants to embrace, like a couple of lions doing a wee waltz.

Aberdeen beat Third Lanark in the other semi-final. So be it. Wheel them on. But, first, some proper preparation was called for. The spontaneous choir had been great; a proper band would be greater. Frontline trumpets, clarinets, trombones were brought out to practise the 'Saints' for that day. In the *Paisley Daily Express* it was mildly suggested that we might be the better for learning some words – not *the* words, our own.

An effusion of verse engulfed the *Express,* for it remains the conceit of Buddies that we dwell on the higher slopes of Parnassus. We fancy our chances with the soul juice. That was aye the weavers' way. It is the basic Paisley joke that when a visiting speaker at a dinner proposed the toast to the Town's Poet (meaning Robert Tannahill), everybody else present rose to his feet to reply.

> Oh, when the Saints go marchin' in,
> The Buddies roar them on to win.
> It's the Lullaby of Love Street,
> When the Saints go marchin' in.

Every verse form was plundered and repainted by the black-and-white minstrels for the occasion:

Tommy Gemmell, the quiet man,
Is the favourite of every fan.
He came to Saints from Irvine Meadow.
There's no right-half can stop the fellow.

A shopkeeper who found a heap of lum hats in his basement sold the lot in a couple of days – when he added white stripes to them. After the 1926 victory, when the players were given a bottle of whisky, David McCrae (who scored one of the goals) resolved not to touch a drop of his until Saints won the cup again. David appeared on the telly with his bottle to show he had been as good as his word. In the backroom of the Bull hostelry in New Street where the excited talk was all about deep strategy to dish the Dons, one of the group barely spoke for several nights. Suddenly he broke silence. 'I've made up my mind. I am going to take the dug,' he declared. Schoolboys built scrapbooks to their stars entitled THE GREATEST TEAM THAT EVER WAS. And there was Davie Lapsley to carry the ball.

Of all the great Saints – Willie Kelly, Willie Telfer, Johnny Deakin, Alex Linwood, Jimmy Drinkwater, Bobby Ancell, John Patrick, Johnny Cameron, Donald Greenless, Michael McAvoy, Dunky Walker – the greatest clubman was Davie Lapsley.

[Finlay Cunningham, that curly-headed lad, deserves a special footnote for how he once bounced the ball off his own goalie's post to jouk past Jimmy Smith of the Rangers.]

Davie Lapsley came from Tranmere Rovers in 1946 as a centre-forward, switched to right-back. He was a gentle ox of a player, with a low centre of gravity (somewhere just above kneecap height, it sometimes seemed) and a high boiling point. He was aroused to anger seldom, but it could be spectacular. When once he banjoed an opponent who irked him it was right out on the track in full sight of the central stand.

The approach of Saturday kick-off times did not set clanging panic bells in Davie's psyche. Young fans used to take it in turns to pace him down Love Street to get him to the dressing-room on time. He missed a match because he missed his bus.

He didnae miss penalties, but. Davie and Jackie Neilson had a formidable formula and when the whistle went for a penalty-kick, Jackie ran and grabbed the ball to place it on the spot, while Davie pawed the ground at the far end. He believed in using every inch of runway available. Sometimes it seemed he must have started his charge out of the west from Caledonia Street or, going the other way, from midway across the playground of the North School. Goalkeepers were beaten before he had roared over the centre line. Davie was a one-man thundering herd. That was our captain.

So we won, of course, rating one other line in the Wee Red Book. That is a lot but it may have been more. With hindsight, that year of 1959 now seems some sort of *annus mirabilis*, or no' a bad year. We won the Second Eleven Cup as well. Paisley Pirates ice-hockey team became British champions. Part of old Paisley that year died, but gloriously.

There was an old-fashioned simple clarity about the geographical battle lines of the final: St Mirren versus Aberdeen, thread against fish. Aberdeen has since become a much more complex place; Paisley textiles have precipitately declined. It has become a mixtie-maxtie town – whisky, mainly, in terms of money and, maybe, motor-cars – compared with what it was and so far as it is, officially, permitted to be a town at all. And going down lonely Love Street these modern Saturday afternoons, you find it hard to tell whether the big team are at home or away.

That night we behaved badly *well*. Packed into Jail Square, steaming like cattle in our wet clothes, we were, in football parlance, robust. Rowdy, if you will. To get the cup unscratched from the team bus into the town chambers they had to throw it over our heads. We made much noise, certainly. It was our crowded hour. Football had put our town together, happily, into the streets, which had only happened once before and that, too, was through football. Paisley again became the right size and in the right place, exactly.

George Carruth, the local football reporter, who travelled back from Hampden with the team, spoke for the town.

'I was kicked in the face by Jack McGugan as his legs dangled from the roof of the open bus – and I hope to bear the mark to my dying day. That's how proud I was,' George wrote in the *Paisley Daily Express*.

Next morning in the *Sunday Post* the back of my head appeared in a picture along with a street-full of other demented heads.

from WE'LL SUPPORT YOU EVERMORE *1976*

Liverpool

BRIAN JAMES

I drive with Emlyn Hughes from Anfield to the club's training ground. He stops first at a doctor's for a prescription for a slight throat infection, bounding in in dirty shorts and red shirt through a crowded surgery. No one seems surprised as he appears: 'Morning Emlyn . . . not too good on Saturday,' they murmur. 'Yeah, rubbish,' he agrees, unmoved. This is the surgery of the club doctor, and international soccer stars jumping the queue are part of the everyday scene.

As we resume the journey, Hughes picks up our conversation from Sunday. 'How do we do it – keep winning? People go on using words like "dedication" as if they were insults. But is it such a crime to do the job you get paid to, and do it as successfully as you know how? I reckon it was even a sort of dedication the number of us who turned up at that "do" on Sunday. The players had given their own party for Callie the night before, so most of us could have done with a night at home. But we'd accepted the invitation . . . also that was it. How many were missing from the first team? Just Kev. And he's a bit of a law unto himself. The rest were there. We do things together. I'd walk into the toughest dockside pub in the world with this lot. Because you know that if things got tough, nobody would "bottle" it, and scoot off.

'You'll be with us all the way now, right along to Wembley. You'll see. Bet it's a bit different already from where was it you started? Toffeedale?'

Contrasts, of course, abound. Hinckley, where this odyssey began, would be delighted to count a crowd each week as big as the throng of Liverpool fans assembled in the Anfield car park at 9.30 a.m. just to watch players arrive for work. Even more are there to watch them drive away after lunch. It is a school holiday, but they are not *all* kids.

Out at Melwood, the Liverpool training ground, boys use their red scarves and bonnets to part-protect their hands from the barbed-wire and glass as they clamber to perches on top of the wall. Two cold hours later, some are still hanging there ... 100 yards at least from the nearest live footballer.

Melwood itself is huge, with acreage enough to have replayed all the qualifying matches we have seen simultaneously side by side. It's hard not to think back to Tividale, probably still doing their training on the town car-park.

At the end of Liverpool's training, players and staff grab cups of tea in a dressing-room the size of a small ballroom. And nearly as ornate. Doors from it lead to a sauna, a gym with more gadgets than the set of Dr Who, and plunge baths that could have swallowed not only Hednesford's 'horse-trough' but also their entire 'admin block' with scarcely a ripple.

Back at Anfield, the players de-bus from a small convoy of coaches and, after showering, make their way to the club dining-room. Quietly lit, comfortable, this is no works canteen: everyone is served soup, steak and mountains of veg, and steamed pudding and custard. Free. The flash-back now is that first meal with Tividale. Chinese spareribs eaten standing in shop doorways.

After lunch, the players take their coffee into the lounge. Here, amid the leather chairs of a room about the size of Matlock's main stand, they meet their friends, talk to their agents, conduct press inter-views and use the phones to make appointments, place bets, fix dates.

The whole place absolutely reeks of status, style and unassuming, taken-for-granted sophistication. Yet my sharpest memory of the morning was to be none of these, but the last part of the training itself. As Hughes had gloomily forecast, it had been a very hard morn-ing's work. 'We all put on a pound or two with those two weekend parties for Callie ... they'll sweat it off. Be sure.' In the gym ... then circuits and sprints ... then six-a-side games.

While the players sweated, Paisley had talked. I have known him for years (he has been with Liverpool since 1939) but until recently his role was to be seen at Bill Shankly's right elbow. When Shankly suddenly gave up the job for reasons even he now seems to find hard to comprehend, Paisley, at 54, took over. Last season he became Manager of the Year, and the recipient of the £1,000 cheque from Bells Whisky that goes with the title.

He has little of the verbal flamboyance of his old boss. But a hesitant manner now and again reveals a vivid commentary on the game. Like this: 'The sort of lad I'm looking for here is a kid who will try to nut-meg Kevin Keegan in a training match . . . but then step aside for him in the corridor.'

Or like: 'We are going for the treble, when to win *one* thing in a British competition needs a miracle. But I reckon that if you're going to try walking on the water . . . you'd better get in and practice lengths of the baths to be on the safe side. That's why we don't shirk training.'

Or like: 'I know they're not angels, or if they are they've changed since I was number two to Bill. My job then was to make sure that if they stepped out of line – say with drink, or women, on away trips – *he* never knew about it. Now it's somebody else's job to hide things from me. If it reaches me it means trouble; if it stops short of my level, then its team-management.'

Or like: 'Oldham? I haven't mentioned them yet. Just as I haven't mentioned last Saturday's game against Derby, either. We were terrible on Saturday, but they know it. So I just hint to them where things were wrong . . . and let their pride punish them. Clubs who use training as punishment are mad.'

Or like: 'I'm hoping somebody says something silly in the papers . . . something I can seize on to stir them up for this cup game. You'd be surprised how often I want to send one of your blokes a fiver for doing my job for me. All players pretend they don't give a damn what anyone writes. But they damn well do.'

About now Paisley excuses himself. 'Got to go. Time for *my* game. We always end training sessions like this, with the training staff mixed up in one of the six-a-sides. It's what keeps me sane . . . reminding myself that this is still what it's all about . . . kicking a ball. Mind you, I'm not as bad as Bill Shankly was; when he was unfit he used to cancel the game.'

So Paisley went off, with Ronnie Moran the trainer, and the rest of the coaches to complete the two teams playing on a side pitch. Ray Clemence was with them . . . like most goalkeepers, loving it at centre-forward. There was Paisley, a portly 56, doing the tricky business on the wing; and there was some kid from somewhere, a triallist, trying to nut-meg Tommy Smith.

Watching, it made me uneasy, suddenly, to remember what I'd heard way back in Tividale about this player or that who 'Had once had a trial with Wolves . . . or been fancied for a time by Coventry.' Looking at these thin, desperately-eager kids from Doncaster and Scunthorpe it was painful to realise that this Tuesday morning's kick-about would be the highlight of some of their lives. Here in this shapeless morass was the nearest one or two of them would ever come to 'making it'. If they didn't impress someone within the next half-hour, perhaps, a life's dream would be ended.

But the real point of the interlude was this: that for forty minutes, the *last* forty minutes of a long, tiring morning, as Paisley and his coaches romped through their daily ego trip, the rest of Liverpool's training went ahead, totally unsupervised. And still every other match goes on with the pace and the commitment unabated; goals are made, applauded, mistakes villified. There are now no coaches around to drive them. There are no referees; every decision is agreed only after much keenly-observed debate. The score is constantly checked, challenged.

And when they come in at the end, they are still arguing, boasting, complaining. Callaghan has his head down: 'We were bloody rubbish,' he mutters. Hughes is happier . . . 'On the champion side again,' he boasts, amid catcalls.

This apparent obsession needed explanation and Hughes, blowing on his tea, tried to supply it. 'Six-a-sides have always been the biggest part of our training . . . because you get everything out of it. Stamina, control, touch, teamwork.

'The thing is, we always mix the teams. Every six has a first teamer or two, a couple of reserves, one or two lads. So everybody is trying to prove something. The reserves are trying to show they should be in the first team. The kids love to put their tricks across the stars. And us, the established players, have to show we still have the edge.

'And there's another thing. We've always bred players here who hate to lose. Tommy Smith is the king of 'em all . . . the best pro I've ever met. He must have played about two million six-a-sides in his day. But this morning he'd have fought his best mate over a throw-in.

'Ask any pro in England and he'll tell you no one these days can win anything unless they can beat Liverpool. Simple as that. I would bet a stack of money on one fact . . . if you go back over the past ten years and find out which team has picked up most points in the last few minutes of a game, it will be Liverpool by a mile. And it all starts here in these six-a-sides. We are such bloody poor losers. All of us. People keep on about how professional we are. And that's right. But at the heart of it is what we are talking about . . . from the manager downwards, we are all like those kids over there hanging over the wall. We love kicking a ball about.'

As we leave Anfield later a gateman, a pensioner, is chasing a kid, perhaps ten, across the car park. He catches him and clouts him, hard. And walks back cursing and limping: "'Ard faced little sod!' 'Easy now!' says Bob Paisley. 'Just keep 'em outside, you can't do more.' As the gateman mutters off, Paisley shrugs: 'You can't blame him. A while back he chased off some of them trying to sneak into the dressing-rooms; they tripped him up and smashed his knee-cap deliberately. Only ten and eleven, some of them . . . but they've got bike chains in their pockets. They're football daft, most of them. But they've another side, worse luck.'

from JOURNEY TO WEMBLEY *1977*

Chelsea

BERNARD JOY

For almost half a century 'poor old Chelsea' provided music-hall comedians with a wealth of material. League champions just once in their long history, they continually earned the unenviable label of the most unpredictable soccer club in Britain as one week they beat the leaders and the next flopped against an inferior side.

Four years ago Chelsea's troubles were complete as they slipped down and down the table week by week and finally suffered the indignity of relegation. What has happened since then could prove to be the final burial of the old image. Chelsea have proved that a collection of eager young players, well-disciplined and well-coached, will not only battle with whole-hearted enthusiasm, but will also win matches – if properly led. The leadership was provided in the first place by Tommy Docherty, the former Scottish wing-half, who, as manager, has guided Chelsea back into the first division and has now fashioned them into championship contenders.

When Docherty took over at Stamford Bridge, he inherited a bunch of able youngsters, who needed to be steered along the right lines. He also had some established players who did not see eye to eye with his policy and in a wholesale clear-out he transferred twenty-one players in a period of twenty-eight months.

Having cleared the decks, Docherty got down to the business of grooming. Every training session was purposeful, aimed at mastering the ball, working out moves, perfecting technique and developing teamwork. The coaching was so hard that fitness followed automatically. He maintained a rigorous discipline, too, and did not hesitate to impose sharp fines for offences, like being late for training.

Pride in the club was fostered by actions like sending a party of colleagues and relatives to watch a Chelsea man in a representative game. A new image of the club gradually arose. Gone forever was the association with the Pensioners (the army veterans at nearby Chelsea Hospital) and the comedians have now switched elsewhere for their material.

In the restless search for improvement, Docherty introduced the foreign idea of a first-team squad of eighteen players, all of whom are on a position bonus, which can earn them an additional £50 for holding the league leadership. Training has been switched from morning to afternoon, as it is with Real Madrid because, as Docherty says, 'We aim to get the team accustomed to peak fitness at the time when matches are played.' And another Continental idea: the team stay together in an hotel on the night before all games in London.

All the planning and coaching would have produced only limited results if Docherty had not found in Terry Venables the man to put his ideas into practice on the field. It is a partnership akin to that between Billy Nicholson and Danny Blanchflower at Tottenham a few years ago – and may eventually be as fruitful.

Venables harnesses the eager enthusiasm of the young Chelsea players and gives purpose to their running power. He holds the team together. He links in midfield with eighteen-year-old John Hollins, while left-half Ron Harris helps to block the middle; provides openings for the striking forwards, Bobby Tambling and Barry Bridges; keeps the wingers out wide and brings the backs up for an occasional sortie. Authority is stamped on his play. He does the simple things quickly, sums up a situation shrewdly, and maintains accuracy under pressure.

Obviously, the receptive background was there when Docherty moved Venables from right-half to inside-left after the transfer of Graham Moore. The switch transformed Chelsea from a run-of-the mill side to potential championship winners.

Chelsea gained fifteen points from the first seventeen games in 1965. Venables was inside-left for the first time against Arsenal on 16 November and the effect was immediate, Chelsea winning eight and drawing two of the next eleven matches. In the forty-two league games –

the same number as a full season's programme – Chelsea took sixty points. This total would have won the first-division title in thirteen post-war seasons.

The truism 'one man can make a team' usually applies to an expensive import like Tony Kay to Everton in their final run-in for the Championship three years ago. A drastic change in fortunes merely by one player's change of position is more unusual and the best parallel is the adoption by Don Revie of the deep-lying centre-forward plan which brought Manchester City the FA Cup in 1956.

Venables has a similar role to that of Revie, except that he wears the No. 10 shirt. He forages deep in midfield to be the focal point of defenders' clearances and the instigator of attacks. What makes his success so remarkable is that he is only twenty-two. Most link forwards do not attain a peak until their late twenties, because experience and know-how are just as important as skill and ball control. But Venables has always taken every chance to learn.

He has a square build and a sailor's roll. The way he sidles up to a penalty-kick, the fastidious wave of the arms as he passes and the peremptory beckoning when in possession, give him an air of cockiness. And cocky he might well have been, except for this deep-seated willingness to learn. When he signed for Chelsea at the age of fifteen, he was already earmarked for stardom. He was a schoolboy international, was labelled 'the second Duncan Edwards', and had been described as 'the greatest player I've seen at his age in fifty years in football' by Jimmy Thompson, the man who had discovered – among others – Jimmy Greaves.

Venables had his first league game, at right-half against West Ham at Upton Park – a stone's throw from his home in Dagenham – a few days after his seventeenth birthday. It was a disaster. The pace was too quick, his tackling was innocuous and positioning crude. With a player whose confidence was shallow, the experience would have been an irretrievable setback. Venables used it as a stepping stone to mastery of the profession.

'You learn more from the bad games,' he once told me, 'they keep you in perspective. I had a spell during that relegation season when Chelsea had no alternative but to drop me. I was playing so badly. Here again I had time to puzzle out why it was happening and what remedies I had to introduce.'

All the time Venables was learning fast. He went to two or three evening matches each week – he still does, for that matter – to study the strength of possible opponents and to assimilate good points. Once he drove to see Pelé play for Santos against Sheffield Wednesday, and drove back overnight so that he could be at training next morning. He talks football by the hour, on the train coming back from away games, in the tea-room at Stamford Bridge or at his mother's café in Dagenham.

It is in creative football that England have lagged behind the top foreign opposition since the partnership of Bobby Robson and Johnny Haynes five seasons ago. Now Venables gives every promise of filling the gap for one of the critical positions in midfield. I made him the only England forward to come through with credit against Belgium at Wembley, and he would have made an even greater impact on the play if the other forwards had run into position as eagerly as the Chelsea attack.

This first full cap enabled him to make a clean sweep of England international honours, having progressed through schoolboy, youth, amateur and Under-23 levels. It is a collection which is likely to stay unique because promising youngsters can now become apprentice professionals at the age of fifteen, and, as such, are not eligible for an amateur cap.

A week after the Belgium match Venables played for the Football League against the Irish League, and so exhausted the list of selection honours open to an English footballer.

Despite all the honours and adulation, despite approaching £100 a week with Chelsea for most of last season, Venables still lives in his parents' council house and travels to training by tube. Had he not made a success at soccer we may still have got to hear of Terry Venables . . . as a pop singer. He also has a miming act, and has appeared at London's Stork Room. Recently he was offered the chance of making a record, but decided football must come first: 'It is more important to be top of the league than top of the pops.'

His example is not lost on the Chelsea players. They, too, have accepted the strict discipline and rigorous training laid down by manager Docherty. By such dedication Venables will lead soccer's Chelsea-set to the top – perhaps not this season, but surely in two or three years' time, when they have fully matured.

from THE SATURDAY MEN *1967*

Fulham

FRANK KEATING

Johnny Haynes was England's captain and unquestionably Fulham's finest footballer. But he was never what we reckoned to be your actual Fulham-type player. For one thing he was far, far too good. For another, he wasn't half eccentric enough. Haynes suffered eighteen glorious, exasperated years for Fulham, carpeting out the world's most sumptuous passes to a motley crew of single-jointed unappreciative nuts; a Brylcreemed Schweitzer among the pygmies.

Going down to Fulham on Saturdays when Chelsea were playing away was part of the corduroy scene in the 1950s and early 1960s. They were, as John Moynihan said in his joyous chronicle of the times (*Soccer Syndrome*, MacGibbon and Kee), 'a Saturday afternoon team, offering a feeling of animated recreation rather than solid professionalism . . . a side of happy, sometimes comic triers watched by garrulous actors, serious actors, pantomime players, band leaders, stuntmen, starlets; tweeds, black leather, green leather, pink anklelength knickers, baggy overcoats over armour-plated suede, cheroots between thumb and first finger.' They were days when a joint was a jazz cellar, LSD was a couple of Friday fivers, a trip was a moonlight bedsit flit – and dope, more often than not, was Bedford Jezzard's latest signing from the Hellenic League.

Liquid lunch, long walk alongside the cemetery past tiny, prim houses called 'Hazeldene' to marvel in wonder at Haynes – and to groan and wring our hands with him when the little men forgot to run on to, or even ran away from, those lancing, expansive long passes. He was too good for us, too; and really we turned up to love the fellows who forgot. What a litany: that loping trier, Maurice Cook, who could never quite fathom what Johnny was at; it was like Laurel and Hardy. Every resigned dismissive shrug by Haynes made Maurice simper with inferiority. And could it have been Maurice who ran out one afternoon with that high-stepping dressage I'll-show-'em swank – and promptly doubled-up with a hamstring and was stretchered off even before the kick off?

Over the years they came and went. But mostly came and stayed: Arthur Stevens, grizzle-haired wingman, who'd be wound up at the start to run the full ninety minutes – but only in straight lines. 'They Also Swerve' we used to plain-chant at him. Arthur was the original subject of the legendary theatre-bill joke – This will run and run' – F. Cashin, *D. Sketch*. Then there was Jimmy ('Give it to the Rabbi') Hill – who, of course, we still know and love. Jim, to be sure, scored many thousands of outstanding goals – but on double-checked reckoning he also muffed about 971 sitters (plus two half chances). One now famous actor said on the terraces that Jim only patented that piratical growth on his chin because he thought it might make him play like Charlie Buchan (don't strain yourself working it out, corny humour's changed too).

And what about Killer Keetch? Blond and butch, fancy in his pointed Eyetie patents, but a devil in boots, no shinpad had an earthly. Horrors, we even loved him that afternoon he got stuck into Bobby Charlton. He'd be jeaned and conspicuously casual down the Portobello on a Saturday morning – after a casual canter down Rotten Row – sniffing out bargains for his junk (sorry, high-class antiques emporium) shop, outstanding headscarfed brunette snuggling into his armpit; at 2.30 (unless stated) he'd wickedly set about some unsuspecting and innocent no. 9 shirt; by 6.30 he'd be downing a few swifties at the Queen's Elm, settling himself up for 10-ish and eyeball-to-eyeball confrontation with outstanding blonde over candles and white tablecloths at L'Ecu de France or some such gracious nosherie. (Why didn't Parky write a book on Keetch, for heaven's sake?)

Earlier, there was Eddie Lowe, the statutory baldy at wing-half, alleged to have lost all his hair overnight through the shock of reading one of Walter Winterbottom's coaching pamphlets on peripheral vision. Or Jim Langley, bow-legged back with convict's crew-cut who, astonishingly, played for England and didn't let us down (though we were terribly worried for him) and then taught that tubby antelope George Cohen all he knew about overlapping and George became the best in the biz.

Our last great joy at Craven Cottage was the young Rodney. In a way Marsh was more of a genius then, simply because he hadn't yet realised it; only we nobodies were telling him and he, sheepish then, thought we were taking the mickey. For one season, just about the final one of those lovely winters, we'd go and watch Marsh in the reserves. Once, the goalkeeper was injured and Rodney excitedly bagged the polo-neck and gloves for himself, but when the first corner came over the dear nut tried to tip it over the top with a flying bicycle kick. Own goal.

Rodney, as a teenager, rated self-education. His bible was *Pears' Cyclopaedia*. He carried it with him everywhere and learned pages by heart. On away train trips George Cohen would solemnly have to hear him – 'Right, ready: World's Longest Rivers. Ready?' – and he'd close his eyes and recite 'Amazon 28 billion yards', or whatever, 'Limpopo 19 billion . . .' right down to the blooming Arno. When Rodney went deaf and almost had to pack up completely after he had nutted the crossbar with an almighty clang, it was sad, era's end – but it was also pure, undiluted Fulham.

But of all of them, most pure and undiluted Fulham was Tosh Chamberlain, winger supreme. It was Tosh who refused to get up after a hard tackle, saying he'd sit the game out 'until that bleeding ref apologises'. It was Tosh who once snapped the flag clean in two when he mistimed a corner kick (if the stick had carried we all bet that Maurice would have nodded it home). It was Tosh who once broke the ribs of his own goalkeeper, Tony Macedo, with a ferocious back-pass. Tosh was the only one who'd audibly swear back at Haynes – indeed once the referee, Mervyn Griffiths, Bethesda Chapel and all that, almost booked him for it.

The team's much slicker now. And there's an impressive grandstand covering the bank from where we used to watch the Boat Race – and invariably miss Fulham's one goal of the month. And they've got two ex-England captains now instead of one. But Tom Trinder, great stand-up comic, still sits down in the directors' box; and the thing to remember about all the foregoing list of loves is that, for all the memory of endearing incompetence, those sides were, more often than not, in the first division – or rather, they were *quite* often there, and once in, it must be said, they spent all their time frenziedly trying to stay there. (Someone once tried to get a new nickname going for them, the Fokker Wolves – 'bloody miraculous how they stay up'.) But they finished tenth in the first division once, in 1960. And they're no newts to FA Cup semi-finals. They lost in a replay in 1962, and in 1958 when Manchester United, rebuilt by Jimmy Murphy after the Munich crash, beat them by 5–3 with all the world praying for a Fulham defeat. The atmosphere was too much for Macedo, whose fine talent in goal had been instrumental (with Haynes) in getting them that far, but on the day he flapped and fumbled like a schoolgirl.

By and by, and hopefully not relevantly, Fulham's present goalkeeper, Peter Mellor has done more than most to get them to Hillsborough tomorrow; but he has been living with a reputation throughout his career as being prone to the most appalling gaffes – his colleagues cheerfully admit to calling him Teflon (non-stick) or Daffodil (he only comes out once a year). But he played a marvellous game in the sixth round, apparently, and if he catches everything tomorrow he will scotch the sniggering murmurs for ever. For himself. And for Fulham.

And if they do get to Wembley, unbelievable thought, the 1950s mob must have a reunion: laughter and memories. Who wouldn't pay a paypacket to hear J. Haynes rollicking Maurice again? Or Tosh showing Les Barrett how to take right-foot away-swinging corners from the left with the outside of his boot: 'The damn trouble is, lad, the damn flagpole makes it so damn difficult.'

from THE SPORTS WRITER'S EYE *1989*

Real Madrid

GUY MILLS

Even when Real Madrid's five-year reign in the European Cup was ended by their top rivals, Barcelona, it was only by a margin of one goal in a final score of 4–3, which included a much-disputed penalty-goal in Barcelona's favour, given by English referee Arthur Ellis in the first leg.

Even after the shock result there were many who were still saying that Real were far from done for; that, in fact, they remained, even in comparative dotage, the finest team in the competition. Real players would seem to have believed in themselves, for within a week or so they returned to Barcelona to slam the home side 5–3 in an important league match!

Yet it could not be erased, that Barcelona defeat in the European Cup, the first crack in a five-year image of invincibility. How much does it mean? And how important is it to football that we continue to have a strong, attractive Real team?

Without doubt, the key men in the Real team are at an age when they should be 'going over the top'. The finest defender, centre-half Jose Santamaria, is turned thirty-one. The two best-known forwards, Alfredo di Stefano and Ferenc Puskas, are thirty-five and thirty-three respectively. Clearly, their best years are behind them and, particularly in the case of Di Stefano, they cannot do quite as much as they used to.

But age, of course, means experience – a quality always, and rightly highly valued by Real Madrid directors. Rarely in their world-wide search for stars do they go for youngsters, and in that context a comment from the club's technical administrator, Emil Oesterreicher, former manager of the great Honved club side, is interesting. Talking of Bobby Charlton, in whom his club have long been interested, he said: 'When the boy's twenty-six or so he will be of the most value to us – in the meanwhile, it is clearly better to leave him with Matt Busby, who can teach him more than we can!'

Experience, then, and skill are the most important assets of the Real team, and age by no means the disadvantage generally thought. Of course, it is more difficult for older players to keep in perfect physical condition, but each one of them is allowed to use his own initiative in training, and he honours the trust put in him. The high rewards and incentives given the players give them a truly professional outlook, and without exception they take great care of themselves.

The present team, in the opinion of most, has at least one more great season left in it. After that, Real's problems may increase. For the Spanish Football Association has tightened its rules regarding the signing of foreign players, and Real's acquisition of the Swedish centre-forward Agne Simonsson in the autumn of 1960 may well be their last for some time.

How much this will mean to them can be shown by the tremendous dividends their policy of contracting at least one big international name each season has paid so far. In 1952, Real contracted Francisco Gento; a year later, Di Stefano, the greatest signing of them all, achieved in his first year of office by the club's brilliant young treasurer, Raimundo Saporta.

José Hector Rial joined in 1954, and Raymond Kopa (later to be transferred back to Rheims of France) in 1955. José Santamaria came from Uruguay – for whom he played in the 1954 World Cup – in 1956, and in 1957 goalkeeper Rogelio Dominguez was signed from the Argentine. The following year saw the arrival of Ferenc Puskas, that 'displaced person' who had been out of football since the

Hungarian revolution two years before, but within a year was fully match-fit and the Spanish league's leading goal-scorer, with that famous lethal left leg!

Didi, the 1959 signing, was not suited to the driving football played in Spain. This gentle, persuasive Negro had been the brain behind Brazil's World Cup victory, but at thirty-two years of age it was asking too much of him to utterly change his style, even, which is doubtful, were he able to have done so. He returned home: wiser – and, of course, richer!

Simonsson was the 1960 signing – and after him, who? But Senor Saporta has already said that if the bazaars of the world soccer transfer market are closed to Real, then 'we shall sign the best players in Spain!' A step in that direction has already been taken in the acquisition of Luis Del Sol, a half-back or inside-forward, from Betis. Del Sol is already a full Spanish international, and his Real Madrid colleagues credit him with a golden future.

But as these stars drop out one by one, with none to take over from the international scene, will Real Madrid keep their unique appeal? One cannot say success, for they will surely continue to have their share of that. But appeal is something quite different.

José Maria Zarraga, the club's handsome captain, said something very telling when pointing out that, in his twelve years with the club, the team had always played much the same style of football. The arrival of the European Cup coincided with Real's big investments in the foreign-player market, and their success in the one has been too easily credited to the other. Yet might it not have been possible that the all-Spanish Real Madrid of a decade back would have done just as well?

We may soon have a chance to test that theory. But there is no denying that the absence of those wonderful international crowd-pulling names will be sadly missed. Their match-winning qualities in themselves have been tremendously important to the club, particularly in the cases of Di Stefano and Puskas. But equally important is the unequalled glamour, the appeal which the presence of so many wonderful players in one team has brought about.

It has permitted the club to ask unheard-of guarantees for its appearances in friendly matches – averaging upwards of £10,000! Yet in every case Real have given good value, as much by simply being there – as if allowing a glimpse of the Crown Jewels – as by the manner in which they play the game, which has heartened every friend of pure football throughout the world. Their style and success has meant a great deal to world standards, and particularly those in Europe.

Of course, they have their detractors – men prepared to dismiss them as a football circus. But what of that? If they can please and entertain and win well, before crowds of 100,000, they are fulfilling the prime purpose of professional sport. What else is this game but a form of art and entertainment? Real Madrid have been the glittering emperors in European football; a constant image that has set the fans talking, and not least, the administrators working.

For has not this club, however unconsciously, been a catalyst in the European game? There had been a general tendency to repress and flatten organised football into a massive mediocrity. Spanish football 'got away', and, independently of so many of the rest, set its own targets, achieved by its own means.

The mood of self-questioning, doubt, and eventually widespread action in English football was brought about by our failures, not our successes – and those failures, and the cause of them, was held up to the mirror of success seen overseas, not least that of Real Madrid. That English players earn more and have acquired greater freedom is the direct outcome of this mood aroused in recent years, not by talk of 'justice' alone.

Real's triumphs in European Cup finals may never now be matched, not even by themselves, for great areas of the soccer world have become aware they were caught napping by this huge and imaginative Madrid club. What triumphs those five successive wins were! In 1956, Rheims defeated in Paris! In 1957, Italy's Fiorentina in Madrid! In 1958, Milan in Brussels! In 1959, Rheims again – this time in Stuttgart! And in 1960, perhaps the finest win of them all, 7–3 over Eintracht Frankfurt before a Eurovision audience of millions, tuned in to Glasgow's Hampden Park!

The quality of the Hampden final arouses more discussion in Great Britain than perhaps any other match since the Hungarians arrived, bewildered us, and conquered us, at Wembley in 1953. The echoes of the image seen then roar through the game even now.

There was no organised Spanish league football until 1928, though Real – a club founded in the main by university students – had first seen the light of day on a site near Madrid's old bull ring, twenty-six years before. So by English standards they are a young organisation. Their fine Estadio Santiago Bernabeu is younger yet, being a post-war construction of the most modern design, to seat 125,000.

Under their able president, in office for many years, Don Santiago Bernabeu, Real continue to exercise a fine virility of outlook. One can be sure that he and his fellow-directors will not, without a fight, allow one jot of the Real Madrid appeal to decline. Even now the club completes a multi-million pound 'Sports City' in the environs of Madrid for use of its members, particularly the very young – and there are 50,000 of them!

One can see that, should they have to develop home-born stars from the cradle onwards, they will do so! Real Madrid have the wealth and imagination to bolster European club football for many years to come. And one feels sure there is nothing the ordinary supporter will look forward to more than his next look at this great team!

from THE SATURDAY MEN *1967*

Ajax of Amsterdam

JOHN MOYNIHAN

Scene: a small, untidy bar in The Hague a few hours after Ajax of Amsterdam had beaten Inter Milan in Rotterdam in 1972 to win the European Cup for the second year running. A spindly-looking youth with a close-fitting red-and-white Ajax cap on the top of his head takes out a pair of false teeth and lays them tenderly on the bar. He leans over his beer glass and gives the bar-girl a long, extended kiss on the cheek. She accepts his boldness, standing firmly on tiptoe with both hands on hips and smiling out at the rest of the customers with a benevolence which goes with local football success and a willingness to share a fellow supporter's joy. She allows herself to be led round to the other side of the bar, where the youth jogs her away into a violent tango to background music from the juke-box. The bar-girl has a stocky, unbending figure and a pimply, homely face, her cheeks bearing the slight pallor of a Dutch cheese. The youth's face, in contrast, is an inflamed sunset colour; his shirt is open and sweat runs down his hairless chest.

Earlier, behind a cage which divided the pitch from the spectators at Rotterdam, he had howled with lusty passion as Johan Cruyff had twice breached the Milan defence in the second half. Without his dentures, the youth's lips are suddenly forced back and from some black inner cave erupts a series of Ajax marching songs. It is a night he will remember as the night he danced and sang for Ajax and the night he got drunk, kissed the bar-girl, and lost his false teeth in some tatty bar, but what did a pair of false teeth matter when his team had won Europe's top football trophy once again and his hero Johan had scored both goals? The maxim that the Dutch are passive souls is hardly apposite on this particular May night – there is more dancing and singing abroad in the Netherlands than at a Rio carnival.

from FOOTBALL FEVER *1974*

The Blue Devils

IVAN SHARPE

'Jimmy-y!' The voice of the 'Wee Blue Devil', Scotland's Alan Morton, soaring over the field at Wembley in April 1928, the day of the finest Association football ever seen in Britain. The day of the Wembley Wizards, most memorable afternoon in the history of the Scottish FA.

'Jimmy-y!' I heard the call for the ball pierce the noise. Perhaps because the English crowd was stunned into silence by the runaway victory of their rivals. The incident shows how perfectly Scotland played. McMullan, left-half-back from Manchester City, had the ball forty yards from the goal-line. Morton, outside-left, called for a pass. No sooner said than done. Between half-back and full-back went the ball, like an arrow. Morton, racing ahead in anticipation, caught it, eased up, crossed the ball a yard from the line and, as it fell in front of goal, Alex Jackson met it in the air three yards from the post and, crash! a volley-goal from point-blank range.

That is football . . . the real thing.

Well, there were five little Blue Devils in this Wembley attack – Jackson (Huddersfield Town), Dunn (Hibernian), Gallacher (Newcastle United), James (Preston North End) and Morton (Rangers) – and one or two more behind.

All because it rained. The greatest display of my time – and J. T. Robertson, captain of the Scottish 1900 team which held the palm, himself described Wembley 1928 as better – arrived because rain on the unused Wembley pitch made the going good for forwards; and the smallest Scottish forward-line gained the biggest victory since 1888. The game was played on 'grease', and the Scotsmen were greased lightning.

Never has the Scottish style of play been more gloriously confirmed in its correctness. I remember saying of England's centre half-back from Huddersfield Town: 'Wilson's head is a great force when the ball is in the air. He must have wondered whether there was any air at Wembley.' The ball was never there when Scotland played it.

On the right, Jackson and Dunn with Gibson of Aston Villa behind them; on the left, Morton and James with McMullan behind them . . . the triangle, prettiest of football 'tunes', was tinkling on both sides of the field. Now we encounter it only at rare intervals.

At centre half-back was Tom Bradshaw of Liverpool, usually called 'Tiny' because he was 6 ft. 2 ins. tall. Of him Mr Harvey Webb, a Liverpool director, said to me: 'He is a wonderful player, but he *will* dribble the ball in front of his own goal. We can't stop him. Once at least in every match he gives his directors a heart attack.'

Scotland won by 5–1. James made the wheels go round; Morton made the goals. At Wembley, 1928, England, with men like Roy Goodall (Huddersfield Town), Willis Edwards (Leeds United), Joe Hulme (Arsenal), Bob Kelly (Huddersfield Town) and William Dean (Everton) in the team, were made to look schoolboyish.

from FORTY YEARS IN FOOTBALL *1952*

Moscow Dynamo

IVAN SHARPE

The preliminary *pourparlers* over, they played Chelsea . . . after queues had started at 8 a.m., mounted police had been pushed aside, 85,000 people had swarmed into Stamford Bridge, thousands had overflowed to the touch-lines, and others had ended up in hospital after climbing roofs and falling through windows.

This, you see, was Victory time. The Nazis were in the dock. All the Russians were valiant. Their footballers, too, were an unknown quantity . . . mystery men. They were a novelty. London did them proud.

They came out to practice fifteen minutes before the time of start, and passed and re-passed the ball to get the hang of things: then retired to get ready. The referee, at the toss-up, had to explain the difference between Heads and Tails to the captain (Semichastny) . . . novelty after novelty. But, by gum, they could play!

Chelsea scored twice before the Russians became acclimatised, but they revived and won 3–2. The fact that the winning goal was quietly queried – off-side? – worried no one: hadn't these darling Dynamos played with the style and touch of the old Corinthians?

Their popularity reached the heights; scores of clubs bombarded the FA with requests to play them.

The newspapers were full of them – and of their secrecy. Their lips were sealed. Not a word would they say. They were almost as mysterious and elusive as the Russians of 1914 with snow on their boots. So when I went to see them play Cardiff City I changed my tactics. Arriving in Cardiff on Friday night I asked a policeman where I could find them. 'Ssh,' he said.

'What's the matter?' I replied. 'This is Wales, part of Britain. They are only footballers. I am a sports journalist. I want to talk to them.'

We had almost an argument. 'All right,' he ended; 'I will let you know where they are, but don't say who told you. They're at a dance at So-and-So,' naming a public hall. What a secret!

So I went to the shilling hop. There I found that tomorrow's team had just returned to their quarters but the reserves and doctor and trainer were still there . . . all looking alike in social standing. Some of them were having a dance.

I was determined to talk to them. So I greeted them and, breaking a rule I have never made to pose as other than a journalist, told them I was an international player and, just before the war, had been on tour near their country in Romania . . . at Bucharest, Ploesti, and so forth. Which was true. They called their interpreter and, soon, I was the centre of a circle of eager Soviet citizens.

For forty minutes I talked to them. Question and answer: question and answer: openly asked and openly answered. But I was not the interviewer. They interviewed me!

What did the British footballers eat? Meat or fish? How much of this? How much of that? What did they drink? Were they all teetotallers? Were they non-smokers?

When did they train? How did they train? Did they work as well as play in normal times?

How much money did they earn? Did the captain get more pay than the other players? Could they all use both feet as footballers? Did they use studs or bars on their boots? How many? . . .

The dance whirled on, and so did the questions. The crowded room was warm, and before the end of the interrogation I was a man in a Turkish bath. Then the signal came, and they all trooped out.

As the doors closed behind them, I mopped my brow and muttered, 'So you won't talk, eh!'

The only question I had been able to ask was whether they were all actually members of one club team, which the public doubted because of their high ability. I was assured that they were, though at home and abroad, the doubt persists today.

The dance continued next day when they waltzed round Cardiff City to the tune of 10–1. Otherwise, everything went swimmingly. Off the field, the Welsh club did the thing handsomely.

But there was a narrow escape before the start. The entrance hall of the pavilion at Ninian Park was gaily decked with plants and flowers. The Russians arrived, and were stepping from their motor-coach when I heard a Welsh voice sing out in alarm: 'Where's Joe? Where's Joe?'

Just in time, the missing centre-piece of the floral display was discovered and placed in position . . . a smiling picture of Josef Stalin.

The Russians' football at Cardiff was played 'on a blackboard': man-to man passing, with always one player, and often two, in an unmarked position to receive the ball. Tip-top attack, but a doubtful defence. 'No finer football ever seen in Wales,' was the Cardiff verdict.

Then came the match with Arsenal – temporarily playing at Tottenham – and trouble over the Arsenal team. 'Why are Matthews of Stoke City and Mortensen of Blackpool playing?' the Russians asked. 'They aren't in the submitted list of eighteen Arsenal players' (*see* Condition L).

George Allison explained that some of his players, on Service abroad, had been unable to get leave. Note, however, that he hadn't filled the gaps with any Matthew Stanleys; he had plumped for Stanley Matthews.

The match proceeded, but what a farce! Fog descended, thick and heavy. Any other match would have been abandoned. But they carried on with the contest no one saw because 50,000 people were in the ground before the blackout really fell.

Throughout the game the Russian referee (Condition F) careered up and down one side of the field, a few yards from the touch-line. The linesmen were blotted out. They told me it was a waste of time making signals as these were seldom seen and invariably ignored.

The match just ran away with itself, and things grew hectic. Some of the heroism was wearing off. Penalty claims arose. They were ignored. A player – it was whispered afterwards – was ordered off the field but, saying 'No savvy,' or words to that effect, disappeared in the fog, and carried on, lost to sight and memory dear.

Arsenal's goalkeeper (Griffiths) had to retire hurt, and the loud-speaker system raked up a substitute (as per Condition H). 'Twas Brown of Queen's Park Rangers.

In a word, Arsenal's 3–2 lead at half-time was turned into a Dynamo lead of 4–3 at the invisible end ... and the footballing Russians were still unbeaten. They had now defeated the great Arsenal FC, though it was the most strange and ill-assorted Arsenal that ever took the field.

This wasn't a football match, anyhow; it was an unseen scramble in a bowl of London 'pea-soup'.

I had wired to Will Struth of Glasgow Rangers that, as it was their turn next, they must see these eleven Russian footballers before they played them. He came post-haste to the Tottenham game, along with Alan Morton.

So now it was up to the Scotsmen. The Dynamos last played the Rangers at Ibrox Park, first ruling out Caskie, outside-left (Condition L). And 90,000 experts at Glasgow soon saw that they could play!

They led at half-time by 2–1 after 'Tiger' Khomich in their goal had saved a penalty-kick. Then something happened – what it was I wouldn't know. But the Rangers came out on the rampage. Now they carried a punch and, from somewhere or other, found the staying-powers the part-time footballers in the other British teams had lacked.

The second half was memorable for its all-out football, as distinct from a test of the traditional Scottish and similarly scientific Russian styles of play.

And nearing the end the Scotsmen claimed a penalty-kick. The English referee said, 'No.' A Scottish linesman in a red coat said, 'Yes' ... raised his flag and, with firm insistence on his knowledge of Scotland's ain game, kept it raised. And the English referee changed his mind, and granted a penalty-kick, and from the spot Young equalised. And the Russians were 'mad'. The Dynamos didn't relish that change of decision. Nor, incidentally, did I. Judging by the way they glared at the man in the crimson coat as they left the field, the Soviet stars saw red and, for once in a way, didn't like their national colour.

At the banquet that evening I sat next to Khomich, the man on the flying trapeze who played in goal. But there's nothing to report. That's the worst of these foreigners: they will speak their own language.

So the Dynamos went home undefeated – an undefeated tour that was followed by a blare of Soviet publicity and claims of superiority. They were duly made Heroes of the Soviet Union and given monetary awards.

from FORTY YEARS IN FOOTBALL *1952*

The Arsenal

BILL SOAR and MARTIN TYLER

The beginning of everything can really be traced to 2.45 p.m. on Saturday 26 April 1930. The place was London's vast Empire Stadium. Two men stood together in the Wembley tunnel, tense with just fifteen minutes to go before the start of only the eighth FA Cup final to be played there.

Soon they were to emerge into the sunlight together, the first captains ever to lead out their teams side-by-side for a major football match. One of those men was Tom Wilson, captain and centre-half of Huddersfield Town, the dominant team of the age. In the brief decade since the First World War, Huddersfield had won a unique hat-trick of league Championships and reached four FA Cup finals. But, though no one could have believed it that day, the parade had already passed Huddersfield by. They would never again win a major honour.

The second man, Tom Parker, captained Arsenal, a north London club of no great distinction which, in nearly fifty years, had won absolutely nothing. And yet in the decade that remained between that April day in 1930 and the start of another world war, Arsenal, originally Royal Arsenal, later Woolwich Arsenal, briefly The Arsenal, would win five Championships, match Huddersfield's League hat-trick and reach two more FA Cup finals. By 1939 they would have become the richest, best supported and most successful club side in the world, a bright shining star that has yet to be dimmed in the football firmament.

For that fleeting moment in 1930 the pendulum stood still. Midway between the two world wars the centre of gravity of English football gently moved south. And, as if to mark such a uniquely symbolic game, the teams not only took the field together but crowded into the same dressing-room at the end to congratulate the winners and even shared the same celebration dinner that night at the Café Royal.

There had to be more to it than that, of course; much more, certainly another reason for such a peculiarly portentous day. The reason was to be found in the slightly portly, commanding figure of the fifty-two-year-old Arsenal manager, Herbert Chapman. It was he who had earlier led Huddersfield to their hat-trick in the mid-1920s, left that team before the end of it and moved to small, struggling, trophyless Arsenal. When he arrived at Highbury in May 1925 he had said it would take five years to build a winning team. Here he was at Wembley, five years to the week later, presumably intending to make good his boast.

In retrospect, with the useful hindsight of half a century, it is easy to see what happened and provide explanations for why it happened. But it was not so clear then. Huddersfield were clearly the better team of the two; Arsenal were in the bottom half of the first division and had survived several close shaves on their way to the final. If the Gunners had lost that day it is not unreasonable to argue that the whole history of Arsenal FC might have been very different. There may never have been the 1930s; we may never have had reason to speak of the marble halls of Highbury; Arsenal may have remained, at best, as they had since their 1927 FA Cup final defeat, a middle-of-the-road first-division club. The 1930 FA Cup final might have been remembered primarily for the dramatic appearance of the German airship, the *Graf Zeppelin*, another peculiarly poignant moment in this symbolic final midway between the two wars. The hopes and fears of years gone by, and of years to come, rested heavily on the shoulders of Tom Parker and Herbert Chapman that day.

It is a measure of this one game, of its remarkable portents, of the future that it promised for one of the two clubs and the past chapter that it closed for the other, that virtually the whole history of inter-war football can be told in its ninety minutes.

And, by the same token, the history of Arsenal FC, which remains in essence a tale of the 1930s, can be related in the day's dominant figure – Herbert Chapman. That is why we must start our story of Arsenal Football Club on this one day, with the life of that one man, and with one single, all-encompassing football match.

Saturday 26 April 1930 had begun fine and warm; temperatures were in the sixties, perfect for the fifty-fifth FA Cup final. The morning papers had said King George V would not be well enough to attend, but he surprised everyone by arriving and was given a rousing reception on his first outdoor appearance since an illness eighteen months ago. The leading story in *The Times* that day had been the arrival home from India of the Prince of Wales, his plane actually touching down in front of the cameras in Windsor Great Park. But even *The Times* took a more than passing interest in the day's football, pointing out to its readers that 'The broadcast from Wembley Stadium this afternoon will begin at 2.30 p.m. with community singing conducted by Mr T. P. Radcliff and accompanied by the band of the Welsh Guards. At 2.45 p.m. Mr George F. Allison will open the commentary on the Cup final match between The Arsenal and Huddersfield Town, and this is expected to last until about 4.45 p.m. The position of the ball in the field of play and the score will be called at intervals by Mr Allison's assistant in the stand.'

George Allison was, as it happened, also an Arsenal director and the club's second biggest shareholder. It was only the fifth time that a game had been broadcast live and the effects of this exciting new medium, wireless, were far from being fully felt. For one thing the Football League still organised a full programme on Cup final day. The crowds who stayed away to listen-in missed some good matches: Wolves drew 4–4 with Bradford Park Avenue, Fred Cheesmuir of Gillingham scored all six goals in his side's 6–0 defeat of Merthyr Town, and Lincoln City beat New Brighton 5–3. Sheffield Wednesday stayed five points clear at the top of the first division with a 1–0 defeat of Grimsby. Arsenal were little concerned about league results. With just two matches left of the season they were in twelfth place and the Wembley crowd of 92,488 was understandably only interested in what was about to happen there and then. Only one London club (Spurs) had won the FA Cup in the twentieth century and the capital had still never applauded a league Championship winner.

As a match, it was one of the better finals, with Arsenal winning 2–0. The Arsenal team was Charlie Preedy in goal, Tom Parker and

Eddie Hapgood at full-back, Alf Baker, Bill Seddon and Bob John the half-backs, and Joe Hulme, David Jack, Jack Lambert, Alex James and Cliff Bastin the forwards. Nine of the eleven had been brought to Highbury by Chapman himself and, with the substitution of Moss for Preedy, Roberts for Seddon and Charlie Jones for Baker the team was probably close to the greatest one of an era that lives on in the memories of those fans still alive over fifty years later.

from ARSENAL *1986*

PART 4

The Players

Glenn Hoddle

SIMON BARNES

I sometimes have moments of terrible vertigo in the press-boxes of football grounds. At the end of the game, I will hear two wise football journalists in conversation: 'For me, Bumstead was man of the match.' 'Didn't put a foot wrong, did he?' And I feel a dizzying rush of confusion overwhelm me: Who the hell is Bumstead? Which side was he on? What did he do in the game?

There is a place in life for solid, steady, professional virtues. When you are at work, for example. But when I go to a football match, I want something else. Genius, glory, inspiration, beauty, joy. All that sort of stuff. When you *play* football, you are happy to mark tight, play ten at the back, and win by a single fluked goal. But when you watch: well, you want something more. At least I do.

And so for years I have carried the burden of being the most devoted admirer of Glenn Hoddle. To confess such an affliction in a serious footballing conversation would always bring a great chorus of pshaws and bahs, and will also bring you hours of vilification. 'Hoddle doesn't tackle, Hoddle doesn't get struck in, Hoddle doesn't chase and harry, Hoddle doesn't defend well, Hoddle is inconsistent.' To all this, I say 'Fiddledeedee!'

Brian Clough is the man to have beside you in an argument about football. 'You don't have to bare your false teeth to show you are a real he-man in football,' he said. 'Some people are morally brave, and Hoddle is one of them. I've heard him criticised for non-involvement, but I'm not sure what that means. If you can compensate with more skills in one foot than most players have in their whole body, then that is compensation enough.'

Hoddle himself says: 'Unlike the Brazilians, we start looking for faults as soon as we recognise a player's skill. I've had it pushed down my throat ever since I was a kid. Of course, the runners and tacklers are part of the game, but people don't have a go at them if they can't play forty-yard balls or go past three men at a time. They don't expect

them to do the things skilful players are good at . . . that is the way
we are in England.'

There is a great mistrust of the exceptional in British football, or
maybe I mean in Britain. There is a great worship of mediocrity: the
most loved heroes are the ordinary blokes who make good by playing
within their limitations. I think the ultimate British sporting hero was
David Steele, the mild, bespectacled batsman who looked like a grocer,
and who was drafted in from nowhere to defy Lillee and Thomson.
His wonderful heroic competence delighted us.

But an athlete of outrageous talent is, in Britain, someone waiting
for his come-uppance. Someone who is so sharp he will cut himself.
In the morality tale of George Best's Progress, it slowly became clear
that Best was not villain but victim, that the public were not his
audience, but his enemies. He was skilful and wondrously gifted, and
the world willed him to fall.

Go to a football ground and hear the great crows of pleasure when
Hoddle, or Nevin, or Barnes, tries to go past a man and blows it. A
great bay of delight echoes round the ground. That'll teach him to
be clever. As Duncan Mackenzie, another man gifted with almost
voluptuous ball skills, once said: 'The attitude in England is the tricks
are okay if they work. If they don't, you're an idiot. It doesn't seem
to have sunk in that if you never try, you'll never succeed.' I don't
think Mackenzie goes far enough. If you try tricks at all, even if they
come off, you're an idiot, and you deserve what comes to you. You
deserve it when some manly chap comes chopping you down from
behind. That's *real* football for you.

One imagines that if Hoddle had been anything in the world except
British, he would have been cherished and made much of in everything
he did. On the field he would have been protected like a quarter-back.
Club and international teams would have been built round him from
the start. Instead, his England career has been, until recently, an in-out
thing. He was played often tentatively and in incongruous positions:
people said afterwards: 'See! I told you he wasn't an international!'

Of course, Hoddle doesn't help his admirers all the time. His temperament is, for all his arrogant moments, rather diffident. He likes
to hang around outside the penalty area when the ball is pinballing
around inside, waiting for a chip shot. He is not an up-and-at-'em
sort of chap and games seem sometimes to overwhelm him.

But Hoddle will always make it up to you. It is remarkable that
England have such a fine player: the whole tendency of the British

game is to shut up such players before they get started. Hoddle is not like an English player at all: but for all that, he is a very English sort of chap. Diffident, as I have said, not pushy. He has talked about playing 'in Europe' for ages; indeed, he has played his last game for Tottenham on several occasions. But he has never quite gone.

On Saturday, he could be playing another last game for them. He has had a new burst of enthusiasm for the notion. He senses that this is his last chance for such delights: perhaps even now he has left it too late. He is twenty-nine, and not, perhaps, the most obvious investment for a major club. Paris Saint-Germain are the latest club to have a think about him: we shall see. No one will be 100 per cent surprised if he is playing another last game for Tottenham next May.

I rather hope that this is the case, because I love watching him play. I love the way that those who worship mediocrity can be made to shut up by a single open-sesame path. There is a football team that lives quite close to Tottenham whose supporters seem rather obsessed with efficiency: with organised mediocrity.

Danny Blanchflower once said: 'The great fallacy is that the game is first and last about winning. It's nothing of the kind. The game is about glory. It's about doing things in style, with a flourish, about going out and beating the other lot, not waiting for them to die of boredom.' Amen to that. And no danger of it happening when Glenn Hoddle is out there and when he is playing like Glenn Hoddle.

from THE SPORTS WRITER'S EYE *1989*

Jim Baxter

RICHARD BRENTNALL

Just down the road from Ibrox, among the stark grey buildings and garbage-strewn streets of Govan, stands a bar on the corner. As befits its environment, it's decidedly not a luxurious place: down to earth, indeed. Its landlord just happens to be one of the finest, and most famous, performers ever to don a football shirt. You could lay claim that our great game, with its creative spectacle and summoning of emotion, is maybe an art-form; or, with its latter-day trend of systemisation, perhaps more of a scientific exercise. What we do recognise to be art can take many forms but no matter how it appears, to be true art it must transmit a state of grace. The man behind the bar had been a true artist. The sign outside announced that this place was 'Jim Baxter's'.

This was a man who epitomised the saying 'Let the ball do the work'. To be sure, even in the most furious combat, the ball had been his plaything. They still talk of his 'keepy-uppy' show during Scotland's Wembley victory of 1963 when before a hundred thousand people and in the midst of England's hectic fight to avoid defeat, he took time off from netting both his country's goals to juggle with the ball just as though he were frolicking in his own back garden. His fans would gleefully say that what he was actually doing sounded similar to that but meant something rather different, and at every Sassenach's expense. When the English FA celebrated its centenary later that year with a match against the Rest of the World Baxter had taken his place alongside Yashin, Di Stefano, Puskas and Eusebio. For Rangers and for Scotland his illuminating skills, expressed with a master's cool arrogance across Europe, had earned him a special niche in Scotland's sporting history. 'Slim Jim' they'd call him.

To see him now! As he pulled pints for his customers, his ruddy complexion and the way his flesh sagged over his belt made you wonder whether his bar profits found their way into the Clyde via his stomach. Living proof that we're all mere mortals, and if we bestow saintliness upon others then that's not their fault.

Mr Baxter looked happy with life, and so he should.

from JAUNT ACCOUNT

Kevin Keegan

HUNTER DAVIES

It was a sunny afternoon in late autumn and the players were finishing off their second training session of the day. Hamburg's training ground is deep in the country, some fifteen miles from the city. There were about 100 spectators, mostly children, straight out of school, plus a few families and old men with nothing to do. They were polite. The team's Yugoslav trainer had only to tell a photographer once to keep well back, and that was enough for everybody.

He gave them a final pep talk and the players then left the pitch, making their way up a long, tree-lined lane to the dressing-rooms. The spectators allowed the players to pass unpestered – except for one, the smallest player in the group of twenty. Every child wanted his autograph. They followed him up the lane, strung out behind him, politely taking turns for him to autograph their glossy scrap-books or the backs of their T-shirts. He was like a diminutive Pied Piper, leading the children of Hamburg.

One girl had the whole of the Liverpool team embroidered down the back of her jacket. How strange that a child in the far north of West Germany should be so loyal to a foreign team. Even more surprising was the fact that Mr Keegan, an English footballer, should be speaking to them in German, a language he knew not a word of just over a year previously. It was pidgin German, with not much idea of grammar, but that wasn't stopping him. His wife Jean knows more German, having taken an A-level in it back in Doncaster, but that seems to stop her speaking as freely as her husband – he bashes on regardless, refusing to use English even with those Germans who can speak it.

Most English footballers are very insular. They travel abroad but see nothing. They believe, with very little personal evidence, that their first division is the best in the world. Their minds have been taken over from the age of thirteen and processed to be footballers and led to belive that nothing else matters.

Keegan had just won the German goal-of-the-month competition for which, unlike the British versions, where a studio panel decides, the voting is done by the public. He decided that for the first time he would be interviewed in German.

So far on German TV he'd used an interpreter. The crew turned up at his house next day and he dealt with all the questions most impressively.

As British footballers go, Kevin Keegan is most impressive. How many people, let alone footballers, would choose to shake up their whole career and their whole life just at the moment when they'd got to the top? This was what he did when he left Liverpool, the European champions, in 1977. He walked into trouble of almost every sort when he moved to Hamburg, but he's now come through it. The previous week, when playing away at Cologne, he'd been clapped off the pitch by the rival supporters.

Hamburg pay him a basic salary of £100,000 a year. The team was currently third in the league and his bonuses meant that altogether they must be paying him about £130,000 a year. After tax he takes home about £70,000. At Liverpool, as their big star, he got around £25,000 a year taking home £12,000.

His outside-football income is even greater – and it goes through his own companies based on the Isle of Man, with all the tax advantages. His annual income, from all sources, must by now be around £250,000. He is certainly on the way to becoming the first millionaire British footballer – if he hasn't already made it.

I asked an elderly German gentleman, who was watching the training, what he thought about Keegan. 'Ver goot player,' he said. 'And ver goot with this.' He made a rustling motion with his fingers. Keegan's salary has been all over the Hamburg papers, along with the other Hamburg players, showing him well ahead, which didn't help him much in the settling-down period.

The previous day Keegan had flown to Liverpool to take part in a testimonial match for Chris Lawler, playing for Swansea against a Liverpool team.

He'd paid his own way to Liverpool, and taken no expenses, and had gone despite a slight injury. He'd gone because he'd promised to go. Kevin doesn't let people down – one reason why the whole sponsorship of footballers in England is now on the increase again, recovering at last from the damage done by G. Best.

Bill Shankly, the former manager at Liverpool, was at the testimonial match and spoke to Keegan afterwards. 'Jesus Christ, you've climbed Everest, son . . .' Keegan was naturally very pleased. 'Now see if you can stay there'.

from MY LIFE IN FOOTBALL *1990*

John Barnes

PETE DAVIES

John Barnes wears Diadora – they pay him to – and he looks good in it. But then, he'd probably look good in oily rags and a tarpaulin.

No other England player has the easy glamour of John Barnes. It's not that he's uniquely more skilled – Chris Waddle or Paul Gascoigne can each, in their way, be equally electric. But no one else is bewitching like John Barnes, no one else has his lazy pace and grace. And when John Barnes moves – when he approaches his man, then elegantly slips him and speeds away like he did it without a thought, like it came as easy as stepping out in the morning to pick up the milk – that's what the people come to see.

He has a way of running with the ball that makes it seem like gravity's not a problem to him in the way it is to ordinary mortals; a flying, dancing lilt in his stride suggests he can go this way, or that way, and either way it doesn't matter, you'll still be there when he's gone. So defenders tumble before him; he induces a bodily panic, they buckle at the waist and back-track frantically, bent double, their arms spread wide trying to fill the chasms of space he opens all around them – because he makes room where there isn't any, and that's what the people come to see.

And yet, and yet . . . Diadora had a poster in Italy of a naked man caught in a strikingly athletic lunge for a high ball. The slogan was, 'Cover Yourself In Glory'. And covering himself in glory is something that John Barnes, with England, has never really done.

He went into the World Cup voted England's Footballer of the Year (by the Football Writers' Association) for the second year running. And he went into it with fifty-three caps – but only ten goals.

The finest of those came when he was twenty years old, in the Maracana stadium in Rio in 1984. He went on his invisible wings of grace and pace past one man, then another; he cut in, lacing his weightless, drifting way into the area – he slipped a third man, and stroked it away . . . he left you, and them, stunned with disbelieving admiration. He'd gone with England into one of the great temples of world football and scored a goal worthy of Pelé at his best.

Not everyone liked it. A fistful of NF thugs followed England on that tour, and though we'd won 2–0 these people (who took the same flight as the squad from Montevideo to Santiago, and barracked Barnes all the way) said the score was only 1–0 because 'Nig goals don't count'.

Fully paid-up members of the human race, however, saw in that goal one of the brightest England hopes of all time. And although since then, as Robson said, we were 'still waiting' for John Barnes – still waiting, six years on – he nevertheless went to Italy as one of *the* great prospects of Italia '90.

In the run-up to kick-off, the Italian papers picked a plethora of 'world teams' from all the stars that were coming their way. Maradona, Van Basten, Baresi – these, of course, were picked time and again. But among England's squad, who did they name? From whom did they expect greatness? Gary Lineker or Bryan Robson, once or twice; Des Walker, not infrequently; and, tellingly, they pointed to Paul Gascoigne now and then. But they picked Barnes pretty much every single time.

So the world waited to see him hit the peak of his career, doing for England what he does for Liverpool every week.

Instead, he was substituted against Belgium, and again against Cameroon – he had a groin strain, and played no further part; he'd not done that much in the previous matches anyhow. It was the saddest of disappointments; and for no one more so than John Barnes.

Gordon Taylor of the PFA told me in Florence that Barnes 'wanted abroad' – that he'd 'wanted abroad' for a good while. But as Italia '90 came to its close, and the Italian papers speculated feverishly in their summer season of transfer madness – linking Walker to Roma, Gazza to Juventus, Bully to Genoa, Lineker to Torino – they were none of them bothering to speculate about John Barnes any more.

from ALL PLAYED OUT *1990*

Bobby Charlton

MAURICE EDELSTON and TERENCE DELANEY

You can play good football for twenty years and never touch what are called 'the honours of the game'. Bobby Charlton had seven England caps, two Cup-finalist medals, and a league Championship medal before he was twenty-two – after three seasons of first-class football. In 1957 he was the baby of Manchester United's team of young veterans. In February 1958 he was aboard the plane that crashed at Munich and destroyed the promise of that brilliant side. In 1959 he was a veteran himself.

Exactly a year after the crash the new Manchester United came to London, and at White Hart Lane, before the kick-off, the crowd and the players stood for a minute in silence. Charlton was one of three survivors in the team – the youngest. He stood on the line of the centre circle, short, fair-haired, solid in the chest and shoulders, impassive. Eight of his team-mates had died at Munich, three of them his close friends; the silence was heavy and disturbing, but we saw no sign of his feelings. He jumped into action when the whistle went; within fifteen minutes United were given a penalty; he drove it in coldly and powerfully. Ten minutes later, near the corner of the penalty-area, he was running fast with the ball, leaning in as he rounded the half-back; the ball was bouncing knee-high in front of him; one had just time to wonder whether he would go on, or check and turn inside; then he hit it, from twenty yards, and it was a goal. It was a most astonishing shot. He had taken it, right-footed, as he ran, without any change of pace or step, hitting the bouncing ball on the volley as it rose away from him with his full force. Yet it was deliber-ately and accurately aimed, and no goalkeeper could have moved a hand to it. This is what Charlton can do, and if he could do noth-ing else he would still be a remarkable player and a rewarding one to watch. By training he has improved his skill in ball control and increased his natural quickness of movement, but his ability to shoot, to hit a ball hard and straight without a flicker of hesitation, this is his gift. Before Munich he exercised it exuberantly. He was a joyful sharp-shooter then; now he is deadly and less light-hearted.

Charlton was jolted into maturity. In his first league season, 1956–57, playing with Byrne, Edwards, Taylor and the rest, he was very much the junior, and looked it. He rarely called for the ball; when it was given to him, shouted instructions came with it. It was good for his team sense, but bad for his confidence and initiative. He played well, but there were times when he seemed uncertain. Yet though he might be caught in the wrong position, or lose the ball through indecisiveness, he always had the goal in his eye. No one had to tell him when to shoot. In his fourteen matches, he scored ten times.

Manchester United led the league all through that season, and finished it, for the second year in succession, as champions. They reached the semi-final of the European Cup and the final of the FA Cup. It seemed they were almost certain to bring off the first double for sixty years. But for the unlucky injury to Wood, their goalkeeper, in the first five minutes at Wembley, they might have done it. It was a great season. Charlton was a new boy, but he had got into a very high class.

It had taken him five years to work his way through United's junior sides into the first team. He joined the club when he was fifteen. In 1953, after he had scored two goals in a schoolboy international, over a dozen other clubs made enquiries about him. There is a story that the representative of one of them followed him into a London theatre, and that Charlton stood up in his seat and said: 'You're wasting your time. I'm going to Old Trafford.' On the ground staff he had the reputation of being a promising little player with too much cheek and not enough interest in work – except with a ball. Apart from football, he liked to go dancing; he went to the cinema two or three times a week, or fishing with David Pegg, the young winger who was killed in the crash. He collected records of pop music, and still does, with Ella Fitzgerald and Frank Sinatra among his favourites. He is a good-looking boy, with a high forehead, a quiff of hair that points forward and upward; his face is long, broad at the high cheek-bones and pointed at the chin, with slanting eyes; it is a face that can be mischievous and Pan-like, or can smooth to an aloof mask, cool and withdrawn.

Before the end of his second season eight of the Championship side were dead. When the airliner crashed at Munich, taking off in bad weather, Charlton was sitting amidships. With the first impact he was thrown out into the snow, and picked up unconscious, bleeding from cuts in his head and hands. The wounds were relatively trivial and soon healed. As to the shock, first of the accident itself, and then of waking up in hospital to hear of the death of his friends, that was a more serious affair, particularly for a boy of twenty. Yet except to those who knew him well, he showed little sign of it. In three weeks he was playing football again.

It would be good for anyone in such circumstances to get back to his job and to normal life as soon as possible. Yet the life of a public performer is not 'normal' at any time. Football helped him, because it is his profession, but he could hope for no privacy. He returned to find that every game was played in an extraordinarily heightened emotional atmosphere.

The new Manchester United drew as big crowds as the old had done, but for other reasons. Spectators with no particular allegiance, and even people who before had only a lukewarm interest in the game itself, were now drawn by the drama of the situation; sympathy took the form of intensely partisan enthusiasm. The team hastily assembled, while Matt Busby was still seriously ill in Munich, by his deputy Jimmy Murphy was welcomed on every ground it visited by long applause, encouraged and cheered on through every game. The players too – the recently acquired Ernie Taylor and Stan Crowther, men of experience, and the youngsters from the reserves – played with a kind of fury. They knew the understanding crowds were there to forgive them if they lost, to compare them with the incomparable, and their fierce response to this made them dangerous opponents.

Manchester United were riding high on this wave of emotion when Charlton returned to football on 1 March 1958, to play in a match that would have been tense enough at any time – the sixth round Cup-tie against West Bromwich Albion. He was no longer the junior. In that game, and from then on, he played with an assurance and a determination that he had never shown before. He played hard now, as if winning was a personal matter. United beat West Bromwich, though it took them two games to do it. They met Fulham in the semi-final and drew 2–2; Charlton scored both goals. He nearly won the game in the last few minutes when he ran right through the Fulham defence and finished with a hair-raising shot that hit the cross-bar. When Manchester won the replay and reached Wembley for the second year in succession, they were applauded as a theatre audience applauds the brilliant performance of an understudy – for their spirit and promise. They had done much more than was expected of them, for in experience, team understanding and talent they were far below the old United. Yet one player at least had established his reputation. Bobby Charlton was now more than a good footballer; he was possibly one of the great ones. Before the final was played he had been given his first cap – in the match of the year, against Scotland at Hampden Park.

The England-Scotland match of 1958, by traditional standards, had no particular distinction; Charlton made it memorable with a goal that many people, – including the Scottish goalkeeper – described as the greatest ever seen at Hampden. It was England's third goal in a 4–0 win. Finney, slowing and spurting with dangerous smoothness, brought the ball down the left wing, and glided calmly through the Scottish defence. From well out on the wing he crossed it hard into the middle; there Charlton, running into the penalty-area, met it on the volley with his right foot, with perfect timing and extraordinary power. It went in chest high, and the net lifted violently as if a gale had struck it.

The new Bobby Charlton was an even more startling phenomenon than the new Manchester United. His sudden appearance in the spring of 1958, with the World Cup finals in Sweden only a month or so away, set all the amateur selectors to remaking the England team. Byrne, Edwards, and Taylor were gone, but here at last, it seemed, was the player we had been searching for for so long, the gunman, the man whose one moment of explosive accuracy could turn a faint hope into a triumph. Without such a player all the scheming and skill is so much pattern-weaving; with him, the most soundly planned defences become nervous and vulnerable. Perhaps, if we were to win the World Cup, we had found Charlton just in time. Against him it was argued that he had a great deal still to learn; his positional sense without the ball was faulty; sometimes he crowded the other inside-forwards; between his power bursts, it was said, he was not hard-working enough; he did not tackle hard enough in defence. The ordinary man's answer to all this was: 'He scores, doesn't he?'

From the point of view of the official selectors there was another problem. If Charlton was to be picked, in what position would he be most useful? Should he remain an inside-forward, or was the middle the natural place for his powerful shooting? There were still three more internationals to be played before the England players left for Sweden. In the first of them, against Portugal at Wembley, Charlton was picked at inside-right. England won by two goals to one, and he scored both of them. He must have felt happy about his chances of a place in the World Cup team. Then came the match against Yugoslavia in Belgrade. The England players went by air – Charlton's first flight since the Munich crash. Engine trouble caused a false start from Zürich, but if Charlton was disturbed, we heard nothing of it. The game itself was something of a disaster. It was played in relentlessly baking heat – nearly 100 degrees in the shaded press-box, something unbelievable in the middle. The England team, just at the end of a hard English season, held out until half-time; they were one goal down then, and three Yugoslav goals had been disallowed. In the second half they were completely outrun and outplayed, and lost by five goals to nil.

This was a bad set-back. There was only one more match to go before the World Cup finals – the first-ever game against Russia. Walter Winterbottom, the England team manager, was said to have made some bitter remarks about players who would not fight, and it was no surprise when four men were dropped. One of them was Charlton. Derek Kevan of West Bromwich Albion was still in the side, a big, strong, wholehearted player; his supporters said his natural instinct for good positioning made him worth his place; against him it was said that he had no subtlety, he was slow-thinking when the ball came to him, and clumsy when he should be neat. England seemed to have decided in favour of the robust, direct style; the half-back line was taken entire from the Wolverhampton championship side – Slater, Wright. and Clamp. The principles of the selectors appeared justified when England made a good 1–1 draw of the match in Moscow; Charlton's World Cup place began to look uncertain. Twenty players were chosen to go to Sweden for the finals, and of these ten were forwards. Charlton was one of the party, and a last-minute choice was Bobby Smith of Tottenham; these two were the only players who were not picked for a single World Cup match. It was unlucky for young Charlton – and, many people believed, unlucky for England, who played four matches in Sweden, drew three, lost one, and scored only four goals. For once the opinion of the ordinary man, the barber-shop critic, seemed to have something to be said for it. We were, perforce, experimenting anyway; why not experiment with Charlton – he was always likely to snatch a goal when it was needed.

Although this ability to take half-chances swiftly and easily is Charlton's great quality, he is considerably more than a shooting machine. As an inside-forward, his true and natural position, he uses the ball coolly in midfield. His big chest and shoulders and his tapering build give him quickness in the turn and make his footwork neat and sprightly. He can be delicate and accurate as well as forceful. He uses this skill to bring the ball sharply under control, more than in dribbling to beat his man. His ability to deceive and pass an opponent is based rather on his sudden speed; running with the ball, he throws the man who is marking him out of his stride by a tricky movement, a characteristic flicker of the feet – a curious subtle feint; for a second it appears that he is about to check his speed or stop dead, but instead he is gone, ten yards ahead, and the man is left. Charlton has been called a lazy player who does not fight hard enough. This seems a superficial criticism. It is true that he does not chase every ball that comes anywhere near him, and that he would rather evade a tackle by skill and speed than spend his time struggling with a tough half-back, but it would be truer of him to say that he saves his all-out spurts of energy for crucial moments. In the England-Scotland match in 1959, at Wembley, he scored the only goal of the game a goal of the kind we have not seen since Mortensen. A high fast centre came over from Douglas on the right. Two England forwards and two Scottish defenders were waiting for it, but Charlton was already racing at full speed, and before it could reach them he sprang high, met it with his head at the top of his leap, and as the ball flew low into goal he went rolling and tumbling after it. One burst like this, and England, not Russia, would have entered the quarter-finals of the World Cup. Apart from scoring the winning goal, Charlton covered ground tirelessly in this England-Scotland game. Though officially centre-forward, he ranged the width of the field, combining in turn with his half-backs and the four other England forwards. No one could have worked harder, but he worked like an artist, not like a labourer.

Charlton was born in Ashington, a mining village in Northumberland. His father is a miner. His mother comes from a family that produced four generations of footballers before Bobby, probably the most remarkable footballing family in the country, the Milburns. Jack Milburn, his great-great-grandfather, was capped for Northumberland in 1888; his great-grandfather – another Jack – had six sons and five daughters, and all eleven of them played football; one of his uncles was the famous Jackie Milburn of Newcastle and England; three other uncles – Jack, George, and Jim – all played for Leeds United; his Uncle Stan plays for Leicester City. An extraordinary family – and Bobby Charlton is likely to be remembered as the flower of them all.

from: MASTERS OF SOCCER 1960

Tom Finney

MAURICE EDELSTON and TERENCE DELANEY

As a schoolboy inside-left, Finney was picked as reserve for the Preston Town boys' team that played in the English Schools Shield. Not yet in long trousers, he went to London for the final against West Ham at Upton Park. The match was drawn, and the trophy shared, and for Tom Finney, fourteen years old, it was a memorable weekend, even if he was only a spectator. At the end of that school term, Preston North End wrote to all the local schools inviting boys who were interested in football to apply to Deepdale for a trial. Finney applied promptly and waited anxiously, but nothing came of it; he was too small. He weighed 5 stone and he was only 4ft 9 in. Luckily for him, his father was just as crazy about football as he was. Mr Finney worked as a clerk with the local corporation, he was a devoted follower of Preston, and he was friendly with the trainer, Will Scott, who later became North End's manager. 'Send him along,' Will Scott said. 'We'll give him a trial and look him over.' Finney was fifteen by then, he had left school, and was earning six shillings a week as an apprentice plumber. The trial came, Preston liked him, and he was offered a job on the ground staff at £2. 10s. a week – and this wealth, as Tom saw it, was not for working, but for playing football, which he would happily have done for nothing. When his father, who had encouraged him so much, would not let him sign, the boy thought he had gone off his head; but Mr Finney knew something about football. 'You may be good now,' he said, 'but who knows what you will be like in five years' time? And at best a footballer's life doesn't last for ever. There's nothing like having a trade.' So Tom Finney went back to his job, but played as an amateur, bitterly disappointed and too young to realise yet how much good sense there was in his father's point of view.

That was the beginning of Finney's association with Preston North End, which has gone on now for over twenty years. There was never a more fortunate connection between club and player. Finney, by temperament and physique suited to be a thoughtful, skilful, careful player; Preston, a club with the highest of proud traditions, playing their football in what used to be known as the Scottish style – close holding of the ball, neat accurate passing, all the work done on the ground. Finney was born, one might say, on the doorstep of the one club most likely to allow him to develop his particular gifts, and to allow him, year after year, to exercise them among players of similar principles.

Finney has played seventy-six times for England, as outside-right, outside-left, and centre-forward; for Preston he has played in every position in the forward-line, but he is primarily a winger, and from preference a right-winger. Yet his first appearance at outside-right came about by chance. In 1938, when he was reserve for the Preston Under-18s, Finney waited week after week for Tommy Hough, the regular inside-left, to lose form or drop out through injury; but Hough, the same boy who had kept Finney out of the Preston Town schools side, went on playing well, and remained irritatingly uninjured. Then, at the last minute one Saturday, Finney was told he was playing – because the outside-right was hurt, and he was the only stand-in available. He had never played on the wing in his life, but Scott the trainer gave him some advice. 'I know you're left-footed, Tom,' he said, 'but try to get your crosses over clean and fast with your right, and if you get the chance, have a go at goal with your left.' He must have had a good game; after it they told him he could forget all about Alex James; from now on he was a right-winger.

Watching Finney today, one would be hard put to it to say which was his natural foot. It is taken for granted now that all first-class players must be two-footed, but it is usually easy enough to detect which one they favour. Finney is rare in his ability to do everything equally well with both. Running clear with the ball, or in a fast dribble, he will control it with the outside or the inside of either right or left, and shoot or pass with either without breaking his rhythm. No one is born with this kind of ability. In Finney's case it is the result of long and painstaking practice. For hours on end, behind the stand at Deepdale, he went through the same moves over and over again, kicking, trapping, turning; at first wearing a soft shoe on his left foot and a football boot on his right, a device many players use to correct a weakness on one side. When he was sure he was equally strong on both sides, he went on practising; forward and back dodged that thin, wiry, concentrated figure; bang, bang, bang, went the ball against the back of the stand. The discipline he imposed on himself then he has never lost. A clumsy Finney is unthinkable.

Finney's great reputation first began to grow in wartime football. In the crowds that watch him today there are probably thousands, now in their thirties and forties, who first saw him with unit sides, and with the famous 'Wanderers', in Palestine, Syria, and Egypt, or after with the Eighth Army team in Italy and Austria. Before that he had one season of wartime football in England, 1940–41. It was a good season for Preston, and Finney's first as a regular member of the league side. The atmosphere of the time was odd and unreal. 'In the event of an Air Raid Warning being received', the single-sheet programme said, 'the Police will instruct the Referee to stop the game, and the players will leave the field. Spectators must take shelter, and remain under cover until the All Clear has been given.' There were unexpected bonuses for these spectators in the appearances of guest players from other teams. In Finney's first league match, against Liverpool, Don Welsh of Charlton was in the opposing forward line, and Stan Cullis of Wolves at centre-half. Preston won the northern section of the league that year, and Finney played at Wembley for the first time – against Arsenal – when they brought off the double by winning the Cup.

In the spring of 1942 Tom Finney, professional footballer, became Trooper Finney, T., of the Royal Armoured Corps. In his matches as a 'guest' and for the FA and Football League elevens, he began to mix with the great. Now, for the first time, playing for the FA against the RAF – both sides full of internationals – he met Stanley Matthews. Matthews had one of his special afternoons in this match, although he was on the losing side; but so did Finney. The comparisons that were to go on for so long began in the newspapers. Was this pale, intent, twenty-one-year-old, whose style was so mature, the successor to Matthews, or was he indeed already his superior? Before the critics had another opportunity of watching the two in the same game, Finney was sent to the Middle East. From that theatre, and its football, to the south of Italy, and from there – no football now – northwards with the advancing tanks of the Eighth Army; when that advance ended at the River Po, touring again with Services sides, coaching, unofficial internationals against Switzerland, short leave in Preston to get married, back to Italy again, and then, finally, demobilisation – a 'B release' as a tradesman.

By 1946 when he returned to league football, Finney was fully formed as a player, unmistakably a right-winger of England quality. However, England had Matthews. For the first full international after the war, against Ireland, Finney was picked as travelling reserve. Matthews had the ill-luck to be hurt in a league match, and Finney took the chance that otherwise might have been a long time coming. England won the game in Belfast 7–2 and Finney scored. The Finney-or-Matthews problem was now *the* controversy of football; whoever was picked, it seemed an offence against good sense to drop the other. Matthews was fit, but Finney kept his place – against Eire, Wales, and Holland. He had now played in four internationals, and scored in three of them. Matthews came back for the Scotland game, on the strength of his wonderful record against them, but it was an unsatisfactory match for England, who got away luckily with a 1–1 draw. So Matthews was dropped again, and Finney played against France; once more he scored. By now the selectors knew that his temperament was as sound as his skill. How much easier their work would have been if he had shown any signs of weakness; instead he had seized his opportunity firmly and confidently. What were they to do?

Their solution was simple enough, but far from ideal from Finney's point of view. In 1947 sixteen men were chosen for the England tour in Switzerland and Portugal. The star match was to be in Lisbon, the first ever England-Portugal international, and the setting one of the greatest stadiums in the world. Portugal were given a good chance to win, and their confidence increased when England were beaten in Zürich. When the England team was announced, Matthews was at outside-right and Finney at outside-left – a position in which he had never played. The story of the game is well known; Frank Swift did incredible things in the England goal, and everything the English forward line touched turned to gold. They won by ten goals to nil.

So Finney was now an outside-left. The reasons that made him one seemed clear enough. He was too good a ball-player to be left out and besides that, his directness balanced the defence-drawing trickery of Matthews on the other wing. Also, he had begun as a left-footer. Against this it could be argued that it was Finney's very 'wrong-footedness' that made him such a good right-winger; he could pick up a pass from behind without having to slow or turn too much; he was always ready to cut in, playing on the back's weaker side; as the angle to goal opened, his shooting was quick and powerful. At outside-left, while his positioning and crossing of the ball was still first-class, he lost a little of his penetration. Finney himself does not care for the outside-left position. For Preston, he remained at outside-right; when, in 1958, the club moved him to the left, it seemed possible that he would ask for a transfer – after twenty years. It was not the first time this ideal long-service club man had considered a change. In 1949, when Preston were relegated to the second division, Finney thought his situation over for some weeks before re-signing, and Blackpool and Manchester United were reported to be itching to pay big money for him. Then, in 1952, a remarkable offer might have taken him out of the country altogether. It came from an Italian millionaire, Prince Roberto Lanza di Trabia, president of the Palermo football club, who met the England players in Florence after their first match of a Continental tour. His proposal was this: if Finney would agree to play for Palermo for two seasons, he would be paid a lump sum of £130 a month, with bonuses of up to £100; he would be given a car, a villa on the Mediterranean, and a free passage to Italy for himself, his wife and family. The prince was also willing to pay Preston North End compensation for Finney's two years' absence, or buy him outright for £30,000. Finney must have been strongly tempted to cable his family to pack their bags and head south at once. With great correctness, however, he made an official request to Preston for release, and the club, naturally, turned it down flat. One wonders if Finney ever thought about this offer on cold January afternoons when the ball stopped dead in the puddles and the hailstones bounced off the roof of the stand.

Preston did not spend long in the second division – two seasons – and it was Finney who had the satisfaction of scoring the goal against Hull that clinched their Championship and promotion in 1951. They seemed then to regain something of their old classic conquering form, and by 1953 they were at the top of the first division. They missed the league Championship by the narrowest possible margin – on goal average – and had the harrowing experience of having to wait to hear the result of Arsenal's last game before they knew they had lost it. The following year was another of achievement and disappointment, this time in the Cup. Preston reached Wembley, but were beaten there by West Bromwich Albion, by 3 goals to 2. Finney's magnificent contribution to Preston's renaissance was recognised when he was chosen Footballer of the Year.

He is the only player to have won this honour twice. His second award was presented in 1957, and this time it was a recognition of his versatility. In that season Preston finished third in the league but they had begun dismally. They lost the first four games, and experimented desperately to evolve a workmanlike and harmonious forward line. Eventually Finney was tried at centre-forward, and suddenly everything fell into place. Finney himself reached a new level of certainty and mastery. As often happens with a mature player, the change brought him renewed vitality and command. He scored twenty-seven goals in cup and league, but more than that his wonderful team sense and instinctively fine positioning made him a great tactical leader. His coolness, his particular kind of intelligence, and his build dictated his method – that of the deep-lying centre-forward. He collected the ball in midfield and held it until the rest of the line were positioned for attack: he drew the defence, and his passes, close or long, were precise and dangerous. To guard against his passing was not enough; his judgement of an opening was deadly, his acceleration and timing of a spirit took him through it like an arrow, he was as tenacious of the ball as ever and hard to rob, and he shot coolly and accurately with both feet. Preston played sixteen games in succession without a defeat and reached their highest total of first-division points, fifty-six. In the following season they were to improve on that record, with fifty-nine points, and still finish second to Wolves. So striking was Finney's success in his new position that he was picked as centre-forward for England against Wales, Scotland, and Yugoslavia, but apart from moments of brilliance he was not a successful leader of the English line.

That Finney should be capable, at international level, of switching from outside-right to outside-left to centre-forward was remarkable enough. Even more surprising was his ability, in 1958, to return to the wing for England while still playing at centre-forward for Preston. By then it seemed that the long duel with Matthews was over. Matthews had played seven times for England in 1957, but in 1958, when the England party went to Sweden for the World Cup, he was not among them – he was over forty, six years older than Finney.

Finney might have been England's great man of the World Cup; he was the one player with the art and experience to steady a difficult and uncertain forward line, to draw out its potential brilliance, the one man capable of the moment of domination that can win a vital game that seems already lost. Unhappily, his part in the competition was limited to one game – the game against Russia that ended in a 2–2 draw; the heavy and unscrupulous tackling he suffered in it put him out of the rest of the series. Yet one moment of the match showed his great quality. With only five minutes to go, Haynes was fouled in the penalty-area. England were losing by two goals to one. When the penalty was given, the Russian players, usually so well behaved, protested violently. As Finney placed the ball on the spot, the atmosphere was so unnervingly tense that Billy Wright, a hardened veteran if ever there was one, turned his back, unable to look; but Finney, apparently completely unmoved, turned, took a few easy steps, and coolly drove the ball in.

from MASTERS OF SOCCER *1960*

Johnny Haynes

MAURICE EDELSTON and TERENCE DELANEY

Football is one of the impermanent arts, practised in public, before enormous audiences – emotional audiences whose memories are short, and whose awareness of what is happening under their noses is limited.

It is difficult enough to mend an electric light fuse with someone standing behind you. To exercise a profession that uses all your concentration, self-control, nerves and physical energy, with anything up to a hundred thousand excited advisers looking over your shoulder, calls for exceptional qualities – or unusual stolidity. The only other artist who performs, week in, week out, before so many eyes is the bullfighter; and one does not need to be in Madrid to be reminded of the bitter remark of a Spanish critic: 'The only beast in the bullring,' he said, 'is the crowd'.

No player can be unaware of the crowd; but, for his own sake, every player must learn, as soon as possible, to ignore it. To hear your own name carried triumphantly on a wind of voices is intoxicating; it can raise you above doubt and tiredness. But every professional knows that the tone of the voices can change, and he knows that the crowd has never made a player, though it has broken a few. But there are others watching, people whom a player as good as Haynes knows he cannot afford to ignore. These are the professional observers – other players, the managers, the old heads. They watch for a purpose, coldly and closely; and by the time a player has had one full season at the top, they know him often better than he knows himself so that in every sense he is a marked man. He finds he no longer has so much room to move; the turn or feint that made openings last year is now anticipated and countered. So, if he is to go on developing, he is forced to start thinking his game out again from the beginning. It may be that Haynes is in the middle of some such process now, so far as league football is concerned.

There is a way to stop Haynes, or any other good inside-forward. This is the recipe: take one good solid half-back, filled to the brim with stamina, not over-spiced with ambition, and stir him gently with assurances of constant employment in the first team. Then subdue any tendency to effervescence by adding an essential condition, that he shall do exactly – but *exactly* – what he is told. What he is told is this: 'Stay with Haynes; stay close; wherever he goes, you go; if you see a wonderful constructive opportunity, never mind; if Haynes goes to right-back or centre-half, don't think about it, do as I tell you. Now go on, son; *stay with Haynes*, and I'll see you next Saturday.' The effect of this is that the second the inside-forward gets the ball, the man is on him, crowding and harrying; before he can set himself free, the ball is gone – anywhere – and the half-back is still there. The inside-forward is blotted out of the game.

Like most footballing plans, this one looks more fool-proof on paper than it is in practice. The man you are dealing with is, after all, an inside-forward, and a good one. Given average material, you can develop a half-back, or any other player; but the inside-forward is a special case. To be first-class at this job it is not enough to be well-coached and well-trained. Good inside-forwards are men born with gifts. The gifts are not aptitudes for special tricks; they are something extra added to, and built into, the normal technical equipment and ability of a hard-working professional. So the dutiful, close-marking half-back may find, in the middle of the second half, that he has been playing out of his class for just a little too long. Then, gradually, we see the inside-forward gaining his freedom, yard by yard; those extra gifts are flowering, and he is commanding the game. Eventually even our merciless commentator in the enclosure notices it, and turns the blast of the nerve-racking voice on to the half-back. 'Look at him!' he says, 'he's on his knees!'

There is no doubt, however, that the plan often succeeds. If the half-back can stay the distance, all a man like Haynes can do is draw him far out of position, pull the defence out of joint, and leave the rest to the other forwards. If they cannot rise to this, the half-back has won.

It is an interesting point that this destructive plan is less often employed in internationals. The aim in international football must always be to use all the gifts of every player. If a half-back – or a back for that matter – is merely a defensive shadow, then he is the prisoner of the man he is marking. His constructive talents unused, he is only half a player. World Cup football requires complete players; in defence or attack, the side must always be able to call on 'the spare man'. Apart from this, the wing-half himself, in this class of football, is likely to be tempted away from his duties as a ball-and-chain by his very feeling for the game. It might be only for a moment, but that can be the crucial moment, then the sacrifice of his other abilities will have been made for nothing.

Haynes is a natural international. There are moments in his great games when the ball comes to him and you seem to see no one else, as if only one figure in the picture was clearly in focus and all the rest slightly blurred and dimmed. Seriously and thoughtfully he makes himself a place to work in, he holds the moment in suspense while he takes his decision, and then the ball leaves him, struck firmly and accurately, flying perhaps thirty yards, precisely into the one possible opening – as *we* see now – precisely into the path of the racing forward, and the game is entirely changed.

This is the most spectacular of Haynes's gifts – his mastery of the long pass. Commonly passes travel five or six or ten yards; fifteen or a little over is long enough, considering the difficulty of accuracy under pressure, and the risk of interception. Haynes will hit a ball twenty yards – and thirty, often more – aim it exactly, and do it regularly, as a normal part of his game. In this he is unique in modern football.

The third of Haynes's peculiarly individual gifts is the quickness of his thinking, and here is another reason why the international is his natural setting, because he is partnered by men whose anticipation matches the sudden changes in his plans.

Fast as his thoughts are, there is an apparent – but only apparent – leisureliness in the way he puts them into execution. There are players who give an impression of great speed and activity because of the nervous quickness of their movements, or the liveliness and aggressiveness of their personalities. There is nothing of this in Haynes. Though he is not thick or heavy, he is strongly built, with solid hips that swing against the swing of his shoulders; he is white-skinned, but there is no fragility or delicacy about him. He gives an impression of youth and seriousness. His hair, thick and dark, is combed back with care. Off the field, you notice the intelligence and sensibility of his eyes, and the humour of his mouth. On the field, he smiles very rarely; when he is not using the ball, he glances round him with an air of controlled impatience, as if he were memorising the position of the pieces on a board. Once with the ball, he seems to have held that clear picture in his mind, the positions and the way they are changing, the places where the sudden, vulnerable openings will appear. He is not the 'willowy' kind of runner, upright and swaying the body; he crouches slightly over the ball, with his feet wide apart. He is always ready to check, and change direction. He turns one way, finds it closed, and then with a hook that is one of his most characteristic movements, brings the ball sharply back, and tries another way. When he is satisfied, he lets the ball go – the beating of the man seems merely incidental.

He has always been a goal-maker, but he seems at some point recently to have taken a deliberate decision to become a goal-scorer as well. His total number of goals for the whole of the 1956–57 season was four; any forward, you might think, should get more than that. In 1957–58 he scored fifteen, a good total for a player who spends so much of his time making openings for other people. Then, after only nine games in the autumn of 1958, he had scored thirteen goals, and, despite a run of injuries, he finished the season with twenty-six. He takes his goals easily. When a loose ball, rattling about in the penalty-area, pops up suddenly in front of him, he simply places it in, with the same coolness that distinguishes his passing. When he is out on his own, and the goalkeeper rushes out to check him, he can wait, gauge his angle, and slip the ball past him. From time to time, nowadays, too, his quick eye spots the chance of a surprise long shot; and he can drive it home precisely from outside the penalty-area, into the particular part of the goal that has been left just a shade too open.

But goal-scoring is a capricious affair. Goals, when they come, come easily; a little bad luck can make a forward try too hard, and then they do not come at all. Goal-making, on the other hand, is Haynes's particular business, and he could flourish in that business for many years to come. He is full of possibilities. His authority, even among older players, his decisiveness, his ability to think the game, to analyse as well as play it, mean he has a future in captaincy, and maybe later in management too.

from MASTERS OF SOCCER *1960*

Len Shackleton

MAURICE EDELSTON and TERENCE DELANEY

For the greater part of his seventeen years as a professional foot-baller, the existence or Len Shackleton was a continuous exasperation and affront to the conventional and the conformists; to the sober hardworking artisans of the game and, above all, to authority and officialdom. One can see why; on and off the field he was incalculable and, occasionally, outrageous. Shackleton was eccentric, an erratic genius, a gifted individualist; a showman who drew the crowds, enter-tained and astonished them, and sent them home with the feeling that football was a game after all, and a wonderfully clever one.

The difficulty of fitting such a man into a prearranged pattern was probably one of the main reasons why Shackleton, a ball-player worthy of comparison with Matthews, was picked only six times for England. Another reason, possibly, was his unfailing willingness to express his opinions. He was not discreet. With a cheerful disregard for the interests of his own career, he criticised the Football League, the FA, players' contracts, the transfer system, international selection, referees, managers, and directors.

He had an impish streak. When he caught himself being orderly and orthodox, a perverse impulse took hold of him. It was as if he looked at the crowd and the directors' box and said to himself: 'They're too comfortable – let's stir them up a bit.' To be well-behaved for the full ninety minutes was beyond him. For two-thirds of a game he would put on a masterly show of inside-forward play that no player in the country could equal – perfect in positioning, bewilderingly clever, and yet direct, constructive, and unselfish. Then, with the side three goals up, he would decide he had had enough of discipline and hard work for one afternoon; he was going to amuse himself. From then on he shocked you. Either you laughed with delighted astonishment at his cheek, or you pressed your lips together and muttered 'Disgusting!' It depended on the sort of person you were, and your motives for watching football.

For example: a high ball is dropping towards Shackleton, who stands waiting for it with his hands on his hips. As it reaches him he raises one foot and traps it dead; apart from this movement his position is unchanged. He stands there, with his foot on the ball, takes one hand from his side and brushes back the loose hair from his forehead. With the same hand he makes the gesture of glancing at his watch. Then he looks towards the trainer's box and says, calmly and audibly, 'How long to go?' This was one of the reasons why the name Shackleton made some well-known people in football red with rage. Another example: in the last few minutes of the game he is taking the ball up the middle towards the opponents' goal, jinking, dodging, evading tackles. He is completely in control. Every swerve and feint touches off a fresh roar of appreciation. He beats one man after another until there is only the goalkeeper left. He fools the goalkeeper into diving the wrong way, and dribbles round him into the empty goalmouth. Then he stops the ball on the line, looks back at the scrambling goalkeeper, and calls out: 'George! It's not over the line yet!' This is why Shackleton's autobiography was called *Clown Prince of Soccer* instead of *How to Win Friends and Influence People*.

from MASTERS OF SOCCER *1960*

Lev Yashin

BRIAN GLANVILLE

Images of Lev Yashin. The semi-final of the 1966 World Cup, on a summer evening at Goodison Park. Yashin dives to clutch the ball. Lothar Emmerich, the West German winger, lunges in with boot outstretched. Ball safely in his grasp, Yashin rises to his considerable height, leans over the prostrate Emmerich and wags an admonitory finger at him.

The same game. Franz Beckenbauer, then only twenty-one, sends a left-footed shot curling round the Soviet Union's defensive wall, to snake its way tantalisingly past Yashin's right hand. Two-nil for West Germany, who go on to the final.

Back to the 1958 World Cup; the Ullevi stadium in Gothenburg; England versus the Soviet Union. Finney has been lamed and England are up against it. And up, up, up goes Yashin with Derek Kevan, the big English centre-forward. Head beats hands, even Yashin's famous hands. The ball is in the net; England have survived.

Strange to conclude that for all his prowess, his majestic consistency, Yashin tended to come unstuck in World Cups. His manager blamed him publicly for Beckenbauer's goal – a poor reward when Yashin had long kept his side in the game after they were down to nine men.

Four years earlier, in Chile, he had blundered twice in the quarter-final match against the host country, in Arica. Two mighty long shots beat him, each a left-footer. After only ten minutes a twenty-five yard free kick struck at an angle from the left by the left-winger, Leonel Sanches, flew home. The Soviet Union equalised, but from thirty-five yards a drive from the left-half, Eladio Rojas, won the game.

That did not stop Yashin being voted European Footballer of the Year in 1963. Nor did those World Cup goals tarnish the image of a marvellous goalkeeper.

That was one irony of Yashin's famous career. Another was that he should have spent the whole of it, as player and coach, with Moscow Dynamo, a club traditionally associated with the KGB. The briefest meeting with Yashin served to dispel any such identification. If, on the field, he radiated authority, off it he was geniality itself. He loved to play football, he loved the game at large and he had great affection for his famous adversaries, like Billy Wright and Bobby Charlton.

He used to say that his inspiration had been a long-forgotten goalkeeper called Sokolov, a Bulgarian who impressed him deeply with his adventurous style. But the man he succeeded in the Dynamo and Soviet goals was Tiger Khomich, hero of the legendary Dynamo tour of Britain in 1945. Khomich and Yashin were two very differet goalkeepers, two very different men. If Yashin was tall and lean, with brushed-back hair and long, straight nose, Khomich was square and squat, almost a peasant figure, though a wonderfully agile goalkeeper in his own way. If Yashin liked to smoke, Khomich, who became a press photographer, liked to drink. What Russian doesn't?

An all-round athlete – boxer, runner and basketball player – Yashin played ice-hockey, too, like so many Soviet footballers of his era, and might have settled down to be a goalminder. As a football keeper, Khomich stood formidably in his way. But Khomich was injured. Yashin was chosen and a great career began.

Yashin thought he had his finest hour not in a World Cup but in the 1956 Olympic tournament in Melbourne, when the full Soviet team, pseudo-amateurs, won the gold medal. Not that money ever seemed much to interest Yashin. If there could be such a thing as a Soviet Corinthian, it was surely he.

As time went by, goalkeeping grew harder. Yashin was wont to complain that the more defensive football became, the more difficult was a goalkeeper's lot. In a packed penalty-box, the keeper was no longer monarch of all he surveyed. Not only was he forced back towards his goal-line, Yashin lamented, but he often saw the ball too late as it came through a forest of legs; frequently deflected.

Yet Yashin continued to be an inspiration to his team, and a terror to his opponents, exemplifying the philosophy of his contemporary, Italy's Giuseppe Moro.

A goalkeeper's saves, said Moro, could be decisive, not only by inspiring his own team, but by demoralising the opposition. Whatever happened in the 1962 and 1966 World Cups, the huge, ominously black-clad figure of Yashin, bestriding his goal like a Colossus, was a daunting sight to an adversary.

That he should die so relatively young, at sixty, and in such pain, was wretched reward for an exemplary career. Thrombosis had cost him a leg; cancer followed soon afterwards.

He stayed with Moscow Dynamo, in one guise or another, after he stopped playing. Football and the club were, after all, the warp and woof of his life. Perhaps the best compliment one can pay him is to say that in his character, his attitude, his altruism, he was a glorious anachronism.

from the SUNDAY TIMES *1990*

Ferenc Puskas

BRIAN GLANVILLE

Now came Ferenc Puskas, one more indisputably great player, who would comfortably co-exist with Di Stefano. He came in the close season of 1958, having got out of Hungary two years earlier. By a massive irony, the Hungarian authorities were hoist with their own petard. They had cracked down on the established clubs of Budapest and made Honved, the Army team, the be-all and end-all of the country's football by inducting a number of stars and giving them phoney commissions. But when they allowed Honved out on tour shortly before the Revolution broke, Puskas, Sandor Kocsis and Zoltan Czibor, three of the club's and the country's finest attacking players, stayed out. All of them found their way to Spain.

In the case of Puskas it was after a couple of years of vagabondage, waiting partly in Milan for his period of 'quarantine' to end. Able now to sign for Real, he looked plump and slow at first but Di Stefano never said to him, as he allegedly did to Didi, then thirty, that he was 'too old and slow' to displace him. They were complementary from the start.

Puskas in fact was thirty-two by now, and a player who had long since entered into the history of the game. Captain of the marvellous Hungarian team which had thrashed England 6–3 at Wembley in November 1953, shattering the unbeaten home record against foreign teams into minuscule fragments, he'd failed to follow up with a World Cup victory in 1954.

Hungary's failure in Switzerland, their defeat in the final, remains a matter of massive contention. Puskas, as domineering a figure as Di Stefano in his day, had been cruelly kicked by Werner Liebrich, the blond West German centre-half, when Hungary thrashed the Germans 8–3 in their initial World Cup game. That put him out until the final, which the Germans, thanks to the vagaries of the competition, reached. Puskas insisted that he play, though he still was not fully fit. Moreover, he allegedly insisted on the exclusion of the right-winger Budai, who had done extremely well till then.

Hungary stuttered and lost, though Puskas probably had a goal quite wrongly ruled out for offside by the British refereeing trio. Now he, and his fabulous left foot, were in Madrid. He had always been not only a marvellous striker of the ball but a superb tactician, playing well upfield in front of a deep lying centre-forward in Nandor Hidegkuti, making goals as well as scoring them.

'I am grateful to my father for all the coaching that he did *not* give me,' he once wrote. 'In Hungary boys, in their own enthusiasm, learn to control a ball almost from the time they can walk.' If I have a favourite, emblematic, memory of Puskas, it involves, curiously enough, a distant and remote city, and it did not occur on the field of play.

It was in Santiago, the night that Chile had won the third place game in the 1962 World Cup, and the streets swarmed with joyful, celebrating Chileans. There, standing in a shop doorway, quite unrecognised, eating monkey nuts out of a paper bag and grinning all over his urchin's face, was Puskas. He had played for Spain in that tournament, but how could it compare with the authentic thing, the Final of '54, when Hungary went down to defeat and his 'goal' was given offside?

It was another Hungarian, Emile Osterreicher, who in fact brought Puskas to Real. He had been added to Real's staff, a downy bird who knew his European football backwards and would sing a diplomatic song: 'I always told Santiago Bernabeu that Real had three great players: Di Stefano, Puskas . . . and Bernabeu.'

'I was charged with being slow after my early matches in Spain,' wrote Puskas. 'Modestly, I beg to point out that this was, and is, an illusion. Spain favours fast, driving football, which is to the appetite of our supporters. I, too, think football should be a fast game – but the ball should run faster than the man! Individual speed is a serviceable advantage. But to run madly and without purpose is of no value. The ball must be moved about quickly, preferably on first contact: to run with it is too often only wasting valuable attacking time.'

Puskas could certainly run with it when the need arose. His offside 'goal' in the World Cup final was an example. So was one of the three he so magnificently but unavailingly scored in the 1962 European Cup Final. But then his technique was such that he could do anything and everything: except, perhaps, head spectacular goals.

When Hungary beat England at Wembley, he scored a memorable goal pulling the ball back with the sole of his boot while England's captain, in the equally memorable words of Geoffrey Green in *The Times*, rushed past him 'Like a fire engine going to the wrong fire.' Puskas insisted, with some justice, that he was 'as fast as the next man when I think it necessary to produce a sprint.'

What was beyond dispute was that he and Di Stefano, two great *maestri*, complemented one another supremely well, and never more so than in the triumphantly successful European Cup final of 1960, when Puskas scored four and Di Stefano three. Puskas was already well used to playing with a deep lying centre-forward, since Nandor Hidegkuti had filled that role for years, not least when he scored three in Hungary's success at Wembley. But Puskas long outlasted him. By the 1958 World Cup in Sweden, Hidegkuti looked a tired and used-up man. Puskas went galloping on for several splendid years.

from CHAMPIONS OF EUROPE *1991*

Danny Blanchflower

GEOFFREY GREEN

He played as he talked, fluently and almost without drawing breath. Delicately balanced and cool as a cucumber, accurate as a slide-rule with his passes, he was always available to his colleagues in an open space, a magnet for the ball. Arthur Rowe, the Spurs manager, who snatched his man from Aston Villa for £30,000 in 1954 – a record price for a half-back at the time – in the face of fierce competition from Arsenal and Wolves, saw in Blanchflower not only all the qualities and attitudes to the game he himself admired, but he recognised in him, too, the powers of leadership. In these terms Rowe once said: 'In nine matches out of ten Blanchflower has the ball more than any two other players on the field. It's an expression of his tremendous ego, which is just what a captain needs.'

Blanchflower's own great hero was Peter Doherty, another Irishman, a wonderful, non-stop inside-forward. 'Always remembering Doherty,' he once wrote, 'I aim at precision soccer. Constructiveness, no matter what the circumstances, ball control, precise and accurate distribution, up in support at all times possible, back in defence to blot out the inside-forward when necessary. I am described as an attacking wing-half, and I suppose that is correct. Sometimes I even score goals.'

Blanchflower practised his profession with all the art, intelligence, craftsmanship and pride at his considerable command. Articulate and persuasive to the point where he might well have taken to law had circumstances been different, he was an intellectual, cerebral player. Only recently someone on television described football as possessing intellectual undertones. The studio audience laughed derisively. Yet football has just that, when performed by certain players. Blanchflower, for one, always projected his mind where others projected their bodies because he always thought and talked about it as constructively as he played it. He became the master of his craft and as such measured his merit and worth clinically, always being an outspoken critic of the transfer system and the men who operated it. Precise and tidy of mind and appearance, he could spread out his game similarly before the opposition like some lawyer spreading out his case before a jury. Often scathing of the English temperament, he was happiest with his own free and easy Irish colleagues. Once, regarded by the Spurs managership around 1956 of having taken upon himself too much authority on the field, he was relieved of the club captaincy for a spell. But a born leader, he regained his position in due course to reach two personal high peaks in the fifties. In 1957 it was his fiery but controlled leadership that took Ireland to an astonishing 3–2 victory over England at Wembley – the first Irish win in the series for twenty-seven years. In 1958 Blanchflower went one better. He captained Ireland to a share of the British Championship with England, was elected Footballer of the Year, and led the Irish into the quarter-finals of the World Cup in Sweden, having accounted for powerful Italy and Czechoslovakia on the way. 'We wouldn't even have reached the World Cup finals without him,' said Peter Doherty, his old hero, then his national team manager.

Most footballers play from habit. Blanchflower was above that. He was able to read a situation, analyse it and try to change the habit or the tactic on the spot. That is why he remains my captain of the fifties. What a partnership he would have made as prompter to Stanley Matthews!

from SOCCER IN THE FIFTIES *1974*

John Charles

GEOFFREY GREEN

He was a Goliath among men, and a footballer of calm authority. Blessed with his physical attributes, his placid nature shunned violence. He always played the ball, never the man. Hence his title of 'The Gentle Giant'. Even the Italians took up the phrase 'Il Gigante Buono'. . . . Yet he took heavy punishment himself from the 'choppers' and spoilers in the game, losing cartilages from both knees before he was twenty years old, yet never retaliating. This dominating impressive, latent power of the man apart, so sparingly used, his real strength and value lay in the fact that he could play a major role in two positions – either at centre-half, or at centre-forward. If many agreed that he was the greatest centre-half in the world, there were those who added that he was also the most dangerous centre-forward to be found anywhere. Many times, indeed, both for Wales and for Leeds, he found himself switched from one position to the other during a match when injury struck a colleague. When he departed to Juventus, the Italians, in fact, used his tremendous all-round power quite cynically and with cold tactical appreciation. In the late 1950s, *catenaccio* defence had already begun to rear its ugly head in the Italian league and the Juventus plan was simple. They would start a match with Charles at centre-forward and once he had scored his inevitable goal (often with his lofty head), he would be switched back to centre-half to shore up defence and keep the 1–0 victory intact.

Charles's awe-inspiring physique made him appear a man amongst boys. Yet his self-effacing streak, his unselfishness as a ball player, all helped to create his entirety as a footballer. Powerful on the ground, quite unbeatable in the air, he was a force of nature, as dangerous in an opponents' penalty area as he was dominating in his own. Both a cool distributor and builder of attacks from the rear (allied to his strength of tackle), he was equally deadly as a finisher of moves when diverted to centre-forward. Deep-chested, powerfully-muscled, upright as a guardsman, Charles was a light-footed Garth, as loose of limb as a Negro sprinter and as deceptively fast. It was in 1952–53 that he switched from centre-half to centre-forward with Leeds, scoring twenty-seven goals in thirty matches. The following year he became top scorer of the whole Football League with forty-two goals. In 1955 Charles reverted to centre-half to bolster the club's defence; by 1956 Leeds were in the first division, the 'Gentle Giant' was already world famous, and by the end of that 1956–57 season Charles (switched yet again to attack) was the first division's top scorer with thirty-five goals.

In the spring of 1957 he went to Italy and at once was drawing record crowds as he had done in England. Juventus immediately won the Italian league (largely through the Welshman's partnership with the flamboyant little Argentinian ball player, Siveri); Charles scored twenty-nine goals (including three hat-tricks) and was voted *Il Campione Preferito*, the Italian Footballer of the Year.

Released, grudgingly, by Juventus, Charles returned briefly in 1958 to take his place at his brother Melvyn's side to help Wales to the quarter-finals of the World Cup in Sweden. Yet, injured, he did not do himself full justice then. Still, he would have won a place in the world side of any generation and is still affectionately remembered in Italy where more than once since leaving those sunny shores he has returned as a welcome guest of Juventus.

from SOCCER IN THE FIFTIES *1974*

Duncan Edwards

GEOFFREY GREEN

How can one measure the loss of life of one person as against another? All, in some degree, should be considered equal. Yet when Duncan Edwards died in the Munich aircrash of February 1958 at the tender age of twenty-one he seemed to symbolise the famous words of George Orwell that some people are more equal than others. Edwards, without question, was the heaviest loss of all to English football. A restless powerhouse, he was a dynamic player who ate, slept, dreamed and loved football. A member of the Manchester United 'Busby Babes' of 1955–58, he was one of a team in the process of developing into the finest club side that Britain perhaps had ever produced. Cut off in its prime as it was, no one can ever prove that point. Yet the critics were unanimous – even Matt Busby himself – that the young United at the time the fates struck could have gone on to dominate both the English and European scenes for the next decade or so. And certain it is that Duncan Edwards, had he survived, would have captained England to the World Cup of 1966.

Height 5 ft 11 in, 13 stone in weight, he was all muscle. Indeed, when I first saw him at an early age, I felt there was a danger of him becoming muscle-bound. But sheer drive, hard training and hard work, plus a limitless enthusiasm kept him within bounds. At heart he was always just a boy, full of fun, spirit and loyalty and a great favourite wherever he went. Once when Busby called him to his office to tell him that the local Manchester schools were playing a five-a-side competition and could Edwards come to present the cup, Duncan's first remark was: 'Sure, boss. And can I play in it?' 'Certainly not, you great bully!' replied Busby, with an understanding smile. Once, too, in the summer tour of 1955 the England team had an afternoon off to watch a bullfight in Madrid. Afterwards Edwards pretended to be the bull: I played the part of the matador. As I was still wafting my handkerchief as if it were the cape, the 'bull' struck me amidships like some tornado. Sent flying, I broke a finger and to this day the swollen joint reminds me of that splendid young-spirited man who would have so flourished in the Elizabethan age.

Edwards, indeed – the master of the forty or fifty-yard pass – played like a tornado, attacking, defending, always wanting to be at the eye of the storm. Many were the great goals he scored, too, as he pounded forward on a solo run like a runaway tank to release a shell from the edge of the penalty-area that would have penetrated a steel wall. Two of these, in particular, still burn holes in the pocket of memory – in the Olympic Stadium, Berlin, 1956, against Germany, the reigning World Champions; at Wembley, 1957, against Scotland. England won 3–1 and 2–1 respectively and each time it was Edwards, ploughing through the defence like a battleship in high seas, who rammed home a twenty-yard broadside. Beyond all this Edwards could play almost anywhere besides his normal position of left-half. For United he appeared also at centre-half, inside-left and centre-forward, always with an appetite for goals. In 1955, when Atyeo was injured at centre-forward in an Under-23 international against Scotland, Edwards was switched forward from left-half and crashed home four goals.

What more can one say of a young man who played only four full seasons in first-class football? Even the stars may finally have not been beyond his reach. By the age of sixteen he had broken into the first division; by seventeen he was in the England 'B' and Under-23 teams; at eighteen and a half he became the youngest player ever to gain a full England cap. At nineteen he won his first league Championship medal and at twenty he played in a Cup final. Three months before his death a panel of leading sports writers in Europe voted him third in their international order of merit – behind Di Stefano and Billy Wright. His talent, his energy, his unselfconscious fun and enjoyment of the chase, his ability to make everything seem possible, all this added up to a volcano of excitement that gripped the crowds and the game wherever he played. For three weeks he fought for his life in a coma. But in the end the gods loved him more.

from SOCCER IN THE FIFTIES *1974*

Alex James

GEOFFREY GREEN

Will there ever be another Alex James? One doubts it! He was as different from David Jack in his approach to life – in this case football – as Puck from Hamlet. His genius and individuality were his own as were his long, baggy trousers and the sleeves of his shirt studiously turned down and buttoned at the wrist. He too 'fluttered' his foot over the ball, and his opponents never knew what trick to expect next, his enjoyment in confusing them being obvious to all. He would scatter defences not so much by what he did with the ball as by what he didn't; he was the conjurer at a children party. It was his quick wits and his sympathy with his partner that beat Huddersfield that afternoon at Wembley.

It all began with a foul. James was bumped and fell. In a twinkling he was up, bent down to place the ball for the free-kick and, without so much as straightening up, sent a quick short pass to Bastin. Moving rapidly into an open space, James took the perfect return and before anyone had realised it – least of all the surprised Hudersfield defence – the ball was in the back of the net. A goal by James at any time was something of a curio, and this one in particular caused a lot of comment. Was the free-kick fairly taken? Yes. James's eyebrows, raised in silent appeal for permission to proceed, had been answered by a wave from Mr Crew, the referee, and quick thinking had gained its reward.

Huddersfield, making strenuous efforts to wipe out that goal after half-time, had the fine Arsenal defence at full stretch for breathless periods, but once again a long pass by James opened the way for Lambert down the middle and Arsenal had made certain of the Cup for the first time.

It was on this sunny afternoon that a long, dark sinister shape floated across the sky over the stadium, throwing its shadow over the field. It dipped in salute and moved serenely away. The players threw a momentary upward glance and played on. It was the German airship *Graf Zeppelin*.

from THE OFFICIAL HISTORY OF THE FA CUP *1960*

George Best

ARTHUR HOPCRAFT

Sport can be cruel to men. Football can make a man more ridiculous even than drink can. Outside the players' entrance at Old Trafford, Manchester United's ground, on a raw and turbulent March morning, the wind blew an old man teetering across the tarmac, wet and flapping, in his overcoat like an escaped poster, and draped him across the windows of my car. His fingers rattled on the glass and he was shouting urgently. He was a thin old man with stubble on his chin and a neck like a cockerel's. There were three people in the car, but he was concerned with only one, the boy in the back who was slight and aged eighteen and who looked no older. The old man shoved his head into the car as I wound the window down and he gabbled through a breathless rigmarole directed solely at the youth. It was one of those football followers' riddles which hinge on one of the laws of the game, in which some improbable incident is invented, such as the collapsing of the ball as it enters the goal and the questioner challenges for the correct referee's ruling. This particular problem was incomprehensible in the old man's hoarseness and anxiety. He kept breaking off to shout: 'I was a referee, you know.' The last time he said it he stopped talking altogether, and the boy he was trying to impress, George Best, of United and Northern Ireland, smiled gently at him and said, 'Cheerio,' and we drove away. Best said: 'It happens all the time now.' Then he put a sweet into his mouth, and his face assumed that seamless, private thoughtfulness with which the decently mannered young excuse themselves from contact with an older generation.

This was the diffident, delicate-looking Best of 1965, not at all self-confident in strangers' company. He spoke when he was spoken to, not at all fluently; the voice came haltingly and sounded barely broken. He bit his lower lip a lot, and looked shyly at his interviewer's breast pocket or over his forehead. He was so unused to being interviewed, or to talking to people outside his immediate circle of friends and fellow players, that we had a substantial problem in communication: not just in terms of words but in the fundamental matter of intention. After about an hour of trying to coax some personal information out of him, and getting little but nods and smiles, I said: 'Well, you're not going to get big-headed, are you?' It was expressed as a rueful kind of compliment. There was an instant blush from him and a flash of temper in his eyes, the first spurt of the pulse I had seen from him off the football field. He had clearly taken the observation as an unwelcome injunction from someone not qualified to give it.

from THE FOOTBALL MAN *1971*

Tony Kay

ARTHUR HOPCRAFT

In January 1965 three of England's best-known footballers were sent to prison for four months after their conviction in what was called The Soccer Conspiracy Case. They were Peter Swan, the Sheffield Wednesday centre-half who had played nineteen times for his country, David Layne, the Sheffield Wednesday centre-forward, and Tony Kay, a wing-half, formerly of Sheffield Wednesday but at the time of the disclosure playing for Everton. The gist of the case was that all three, while playing for Wednesday, had conspired to prevent their own team from winning a match to facilitate a betting coup. A few months after the case the three players were suspended from football for life by the Football Association, which meant that any form of officially recognised football anywhere was barred to them. Kay and Swan had pleaded not guilty in court.

The case made a wretched winter for British football. Seven less well-known players and former players were sentenced at the same time on similar charges to terms of imprisonment ranging from four years to six months. The exposure was the work of the *People*, the Sunday newspaper, whose reporters did their job resourcefully and ruthlessly, and the dirty shrapnel of the explosion nicked and wounded people all round the game. Such a revelation was bound to make the public ask each other, blackly, how much 'fixing' of matches was going on which was never discovered. This fear struck at the very roots and heart of football. The footballers, once found guilty, were bound to suffer the complete punishment.

While the tale was being told little sympathy was invited fot the men concerned, although Mr Justice Lawton, passing sentence, said he accepted that the Sheffield Wednesday players were involved 'really by chance' and on one isolated occasion; they presented him, he said, 'with the most unpleasant part of my duty'. Excuse may never be possible, but at least the personal tragedy of the event should be acknowledged. The fallen, ruined hero is no figure for callous scorn. Some respected men in the game have given their names to appeals for the players' reinstatement. There is kindness here but also, I think, a failure on their part to recongnise the significance of the case. Perhaps it is a matter of being too close to the game to see the extent of the damage. A court conviction on a charge of 'fixing' football is not just a nasty blotch on the wall, but a jagged hole in the fabric. Two or three more like that and the whole structure falls in rubble.

Of the three men I have named, Kay was the most colourful player, and he was notably articulate. He was twenty-seven at the time of the case, and he had played once for England, against Switzerland. He was an extremely tough, quick, enterprising half-back, of the combative, all-action kind: very much the type of player whom Sir Alf Ramsey developed in Nobby Stiles for England's World Cup victory. Stiles played magnificently for England. It is fair to ask whether he would have been given the chance if Kay had been available. That thought was very sharply in my mind when I went to see Kay in Liverpool in 1967.

He looked haggard, although not in the debilitated sense of a man gone to seed. He looked what he was still: a hard-driven athlete, the flesh tight on the bones. He had red, scrubbing-brush hair, and he wore thick-rimmed glasses. He exuded an exaggerated ruefulness, a bitter and aggressive self-mockery. There was a distinct television-age, showbiz edge to the back-street wit. 'The cops have it in for me; must have,' he said. 'Have you ever heard of anyone being booked for parking by a copper on a horse? That's Anthony's luck.'

Kay was brought up in Sheffield, where he learned about life and football, which amounted practically to the same thing for him . . . He knew working-class austerity as people know sweat, through the pores, not book-learnt or observed in passing. Money was important because there was not much of it about. Everton bought him from Sheffield Wednesday for more than £55,000.

The face has a flare of insolence, and now that he had much to regret he played up this component in his personality, telling stories of the persecution and recurrent disaster in his life with a chirpy, gritty comicality. 'Wasn't I always in trouble?' he said. 'Well, I nearly got killed more than once, didn't I? Look how the crowds used to get at me.'

He launched into a story about a match in London, which ended with a mob of the home crowd's fans yelling for his blood round the exit. He walked out disguised in the home team manager's long overcoat and trilby. He said: 'When I got in the coach I took 'em off and tapped the window at the crowd. You should have seen 'em,' and he bared his teeth wide and crooked his fingers on either side of his face, like talons.

Then he said: 'There was that time in Italy when the crowd was at me. "Kay, Bastardo, Bastardo." They were behind this wire grille (bared teeth and crooked fingers again). I banged the ball at their faces. So what happens when we come off at the end? I'm there, with our team in the dressing-room, and I'm standing at the tunnel thanking everyone, and I go up to this Italian trainer, who's only about 7 feet tall. I hold my hand out, and what does he do? He's only got both me arms pinned behind me back. And all the Italian team's giving me one as they go off the field.'

The resentment poured out of him, as he built up a picture of a victimised upbringing. The voice teetered up into a thin malevolence, the voice of childhood's tormentors: 'Right, you've been very, very naughty, and now we're going to rattle your little arse. Whack. Sort that out.'

Kay, the bolshie; Kay, the whipping-boy; Kay, the misunderstood; Kay, the unlucky: he overstated his battering from life, and his tumbling resistance, with the skill of a natural comedian who is beginning to believe the letter as well as the spirit of his material.

'I've always hated referees,' he said. 'To me they're all no-marks. Otherwise, they wouldn't be there. Who are they? All the week they're sitting there in offices, scribbling away, scribble, scribble, and on Saturday afternoons they're on the field with all the big men, and they're saying, "Right, now you do what I tell you or you're going in my little book."' He did a wickedly observed impersonation of a hunchbacked, myopic referee writing in a notebook, his hands up by his nose. He said: 'I've seen blokes kicking lumps out of each other, and what's the referee doing? He's wagging his finger and making a great production out of moving the ball three foot back for a free kick.'

Kay's sadly funny performance was the more disturbing because in his comment on authority, and its view of him, there was a strong thread of truth. As a player he was undoubtedly one of those eruptive influences which infuriate referees. He was known for his bitter tackling and only tough men were prepared to take the consequences. Kay insisted to me that he was a marked man not only in the opposition's dressing-room but in the referee's as well, and he added that he did not mind telling referees so. One of his troubles was that he was never discreet in what he said or what he did. He said to me: 'I was naive.' He was right. He knew most of the tricks of the trade, but not the most important trick of all, which is to appear not to.

The more Kay talks the stronger is the conviction borne in on the listener that his misfortunes were impelled from inside him. Like everyone else the influences he assimilated from his environment were an imperfect blend; but is it the mixture or the chemistry which makes a man? Kay was embattled against the world, pretty well all of it, so that ultimately he was working against himself. Even in trivial, everyday matters, such as his relationship with road traffic, his progress was interrupted by violent incidents of bizarre complexity, in which his saving grace was to be found in his comic, fatalistic hindsight. One accident, as he described it, involved the inexorable will of some dauntless old lady, launched come what might for the distant haven of the opposite pavement. There was also snow and a steep hill. Then: 'So all of a sudden I'm waking up in me mini, upside down, and this geezer's shouting all sorts at me out of his bedroom winder.' On another occasion the slapstick disaster ends: 'So here I am, can't move a limb, being wheeled about the station by a porter on a trolley.'

Kay managed to squeeze a few wicked, retaliatory jokes out of his prison sentence. He said that the prison governor was 'a wild football fan, and he couldn't get enough of the game'. Kay said that he and his friends were given full rein to train the prison football team, and that the governor refereed most of the matches himself. 'We only lost one game out of fourteen,' Kay said, adding with a look of feigned distate, 'and that was because the other lot brought their own referee: the game was *bent*.' He laughed. He said that the first warder he met in gaol was a little man – most villains in Kay's life are little men – who greeted him with: 'Yes, it's through people like you I never win the pools.' Kay said: 'I thought to myself, "Hullo, Anthony, you've found yourself one here. It's your luck again."' He encountered the warder later when the man was a linesman at one of the matches. The story is a symettry of irony: 'The governor was sold on us. I gave 'em all hell, you know. He used to say, "Well done, young Kay." Well, this little warder – the bad one – he kept sticking his flag up and shouting at me every time I touched anybody. After a bit I said to him. "Why don't you piss off?" He was furious. He said, "I'll have you yet." So I ran across to the governor – he was refereeing again – and I said, "Excuse me, Sir, can't you do something about this linesman? He keeps on at me. I can't concentrate." So the governor went across to this warder, and he said, "Not so much noise, please, Mr So-and-so."' Kay's eyes glinted at the memory.

To judge from Kay's conversation, his attitude to authority always had that cynicism. He reminds one of the bad lad at the back of the class, or the hard case in the barrack-room, who recognises the sneaking respect, and often fear, that the man in charge has for the ones who won't conform. Such men seldom appeal for help, and when they do it is to exploit the boss's sense of importance. Kay told me this story about a match against Fulham: 'I was up against Jimmy Hill, and he was up there towering above me. Every time I went up for the ball there he was, just leaning over the top of me. I thought, "Right, I'm not having this all the game. Next time we go up I'll have his shorts off him." Well, up we went, and I shoved me hand out and I missed 'em. Instead I caught him right between the legs. He screamed the place down. But he kept with me afterwards, all over the field. I went to the ref. I said, "Hey, ref, look at this maniac with the beard. Look at the way he's after me." It worked.' Kay's relished little triumphs can only be properly understood by someone brought up where people never play cards for matchsticks.

I was warned before I went to see him that Kay might be sad; that if the gloom was on him he might even weep. He anticipated my wariness. He had stopped crying, he said, although when he was first told that he could never play football competitively again, he confessed: 'I never cried so much in all me life.' He said it looking straight at me, using the words like a showbiz catchphrase, but not smiling. He knew he had been overdoing the clowning. 'It just hides the tears,' he said. 'You can't cry all the time. You get a reputation for it. No one wants to know after a bit. They say, "Oh Christ, I've got to put up with this crying gett again." You can't just give up, can you?'

It was plain that he had been deeply hurt by what had happened to him; he was convinced it had been imposed and not brought upon him by himself. Every six months, he said, he wrote to the FA, asking if they would reconsider his registration. He did not really think they ever would. People in Liverpool, he said, were friendly and sympathetic towards him. That salty city would never snub a man like Kay. He was as much one of Liverpool's own, pugnacious and at least pretending cunning, as if he had been born there.

But his life was not pleasing him, to say the least of it. At the time I was talking to him he was a family man living away from his wife, and a bookmaker not sure that there would be another year's wages out of his betting shop. What had he been doing since prison? 'Just going round in circles,' he said. 'Getting nowhere.'

He had been playing football, surreptitiously, in scratch matches, giving another name when he was asked, keeping an eye open for men hanging about with cameras. He was training twice a week, and I could believe it when he said: 'I really push myself.' He did much of his training at a school gymnasium, often giving practical instruction to the boys. He said, the edge going out of the voice for the first time: 'They all want to take me on, you know. They think, "Oh, this old Tony Kay, he's finished." I like to get 'em trying to get past me on the outside, and I'm leaving 'em behind, and I'm shouting, "Come on, what are you waiting for, you lads?"'

There was a lot of heart in Kay as a player. Professional sport made him, tested him and broke him. He is one of football's tragic casualties because he was so strongly equipped in nearly all his aspects. His counsel said in court, after his conviction: 'He has given up for £100 what has in fact been one of the greatest careers of any footballer. He was tempted once, and fell.'

from THE FOOTBALL MAN *1971*

David Jack

BERNARD JOY

Buchan's departure from Arsenal left a void in the strategic as well as playing sense and Herbert Chapman knew that he had no alternative but to find one as near his counterpart as possible. 'Find the right man,' he instructed his scouts and he examined himself – and rejected in turn – the claims of such outstanding players as McGrory (Celtic), Smith (Ayr), Gallacher (Newcastle) and Hampson (Blackpool).

Finally, only one man measured up to the requirements: twenty-nine-year-old David Jack, the elegant English international inside-right of Bolton Wanderers. Tall and graceful, he dribbled as though the ball was magnetised to the flow of his body. He used to swerve by a sway of the shoulders towards an opponent and then go straight on, high-stepping disdainfully over his bewildered and stumbling foe. He might easily have been a Chelsea player, because he 'guested' for Chelsea in the 1914–18 war, but when his father Robert, a former Bolton outside-left, became manager of Plymouth Argyle he took his son with him. David Jack was Bolton-born and Bolton had to pay £3,000 to Plymouth to secure his return in 1921. He had the distinction of scoring the first goal in a Wembley final, for Bolton against West Ham in 1923, and he was in the 1926 final as well. By 1928 he was accepted as one of the greatest inside-forwards of all time and an automatic choice for England.

Just the rumour that Arsenal had made inquiries for him was sensational. Shortly beforehand, Bolton had circularised that they had players available for transfer, but they added the proviso that David Jack was the one man who would not be leaving. It took twelve hours of negotiations to secure him. After Bolton had been persuaded to consider the proposal they staggered Herbert Chapman by asking for £13,000, which was exactly twice the previous record fee, that paid by Sunderland for Bob Kelly. At two o'clock in the morning the clubs agreed to a fee of £11,500 and then Chapman had to go to Jack's house for his consent. The matter was not ended there because Jack telephoned his father in Plymouth for advice.

People derided the folly of paying such a sum and sneered at the 'Bank of England' methods of team building, but Arsenal had no regrets. Jack was one of the influential factors in the momentous years ahead and at Highbury he succeeded in adding to his great reputation.

from FORWARD ARSENAL *1954*

Three Liverpool Goalkeepers: Teddy Doig, Sam Hardy, Elisha Scott

STEPHEN F. KELLY

I was pleasantly passing the time of day last week with a former international goalkeeper. We were watching a couple of young apprentices practising their solemn art on a rainsodden pitch in Lancashire. The wind howled about the open spaces, curling and twisting the ball like a chinaman delivery while magpies nosed and fooled around in the pools behind the goals. 'Neither of them will make it,' he grunted. 'They've got technique but that's not everything.' I expressed some surprise at his reservations. 'Naw,' he drawled, curling his lips. 'Goalkeepers fall into two categories. They're either self-assured and cocky, or worriers. Just look at Neville Southall. Keeps himself to himself. A worrier if ever there was one. Then there's Bruce Grobbelaar. They don't come any cockier than him. Remember the way he clowned about in that European Cup penalty shoot-out. Takes bottle that. These two lads are neither one thing nor t'other.'

There's no doubting that at Anfield they pride themselves on knowing a thing or two about goalkeepers. In the days before fax machines and mobile telephones the telegraphic address of Liverpool Football Club was 'Goalkeeper'. It was a name almost certainly conjured up by that long-serving manager-secretary, Tom Watson, a man who reared the three finest goalkeepers of his generation.

Watson introduced many a fine player to Anfield yet it would be for his goalkeepers that he will always be remembered. In his day he brought to Liverpool the three greatest goalkeeping exponents of the Edwardian era, and all three from different corners of the land – Ned Doig from Scotland, Sam Hardy from England and Elisha Scott from Ireland. And sandwiched somewhere in between was Kenny Campbell, another Scottish international.

The first to arrive on the Anfield scene was Teddy Doig, who had been carefully nurtured at Roker Park by Watson in his early days as coach of Sunderland. An Arbroath lad, Doig had begun his professional career with Blackburn Rovers, at that time the most famous of all English clubs, but had moved to Wearside in 1890 where his arrival coincided with Sunderland's finest achievements. Three times they picked up the league championship in the space of four years and at the blunt end of it all was Ned Doig. Lanky, barrel-chested and moustached, Doig spelled the difference between success and failure. He served Sunderland well but when his mentor packed his bags and took off for Anfield in 1896 Doig found himself a lone protagonist of the goalkeeper's art. Without Watson the Team of All the Talents fell apart and slid painfully out of the honours.

Watson had transferred his wizardry to Anfield and within a few years they had clinched their first league title. But just as suddenly triumph turned to disaster as they conceded sixty-two goals and plummeted towards the second division. It was time for Watson to call on Doig. By the beginning of the 1904 season Doig was firmly in place, still sporting his cloth cap peaked at its usual jaunty angle to hide his receding hairline and as Liverpool clinched the second-division title the Arbroath lad conceded a mere twenty-five goals. A year later they were league champions.

By then Doig was well into his thirties, his bones creaking, his agility visibly failing and his hairline now well out of sight. Watson reluctantly sensed the need for change. But who could possibly replace Doig? Earlier that season Watson had watched in the drizzle of Anfield as six goals flashed past a young Chesterfield keeper. Not the kind of performance you might expect to excite anyone. But six goals or not Watson was impressed and within weeks the young man, Sam Hardy, had crossed the Pennies to join the Reds. He made his debut a week later on a muggy autumn afternoon, standing defiantly in front of the Kop. The ageing Doig had conceded twenty goals in the previous eight games. Hardy would play thirty-five times that season and concede just twenty-two. By the time he left Liverpool, seven seasons later, he was something of a folk hero.

Hardy was majestic. You'd risk your life in his hands. Confident, reassuring, his positioning was impeccable, always in the right place at the right time. He was the cocky type. No need for acrobatics, just a shimmy of his slim hips and he was there to take the ball squarely on the chest. He was still a young man when he left Anfield for Aston Villa and had already clocked up 239 games for the Reds and would go on to play another 500 league games and win twenty-one England caps before injury forced him into retirement. Liverpool should never really have let him go but guessed that in Scottish international Kenny Campbell and the newly signed Elisha Scott they had more than adequate cover.

If some goalkeepers are worriers then Elisha Scott was the prince of them all. He was the very opposite of Hardy. A twitcher, always first in the dressing-room, changed and ready for battle long before anyone else had even arrived. And then hurling the ball against the wall for an hour, springing first one way then the other as he flexed his mighty muscles. Scott arrived on Merseyside in the footsteps of his elder brother Billy, an Irish international who was keeping goal over at Goodison. Everton took one look at the slip of a lad and, like Linfield before them, decided he was not only too young but also too small. Fortunately Elisha grew not only older but also sprouted, though he never managed much beyond 5ft 10ins. It was brother Billy who advised him to try across the park where they knew a thing or two about goalkeepers.

Scott made his debut against Newcastle United on New Year's Day 1913. It was rumoured that Newcastle were keen to sign him and on the train north Scott pleaded with Watson to let him go. He could see no future at Anfield with the splendid Kenny Campbell firmly entrenched between the posts. But Watson shook his large head. 'Nay lad, bide thi time,' he said, pursing his lips, just allowing himself a thin smile. In those days you didn't argue. His break finally came during the 1914–15 season when injury to Campbell threw him a lifeline. He made twenty-three appearances but then war annoyingly intervened and off he went to do service for his country. He was absent from Anfield for most of the time but returned in 1919, expecting to take over from Campbell. But he was rusty, Tom Watson was by then dead and Campbell had kept goal throughout the war. So Scott had another wait though for only a year. Patience held its reward. The job was to be his for the next fifteen years.

Willowy and delicately built, Scott could just as easily have been a ballet dancer. Or given his penetrating handsomeness, a Hollywood hero. A square angular chin, proud Roman features with flashing dark hair pasted back to reveal a broad dome of a forehead, it was said that Scott had the eye of an eagle and the pounce of a panther. When he bumped into Dixie Dean in the street one day the Everton man casually nodded to him, only to see the giant Irishman fling himself to the ground to save some imaginary shot. Well that's what they say. You see, their tussles were legendary. They loathed him so much over at Goodison that in 1934 they tried to buy him but the protests poured in to Anfield and the local papers. So instead Liverpool shipped him back to Ireland where he became player-manager of Belfast Celtic. He had played over 450 games for Liverpool, winning two championship medals and a record thirty-one international caps. He was what heroes are made of.

from THE FOOTBALLER *1991*

Kenny Dalglish

STEPHEN F. KELLY

Sean Fallon had promised to take his wife out for their wedding anniversary. It was the 4th May 1967 and half Glasgow was still celebrating Celtic's famous European Cup-final victory against Inter Milan. The Fallons had been married four years. It was an anniversary that had to be observed and Sean was not one to forget the importance of such occasions. He had booked a table at the Seamill Hydro, a pleasant friendly hotel on the Ayrshire coast, close to Largs. It was a regular spot for the Celtic football team. Prior to Cup finals and other major games, Fallon and the Celtic team would often spend the night at the quiet hotel, ideal preparation for the forthcoming day especially with its spacious lawns and rousing view across the Firth of Clyde towards the Isle of Arran. It was just thirty miles out of the city, no more than an hour's drive but far enough to be away from the buzz and distractions of Glasgow. Fallon liked the hotel and the Ayrshire coast on a late spring evening was always refreshing. He felt relaxed there, not like some of the grander hotels in town where you were always likely to bump into people you knew.

Sean Fallon was a popular man who had joined Glasgow Celtic on, appropriately, St Patrick's Day 1950 from the Irish league club

Glenavon. Three weeks later he made his Celtic debut though when he put into his own net after just thirty minutes it seemed his brief career was set to come to an abrupt end. But it didn't and Fallon went on to play more than 250 games in the green and white hoops. He was part of the fixtures and fittings at Parkhead and it was hardly surprising when, at the end of his playing days, Celtic decided to keep him on, eventually making him an assistant manager to his old chum Jock Stein.

Fallon and his wife piled their three children into his car and left their Glasgow house in good time to reach the Ayrshire coast. Their journey would take them close past Ibrox and as they drove down the Paisley Road West, Fallon deep in thought, suddenly had an idea. It was to be an inspired moment.

'Do you mind if I drop off at someone's house for a minute?' he asked his wife Myra. 'There's a young lad I want to see. I'd like to have another chat with his father and he might just be in now,' he said glancing at his watch. 'We've been trying to sign him but he's a bit reluctant. I think if I can have another go at his father I might be able to persuade him. It shouldn't take long.'

The wives of football managers need to be patient, long-suffering and remarkably tolerant of their partners' enforced absences. Mrs Fallon had already learnt in the four short years they had been married that there was little point in arguing when it came to football. She might just as well accept that her husband was married to Celtic Football Club as well as to her. And so she reluctantly agreed.

Some months before, after a particularly strenuous morning's training, Sean Fallon had walked into his Parkhead office and had sat down to open the mail. Outside the rain was beating on Parkhead, sweeping across the terraces and cascading down the gutters of the stand. Inside it was warm and steamy. There was a letter from a Mrs Davidson. He had no idea who she was. 'Come and see my boy Victor,' she wrote. 'I think he has the potential to be a footballer, everyone says so and he so wants to play for Celtic.'

'I went myself and saw the boy in a game against some other team, I can't remember which. But he was playing for Glasgow United. The lad was about fifteen and he was impressive. I decided that I liked him and told him that I would like to see him and his father. I invited them up to Parkhead for a chat.' Eventually Victor Davidson signed for Celtic and went on to have a distinguished career with the club which might have been even more illustrious had it not been cut tragically short by injury.

'But while I was watching Davidson that day I saw this other boy. He was a pal of Victor's, playing on the same side. He had magnificent balance and his attitude was unusual for one so young. Even then he was strong and the other players clearly had problems getting the ball off him.'

Fallon decided he wanted to talk to the other boy as well, so he invited him to Parkhead for some training. But the lad seemed hesitant. Nevertheless, he showed up at Parkhead one day, did a spot of training and Fallon decided to try and sign him. He asked him if he would be interested in joining Celtic but he was noncommittal. Fallon was surprised. Most lads his age would give their right arm to play for Celtic. Unless, of course, they came from the wrong side of the great divide. Fallon ought to have guessed but he didn't. Although Fallon did not know it at the time, the lad had set his heart on playing for Rangers. After all they were his team. He had been repeatedly told that Rangers would come in for him and that one day he would wear the blue of the Gers, but so far they had failed to make a move.

Sean Fallon was not a man to be put off his stride. The more he saw of the youngster the more he liked what he saw. He had set his heart on signing him and for some weeks had been promising himself he would go and see the lad's father, as soon as he had a free moment. Give it one more try, see if I can't talk sense into them, he thought. The parents are always the key and it was important to see the family in its own setting. And there they were with Sean Fallon on his wedding anniversary driving past their house. It was early evening, tea time. Yes, his father was sure to be in.

'I won't be long,' he promised his wife as he parked the car and slammed the door. Fallon found the flat and knocked. They had just finished their tea. 'I could sense there was something wrong,' he explains. 'I don't know what it was but I felt that maybe they had had a row. It felt awkward.' When the boy saw Fallon at the house he was petrified. His bedroom walls were covered with blue-shirted players. If Fallon should come into his room and see them, he would surely walk straight out and that would be the end of Celtic's interest. The lad sneaked into his room and while Fallon chatted with his father he tore down the photographs of Jim Baxter and Ian McMillan, tossing them into a drawer. And with that simple gesture he ended his boyhood association with Rangers.

'I didn't say anything about signing for Celtic,' says Fallon. 'I just sat there and talked about football, this and that, the great players,

Jimmy Johnstone, Charlie Tully, Bobby Evans, even a few Rangers players, Baxter, George Young. They were clearly troubled about what the lad was going to do with his future, where he was going to work. I don't think his father was too keen on him becoming a footballer. It doesn't always work out, you know. Time went by. I didn't hurry things along.'

Mrs Dalglish made a pot of tea, the two men chatted, and the youngster hovered. Fallon needed to be sure as well, to know the kind of background, his father's attitude and the depth of relationship between father and son. He quickly realised the closeness of the family, its respectability, and liked what he saw.

'I didn't feel it was right to broach the subject of signing for Celtic straightaway but eventually after about an hour and a half of all this idle chat, I finally put my cards on the table. "I wanted the boy to sign for Celtic," I told him. It took me two hours, but I finally got the father's agreement. He could join Celtic.'

Mrs Fallon was furious. She had been sitting in the car the whole time with three wailing bairns. They were starving, she was hungry and it wasn't exactly warm either. The spring day had turned into a chilly evening and the best part of it was now gone. Their wedding anniversary was ruined. When her husband returned she hit the roof.

'I want to go home,' she shouted. There was little Fallon could say to appease her and they hardly spoke the rest of the evening. She just asked one question later that night. 'What's the lad's name?'

'Kenny Dalglish,' replied Fallon.

'He'd better be worth it,' she muttered.

from DALGLISH *1992*

Goodbye, Mr Lucky

WILLIAM LEITH

The door is open. I turn in from the pavement, put my foot on the first step.

'Hey! Who are you?' A man is moving towards me from a car parked on the kerb.

'What are you doing?'

'I've come to see Gary Lineker.'

'There's a film crew in there at the moment. We're making a documentary . . .'

The place is crawling with media. Well, what do you expect? This is the house of the man who, in a way, represents football. The football world needs him to feed to the media; he is its best asset, the main attraction for potential sponsors; he and his wife Michelle are practically public property. When their son George was born last year, they got the front page of the *Sun*. When the boy fell ill with acute myeloid leukaemia, it was a national tragedy. And when George's condition stabilised, Gary Lineker did the only thing he could have done, under the circumstances – he called a press conference. Now he's preparing to play for England in the European Championship in Sweden, his last appearance in the national colours; after that, he will become the first British footballer to join a Japanese team, on a two-year contract that will take him to retirement. So naturally his house is crawling with media.

But I have an appointment, so I walk up the steps, through the door, into the hallway. The hall! It's extraordinary. It is lined with trophies, plaques, medals, football boots sculpted in metal and mounted on plinths, models of little men kicking balls. These are the prizes Lineker has won for doing something which, in the world of football, is highly specialised and utterly revered – scoring goals. This is Lineker's talent, the thing that has taken him from the Leicester City reserve team to here, the lovely house, the swarming media. It's the thing he does. At an average of 0.62 goals a game, one every 2½ hours of playing time. Nobody does it more.

Gary is in the garden, taking a walk across the lawn with his old friend, the snooker player Willie Thorne, the two of them walking abreast, heads close together, eyebrows raised. But he's not really walking across his lawn talking to Willie Thorne; he's pretending to a walk across the lawn talking to Willie Thorne.

'All right, cut. That's fine. We'll just do one more of these.' The director stands back. Lineker walks straight over, shakes my hand. He says 'Sorry. We're just finishing off this thing – it's a documentary about friendship.' As he says it, his voice is quiet, without much expression, but his eyes are rolling all over the place, as if he's trapped in a persona and is anxious to communicate the fact. 'Hang around if you like,' he says.

*   *   *

The year is 1979. Gary Lineker, 18-year-old Leicester City winger, who has a good turn of speed but who keeps falling over when he gets the ball, arranges an appointment with Jon Holmes, a financial adviser based in Leicester who is already advising two England foot-ballers, Peter Shilton and Tony Woodcock, and the future England cricket captain, David Gower. Holmes says: 'He came to see me because he thought he wanted some advice. He hardly said a word. He brought his team-mate Andy Peake with him, and Andy did all the talking.' How much was Lineker on? 'About fifteen grand a year, maybe not as much – maybe ten. Not very much.'

Holmes became Lineker's agent, at first on a casual basis, then more formally. 'He was really, really ambitious,' says Holmes. '*Extremely* shy. But he wanted to get on, and this is what he did about it, aged eighteen.' Holmes, who has since flourished as a sports agent, has advised Lineker for every step of his career, and now also represents his international colleagues, John Barnes and Neil Webb, and Will Carling, the present England rugby captain.

But it was taking a while for Lineker to shine at Leicester. 'His first touch wasn't so good,' says Gordon Milne, then Leicester's manager. 'He'd try to turn, and he'd fall – playing with his back to goal wasn't his style.'

Terry Shipman, Leicester City's chairman, says: 'When Gary first came to the club, he looked all right, but he didn't look as if he was going to make a first-class footballer.'

'He isn't a naturally gifted player like Cruyff – he's picked up his skills on the way,' says Steve Humphries, who was an apprentice goalkeeper at Leicester with Lineker at the age of sixteen. 'Gary learned from his education with Everton, Barcelona, Tottenham and England, and he's been very astute off the field.'

So when did the Gary Lineker that everybody knows emerge? Not until several years later. He was an apprentice, a lad in the reserves, a dodgy first-team youngster. But he kept trying, kept plugging away. He was at Leicester for eight years; it was only in the last three that he began to do his stuff, averaging more than twenty goals a season. He was a late developer. 'And that was good for him, in a way,' says Jon Holmes. 'He didn't get too much too soon, like some of them do. He could handle everything as it came up.'

That's one of the main things about Lineker. He isn't an impulsive, creative genius like Paul Gascoigne or George Best, men who are always being surprised by their own genius, whose brilliance is linked to the fact that they can't control themselves. Lineker is a worker, a tryer. I asked him if he ever felt inspired when he was playing, and he looked at me quizzically again, and talked about sometimes not being inspired, but plugging away, getting through it. 'What it's all about when you're playing,' he said, 'is keeping control of yourself.'

He'd been born in Leicester in November 1961, the son of a market trader. His mother, Marie Lineker, says: 'It was Gary's ambition from five to make the grade at football – there was never any other work. Mind you, it's a good job there wasn't because Gary's good with his feet, but not so good with his hands.'

At fourteen, two years before he joined Leicester City, Gary's end-of-year school report at City Boys, his Leicester comprehensive, read: 'His work has shown energy, intelligence, and control. One of the clear leaders in this group. He must keep aiming high, and not rest on these laurels. Overall these reports indicate his approach to academic work is handicapped by excessive juvenility. It is time he worked out seriously his objectives in life.'

He did. Gary wanted to be a footballer, to play for the youth team, for the first team, for the national team. 'He was a lot more ambitious than people realise,' Holmes says. 'He wanted to know how things worked, how he could get on. When he realised I looked after David Gower, he was fascinated – he'd ask me how I did this, how I did that. How did we handle the press, that sort of thing. I remember I once introduced him to a TV producer – you should have seen him. He was riveted to what this guy was saying. He wanted to know everything – talking to camera, sound, lighting. He knew what it was going to take.'

When he was twenty-four and still living at home, Lineker discussed with Holmes the possibility that he might move to a bigger club. He'd already played, and scored, a few times for England, but his international place was far from secure; he was competing with some older players – Trevor Francis, Tony Woodcock, Paul Mariner – and two other strikers, Lineker's peers, were breathing down his neck: Kerry Dixon of Chelsea and Peter Davenport of Nottingham Forest. Lineker wanted a transfer to a bigger club. If he stayed at Leicester City, it might hold up his career.

'It was important, if he was going to go, to go at the right time,' Holmes says. 'For one thing, this was 1985 – a World Cup season. You want to be settled throughout the whole season, not to have to move house in the middle. A few clubs were showing some interest – Liverpool, Everton, Manchester United. So we talked about it. Liverpool was a good option, but I said to Gary that it would be hard for him there, he'd have to fit in with the Liverpool style of play, he might be on the sidelines for a bit while they groomed him. And Manchester United didn't seem *quite* so keen. So we decided on Everton.

'I called Gary's dad and told him, and we all talked about it. Everton seemed the best idea.'

So the negotiations began. Howard Kendall, Everton's manager, says: 'Gordon Milne said to me: "You don't know how good a player you're getting." Jon Holmes said to me: "You know about his disciplinary record, don't you?" I immediately thought, "Oh, no, he must have been booked several times; he'll miss the start of the season." Jon told me that, on the contrary, he'd never been booked. And that gave me even more concern. I thought: "Is there a doubt in terms of his character – is it that he's not passionate enough, not aggressive enough?" But it's just that he's got that nature, he's that type of person.'

Lineker still hasn't been booked or sent off the field, for club or country. David Elleray, a senior referee, says: 'He has a great skill of keeping out of trouble, when trouble is going on. He just doesn't get involved. He neither provokes nor reacts; rather like a British diplomat, I'd say. He's got a very stable temperament. He's worked out that dissent doesn't do any good.'

Lineker's move to Everton, for a fee of £800,000 was a huge success. He moved from his father's house to a converted barn in Southport, doubled his salary from around £35,000 to around £70,000, and scored forty goals, including one in the FA Cup final. And then, at the end of the 1985–86 season, Barcelona, the richest club in football, made a bid of £2.4m for him. Lineker wanted to go – the Spanish league is, after Italy, the most glamorous and cosmopolitan in the world. Playing in Spain would sharpen him up for international football. So he signed, and flew out to Mexico to play for England in the World Cup.

He'd had a poor run, not scoring in four matches, and didn't get a goal in the first two World Cup matches. For the third and final qualifying game, England were to play Poland. England needed to win to stay in the competition. As it turned out, he played the match of his life.

He scored a hat-trick, and all three goals were typical of him. They were a poacher's goals, goals that really shouldn't have happened. For the first, a team-mate put the ball right across the face of the goal; Lineker, with an astonishing burst of speed, got a few inches ahead of the defender, stuck out his leg, and turned it in. For the second, a hopeful pass came into the penalty box from deep on the left; Lineker who had two men between him and the ball, squeezed himself between them and made contact with the ball at the last possible moment. The third was a goalkeeper's fumble; he fluffed the catch from a cross and Lineker, waiting behind him, took advantage.

This is what Linker does. He waits, as near to the opposition's goal as he can get without being offside. Then, when his team are attacking, he makes a sudden darting run, trying to lose the defender who has been assigned the task of staying as close as possible to him. Lineker doesn't run for the ball – he runs for a space. Then he hopes the ball will come to him.

Terry Butcher, also an ex-England team-mate, and a defender who has marked Lineker at club level, says: 'He's like a spider, dragging you into the wrong position. It's the mental awareness that makes the difference – he's so sharp. He's got his back to goal, and you're behind him, and he gets you to think that he's about to receive a pass, gives a little run, so you move forward, towards him, then the pass will come, a split-second later, and he'll have spun into the space you've just left. He knows *exactly* where his opponent is.'

It was playing for Barcelona among the tight defences of the Spanish league that changed Lineker's playing style; and it was here that he sharpened up his other asset – his friendly relationship with the media. Of life in the Spanish league, his former Barcelona team-mate Mark Hughes, now with Manchester United says: 'I tried to get the better of them physically, which was probably the wrong way to go about it, whereas Gary would try to do it with a bit of guile.' Off the pitch, Lineker learned Spanish; in a few months he was giving TV interviews in the language.

After two seasons, Lineker came back to England to play for Tottenham under Terry Venables, the manager who had taken him to Barcelona. And now, after three successful seasons in north London, he is going to Japan. 'It's the perfect way to end,' says Jon Holmes. 'The European Championship, and then Japan. Japan is a really strong financial deal. It's a hell of a lot more money than he was getting at Tottenham.'

*   *   *

Gary Lineker, sitting on his pristine sofa, wears a short-sleeved shirt with a button-down collar, grey trousers, black shoes with a buckle. He's always been the best-dressed of footballers, only a tiny bit flash, colours co-ordinated, nothing too outrageous. You should see what the England squad looks like in the check-in queue at Luton airport. Some, like John Barnes, wear the most expensive designer stuff they can find. Others, like Alan Shearer, tipped as the next Lineker, haven't been dressing up for very long – the shirt doesn't quite go, the shoes are scuffed. Lineker, by contrast, always looks comfortable.

Some of the others, particularly the younger ones, cruise around him, hoping for a quick word, or just hoping to be seen passing the time with him. They want to be like him; in other words, they want to be unlike footballers. And they all speak of him with the sheerest admiration. Peter Beardsley, his favourite partner at international level, says: 'He's a gentleman; he knows how to handle life; he knows what he wants. He's such a clever person – he looks immaculate every time you see him. Most people would like to be in his position.'

Lineker says: 'It's so difficult for footballers to look good to the media. Imagine what's happening – you're coming off the pitch, after a match. You're not thinking in words, you're totally taken up with how you feel about the match. People are all around you, saying things – you're reacting, looking at them. Then someone pushes a microphone in front of you. It's difficult to be coherent.'

'How come you're more coherent than the others?'

'I've learned to avoid the traps. Remember, I've had a lot of practice. The traps are the clichés – "over the moon" and so on. I mean, if a politician said he was over the moon, nobody would notice. But a footballer would get slaughtered. You just have to say what you want to say; ignore the question.'

'What's the worst thing about British football?'

'They make you play twice a week. It's too much. In Spain or Italy, you play once a week, so the match feels like a big occasion, and the club can charge more. Also, the players are fit, they give 100 per cent. Here, you can't do that. It's the wear and tear on the joints.'

'Do you feel old?'

'Well, I'm not like I was. I can still do it, but it's beginning to wear me out. I can't do anything the next day – I hurt all over, I'm stiff. I used to be able to play two games in two days. I couldn't do that now. I don't mind getting kicked so much. You can run that off. But after a game, I'm *so* tired, just stiff everywhere, I hurt everywhere. So I can still do it, but I'm . . . on the brink.'

Lineker smiles again, rolls his eyes around in his head again. Gordon Milne, his first manager, told me that he's met Lineker recently for the first time in a long while. 'He's just the same as he was when he was a lad,' Milne said. 'Just the same straightforward lad. All this hasn't changed him, you know. There's still no edge to his character.'

Lineker says: 'My life's been incredible, it really has. I've been very lucky. Each step on the ladder, each step I've taken, it's been incredible – being an apprentice, getting in the reserve team . . . all the way up to international level. All these things I've desperately wanted to happen, but I never thought they would.'

'Did you never feel worried, then, that you'd be like a lot of other footballers, who have short careers and end up with nothing?'

'No. Because you always have some sort of belief in yourself, or at least hope. Some part of you believes things will work out.'

They didn't work out two Sundays ago, in Lineker's final Wembley appearance for England, when he took a penalty against Brazil, needing one goal to equal Bobby Charlton's England record. What a way to go out! He stepped back from the ball, took four paces towards it, and . . . not the usual Lineker penalty, hit smartly to the goalkeeper's right, rising five feet off the ground. Lineker stubbed his toe, miskicking the ball almost straight at the goalkeeper. For the first time he looked as if he was struggling, older than the rest of the lads, a little heavier, his face a little less alert, his mind drifting.

'This has never happened to me before,' he says. 'I changed my mind during the run-up. I was going to kick it one way, and the goalkeeper moved. So I changed my mind . . .'

'Gary, can I have you now?' It's the TV director, who has been in the garden the whole time. Lineker sees me to the door, smiles, rolls his eyes, pulls his tie-knot a little tighter, and walks away, keen to pursue his new career.

from the INDEPENDENT ON SUNDAY *May 1992*

Roger Milla

JOE LOVEJOY

The indomitable Lions of Cameroon are fondly remembered for brightening a grey World Cup with what grateful hosts called a touch of fantasy, but dreams are essentially ephemeral, impossible to recapture, and we should not expect too much tonight when they become the first African team to visit Wembley.

Since that memorable quarter-final in Naples, when they turned Bobby Robson into Dorian Gray, it has been bad luck and trouble all the way. The manager and his boss, the president of the football federation, went, and morale went, too – destroyed by endless bickering over World Cup bonuses and a run of five games without a win.

Lions? Beaten 6–1 by Norway and 2–1 by the Congo, and able only to draw with Mali, Sierra Leone and Botswana, they arrive more like lambs to the slaughter.

For the Great Corinthians of Italia '90, the magic went out of the window when money came through the dressing-room door. Or rather didn't. Part-timers picking up £150 a week at home found their heads turning like something out of *The Exorcist* when told that they had earned their country £1.5m in less than four weeks. When the Lions' share wasn't, there was mutiny in the air. Strike action was threatened before bonus payments of up to £55,000 per man were finally agreed on 29 December.

When the money became available, so did the players. Seventeen of the eighteen on parade tonight are World Cup thoroughbreds. For the goalless draw at home to Mali, the figure was just one.

All is now sweetness and light? Not exactly. The manager in Italy, Valeri Nepomniachi, returned whence he came, to the Soviet Union, to be replaced four weeks ago by a Frenchman of modest attainment. Philippe Redon, 40, who had coached three French second-division teams, is said to owe his appointment to the ubiquitous Roger Milla, with whom he played at St Etienne.

Old Snakehips, just back from an ambassadorial trip to China and Japan with a Cameroon trade delegation, enjoys enormous influence in government circles, and was instrumental in the selection of a manager just one year his senior.

In return, Redon indulges his mentor's every whim. Milla plays no club football, trains when he likes and had no sooner arrived in London than he was threatening to fly out again, to collect yet another award, in Spain. These days, he refuses to discuss his age ('It doesn't matter. How old was your Stanley Matthews when he retired?') and says the World Cup was no big deal. 'I was already an international superstar before that. It was just that the Europeans didn't recognise it.'

He is certainly acting the part, demanding £50,000 appearance money to play at Wembley, jibbing at the fee for appearing on Monday's *Wogan* and turning his back on photographers at the team's photocall.

The captain, Stephen Tataw, was more accommodating, but then he had reason to be. Left behind in the mercenary exodus, he wants a piece of the action in Europe.

The powerfully built full-back is still bemused by an eleven-day trial he had with Queen's Park Rangers in October. 'The manager, I forget his name [Don Howe], said I was good – excellent – but he was full up. I was a right-back and he did not need one. Why did he not tell me this before I came? Ask him. I was excellent. Maybe if I play well against England there will be another chance.'

Tataw earns £60 per week from football and another £100 from a sinecure with Cameroon television, but it is not only for financial reasons that he wants out of Africa. His club, Tonnerre of Yaounde, play on a baked-earth pitch in a stadium which has no showers or dressing-rooms. Players change either in cars or preserve their modesty in the long grass behind the goals. Conditions in Cameroon are primitive, with no decent facilities for internationals, let alone young boys learning the game.

'I started in exactly the same way as everyone else,' Milla says. 'By kicking a ball around the streets. And when I say a ball, sometimes it was a stone wrapped in banana leaves, or even a grapefruit or a pineapple wrapped in rags. It gives you an advantage when you come to play with a real ball. It seems easier to control.'

Michel Kaham, a member of the Cameroon World Cup team in 1982, and their coach in Italy, believes the lack of decent pitches at home cost them dear last summer. Poor defensive technique got them into trouble time and again – decisively against England, when two unnecessary penalties enabled Gary Lineker to prise victory from the Lions' jaws.

'Our tackling cost us the game,' Kaham said. 'In Africa we play on hard-baked pitches, and nobody likes to tackle. On your soft grass it is easier to tackle, so you are better at it.'

The visitors have other difficulties to overcome tonight. 'Our season at home has only just started, and it is 32 degrees. I mean the right degrees. Your cold weather is a big problem for us. In Cameroon, the temperature only gets as low as 15.'

We have been warned. Do not expect too much of the Lion in winter.

from the INDEPENDENT *1991*

Stanley Matthews

J. P. W. MALLALIEU

His name has become a magic which for the moment can still a child or stir an old man, which even on the bitterest day can draw nearly all of us from our firesides.

Yet there is nothing remarkable about him. There is no oddity about his dress, except perhaps that the laces in his boots look new and always are new – for Matthews' feet and Matthews' boots must be as one, and new laces play a part in ensuring that end. Otherwise you'll notice only that as he comes on the field his head is not down contemplatively but forward expectantly. No, there is nothing striking about Matthews. Yet on Saturday, when the Bolton and Blackpool teams emerged side by side from the dressing-room tunnel, one hundred thousand pairs of eyes looked mainly at him, and there he was, fifth – or was it sixth? – in the Blackpool line, coming bump, bump, bump, leaden-footed on to that springy turf, shoulders bent and head forward, like a porter already feeling the load of baggage he has been sent to carry.

Why does the whole football world and many outside that world look for Matthews whenever he plays?

Have you ever watched a lizard suddenly shoot his tongue at an insect? I have watched many times while Matthews has stood motionless with the ball at his feet and facing a barrier of opponents. Then suddenly there has been a stab from his foot quicker than a lizard's tongue and the ball has shot through some unimagined space between the forest of legs. Have you ever watched a dragon-fly, how it hovers in one spot with its wings vibrating and then apparently, without changing gear, darts away at top speed? Many times I have seen Matthews, the ball as ever at his feet, hemmed in by a watchful opponent. There has been no room to move so Matthews has hovered, his whole body vibrating, while his opponent watched. Suddenly Matthews has made his dart to the right, and his opponent has darted with him. It is only seconds later that we and his opponent see that Matthews has in fact darted to the left. Have you ever watched a racehorse lope along until at a touch from his jockey he streaks away from the field? Time and again I have seen Matthews loping down the wing, apparently no more conscious of the ball he is dribbling than of the boot he is wearing. His head is up now, looking for a friend in position, watching the swarm of opponents scurrying back to bar his path. Suddenly, just when the circle of opponents seems to be closing, Matthews has tapped the ball with the outside of his foot, shot through whatever gap remained at a speed MacDonald Bailey would envy and placed his centre with an accuracy which would do credit to Joe Davis. But I have never once seen him lose his temper, or be anything but gracious. Full-backs who have floundered before his dancing feet, half-backs who have been sent the wrong way throughout the game, goalkeepers who have been mesmerised into immobility will tell you after the game that Matthews is the greatest footballer they have ever tried to face. They'll say of him: 'If we go into the tackle, he shoots the ball between our legs. If we hem him in he catches us on the wrong foot, and he's in the goal-mouth before we can pull our foot out of the ground. If we hang back and give him room, he runs round us or centres over our heads. The only way to stop Matthews is to puncture the ball.' Above all, they will add, of this man who makes them look foolish every five minutes, 'He's a gent, is Stanley.' It is no wonder that crowds love him; but it really is surprising that his fellow players love him too.

This then is the man that nearly 100,000 spectators went to see last Saturday. What in fact we saw was not merely the greatest footballer of all time playing at the peak of his form. We saw the greatest footballer, suddenly and almost visibly, begin to glow with genius almost as if a hand had come from the skies and touched his shoulder. This was how it happened.

At half-time, despite injuries, Bolton were leading 2–1. They were the better team. Ten minutes after half-time Bolton made it 3–1, and when, four minutes later, Matthews put a centre slowly along the ground, across an open goal and two Blackpool forwards, one after the other, missed it we felt that the match was over. How could a team, two goals behind, recover from such an appalling miss? But with twenty-two minutes left, Matthews sent over a high centre which spun towards the top far corner of the net. The Bolton goalkeeper could only scrape it with his fingers, and Mortensen, touching it with his head, had it safely home. 3–2. Then Matthews felt the touch. Before he had beaten opponents sometimes by craft, sometimes by speed. From now on he beat them by craft and speed brilliantly combined in the same movement. He sought the ball everywhere, now in the centre, now on the left wing, now back on his own right wing, and every time the ball touched his toe at least 80,000 spectators screamed in high-pitched expectancy. Twice he cut perfect openings, and twice more his colleagues failed him while the minutes ticked by. Then, three minutes from time, Mortensen took a free-kick just outside the penalty area and, unbelievably, slammed the ball home. 3–3. Three minutes to go, not a seat at Wembley in use and a roar unbroken. With thirty seconds to go, near the half-way line, Taylor passed to Matthews and Matthews passed it back. Taylor at once sent it through to the right, and while the defenders turned Matthews swerved inside. Another defender hurled himself in the way. Matthews cut outside him and went at great speed to the goal-line. Two yards from there and still at top speed, he pivoted on his left foot and with his right sent back a diagonal centre; and while the Bolton defence were still jerking their heads from left to right, Perry put this centre into the net and the world exploded.

from SPORTING DAYS *1955*

Pelé

DAVID MILLER

The brown eyes are dreamy under heavy lids. Like a lion asleep in the sun, he has that total relaxation that characterises every great Negro athlete. In blue woollen sports shirt and pale grey slacks, a mere five foot eight, you would never guess he possessed the power once to have scored a goal from the half-way line. It is only out on the field that those limbs become poetry in motion.

This is Pelé, pride of Brazil and a budding dollar millionaire at twenty-five. There have been other players who either could run faster, were stronger, possessed such body swerve (though that is doubtful), or could shoot or head as hard. But never have so many qualities been combined in one man. In the Maracana National Stadium in Rio a plaque commemorates the day he dribbled the length of the field through the entire opposition to score a goal. He is the only player ever with the timing and finesse consistently to draw his man and at the last moment pass the ball *between* his opponent's legs. Regularly he deceives them by deliberately kicking the ball against their shins and then sweeping by on the rebound faster than the eye can follow.

When he takes penalty kicks, the speculation is not whether he will score but where he will put the ball. Often the goalkeeper dives in the opposite direction to the ball. Even under pressure, when other players would be doing well to get in a shot, Pelé can feign a first shot and then a split second later put the ball the other way. The left foot is as devastating as the right.

In an era of excessively defensive football, dominated increasingly by tactics, less and less by individuals, Pelé remains the supreme attacking individualist, the greatest crowd-puller the game has known. Over 100,000, the biggest attendance of the year, flooded into the Bernabeu Stadium in Madrid last Tuesday for the friendly match against Atletico FC, and were rewarded by seeing Pelé score three goals and make two others. When he puts his mind to it, he is untouchable.

Yet now, at the peak of his fame, he is already thinking of retirement. After nearly 1,000 games in ten years, he has had enough, though he would normally expect to have at least two more World Cup competitions – eight more years at the toughest top – ahead of him. I talked at length to Pelé last week in Madrid, where Brazil were completing their preparations for their defence of the World Cup, which begins in Liverpool, against Bulgaria, on 12 July. His startling news came out in the most casual way, without any fuss, for Pelé is the most modest and humble of men, not given to self-dramatisation.

Knowing the strain he has experienced recently, with over 100 matches a season for his club, Santos, and the national team, I asked how long he might stay in the game, expecting no more than a conventional reply. The swiftness of the answer suggested it was something he had thought much about.

'Perhaps, if I'm able, I might stay another two or three years, until I am twenty-eight. For me there can be no greater experience than the World Cup in England, the home of the game. Whether we win or not, there can be nothing left to achieve. I have no reason to want to play anywhere else after England. It was a terrible disappointment to me when my club prevented me playing for the Rest of the World in your Centenary match in 1963. My only ambition now is to win, if we can, next month at Wembley.

'Maybe, if I was needed badly, I might play in the World Cup in Mexico in 1970, but I don't think so. I would like soon to play just now and then for an amateur club. I want more time with my family. Playing is not the problem, it is the travelling. I can't remember when I last spent a whole week with my family. My honeymoon in Europe a few months ago was the first holiday I've ever had. The only time I get days off is if I'm injured. Slowly, I will drop out of the game, spending more time on my businesses. Not that money is any problem, but I must still have some occupation.'

This news will come as a revelation to Brazilian football followers, for as Pelé has risen to fame, so has the national team. When Brazil went to Sweden for the World Cup in 1958 Pelé had played only five international matches. He helped to carry them to victory in the final with a goal of breathtaking brilliance and impudence.

Pelé was born Edson Arantes do Nascimento of humble parents in the small town of Bauru. 'My father was a professional with the Atletico team of Minas Gerais. Until I was ten I used to play with the other boys barefoot in the streets, often using a bunch of woollen rags for a ball. At eleven, I had my first pair of boots, and Valdemar de Brito, the old international and a friend of my father and trainer at the Bauru club, took me along to play for them. I stayed as a junior with the club for four years. I can't remember learning anything special, except that Valdemar impressed on me the importance of being really fit. These days, my weight goes up when I'm in training, and down only when I am not playing, so finely balanced is my fitness. When I was fifteen, Valdemar took me to join the famous Santos club, which meant I had to leave school and my apprenticeship as a shoemaker.'

Up to then, as far as he was aware, Pelé had done nothing special. When did he first realise that he was a remarkable player? 'I had been with Santos about nine months, and was still sixteen. They told me I had been chosen to play for Brazil. I thought to myself: "Well, you *must* be good."'

from THE SPORTS WRITER'S EYE *1989*

Tommy Lawton

JOHN MOYNIHAN

We used to wait for him in the car park at Stamford Bridge. Greasy schoolboys with greasy autograph books. The crowds came through the turnstiles fanning out towards the terraces and we got buffeted if we got in the way.

Near the club offices was the players' entrance and we got as close to the mouth as the on-duty official would allow. 'Go away, sonny. Move on, sonny. Come on lad.'

Half an hour before the kick-off the players would drift in and we would pounce on them saying: 'Please Mr Goulden. Sign Mr Walker. Please Mr Harris.' They came in with friends, wearing long overcoats and scarves, their hair well oiled and pulled back over their ears. Tommy Walker, the pre-war Scottish international inside-right and described, not inappropriately, as 'the first gentleman of football' was the kindest. He was not a tall man and we could crane up near his face and he would smile hugely and sign all our books.

Len Goulden, the other inside forward, who had played for West Ham and England before the war, was brisk and forthcoming but he signed our books as he strode towards the dressing-room under the main stand talking to his friends as he walked in broad cockney, his hair parted in a thin line down the middle. John Harris was equally kind, a small smile on the edges of his mouth, a mild Scottish purr. 'Quick son. Kick-off's soon.'

They were our gods, they and the goalkeeper Harry Medhurst, the present Chelsea trainer, who bounded into the ground like a small ostrich. Harry still shows that bounding walk as he leaves the pitch after treating an injury.

The Chelsea footballers were not dandies in those days. They dressed as well as they could afford on £12-a-week maximum, which came into effect early in 1947, long overcoats with slightly spivvy shoulders, polished, solid shoes and gaudy ties.

We waited for them and for visiting players, especially if they were Stanley Matthews of Stoke, or Tom Finney of Preston, or Billy Wright of Wolves, or Stanley Mortensen of Blackpool, or Billy Steel of Derby County, men in slightly crumpled, double-breasted pin-striped suits with splashy ties that gangsters wore in Hollywood films.

But in the winter of 1946 we waited most of all for Tom Lawton, the hero of Chelsea and Stamford Bridge, and indeed, of all England.

Tom was the great professional, the goal getter, the towering athlete with the elastic head in the number nine shirt. He was unmistakable on the field, shoulders slightly uncloaked, his hair greased back into a solid flattened, blob of black, his long legs dangling across the pitch, his arms flung out to take a tackle, his cheeks puffed out when he unleashed a shot. At the players' entrance we always waited for Tom.

He would come swinging through the entrance, a towering figure to those of us who had only achieved half of our ultimate height. Tall, strong, his craggy Lancashire face jutting forward slightly, his long overcoat hanging down near his ankles and done up untidily with a loose, flapping belt, his hair soaking with oil so that the central parting stood out like the lane of a city highway.

Around Tom Lawton came the hangers on. I remember them in the cold weather with their neat trilbies and demob raincoats, and in the spring with wide pin-stripe suits, usually brown. and shirts with no ties with the white collars outside the jacket collars. Perhaps Tom knew them or perhaps he didn't. But they followed him devotedly in packs, one or two of them chewing matchsticks from a corner of their mouths.

Tom soared forward and we tried to stop him but he moved on gangling above us to look in on the way to the dressing-rooms at the Chelsea offices. He would come out after a few minutes and the pack would move off, the hangers on lounging at his side saying: 'Good luck, Tom', 'Bang two in, Tom'. And we would go along also, but smaller and less obvious, until we lounged into the centre-forward's belly, bearing our books.

'Please Mr Lawton. Sign Mr Lawton. Oh, please Tommy.'

Mr Lawton was usually in a hurry. Although he was my hero and I dreamt of him, I never found him a sympathetic character in those days when he was a football warrior of England. I never got his autograph and rarely saw him sign one for the kids. The odd one perhaps. But he didn't make a habit of it. He pushed me aside once and wouldn't sign. 'I'm in a hurry, son,' he said in broad Bolton.

Tom Lawton may have had his reasons for seeming morose. In 1946 and 1947 he was playing for Chelsea but the side was not particularly distinguished; particularly on the wings and at wing-half; Dickie Spence was in the veteran stage on the right-wing and there was virtually no left-winger to speak of: Dolding, Paton, ran themselves into the ground but they lacked class. Chelsea's saving strength lay at inside-forward where Tom Lawton had Len Goulden and Tom Walker working to make him goals, and at centre-half where John Harris, the captain, was calmly efficient.

The Chelsea side under the secretary and managership of Mr William Birrell hovered round the middle of the table that season although Tom Lawton broke the club's goal-scoring record with twenty-six goals. What was evident was that he had incredible drawing power. The crowds, starved after five years of war, flocked to Stamford Bridge to watch the resumption of Football League soccer.

Lawton was a moody player at that time, often staying sulkily out of the game for long periods but when he did respond the effect was devastating. There would be a huge bulge in the opposition's net and Lawton would stride away with a shrug of pleasure.

The vast, open slug of a main terrace at Stamford Bridge was usually spread like a ham sandwich with humanity when Tom Lawton was on Chelsea's books. Entertainment was restricted, apart from the cinema, and soccer was one of the few attractions available. Tom Lawton playing down the Fulham Road provided one of the few pin-ups of a jaded metropolis. That soccer had lost none of its pulling power because of the war had been proved a year before at Stamford Bridge when the Moscow Dynamos attracted over 82,000 people to the ground and many more who struggled over the barriers and stood on the roof of the main stand.

Lawton had scored an exquisite goal that day in a 3–3 draw and the London crowd had taken an instant delight in the appearance of the centre-forward who had taken over from Dixie Dean at Everton before the war and lived up to the great man's reputation as a killer inside an opponent's penalty-box.

from THE SOCCER SYNDROME *1966*

Horatio Carter

MICHAEL PARKINSON

Great inside-forwards, like blissful marriages, are made in heaven. They are fashioned out of gold and sent on earth to win football matches and weave the stuff that memories are made of. Their deeds are branded on the mind. They are the architects who design a game, the artists who adorn it. Wingmen are more spectacular, centre-halves more pugnacious, goalkeepers more idiosyncratic, but inside-forwards, like leg-spin bowlers, are the connoisseur's delight.

My first clear memory of football is of a great inside-forward at work. His name was Horatio Carter and I don't know how old I was when I first laid eyes on him, but I do remember that it was in the days when he played with Sunderland and he came to Barnsley and I stood on a tin can to see over the heads of the spectators in front of me. He strode alone on to the field some time after the other players, as if disdaining their company, as if to underline that his special qualities were worthy of a separate entrance. The Barnsley fans gave him the sort of reception they reserved for visiting dignitaries. You know the sort of thing: 'Big 'ead' and 'Get your bleedin' hair cut, Sybil'.

He treated the crowd and the game with a massive disdain, as if the whole affair was far beneath his dignity. He showed only one speck of interest in the proceedings, but it was decisive. The scores were level with only a few minutes to go when Carter, about thirty yards from the Barnsley goal and with his back to it, received a fast, wild cross. He killed it in mid-air with his right foot and as it dropped spun round and hit an alarming left-foot volley into the roof of the Barnsley goal. At least after he was seen to kick the ball it was seen to appear in the net, but no one on the ground, least of all the Barnsley goalkeeper, could say just how it arrived there. Carter didn't wait to see where the ball went. He knew. He continued his spin through 180 degrees and strolled back to the half-way line as if nothing had happened. Normally the Barnsley crowd greeted any goal by the opposition with a loud silence, but as Carter reached the half-way line a rare thing happened. Someone shouted: 'I wish we'd got eleven like thee, Carter lad.' The great player allowed himself a thin smile, as well he might, for he never received a greater accolade than that. In the following years I saw him whenever I could, first with Derby County, where with Peter Doherty he made up the most attractive and deadly pair of inside-forwards possessed by any club side in post-war England. Then in his later years I watched him give his spectacular one-man show with Hull City. The sight of one man conducting the fortunes of his team is the most warming spectacle in football. It's an heroic situation in which the individual takes on the awesome-qualities of the silent stranger in the cowboy film, the man who rides slowly into town and plugs all the baddies. Carter's performance at Hull contained all the heroic qualities but they were embellished by the man's sense of showmanship. During the course of his demonstrations of the art of football to the citizens of Hull, Carter took all the corners, all the free kicks, all the throw-ins, and, of course, all the penalties. Such was his domination that when one arrived at the ground one half expected to see Carter at the turnstile taking the gate money.

from FOOTBALL DAFT *1968*

Skinner Normanton

MICHAEL PARKINSON

Normanton, I suppose, personified Barnsley's cup-fighting qualities. He was tough, tireless, aggressive, with a tackle as swift and spectacular as summer lightning. In the family tree of football his grandfather was Will Copping, his godson is Nobby Stiles. And just in case anyone is still uncertain about what kind of player he was, he could claim a distant link with Rocky Marciano. He was a miner and built like one. Billiard-table legs and a chest like the front of a coal barge. He was so fearsome that there are those who will tell you that naughty children in and around Barnsley were warned by their parents: 'If you don't be good we'll send for Skinner.'

The other legend about him, probably equally true, was that certain inside-forwards of delicate constitution were known to develop nervous rashes and mysterious stomach disorders when faced with the prospect of a Saturday afternoon's sport with Skinner in opposition.

Cup-ties were his speciality, inside-forwards with international reputations were his meat. He clinched one game for Barnsley in a manner all his very own. There was about ten minutes to go, the scores level, and Barnsley were awarded a penalty. The inside-forward placed the ball on the spot and as he turned to walk back Skinner, from the half-way line, set off running. The inside-forward, ready to turn to take the kick, saw Skinner approaching like an odds-on favourite and wisely stepped aside. From that moment the grey, dour ground was lit with the purple and gold of pure fantasy. Without slackening speed Skinner kicked the ball with his toe-end. And, as he did, many things happened: the bar started shaking and humming, the goalkeeper fell to his face stunned and the ball appeared magically in the back of the net. What in fact had happened was that Skinner's shot had struck the underside of the crossbar, rebounded on to the back of the goal-keeper's neck, flattened him and ricocheted into the goal.

Barnsley, by virtue of Skinner's genius in scoring with the penalty and at the same time reducing the opponents to ten men, won the game.

It was soon after, though, that Skinner for the first and last time met his match. Again it was a cup-tie and this time Barnsley were playing Arsenal at Highbury. Going down on the train with the crates of light ale under the seat, we agreed that if Skinner could frighten them Barnsley had a chance. But we didn't know that Arsenal had someone just as hard as Skinner and twice as clever. His name was Alex Forbes, and Barnsley lost. Going sadly home, we agreed with the thought that if Barnsley had Forbes they'd soon get into the first division. What we left unsaid was that they'd probably make it by default because other teams faced with the prospect of playing against a side containing both Skinner and Forbes would probably give Barnsley two points to stop at home.

Anyway, things have changed now. Skinner has retired and there's no one to take his place. The last time I saw Barnsley in a cup tie things were different. They played Manchester United at Barnsley and went down ever so politely by 0–4. United played as if they had written the modern theory of the game and Barnsley as if they'd read it backwards. There were no fights either on or off the field, Denis Law shimmered like quicksilver and scored as he pleased, and a young lad called George Best played with the instinctive joy of a genius. There was only one flash of the old fighting spirit. As Law cheekily and magically dribbled round the wing-half, stopped, showed him the ball, then beat him again, a bloke standing near us shouted, 'Tha' wouldn't have done that to Skinner, Denis.' Those who remembered smiled. But knowingly.

from FOOTBALL DAFT *1968*

Ted Drake

IVAN SHARPE

'A prize every time!', the cheapjacks shout in the market. It was like that with Drake yesterday. Every time he shot, he scored! One, two, three, four, five, six goals came his way inside an hour! Amazing. You had to pinch yourself to make sure it wasn't all a dream.

Six shots – that's all he had in this time – and six goals in succession! No need to say that these six goals from only six shots beat all records. In all my experience I have never seen anything like it. Nor has anyone else. Then close on time Drake gets a seventh to crown the performance of his career.

Marvellous from one point of view. Truly tragic from another, remembering how the Villa have poured out wealth, sparing no expense to get them out of their troubles, and with the latest Scottish international acquisitions in their defence, surrendered five goals at Manchester, and now seven at home in successive games. What a send-off for Massie! In his first two and a half hours' play for his new club Massie has seen eleven goals go into the Villa net before his colleagues have got so much as a consolation goal, and twelve in all.

For the rest of the Villa's woes in defence consult the league table. It now tells a terrible tale. The Villa must be convinced that they have done something to enrage the gods of the game, for things went wrong for them from the start.

It is a fact that they were doing most of the attacking up to the point when, thirty minutes from the start, they were in the awful position of being three goals down. That's how the teams crossed over. Then when Drake came along with a fourth goal immediately after play was resumed their plight was pitiable. They stuck it out, but what must have been in their thoughts? Team last in the table; money poured out like water for a recovery campaign; and now 1–7 down at home. One just had to sympathise with the team, who, of course, are worthy of better things – much better. But let me recite the story of Drake's day out.

Thirteen minutes: he positions himself splendidly to take a long pass up the left wing. It comes from Beasley. Drake is fortunate enough to put the ball between Griffiths's legs, and then he runs forward a few yards and shoots. He tops his drive a trifle, and the ball bounces in front of goal and beats Morton. One up.

Twenty-six minutes: Drake collects a forward pass from Bastin ten yards over the half-way line, shoulders off Griffiths and Cummings, and shoots a glorious goal – about the best I have seen this season. The way he collected that pass was wonderful. Two up.

Thirty-one minutes: slow play by Cummings on the Villa's left flank in defence lures Blair out of position. The ball is crossed to Blair's wing, and Beasley shoots. The ball strikes Blair and goes to Drake. The rebound has put Drake on-side. He accepts an open goal. 3–0 at half-time.

Forty-seven minutes: a centre falling near goal. Drake deceives Griffiths and scores a surprise goal. 4–0.

Fifty minutes: scrimmage on the corner-line. Ball passed back to Drake, who drives it home with deadly accuracy. Five up.

Fifty-five minutes: the ball bounds out of a tussle twenty yards from goal to Drake, who shoots first time and sees the ball fly home like a bullet. Six up.

Fifty-five minutes: here the Villa got a goal, a header by Palethorpe.

Eighty-seven minutes: a cross-field pass by Bastin, and Drake has an open goal. 'Seven,' says Master Drake, 'is my lucky number,' and home again the ball goes.

Poor Villa! What can one say about all this? The ball ran the Arsenal way at the start and ultimately the Villa became demoralized.

Morton in goal must have been saying most of the afternoon, 'Where did that one go?' Of a pair of unsuccessful backs, Blair was decidedly the better. Somehow Cummings never got into the game. He was so indecisive.

The Arsenal need no praise. The score speaks for itself. They were always a better-organised team, the defence being as sound as a bell. But I must add a pat on the back for Beasley, who fitted in well with Bastin and was a menace from first to last. For Drake it was a joy-day – the day of his life. His foot could do no wrong.

And what problems are left for the Aston board! Mark one of them: Allen, £10,775 centre-half, is dropped. A newcomer arrives, a man in whom the football world as a whole has faith – and here are seven goals from a centre-forward following that haul of five by the Manchester City line the week before. Ye gods!

ASTON VILLA: Morton; Blair, Cummings; Massie, Griffiths, Wood; Williams, Astley, Palethorpe, Dix, Houghton.
ARSENAL: Wilson; Male, Hapgood; Crayston, Roberts, Copping; Rogers, Bowden, Drake, Bastin, Beasley.

from the SUNDAY CHRONICLE *1935*

Armando Picchi

KENNETH WOLSTENHOLME

It was in the autumn of 1963 when Picchi first made his mark in England. He was a member of the Inter Milan side which played Everton at Goodison Park in the European Champions Cup. The result that night was a goalless draw – just how many of them have Inter Milan played? – and most people who saw the game talked of Suarez or Szymaniak (who wore no. 11 but who operated in midfield), or of the way Everton had done all the attacking without scoring. Everton fans put that fact down to bad luck, proving that not for the first time Picchi had done his job superbly without being noticed. Perhaps that was the very essence of his job . . . not to be noticed.

Picchi has become accustomed to doing his job efficiently without receiving any praise for it. In fact he is quite convinced that there are few who understood the role he had to play for Inter. Those who still cling to the old-fashioned naming of positions on the football field find it totally impossible to fit him into a slot. He wore no. 6 for Inter but never played like a left half-back. He wasn't a centre half-back, either, because he never made the slightest effort to mark the opposition's centre-forward. Nor was he a full-back because he ignored the opposing wingmen.

Armando Picchi was the first of the sweepers, or, as the Italians call them, *libero*. His job was to stay behind the main line of four backs and pick up anything which got through. He never specifically marked anyone, yet he marked everyone. He never ventured upfield. He never had a static position, yet he had all positions.

If a player got beyond the line of four backs, either by dribbling his way there or by creating space with a one-two passing movement with a colleague, he would be confronted by Picchi. Any player who ran through to pick up a long pass would be confronted by . . . Picchi. Any high lob or centre which was floated into the Inter Milan goal-mouth would be picked off by . . . Picchi. It became a feature of the Inter Milan side that whenever one of their players was beaten he didn't worry. He knew Picchi would be there.

Then suddenly the whole pack of cards collapsed in a heap. Inter Milan found themselves in the European Cup final of 1967, but under heavy pressure in the Italian league. Their route to the European final had been cruelly hard – they had had to meet the champions of such leading countries as Russia, Hungary and Spain. For the first time, Inter Milan began to feel the strain.

They got through to the final because of the superb performance of the defence and skilful counter-attacking. That meant Picchi had done a wonderful job, but, as usual, no one talked about it; no one put his name forward for an 'Oscar'.

Then came Lisbon and the 1967 final against Celtic from Glasgow. For the first time a team refused to play Inter's game. Celtic would not pump long passes into the heart of the Inter defence, or sling across high centres. They knew that Picchi would pick off every one of them. Celtic tried it the other way. They attacked in small packs with short, accurate passing. They used the individual skills of players like Johnstone to take on the Inter defenders one by one. They shot into the packed defence. And they played quickly across the field to get the defence on the wrong foot before coming through to strike.

For the first time the Inter Milan defence began to creak.

Picchi swept up like a hero, but he had so much to sweep up. The line of four backs, behind which he was supposed to operate, was pushed back until it was on his toes, cramping his style. And before the end, the rout was complete. Inter Milan were defending simply by weight of numbers. Tactics had flown out of the window.

The defeat by Celtic was followed by the failure to win the Italian Championship and defeat by a second-division club in the semi-final of the Italian Cup. The Inter Milan crash was a spectacular one.

In Italian football you live by your success. Failure means extinction.

So Helenio Herrera picked up the big axe. One neck it fell on was that of Armando Picchi. The man who had never received the credit for being such an important part of the success was the first to be blamed for the failure. He was transferred to Varese.

He wasn't bitter, although you could not have blamed him if he had been. He just smiled and said, 'When things go right it is always Herrera's brilliant planning. When things go wrong, it is always the players who are to blame.'

But Picchi's sacking by Inter Milan will never erase the fact that Armando Picchi is one of the greatest defenders we have ever seen. He will go down in soccer history as the first – and the best – of the sweepers.

from THE PROS *1968*

Maradona

IAN WOOLDRIDGE

For a gasping and unworthy moment here yesterday I felt that England's footballers might storm on towards the World Cup final on the strength of a tragic act of fate.

As the little bull-like figure came bustling round a corner – pursued by a running horde of reporters and about to be ambushed by an encircling wall of cameramen – he trapped his right leg in a heavy metal spool used for storing hoses.

For an eye's blink he began to fall. But then the phenomenal balance that is the secret of his artistry saved him. He recovered and strode on, the swarthy face darkened by fury at the fool who'd left it there.

Never mind a broken leg. A ripped ankle would have made blazing headlines around the world and plunged Argentina into national mourning. It may well have transformed the entire destiny of this World Cup.

The leg's owner, of course, was Diego Maradona, whom England's defenders have the monumental assignment from high noon here tomorrow of attempting to reduce to mortal stature.

Stop Maradona and they can surge on to win the World Cup. Lose him and they will look like blundering artisans condemned to the next plane home.

There are great stars here of the brilliance of France's Michel Platini and Mexico's Hugo Sanchez but of none but Maradona is it said that on his day – and such days are so frequent that his market value is now £7 million – he can win the World Cup alone.

He *can* be stopped, of course. The Italians stopped him dead in his tracks in the last World Cup in Spain by cynically kicking him from groin to ankle whenever they could lay a boot on his passing figure.

I hope, pray even, that England have no similar thoughts in the darkest recesses of their minds. Such tactics would be interpreted here as nothing short of a flare-up of the Falklands war and, amid a passionate short-fused Latin crowd, no Briton would be safe.

Maradona will not be drawn into admitting there has ever even been a tiff to ruffle the long history of friendship between Argentina and Britain. 'I am here,' he repeated in a hundred interviews yesterday, 'to play football.'

Carlo Bilardo, Argentina's coach says: 'Among his team friends he is a very humble man who wishes only for the team to win.'

Argentinian journalists smile at this diplomatic evaluation of a star whose postures and temperaments they know so well and, when out of earshot, they confide that there was not universal dismay when Maradona packed his bags, rounded up his coterie of hangers-on, his rude and bloated business manager, and headed off for Europe.

Europe was where the money was. Barcelona, where he arrived in 1982, is also where the culture is and where the fans expect their idols to act with style. Maradona and clique roared around the gracious city as though they were cowboys in downtown Buenos Aires.

The favourite trick, with money to burn, was to hire out an entire restaurant for an evening and have the public excluded. This outraged the proud and formal Catalans and Maradona's star was soon in the descendancy. For a while his football talents followed it.

Two years later he was to meet his match: a London cockney quite as street-smart as he was. For a while, when he took over as manager of Barcelona, Terry Venables quietly assessed the character and life-style, the habits and the roistering friends of the world's greatest footballer.

He then decided that Barcelona was not big enough for both of them and performed the unthinkable: he sold Maradona to the Naples club in Italy.

There was scarely a whisper of protest in Barcelona for what turned out to be not only a stroke of great perception but an act of salvation. Barcelona won the Spanish league championship. Maradona fired his business agent and began to recapture the football form that, at its height, has the bewitching quality that transforms mere spectatorship into a trance-like experience.

Now a mature twenty-five, he has brought that peak of form to this World Cup. You find yourself holding your breath and not blinking as he bullets himself and ball into a labyrinth defence, weaves through non-existent spaces and then emerges, still with ball, running clear from a scene of carnage.

When the Argentines opened their training camp to the world's press, Maradona displayed none of the churlishness which for so long has come so naturally. He wasn't charming, for it's hard to be charming with milling media men shoving microphones, tape recorders and cameras into your face. But he was patient, compliant and polite – and very wary. He is always wary of crowds, for twice in his career he has been seriously kicked by hostile fans hoping to injure him before a vital game.

The biggest fortune ever yet amassed from football is still invested in those legs, which accounted for the murderous look which crossed his countenance when he collided with that very heavy lump of metal yesterday.

from SPORT IN THE EIGHTIES *1989*

PART 5

The Managers

Gerry Francis

CYNTHIA BATEMAN

Six bottles of champagne followed Gerry Francis into the dressing-room at Old Trafford, and not just because it was New Year's Day. Ninth from bottom, Queen's Park Rangers had just beaten the league leaders Manchester United 4–1, leaving Alex Ferguson shaking his head in disbelief. They meet again today.

'We hadn't started when they had scored two. It was a nightmare. I hope for my players' sakes it was a one-off,' said Ferguson of United's worst defeat at home for thirteen years.

It was no one-off for Queen's Park Rangers. They went on to bite the legs of the rest of the title contenders: Leeds crashed 4–1, Manchester City were sent packing 4–0 and Sheffield Wednesday counted themselves lucky to draw. But what seemed like a flickering into life for QPR was the start of a sustained run in which they have lost only one in eighteen games.

'We have only been beaten nine times in the league all season. Only five teams in the first division can better that,' said Francis. He once said about his previous club Bristol Rovers: 'When I went there, they didn't think they could win. When I left them, they didn't think they could lose.' He has swiftly worked the trick at QPR.

He took over in the summer having turned down nine other management opportunities and having seen out his contract at Bristol Rovers. 'I'm basically a loyal person. I don't think I would have left if they had been able to get a stadium.'

But Queen's Park Rangers had always tugged at his heart – not just because he had the best twelve years of his playing career there but because he was born just round the corner at Chiswick. 'We supported Brentford, where my dad played, and QPR on alternate Saturdays.'

He made his league debut for them aged sixteen, against Liverpool. It needed only four games with England for his leadership qualities to be recognised, and he was given the captaincy. A bad back injury killed his chances after only twelve caps. Is now the time for a second chance of real football success at the top level? There are those who consider him the best manager in the country. But elbow grease and commitment may not be enough.

'The last time Queen's Park Rangers won a major trophy was in 1967 when we won the League Cup, when a couple of first-division teams didn't enter,' says the forty-year-old Francis. 'Queen's Park Rangers have never won the Championship in their history, and they have been in the top three only once – in 1976 when I was captain.'

QPR have no money to spend on players and Francis was straightaway forced to sell Paul Parker to Manchester United for a club record £1.7 million. 'It was a case of having to. I knew the financial situation before I arrived. But how many managers have been forced to sell £3 million worth of players, and spend less than £1 million on five different players from lower divisions, and still be expected to be successful?'

At Bristol Rovers Francis, who has successful business interests outside football, improved a low-budget side by lending the club £10,000 to buy the midfielder, Ian Holloway, who has now joined him at QPR, as has Dennis Bailey, the Birmingham City player he twice had on loan at Bristol.

Bailey, now QPR's top scorer with eleven goals in twenty-two games, scored a hat-trick against United in that New Year's Day debacle. Otherwise Francis has a mix of experience – built around Alan McDonald and Ray Wilkins – and home-produced youth (Bradley Allen, Andrew Impey and Karl Ready), thrown in at the deep end as QPR faced up to seventeen senior players injured from their thirty man squad. 'Our injury list was probably worse than Liverpool's but they had all the publicity. Nobody is interested in Queen's Park Rangers from that point of view.'

But once Francis had 'coaxed, cajoled and bullied' the players into his way of things and persuaded them to drop the sweeper system, the results started to come. He has no doubt the success can be sustained.

'This is exactly the same as Bristol Rovers. When I went there, they had no hope, no ground, no nothing. The last match of the season they avoided relegation. Two seasons on, with a team costing £100,000, with no stars but with everybody working hard for each other, we went to the play-offs and lost in the final. The year after that we went to Wembley again and also won the third-division championship. So when you ask can we keep it going, I think that proves it.

'But most important, a team must be consistent. Beating Manchester United, Leeds and Manchester City was lovely. But the thing I'm most proud of is the eighteen-game run with only one defeat.

'The irony of the win against United was that three or four days later we played absolute rubbish at Southampton. I had to really liven one or two up – to put it nicely – at half-time for us to come back and nearly save the game. But we lost and went out of the FA Cup. Now that is what I don't want and will not stand for. The old QPR would go and beat Liverpool away and lose the next eight games.'

The new consistency has put them ninth in the league behind some very big guns. Ferguson's warning against complacency fell on deaf ears last time. United, trying to reclaim top spot, should need no reminders today.

from the GUARDIAN *1992*

Graeme Souness and the Liverpool Boot Room

STEPHEN BIERLEY

Before Bill Shankly was appointed manager at Anfield on 1 December 1959, the newspapers of the day played the usual game of name the successor. Harry Catterick, Jimmy Murphy and Jimmy Hagan were all in the frame, as was a little-known back-room boy – one Robert Paisley. And in the back room, or perhaps more properly the boot room, Paisley remained for another fifteen years.

There is a lovely photograph of Shankly, not quite able to bring himself to smile for the camera, standing somewhat gauchely alongside his Anfield henchmen: Paisley, Ronnie Moran, Joe Fagan and Reuben Bennett. This simple black-and-white snap, much more than a thousand words, brings into startling clarity the red thread of continuity that has run through the club since that momentous winter's day when Shanks said, 'I will'.

On his first morning he told the staff he would be introducing no new assistants. 'I'll give you loyalty if you give it me.' There was never any question.

Paisley, who had joined Liverpool from Bishop Auckland in 1939, described the pre-Shankly Liverpool days as 'easygoing'. A born winner, he collected a league championship medal in his first full season at Anfield, 1947, yet remarked: 'We were not a team of real winners in those days. There was a feeling we belonged in the middle of the table. But Bill changed all that.'

Nearly thirty-three years and twenty-seven major trophies later, the feeling of uncertainty, both inside and outside the club, are perhaps greater than they have ever been during the last three staggeringly successful decades.

Such doubts may be no more than the pulses of underlying unease caused by fifteen months of, in Liverpool terms, quite astonishing flux, set off by the enigmatic departure of Kenny Dalglish.

Paisley and Fagan had been promoted from the ranks, in seamless succession to Shankly. Dalglish, with Paisley still very much at his elbow, had jumped over Moran and Roy Evans in being appointed in 1985, but his promotion was nevertheless within the delineated requirements of internal accession to the crown.

The arrival in April last year of Graeme Souness, albeit the club's former player and captain, was an 'outside job'. And, unlike Shankly, Souness brought an assistant, Phil Boersma, who thus gained automatic entrance to the mystical boot room. Noses were immediately and obviously put out of joint.

On the day Souness was paraded, Moran made a short speech of welcome, publicly stating he would do everything to help. But there was little conviction in his voice or joy in his eyes. Whatever disappointment he had felt when Dalglish took over from Fagan had been well hidden. Not so now.

Souness changed the locks on the manager's door, and Moran has not bothered to learn the combination. Telephone calls by him to the Cheadle hospital where Souness has been recuperating have, for reasons unexplained, frequently not been returned. Outwardly Moran remains loyal but the deep, organic trust of the boot room is being severely tested.

This pokey little cubbyhole under the main stand where the boots of the first-team players are stored has, since Shankly's days, become a potent symbol of the club's tight-knit homogeneity. It is, perhaps, the equivalent of a church vestry where, in strict privacy, the vicar can discuss everything from the thinness of the communion wine to why Mrs Smith's husband has been missing for three of the last four evensongs.

Neither Shankly nor Paisley were pulpit or manager's office men. They both knew when to be formal but the socialist gatherings (cabinet by consultation, if you prefer) in this cramped room were where policy, style and the way forward were thrashed out. All for one, one for all.

Trust was and is paramount. Those upstairs – Peter Robinson, the chief executive, and the board – could sort out wages, contracts and sundry other fiscal matters but, down in the boot room, little other than the game itself was talked about. Thus it was, whenever Dalglish faced potentially awkward questioning about team or tactics, he would say quite simply, and *ad infinitum*, that 'such matters would be dealt with internally'. It is now possible to argue that he used the 'secret' fabric of the Anfield set-up to hide or mask his own inadequacies as a manager in the final year and a half when the team were showing sharp signs of decline, his tactics became increasingly curious and his purchases often bizarre.

What may have been forgotten amid the shock of Dalglish's resignation – because of 'pressure' – was the decline in the quality and influence of the boot room itself. Fagan, deeply scarred by the Heysel tragedy, had gone, and Paisley's gathering illness further isolated Dalglish from the wealth of the past. Not that he was a great one for advice in any case.

Souness, via a French magazine interview last October, spoke of complacency and the need to regenerate the spirit of old. It was assumed he was talking only of the players. It may not have been so.

And so the rumours have strengthened of Souness wanting a clear-out from top to bottom. A number of players – McMahon, Ablett, Speedie, Carter, Staunton and Beardsley – have gone. Others will follow this summer. But what of the boot room? What of Moran? Here the true power-play will be decided. There is every reason to suppose that the leaking of the manager's alleged wish to get rid of the long-serving Moran, and the resultant anger in certain areas of the board, was carefully orchestrated from within.

Such is the pervading uncertainty that when Souness briefly left hospital on Thursday and was driven to Anfield by his solicitor, the knee-jerk conclusion was that he was about to resign. And this two days before an FA Cup final.

Souness is a man with scant regard for tradition when tradition stifles progress, as his signing of the Catholic Mo Johnston at Rangers testifies. He can also be a man of instant decisions, not all of them right. His selling of the story of his heart operation to the *Sun* was a clear case in point, an awful misjudgment.

Tommy Smith, talking of Liverpool's so-called magic formula, once said: 'When you play professional football there are one or two basics and if you stick to them you don't go far wrong. The system only breaks down with individuals.'

There is no mistaking Souness's individuality, nor is it in doubt that some members of the board now believe his appointment was an error. He has the full backing of the chairman, David Moores, but that may not be enough. Much of Liverpool's future will depend on his future health. His operation has merely added to what has been, since Dalglish's departure, a continuity of uncertainty. But it was always possible, given Paisley's quite outstanding gifts, that once he went nothing would ever be quite the same again.

Only the best was good enough for Shankly and Paisley. Today the best is becoming increasingly hard to find.

from the GUARDIAN *1992*

Tommy Docherty

BRIAN CLARKE

Milan dominated the game in Italy but a George Graham goal in injury time gave Docherty real hope that his team could finish the job at the Bridge in the return leg. Their performance inspired Chelsea for the FA Cup-tie with Leeds which they won with the only goal of the game from Bobby Tambling to move into the fifth round and a clash with Shrewsbury. So far so good.

But the on-going success was putting more demands on the Chelsea youngsters. A 2–1 victory over AC Milan at the Bridge levelled the Fairs Cup-tie at 3–3. Chelsea lost the toss in the boardroom for the choice of venue for the play-off and so it was back to Italy again. Amid heart-stopping drama they came through that game to round off a splendid spell for Chelsea, who had now beaten Liverpool and Leeds United to reach the fifth round of the FA Cup and had knocked out Roma, Weiner and mighty AC Milan in the Fairs competition. However, Docherty's determination to be the only boss in the dressing-room brought a long-running feud with his skipper Terry Venables to a head.

Venables had always set himself up as something of a dressing-room spokesman. He started to challenge my authority in training. He would make sarcastic comments about what I was trying to put across. I would have welcomed constructive comments but Terry would tend to dismiss what I was saying. He wanted to be Mr Big in front of the lads, but what they didn't know was that he would often come to my office after training and apologise, saying he didn't mean any disrespect.

Just before the play-off against AC Milan in February 1966 Docherty acted swiftly to curb the disruptive influence of Venables and put him on the transfer list. 'This club's not big enough for the two of us,' he warned his twenty-one-year-old skipper, who was also dropped from the team and told he would not be going to Milan. Docherty was willing even to put his own career on the line over the Venables issue, giving his chairman an ultimatum to back him or he would quit. Mears was saddened and had hoped it would not reach such an impasse but pledged his support for his manager, and Venables, a crowd idol at the Bridge, was put up for sale. A barrage of criticism rained down on Docherty but he countered by saying that constantly having his authority challenged was not acceptable: 'In any case Terry had been playing for himself, not the team.' To the press he responded defiantly: 'When I start worrying what people think of me I'll give up. It's my job to manage and do what I think is best for Chelsea Football Club.'

He was left in no doubt what Venables thought when Docherty was the only person on the staff at Chelsea not invited to the young man's wedding.

In Milan, Peter Osgood was given his chance to fill the role of Venables and proved the wisdom of Docherty's thinking when he combined with George Graham to set up a crucial goal for Barry Bridges to give Chelsea the lead. It was only in the closing seconds that Milan equalised through Fortunato – 'he was well named,' laughs Docherty now. It happened when three Chelsea players, confidently expecting a goal-kick, hovered and guarded the ball as it crossed the goal-line, but the referee awarded a corner. In the ensuing – and unwise – argument the Italians raced to take the kick which found the head of Fortunato and the defenders well out of position.

After thirty minutes of extra time the teams were still locked together and the players slumped to the turf in sheer exhaustion. The two captains now had to toss a coin to decide who would go through to the next round. Milan's Maldini and the Chelsea skipper Ron Harris watched nervously as the coin was flipped.

Standing at the side of the pitch Docherty knew the winner instantly as Harris threw his arms into the air in a gesture of delight. The young Chelsea team was through to the next European round against TSV Munich.

from DOCHERTY *1991*

Brian Clough

HUNTER DAVIES

There were shouts of delight as he arrived home in his Mercedes. He was slightly late for the party, but they were all waiting for him, sixteen eight-year-old boys. The party was for Simon, his eldest. He has another son, Nigel, six and a daughter Elizabeth, who is five. He went in, clapped his hands and told them to get ready. He has had fourteen kids in his Mercedes, but he decided sixteen was too many, so they all set off down the suburban street, running behind him, shouting: 'We are the Champions.' We got to a park and he arranged two sides and started them playing. He was to be the referee, though Elizabeth was to stay beside him and do the actual whistle-blowing.

An onlooker could easily have thought he was slightly deranged. He wasn't running a children's party game between two sets of eight-year-olds. It was deadly serious. He treated the kids as real professional footballers, which of course they responded to. He padded up and down in his carpet slippers, screaming out instructions, like that schoolmaster in the football match in *Kes* who was convinced he was running Manchester United.

'Do that once more, Si, and you're off!' he shouted at his eight-year-old son. 'Who said you could pick that ball up? The whistle didn't blow for a throw-in, did it? No, it did not. Handball!'

He let them get away with nothing, not even foul throw-ins, though their little arms weren't really up to it. He made them line up while he demonstrated the correct way.

Even his five-year-old daughter, Elizabeth, who was supposed to blow every time he told her, didn't escape his wrath. 'I've warned you, Lib. If you bugger around any more I'll take the whistle.'

His wife Barbara was duly grateful when they all trailed back to the house for the birthday tea, all nicely quietened and exhausted. He watched them getting stuck into the goodies then went into his front room and opened a bottle of champagne.

'What do you mean, I'm now coming on all middle-class? You can say I live in a middle-class house. You can say I've got a middle-class car. Say what you bloody like. It's only your opinion. This house isn't middle-class. It's bloody Buckingham Palace.

'I'm still a Socialist and always will be, but that doesn't stop me having the best car. I can get our three kids in it, plus the wife and me Mam and Dad, all in comfort, that's why I have it. The club car when I came here was a Vauxhall Victor, but I didn't want that. I asked them to buy me a Mercedes last year but they wouldn't. So I said stuff it, I'll buy one myself.'

He says his Socialism is from the heart, not his head, and always has been. Over the years he's been asked several times to stand as a Labour MP and has seriously considered it. He has a charity box for leukaemia research on the bar in his office. He's talked all his staff into giving up part of their salaries to Oxfam. During the miners' strike he gave out free tickets for Derby matches to the pickets.

'I just have to read the papers to know I'm a Socialist. Look at all the millions not being fed. Look at the political prisoners. Look at the discrimination everywhere, not just colour but class, education and privilege of all sorts. I'm lucky. I've got three well fed, superbly looked after kids. When I saw the pictures of those dead kids in Biafra I burst into tears.

'People in football are surprised I'm a Socialist. Their apathy generally is staggering, which I think is an indictment of my profession. They say sport and politics don't mix, which is rubbish. It's like saying you don't need oxygen to breathe. You can't have one without the other on this earth. I think people who want to keep politics out of sport are a bit simple.'

In practice as a manager he tries to follow his principles, such as never discriminating, except against the louts and skivers. There's one London team which has him frothing at the mouth, just because he maintains a spiv element has been allowed to take over. 'If you threaten certain spiv players, you must carry it out and not let them get away with it. A football team has only eleven players. It just needs one bad 'un to affect the rest. In ICI, with thousands and thousands of people, you can afford to carry some scoundrels. Not in a football team.'

He's fanatical about education, insisting that each apprentice who joins the club at fifteen goes to the local Polytechnic for one full day and two evenings each week till he's a full professional. Most managers allow young players time off for study, but not many make it compulsory. 'I can't guarantee to turn boys into professional footballers at Derby, but they'll end up well educated. I've got one boy, sixteen-year-old Steve Powell, who's doing three A-levels. I've got another doing a degree. In this democracy in which we live, education is available to all despite the public schools trying to make it exclusive. Give me any time a talented football player who's also intelligent. Show me a talented player who's thick, and I'll show you a player with problems.

If his heart is therefore in the right place, if he's kind to children, contributes generously to charity and always helps dumb footballers across the road, why then do so many people dislike him?

It's all to do with his TV appearances. One minute he says he loves it, admitting he laps it up and yes, he must be vain, and the next he's trying to pretend he does it as a duty, because it's an honour for Derby. 'There are ninety-two football managers, give or take the six or seven who are about to be sacked every season, so I think it's a compliment to Derby that the BBC should choose me for their football panels.'

There's no doubt he loves it, despite all the abuse he's had to take over the years. 'I have had some terrible stick. I know many viewers say bloody hell, not that bugger again. But there's now been a complete switch. I'm not bulling you, because I never bull, but I promise you letters have suddenly changed. They now say I'm right.

'The thing is, people never listen to what you say on the telly. All they notice is your manner. I can't help my voice. I can't help my manner. I can't help how I look. If people disagreed with what I say, that would be one thing, but it's how I say it that gets them.

Internationally, his manner has led to a few rows in the BBC. He's not very good, for example, at controlling his bad language. He called Sir Alf Ramsey 'a stubborn bugger'. During the World Cup they put him with a panel of nine, which he thought was ridiculous. 'It was a silly set-up so I just messed round. They then saw sense and agreed with me.

'I'm against any rehearsing and always refuse to do it. I've also refused to have Bob Wilson talking about managerial problems, not when I'm on anyway. He's a player and he knows nothing about management. I won't have it.

Now and again, when he sees himself as others see him, he's a bit appalled. 'I came home once and watched a recording of a sports programme I'd been on and I thought, bloody hell, that's not me, is it? What a big-headed, dogmatic bastard. So next time I tried to calm down. It meant they got themselves a crappy interview.

'I only get upset if the wife's upset. She did once say I'd been extremely rude to someone. Sometimes I do set out to be rude, but that time I hadn't meant it. I hate me Mam getting upset, that's even worse.

'I suppose I've got more intelligent and wiser over the years, but I'm not going to try and change myself now. It doesn't bother me what people think.

'They say I've got chips on my shoulder, but I don't think so. I just believe in giving my opinion. I don't say it's the right opinion. I just say it's mine. They tell me that in giving my opinions I shout, that I say things other people wouldn't say, but bloody hell, you've got to shout, when kids in Vietnam are having bombs dropped on them. OK, I have got a chip on my shoulder, if it means shouting out about what's wrong with the world. And OK I'm stupid and ignorant enough to think my opinions are right. Have some more champagne. To absent friends, those buggers in London. You wouldn't believe the pleasure I've had out of drinking their health.'

from MY LIFE IN FOOTBALL *1990*

Matt Busby

EAMON DUNPHY

The Football League tried to intimidate Manchester United out of entering the European Champions Cup – they were reminded of their first duty, to the Football League – and warned that no excuses could be accepted if this 'gimmick' called the Champions Cup caused any disruption to their first-division programme. The League was politely but firmly rebuffed.

Busby had no difficulty persuading his board that Europe was a wise option. But now he dominated board meetings although protocol insisted that he sat in only to advise. Alan Gibson obeyed his father's wish and voted with Mr Busby. The chairman, Harold Hardman, was a flinty little man, Manchester's rigorous English Masonic face, and he and Busby were respectful rather than fond of each other. Hardman did not approve of the characters his manager socialised with, but he did approve of the football club of which he found himself the titular head. He remembered the bad old days and continued to watch the pennies, but as he wryly remarked, 'Our manager advises us and then tells us what to do.' The quote is apocryphal yet an accurate reflection of Busby's unique influence. No other manager before or since ever wielded the power that Matt Busby did at Old Trafford.

His rationale for engaging in European competition was threefold. First, it would provide money to pay for the floodlights United had still to install, and for the large, ever-expanding wage bill rising in proportion to the number of first-division quality players on United's books. Second, the extra competition, seen as a problem by the Football League, was a blessing to Busby – players could be kept happy and gain experience playing in the Champions Cup. His final reason was more abstract than practical. He understood how irrevocably the balance of power was shifting away from the English game, and saw that football in the future would be an international game. The world was contracting, travel was easier, people were curious about abroad. As a football man he was intrigued by the international game. Football as played by the Hungarians was his kind of game.

Billy Whelan beat Bobby Charlton into the first team. Whelan started the 1956–57 season at inside-right in a side that began the defence of its title confidently by running up a sequence of twelve games without defeat. Bobby Charlton was desperate. At the end of September Edwards and Taylor were injured.

'I always remember that week,' Charlton declares. 'Three weeks before, I'd been injured at Maine Road in a reserve match. I twisted the ligaments in my right ankle – it's still bigger now. It took me two weeks to start running again. The week the lads got injured the Boss says, 'How's your ankle?' And I knew this was my chance. So I said fine. It was sore as hell, not when I ran, but when I turned on it or tried to kick the ball. But I knew I had to get in. I was desperate. I played against Charlton at home, and scored two goals. I never kicked the ball with my right foot all day.'

That level of enthusiasm existed throughout the club. 'I was left out again when Tommy was fit,' Bobby recalls, 'but I got fourteen games that season which meant I got a blazer. You had to play fourteen games to get a blazer.'

Charlton, desperately worried about his future, was eighteen. He scored consistently whenever he played, including a hat trick in the return fixture with Charlton at the Valley. Bobby was the young player with everything: power, wonderfully fluid movement and two great feet. He could score goals and link up in general play to devastating effect. His long gloriously flighted passes raked holes in the opposition defence. He could shimmy past defenders and once away was uncatchable. Bobby Charlton was a sensation. And he could hardly get a game.

John Giles had arrived at Old Trafford. John was, in Billy Behan's opinion, the best schoolboy footballer he had ever seen. A stocky, well-built little Dubliner, Giles was beautifully balanced, had two good feet and remarkable vision. From a renowned Irish football family, Giles was also impressively self-possessed for a youngster. Watching Bobby Charlton play for United's reserves caused Giles to doubt himself. 'I'd never seen anything like him,' John says. 'I remember sitting in the stand at Old Trafford one night watching the reserves with my dad. I don't know who they were playing, but they won something like eight or nine nil. Bobby scored five. I'd never had the slightest doubt that I'd be a player, but I turned to my Dad and said, "I don't know about this."'

Dickie Giles, a great old football man himself, offered his son reassurance. It was badly needed. 'Bobby was unbelievable, even in training. It was an intimidating atmosphere at Old Tradford at that time. There were so many great young players desperate to get in the side.'

The team matured as expected. Confidence now infused all the other qualities. Wherever they played attendances were inflated. This was particularly true of London. A crowd of 62,000 saw United win at Highbury; 57,000 turned up for the Spurs fixture at White Hart Lane. There was never any doubt that the Championship would be retained. Everywhere they played they attacked. They loved the applause: Colman, Byrne, Taylor and Viollet responding with deft little improvisations. There was something inspiringly joyous about this team. They were exhilarating, carefree, unconventional. And British, not Hungarian. Of this Britishness – or more accurately *Englishness* – the intimidating competitiveness of Duncan Edwards was a perpetual reminder. He *didn't* play to the crowd. He hardly seemed to notice.

In Munich the news of fatalities was kept from Matt Busby for almost a month. Professor Georg Maurer insisted that the shock of learning about Tom Curry, Bert Whalley, Willie Satinoff and the players he'd led on this great European adventure might sap his will to fight for his life. Jean, Sheena and Sandy lived anxiously lest they betray their dreadful secret. Frank Taylor, the only sportswriter to survive the crash, recounts a visit to Busby's hospital room a month after the tragedy: 'Matt was a shattering sight. He lay silent, stretched full length as though asleep, the plaster on his right leg bulging the blankets. The bushy, once sandy hair was now grey and tinged with streaks of white. The eyes opened in recognition; the pale waxy face which belonged to a man of seventy brightened; a thin pitifully emaciated hand advanced haltingly over the white cover on the bed, found mine and gripped it weakly. "Hallo, my old pal, how are you, Frank lad?"' Within minutes Busby had lapsed into slumber.

Busby knew that something awful had occurred. Lying weakly in his bed his powerful instincts still functioned. He didn't press the questions for in truth he was afraid to know the answers. Finally it was Jean who broke the news. Sheena and Sandy listened as Matt held her hand and listed the names of those who'd boarded Flight 609 with him. When he named a survivor Jean nodded and squeezed his hand. When he asked for those who'd died she shook her head. Words seemed pointless.

Subsequent claims that Matt Busby decided to quit football after the Munich air crash are inaccurate. Thinking aloud he talked to his family about the absurdity of the game's obsessive quest for results and trophies when measured against life's realities as they had just experienced them. Understanding power as he did, Matt Busby also reflected on his decision to seek the glory of European football, his defiance of those who argued against the new idea. He had been impatient, resenting the timid, narrow-minded counsels of caution. Europe had been his vision. This thought prompted reproach. However, on reflection, he recalled his young team's enthusiasm for the challenge he'd posed them, their hunger for the new experience, their desire to fulfil themselves beyond the parochial English game. They could have been the best in the world, but not unless they went in search of Real Madrid and others like the Hungarians of mythology. That was what he wanted, the dream his players shared.

Thus, remorse gave way to deep, abiding sadness. On 19 April 1958 Matt Busby left Rechts der Isar Hospital to return home. That afternoon Bobby Charlton marked his debut for England against Scotland at Hampden Park, with a spectacular goal volleyed from a Tom Finney cross. The same day Billy Meredith died in Manchester aged eighty-three. Professional soccer's first great star died almost destitute. During his last years Meredith eked out an existence with small donations from the Professional Footballers' Association. Thanks to Matt Busby and United he kept a roof over his head. He had met Duncan Edwards, Tommy Taylor and Eddie Colman who had called to see him to pay their respects. The Wizard and the 'Red Devils' had much in common. Like him their hearts were always full of football. They died on a maximum wage of £17 per week, less in real terms than Billy had earned fifty years before. In newspapers dominated by Matt Busby's return home and Bobby Charlton's stunning debut for England, the passing of professional football's first hero was a small story. He would have understood, for nobody knew better the nature of the glory game.

from A STRANGE KIND OF GLORY *1991*

Johan Cruyff

GUY HODGSON

In the numerous small bars leading to Barcelona's Nou Camp Stadium there was not the unanimous acclaim you would expect for a man who has guided the local club to the European Cup final. The majority gave Johan Cruyff his due, but a significant minority did not.

'He was a fantastic player,' one malcontent said, 'but as a coach, no good. He changes players from their best positions and ruins them. Gary Lineker is the best example. He is a great goalscorer, one of the best, but Cruyff wanted him to play on the right. Hopeless.'

A second used another striker, the Bulgarian Hristo Stoichkov, as a rod to beat the Barcelona coach. 'He is the best striker at the club yet he is played on the left. On the left! And he is always being substituted. If Barcelona fail to win a trophy this season I expect Cruyff to leave.'

If the doubts about a man who was regarded by many as the world's greatest player and who as a coach has led Barcelona to three European finals in four seasons are a surprise, they merely mirror the uncertainty surrounding Cruyff's position at the club. Barcelona will claim the Champions Cup for the first time in their history if they defeat Sampdoria at Wembley on Wednesday, but Cruyff is not a happy man. On the brink of the highest honour possible for a European club coach (on the Continent the position of coach is equivalent to that of the British club manager), he is dissatisfied to an extent that jeopardises his future at the Nou Camp.

'It is not certain I will still be here next season,' he said last week. 'It is not a question of whether we win or lose at Wembley, it's the organisation here. Barcelona is a volatile club, very volatile. Things are wrong, little things that to an outsider are very difficult to explain, but things are erratic. It's something to do with the mentality here, the character of the people and the way they work. If things are not changed then I have to make my decision whether to continue.'

From his exterior there was nothing to suggest Cruyff has anything but a tranquil mind. At forty-five he has a leanness given to athletes and those who have come face to face with their own mortality as he did in February last year when he underwent a double-bypass heart operation. On television he can look grey and gaunt, but in the flesh he exudes health.

Even on the training pitch last week he was the epitome of calm. The Dutchman sat impassively on a ball on the sidelines while the players prepared for last night's league match against Real Mallorca and Wednesday's final. He issued the occasional command, but generally remained silent and still. He sprang to life only when he talked about the power struggle within the club that might terminate his contract – rumoured to be worth around £1.4 million a year and due to run until June 1993 – twelve months early.

On the one side is the traditional structure of a club that boasts more than 100,000 members and probably the powerful president Jose Luis Nuñez, and on the other is Cruyff, who wants a greater say in the running of the organisation. 'I believe there is no point taking part unless you think you can be the best,' he said. 'That's why I say to Mr Nuñez we need to alter the organisation, otherwise it will be impossible to maintain the highest standards. I have all kinds of ambitions stemming from the main priority of wanting to win. If you are trying to succeed you need incentives, you have to change things all the time. You can't stop and congratulate yourself because as soon as you do it's over. That's why we need to look at the structure of the club. Otherwise you can't go on.'

Managing any big club has its pressures, but nothing is quite like running one of the great football institutions in Spain, where power struggles are a way of life and job security is almost non-existent. Just as many people must wonder why on earth Graeme Souness would want to continue as manager of Liverpool after his recent heart operation, so it is tempting to suggest that Cruyff should opt for a quiet life basking in the glory of his past achievements.

As a player with Feyenoord, Ajax, Barcelona and the New York Cosmos, his reputation is safely established. Three times European Footballer of the Year, he was blessed with pace, bewildering skills and a striker's instinct to arrive in the right place at the right time. Yet he was far more than just a gifted individual. With Ajax and the Netherlands he was also the conductor of the orchestra, able to beat defenders at will but regularly preferring to seek the pass to free colleagues. He scored thirty-three goals in forty-eight appearances for the Netherlands before his early international retirement.

Alongside colleagues like Neeskens, Krol and Rep, Cruyff and the Netherlands developed a style that had a pattern but a frequently changing one: 'total football' ideally complemented Cruyff's abilities and took Ajax to three European Cups (in 1971, 1972 and 1973) and the Dutch to the 1974 World Cup final. The fact that the national side lost that match and also the final of 1978 (without Cruyff) has bracketed them with the Hungarians of 1954 as the finest team never to win the World Cup.

Until recently, there was no real tradition of the truly great players becoming great managers, but perhaps Cruyff is intent on emulating one of his contemporaries, Franz Beckenbauer, who two years ago led Germany to victory in the World Cup. Cruyff, not surprisingly, has already been linked with the job of Dutch national manager.

He certainly has little to prove as a coach at club level. He has won the European Cup-Winners Cup with both Ajax and Barcelona, whom he also led to the Spanish league title last year, and his teams have played with all the style and flair you would expect of a former player with his pedigree.

So why does a wealthy but not totally healthy man continue to work in what appears to be a highly stressful and, by his own admission, not entirely helpful atmosphere? 'For one reason,' he said. 'I enjoy it. Or I would with a few changes. I don't see being a coach as a career, because that would mean I would have to be willing to go anywhere and I'm not. I just want to do what I like to do, choose the clubs where I want to go. Otherwise I wouldn't be in the job.

'In any case my health is very good. I didn't have a heart attack as was reported in some newspapers, it was an internal problem in the heart. The bypass operation affected me in a sense that it made me more realistic but I'm not afraid. I run around as much as I used to and the only change is that I have given up cigarettes and other little things that, added up, could become important. I had to choose between tobacco and football and I chose football.'

Cruyff, who smoked forty a day before his operation, may get his wish for more influence if Barcelona secure their holy grail, the European Cup this month; the man himself is less confident. This reaction stems from a stormy year even by the tempestuous standards of Barcelona, where 'excess is not enough' could be the motto.

Cruyff's illness did nothing to moderate a man who walked out of Ajax – the club he had joined first as a ten-year-old – in 1988 for much the same reasons he is unhappy now. In December, bitterly angry with his players, he threatened: 'Either things improve or I leave.' Two weeks ago he accused his charges of surrendering the league title with a slipshod run of six matches, an assessment made premature by Real Madrid's lapse last weekend.

The anger has not always been Cruyff's. Two months ago Nuñez was infuriated by newspaper reports that his coach had agreed to lead the Netherlands team if they reached the World Cup finals in the United States. 'I'm not going to negotiate with people who already have their future planned out,' the president thundered. 'I don't believe in half days, like those who work in one place in the morning and another in the afternoon. If Cruyff wants to renew his contract I would demand of him total dedication to Barcelona and more hours.'

Add to that occasional bust-ups with the likes of Stoichkov and his fellow striker Michael Laudrup, and it is no small wonder that Cruyff has been a success. Only recently the Barcelona ship was rocked once again with the news that Stoichkov has been having discussions with Napoli with a view to a £6m transfer in the summer.

'I have a good relationship with Stoichkov, more than good,' Cruyff maintained. 'But if you play twenty-eight games as a striker you have to score more than eight times. That's it. Don't talk about relationships, those are facts. If it's my best friend or my biggest enemy, if you don't score enough in his position then you're out. It's exactly the same with Laudrup. If he goes eight or nine games without scoring, very unusual for him, he'd be dropped.

'Stoichkov has been linked with Napoli but it doesn't interest me. That's next season. What's important to me is this season and that he continues producing for me now.

'As a coach all you can do is pass on your experience. Being a good player, and I consider myself to have been a good player, is not enough. You need more, to learn little details and explain them to the players. Eventually they understand them and together they become a stronger team.'

Now comes Wednesday's match and the trophy the club's followers crave most. More than 20,000 Catalans will travel to Wembley to add support to a quest made the more passionate by the success of their rivals Real Madrid in the early years of the European Cup and the inability of Barcelona to win it.

At least the omens are good, because Cruyff has gone a full circle. It was at Wembley that he first sampled international success as a player at club level, winning the first of three successive European Cups with Ajax by beating Panathinaikos. 'I have very good memories about Wembley,' he said. 'The stadium is beautiful, a cathedral to football. The English fans were very honest with me, they enjoyed the way the team played and the way I played. There was a lot of mutual respect. I think the English supporters will support Barcelona because we will be doing the attacking. That's our way of playing.'

Barcelona have reached the final twice before, losing in 1961 to Benfica and in 1986 in Seville to Steaua Bucharest, when Terry Venables was in charge of the Spanish club.

'Losing to Steaua was felt deeply by the supporters,' Laudrup, Spain's Footballer of the Year, said. 'They lost interest the following season, attendances were down to 25,000 and 30,000.' The Nou Camp capacity is 115,000.

Cruyff is anxious to make good that failure, with interest. 'I'm very excited about Wednesday's match,' he said, 'because I believe we will win it. And if we take the European Cup we want to continue winning it.' And emulate Real's five in a row? 'Whatever's possible', he said with a smile. 'That's why you are working.

'The team is playing quite well, the average performance is good, but in several games the final touch has been missing. We have played much better in European matches than we have at times in the league. My job is to make sure the highest standards are maintained in every match.'

Barcelona beat Sampdoria 2–0 in the final of the European Cup-Winners Cup three seasons ago and their lapses since have been rare. One came twelve months ago, when they lost to Manchester United in the Cup-Winners Cup final in Rotterdam and were limp excuses of a team exceptional enough to win the Spanish league by 10 points.

'The biggest problem against Manchester United was that everybody was already satisfied because we had won the Spanish championship and had the opportunity to play in the European Cup,' Cruyff said.

'In this club, when something happens everything is exaggerated. It's never normal, either big ups or big down. So when they won the league everyone was so happy that the Cup-Winners Cup became unimportant. The league here is very, very important.'

from the INDEPENDENT ON SUNDAY 1992

An Argument with Tommy Trinder

JIMMY HILL

Why did I have a row with Tommy Trinder? Well, I didn't know then and I still don't know. It came as a bolt from the blue and for a moment I was shocked. Let me tell you how it came about. A week previously, Fulham's team had been 'special training' at their favourite haunt at Worthing and I had been with them. On the Friday evening I had been invited to do a television programme for Granada called *We Want an Answer*. It was to be televised in Manchester and I had to obtain permission from the club to fly to Manchester for the programme. It was granted, provided I got back to Worthing the same night. Fortunately I wasn't the only one of the players to be so privileged; if I had been I could have understood the chairman of the club being upset at my singular concession. As it was, two other players, Roy Bentley and Graham Leggatt, had been allowed away from training quarters at Worthing on the Thursday evening, to coach in London. They also were told to get back the same night.

The programme itself was very innocuous. A group of teenagers asked questions about a subject that interested them. It wasn't strange that it was football and, although some of their questions were searching, I wouldn't say that my answers were the sort to excite any officials of the Football League or the director of a football club (I had been pre-warned that my answers should not be too controversial. This was an anonymous top-level instruction). I answered the questions factually, although naturally, as is my responsibility, I tried to present the facts in a way that would be to the advantage of professional players. Unless you can remember the programme, there is no reason for you to believe this, but it can be substantiated.

At the time of the programme, Mr Charles Dean, also a director of Fulham Football Club, and his wife Margaret, were in the studio in Manchester. Afterwards they were profuse in their congratulations of the way I handled the questions. I think we were all pleased that the programme had gone off without a hitch. Twenty minutes' questioning can be very searching indeed. It fathoms the depths of your personality and tests the sincerity of your beliefs and the extent of your knowledge. I didn't realise quite how exhausting this could be until I landed at London Airport, having travelled on the plane with Miss Elaine Grand, the chairman of the programme, and got into my car to drive back to our training headquarters at Worthing.

I felt exhausted as I drove down and there was a great temptation to stop off at my home at Worcester Park, stay the night there, and rejoin the team as they came through the next morning to go to the match; but my orders were to return to Worthing on Friday night, although I knew that I wasn't playing in the Saturday match. I appreciated that discipline had to be maintained and for this reason I pressed on to Worthing, arrived about 12.15 a.m. and sank exhausted into my bed. Saturday was a lovely spring day and as we drove up from Worthing, stopping at a Dorking hotel for a steak, no one, least of all myself, had the slightest idea of the thunderbolt that was to fall later in the afternoon. It turned out to be the calm before the storm.

The match was against Bristol City. It was a bad one for Fulham in every way, except that we won 1–0. The team had not played at their best and there was an unhappy, dissatisfied atmosphere in the dressing-room after the game. I was standing there chatting to the boys, discussing the match, when Tommy Trinder burst in and, in his first sentence, accused me of making him look an absolute mug in front of friends, including Mr Christiansen, past editor of the *Daily Express*, whom he had been entertaining the evening before. He said he had taken down on his tape-recorder, word for word, the answers I had given on television.

Apparently I had made Tommy feel foolish by the answers that I had given, and one he particularly complained about was when I was asked how much footballers earned. I had said that the maximum wage was £20 a week in the winter and £17 in the summer. He argued that I earned more than that and so did the other Fulham players, because of the win bonuses and benefits we received from time to time. Of course, his facts were accurate. If I had been asked on the programme if there were any additional payments, I would surely have given them. It would have been equally incorrect for me to have answered: '£14 a week', which is in fact the average standard wage of footballers, and far less than the £20 that I had mentioned. This seemed to me an inconsequential reason to spark off such an outburst. Since I was chairman of the PFA, it was natural that I should present my case in this way. I certainly didn't intend to supply evidence to support the Football League Management Committee.

Tommy then switched his argument to another tack, saying that footballers were lucky, anyway, to get £1,000 a year and the majority of them, if they couldn't earn it through football, would be hard put to squeeze a living in any other occupation. He mentioned the example of a Fulham player, saying that if he were not a footballer, his intelligence would hardly enable him to survive in the outside world. This made me see red because this sort of argument levelled against footballers really upsets me. I asked Mr Trinder whether he thought there was a difference between a person who had some particular talent on the stage, that didn't really require intelligence, and a professional footballer. Should there be a maximum wage in football, though there was none in his profession? Was it because he thought that he was a human being and that footballers were animals that he advocated such distinctions in their respective prerogatives?

I didn't get an answer to any of these questions, and anyway, perhaps most of the hard words on both sides have by now been forgotten. I still remember the ending, which went like this;

Mr Trinder: 'The trouble with you is you talk too much.'

Mr Hill: 'And if I may say so, Mr Trinder, the trouble with you is that you shout too much.'

from STRIKING FOR SOCCER *1963*

Terry Venables

KEN JONES

To know Terry Venables even slightly requires some acceptance of conflict, the understanding that his attitudes are shaped by nothing less than an extended confrontation with life. Beyond perceived brashness, the courage, imagination and restless wit that helped to make him a brilliant coach, there is something else, inner and supremely private.

He runs conversations like a clever bowler runs an over, never giving you quite what you expect. He makes phrases, often memorably humorous ones, although lately he has been more serious than I remember.

As a player who fell marginally short of the highest class, Venables ran races against himself, matching, or, ideally, surpassing his last performance. With his young athlete's body, his determination and drive, he learned what he wanted. He was arch and opinionated but never shifty and reporters often sought him out.

Approaching forty-nine, the wunderkind of Chelsea days now a grandfather in middle age, Venables has had more interviews than he remembers. Now, long after the last canny pass, and though prepared to defend passionately held principles, he is not going to speak about the game or even Tottenham Hotspur's prospects. He is going to talk about being a major investor and chief executive.

We were sitting in the dining club Venables has acquired close to his Kensington home, and it was about two o'clock in the afternoon. Since arriving from the Tottenham training ground an hour earlier he had already attended two important meetings and taken numerous calls. Nicely groomed in an expensive dark blue suit, and confident, he lifted a white telephone and dealt quickly with another urgent interruption. 'Sounds good. Let's set it up for Wednesday.'

I think this is the way to start telling you about Venables, but I'm not sure. Maybe I should tell you about the time, a little more than a year ago, when the death of his Welsh mother raised immense sadness and manifestations of Celtic gloom in him. 'Some days are better than others,' he said, 'but it is a hard thing to cope with.'

No depth of perception was required to sense that Venables was less sure of himself then than at any time since finding it difficult to settle down as a Tottenham player in the 1960s.

After returning from Barcelona to manage the club, he had brought about steady improvement and could send out players capable of upholding an admirable tradition. But if things were going well on the field, it was a different story in the boardroom. There it was one of mounting debts; potential disaster.

Fully aware of serious corporate problems, Venables was also at odds with Irving Scholar, the avid Tottenham supporter who became chairman in 1982 after using his business acumen to gain control of the club. Scholar had offered to extend his contract, but as the terms included a reduction in basic salary they were unacceptable. Venables, encouraged by entrepreneurial inclination, began to look elsewhere, even outside the game. His responses contained unavoidable flickers of frustration as though the deep-rooted enthusiasm that marked him as a player and a coach had been seriously undermined by increasingly burdensome responsibilities.

The experience of being fired by Barcelona after winning the Spanish championship and, almost, the European Cup, left no scars because in Venables's mind management is a high-risk occupation and he had been handsomely rewarded. I remember him saying: 'Trouble is that the majority of our clubs are reluctant to make it clear that the manager has little or no influence outside the dressing-rooms, putting him up as the only one to be shot at.'

In that sense Venables, although still the most visible figure at White Hart Lane, is no longer in the firing line. The corporate turmoil that ultimately satisfied what had remained a vague ambition is well documented by Alex Fynn and Lynton Guest in *Heroes and Villains*, a vivid account of the 1990–91 season at Arsenal and Tottenham. It can be taken up here at the point where Venables and Alan Sugar took over. 'On Saturday 22 June, Terry Venables and the boss of Amstrad Electronics, Alan Sugar, called a press conference to announce that they had reached agreement with the board of Tottenham Hotspur and the Stock Exchange to purchase the shares of Irving

Scholar and Paul Bobroff, and were assuming control of the club. If things went well, a rights issue (due to be announced last week but held over) was to follow, which would raise £3.75m. This would put the cost of the takeover at £7.5m. In the new order, Sugar would become non-executive chairman of the plc with the task of "getting the balance sheet into shape", while Venables would take over the role of managing director.'

Throughout the months that have followed, Venables has trodden carefully, bringing back Peter Shreeves to manage the team, and concentrated on financial affairs. Not that he ever intends to be a pervasive presence. 'I appointed Peter because he was here before and has a Tottenham mind for the game. It is his team and I never interfere. I have meetings with him and the coaches, something that I intend to develop in the future, but only to establish policy.'

He indicated a place tucked away in the corner of a long dining-room and led the way jauntily as he did when a precociously assertive inside-forward in Chelsea's colours. Called to the telephone again, he sighed and looked across the table, a friendly and comforting man.

He has felt this restlessness all his life, set apart from his fellows by ambitions that ranged beyond what could be achieved within the white-limed markings of a football field. 'I quickly realised that footballers have a lot of time on their hands,' he said, 'and I couldn't see much sense in hanging around snooker halls.' On Sunday mornings in his youth, developing an instinct, he did the book-keeping for his parents, who ran a public house in Essex. With Gordon Williams, the author, he helped compose a futuristic novel, *They Used To Play On Grass*, and detective stories that became *Hazell*, a successful television series.

With George Graham, the Arsenal manager, and I as partners, he lost money in a tailoring venture that quickly went under. 'I learned from getting my fingers burnt,' he added. 'It was important to have an idea of business. As I recall it, we set out with a great deal of enthusiasm but didn't apply ourselves properly. It might sound fancy, but I look upon life as a mystery. The trick is to be ready, a jump ahead. You've got to be on patrol every morning.'

Venables loved playing, 'the cut and thrust of a game, trying to outsmart the opposition, pitting your wits against them, but I don't miss it. I got a tremendous kick out of coaching, and working with outstanding players. But that's also behind me. Sometimes when I'm watching one of our matches I have to suppress an urge to get involved. My responsibilities lie elsewhere and when we can see a bit more daylight I shall probably go off and watch other teams.'

Venables had no intention of taking over at Tottenham. 'It came on gradually,' he said. 'The club was clearly in deep trouble and I thought I might know someone who could help.' As a result, he soon found himself operating on two fronts. The team in the morning, business in the afternoon. He was negotiating on the eve of the Cup final. 'That's why I look upon winning the Cup as my biggest achievement,' he said, 'more uplifting than taking Barcelona to the Spanish championship and the promotion seasons at Crystal Palace and Queen's Park Rangers.'

Problems remain at the bank and on the field. Once again Venables is striving to get his head in front. Nevertheless, he feels that Tottenham's supporters may be the first to realise the importance of finance. 'I've never flinched from taking a risk,' he said. 'But at times it is sensible to accept that you can't have what you can't afford. Things are tight, no question about it, but we are getting by, and with luck we'll get better. It isn't easy to think long term because loyalty went out of football a long time ago and I'll never blame a player for wanting to move on at the end of his contract. That's the way life is now, but the important thing is the club. People, players, managers, directors, supporters come and go, but the club is always there, the only thing that's permanent.'

Still charged with an unfettered energy, Venables rubbed his hands, thinking about tomorrow's match against Arsenal. He is, as he frequently demonstrates, quick to direct attention to the significant.

from the INDEPENDENT *1991*

Herbert Chapman

BERNARD JOY

Herbert Chapman became a manager by chance. As a player, he was a hard-working forward with experience of several clubs and one claim to distinction, that of wearing bright yellow football boots. He was sitting in the bath at White Hart Lane after playing for Tottenham in their last match of the 1906–7 season and talking to Walter Bull, the centre-half and captain. Bull had been offered the post of player-manager of Northampton Town, the Southern League side, but confessed doubts as to whether he had the temperament for the job. He turned to Chapman. 'Look, Herbert, you're more suited than I am. Why don't you take it.'

Chapman did. His influence on Northampton was remarkable. They were a struggling club when he took over but soon were at the top of the league, which was then the equivalent of the third division south, with an ample points margin and a roaring goal average. They did well, too, in the FA Cup against teams like Newcastle United and Sheffield Wednesday.

The successful touch accompanied Chapman to Leeds. The club won everything that was going in the emergency competitions of the 1914–18 war, until some internal irregularities came to the notice of the Football Association. The directors were suspended and although Chapman was not directly involved, he was suspended too.

Chapman returned to soccer with Huddersfield Town and immediately helped them to gain promotion to the first division in 1918–19, the first full season after the war. A year later they reached the Cup final, to be beaten by Aston Villa at Stamford Bridge. The league Championship fell to Huddersfield twice during Chapman's regime, in 1923–24 and 1924–25.

A move to London was inevitable. It alone could give full scope to the breadth of Chapman's imagination and ambition. Arsenal appealed to him most because it was a struggling club, something he could work on and make a power in the land. Knowing how crowds followed success in smaller areas like Northampton, Leeds and Huddersfield – the last a Rugby League stronghold at the time – he realised that a winning team at Highbury, which is only a few minutes away from the heart of London, would bring unparalleled prosperity and acclamation.

His decision to apply for the post of manager of Arsenal in 1925 and then to pull every string to further the end, showed his character. He was ambitious, determined and far-sighted. He was a fighter, and the harder the fight the more he revelled in it. Quiet, stocky and of average height, he might easily be unnoticed in a crowd but the energetic and purposeful walk and the mastery in the steely-blue eyes revealed the human dynamo underneath.

from FORWARD ARSENAL *1954*

The Greenwood Academy

JOHN LYALL

Probably the most exciting and stimulating period of my career were the years I spent learning the basics of coaching from Ron Greenwood. He was a constant source of inspiration to me. I had not set out to be a coach; when my playing career was prematurely ended by injury I went into coaching with little practical experience and even less knowledge. But suddenly, under Ron's wing, I discovered that I couldn't learn enough. I had a completely open mind on coaching and I devoured everything he said. I could listen to him talking about the game for hours. He created pictures of situations for his players. He told me that every time I took a training session I should do likewise – create the picture that helped the players understand what was required.

I began to pick up the phrases Ron used daily in his coaching sessions. They have stuck with me all my life. One of the earliest, and truest, was 'Simplicity is genius'. I was beginning to realise that the best football, like that played by the modern-day Liverpool team, is the simplest. That phrase became one of the rocks upon which I built my own coaching reputation. I like good players who do simple things well.

Ron also liked players with 'good habits'. This didn't mean that they held a teacup with the correct degree of finesse, though he admired good behaviour and good manners in his players. He meant that players who consistently do the right things on the playing field develop good habits and become good players. Those with bad habits, he would argue, become inconsistent players. Yet he also felt that one of the most important arts of the game was the ability to improvise. the ability to surprise the opposition with the unpredictable. The complete footballer was the one who could combine good habits with improvisation.

He used to tell all his players: 'You must leave the ball playable.' This meant that when making a pass the receiving player had to be able to play the ball first time. This was a good habit. If the pass was perfect, the receiving player could play the ball, spin away from his marker and move into space to collect a return. This was improvisation. This was what he taught at West Ham, and it was a joy to watch him at work with players of the quality of Bobby Moore, Martin Peters, Geoff Hurst, Johnny Byrne and Ronnie Boyce.

As a player with an enquiring mind, Ron had been enormously impressed by the wonderful Hungarian side that beat England 6–3 at Wembley in 1953. It was a historic defeat, the first England had suffered at Wembley against a foreign team. That Hungarian triumph proved to him that football could be a game of beauty and art, as well as a muscular science. He once said that he came away from Wembley that day with a little insight into how Paul must have felt on the road to Damascus. He applied many of the features he saw in that Hungarian side to his own West Ham teams over the years. One tactic used by the Hungarians in later years also had a big influence on Ron, and he was to use it with enormous success at West Ham.

He had recognised the value of the near-post cross used by the Hungarians, and embedded that tactic into the framework of West Ham's attacking game. The near-post cross, an innovation in the English game, became a Greenwood speciality. The essence of the move was that the ball was whipped in quickly from the flanks to unmarked space at the near post. The key to the move was that the central strikers anticipated the flight and timing of the cross and ran into the empty space as late as possible to head or volley the ball towards the goal. He first developed this move with Martin Peters, Peter Brabrook, Johnny Sissons and Geoff Hurst, with Bobby Moore also involved as the player feeding an early pass out to the flanks. The delivery of the ball into the penalty area had to be perfect but, equally important, Hurst, as the main central striker, had to get the timing of his runs to the near post exactly right. I remember spending months and months on the training pitches at Chadwell Heath perfecting the tactic. Ron had the training-ground maintenance staff stick a couple of posts in two huge paint tins filled with concrete. These posts were positioned out on the flanks and acted as markers. The wide players, Sissons and Peters (and, later, Harry Redknapp and Johnny Ayris – Ron insisted that all players at all levels learned the move), had to run at the paint tins, pretending they were markers. The players then had to push the ball outside the tins but, before they went beyond them, had to curl their cross round the tins to the near post. The central strikers would start their runs from the far side of the penalty area. They had to leave the space at the near post empty for as long as they could, otherwise the defenders would follow them and the element of surprise was lost. Hurst, for instance, perfected his dummy run at this time, lingering on the edge of the area before making a decoy run. The marking defender would follow him, and Hurst would suddenly change direction and sprint into the space at the near post, arriving just in time to meet the ball from the wing.

That move brought West Ham literally dozens of goals over the years and, inevitably, was widely copied by other teams. Perhaps the most memorable example of Hurst's near-post expertise came at Wembley in 1966, not in West Ham's claret and blue, but in England's red shirts. England were trailing 0–1 to West Germany, when Overath fouled Bobby Moore. The England captain took the West German defence completely by surprise with a quick, long and accurate free kick from out on the left. Hurst, almost programmed by now to expect such a ball to the near post, timed his run from the right immaculately, gliding the ball with his head past Tilkowski. It was a goal that had its origins on the training ground at Chadwell Heath. It was as if the relationship that day between the three West Ham lads, Hurst, Moore and Peters, was telepathic. Ron put it more simply. It was good habits.

The longer I worked with him, the more I realised that one of his greatest strengths was his ability to spot the central problems every time. He would sit the players in the dressing-room and say, in quite straightforward terms, that this is where we were at fault and this is what we had to do to rectify the problem. There were times when he could be dogmatic, but I think a good coach has to be like that. But he would always put his ideas across in an intelligent and creative manner. If you had any football brain at all he was easy to understand. You have only to look at the number of his players who went on to become internationals, and then coaches and managers themselves, to realise that the vast majority of them learned a great deal from Ron Greenwood.

He taught them, too, about life and how, as public figures, they should behave and handle themselves. He taught me always to talk to the people who guide you to the car-park, open the door for you or give you your match programme. He believed in respect and good manners. He was a kind, caring and thoroughly decent man who loved his job – and football – in all its aspects.

from JUST LIKE MY DREAMS *1989*

Jock Stein

HUGH McILVANNEY

The larcenous nature of death, its habit of breaking in on us when we are least prepared and stealing the irreplaceable, has seldom been more sickeningly experienced than at Ninian Park in Cardiff on Tuesday night.

Those of us who crowded sweatily into the small entrance hall of the main stand to wait for word of Jock Stein's condition will always remember the long half hour in which the understandable vagueness of reports filtering from the dressing-room area lulled us into believing that Jock was going to make it through yet another crisis. The raw dread that had been spread among us by his collapse on the touchline at the end of the Wales–Scotland World Cup match gave way to the more bearable gloom of acknowledging that the career of one of the greatest managers football has known would have to be ended by immediate retirement.

Then – off in a corner of that confused room – Mike England, the manager of Wales and a deeply concerned first-hand witness of what had been happening to Stein, was heard to say that he was still 'very, very poorly'. There was no mistaking the true meaning of those words and suddenly the sense of relief that had been infiltrating our anxieties was exposed as baseless. We felt almost guilty about having allowed ourselves to be comforted by rumours. Then, abruptly, we knew for sure that the Big Man was dead and for some of us it was indeed as if our spirits, our very lives, had been burglarised.

Of all the reactions to Stein's death, none meant more than that of the thousands of Scotland's travelling supporters who learned of it haphazardly but with eerie swiftness as they got ready to celebrate a ragged draw against Wales that should guarantee their team a passage to the World Cup finals in Mexico next summer. They are, given half an excuse, the most raucously exuberant fans in the game but as midnight neared in Cardiff on Tuesday they wandered through the streets in subdued clusters, sustaining the unforced atmosphere of mourning that pervaded the hundreds who waited silently in the darkness outside Ninian Park after the last hope of reviving the stricken man inside had been abandoned.

There is no doubt that the Scots have a highly developed capacity for the elegiac mood, especially when there is a bottle about, but what was to be encountered in South Wales last week was no cheap example of the genre. When travel-soiled units of the tartan expeditionary force interrupted their morose drinking to propose toasts to the lost leader, anybody cynical enough to see such behaviour as just another maudlin ritual doesn't know much about the way the power of Jock Stein's nature communicated itself to millions of ordinary people.

His achievements in football were monumental but they can only partially explain his impact upon and relevance to so many lives. Perhaps he was profoundly cherished simply because he was a true working-class hero – and that is a species which is disappearing almost as fast in industrial Scotland as elsewhere, if only because the values that governed its creation are being relentlessly eroded day by day. Even the common misery of unemployment has not halted the fragmentation of a sense of community that once seemed indestructible.

In an age when, if I may quote a line from my brother William's latest novel, it is as if 'every man and his family were a private company', Stein was the unpretentious embodiment of that older, better code that was until not so long ago the compensatory inheritance of all who were born of the labouring poor. No one was ever likely to mistake him for a saint, or even for a repository of bland altruism. He could look after himself and his own in the market place or anywhere else, but there was never the remotest danger that he would be contaminated by the materialism that engulfs so many of those who find prosperity through sport or other forms of entertainment.

These days it is hard to avoid having the eardrums battered by some unlikely pillar of the New Right who – having persuaded himself that a largely fortuitous ability to kick a football or volley a tennis ball or belt out a pop song or tell a few jokes more acceptably than the next man is actually evidence of his own splendid mastery of his fate – insists that the dole queues would fade away overnight if people got off their arses, got on their bikes and showed the enterprise that has carried him to what he imagines is glory. Stein's whole life was a repudiation of such garbage.

He was utterly Scottish, utterly Lanarkshire in fact, but his was the kind of loyalty to his roots that made his principles universal.

His father was a miner who was a miner's son and Stein himself worked underground until turning belatedly to full-time professional football at the age of twenty-seven. During a long, incalculably rewarding friendship with him, I heard him say many memorable things and some of the most vivid were inevitably about the game he loved and the great practitioners of it, but he was most moved and most moving when he talked of that earlier phase of his working experience.

There was a dynamic, combative quality to most of his conversation (mischievous wind-up was a favourite mode and, though he did not drink alcohol, he occasionally dipped his barbs in curare) but when the subject was mining and miners a tone of wistful reverie invaded his voice.

'I went down the pit when I was sixteen (at first I was working with ponies – it was still that era) and when I left eleven years later I knew that wherever I went, whatever work I did, I'd never be alongside better men. They didn't just get their own work done and go away. They all stayed around until every man had finished what he had to do and everything was cleared up. Of course, in the bad or dangerous times that was even more true. It was a place where phoneys and cheats couldn't survive for long.

'Down there for eight hours you're away from God's fresh air and sunshine and there's nothing that can compensate for that. There's nothing as dark as the darkness down a pit, the blackness that closes in on you if your lamp goes out. You'd think you would see some kind of shapes but you can see nothing, nothing but the inside of your head. I think everybody should go down the pit at least once to learn what darkness is.'

Phoneys and cheats did not flourish in his company during four decades of involvement with senior football. As a player he was shrewd, well organised and strong rather than outstandingly gifted, though he made a fundamental contribution to the rich streak of prize-winning enjoyed by the Celtic team he joined unexpectedly for a fee of £1,200 after modest seasons with Albion Rovers and a motley troupe of non-league men at Llanelli in South Wales. He became an influential captain of Celtic and when his playing career was ended by an injury to his right ankle that left him with a noticeable limp for the rest of his days, it was clear that he would make a manager.

His old employers were certain to be impressed by his successful introduction to the trade in charge of Dunfermline, for he gave that humble club the Scottish Cup by beating Celtic in the final tie, and after a further rehearsal period with Hibernian he went back to Park-head as manager in 1964. It was a genuinely historic return, perhaps the most significant single happening in the entire story of Scottish football.

All of Stein's family associations, centred on the Lanarkshire villages of Blantyre and Burnbank, were vehemently Protestant but he had never hesitated for a second over first identifying himself with a club traditionally seen as carrying the banner for the Catholic minority in Glasgow (and throughout Scotland) and when he emerged as Celtic's first non-Catholic manager he became a living, eloquent rebuke to the generations of bigotry surrounding the Rangers-Celtic rivalry.

Under him, Celtic dominated the whole range of Scottish domestic competitions to a degree that stamped him, in his context, as the supreme achiever among the world's football managers. Nine league championships in a row is in itself a record no one can ever hope to equal but it was the triumphant lifting of the European Cup in Lisbon in 1967, a feat that had previously proved beyond the most powerful British clubs, that set him totally apart in the annals of the sport. That other legendary Scot, Bill Shankly, got it just about right when he held out a fellow miner's hand to Stein after the brilliant defeat of Inter-Milan and said in his coal-cutter voice: 'John – you're immortal.'

Celtic in Lisbon performed with irresistible verve, representing per-fectly Stein's ideal of blending athletic speed and competitiveness with imagination, delicacy of touch at close quarters and exhilarating surges of virtuosity. Of course, when all Stein's technical assets had been assessed – of the vast tactical awareness that owed nothing to coaching courses, the precise judgment of his own and opposing players, the encyclopaedic retention of detail, the emphasis on the positive while eradicating the foolhardy – the essence of his gifts as a manager was seen to reside in something more basic and more subtle: in his capacity to make men do for him more than they would have been able to do for themselves.

Stein's allegiance to Celtic withstood more than one attempt to coax him to switch dramatically to the manager's chair at Rangers and it was sad that when his connection with Parkhead was eventually severed in 1978 he should leave with a justified feeling of grievance about how he had ultimately been treated. By that time he had survived a warning of skirmish with heart trouble and a car crash that almost killed him in the summer of 1975. Many men would have throttled down there and then but he had been a compulsive worker around football most of his life and when the manager's job at Leeds United was offered he decided, at the age of fifty-five, to move south.

However, two months later he received the call millions of admirers believed he should have had years before and was given control of the Scotland team. He took them to the World Cup finals in Spain in 1982 (the Soviet Union kept them out of the last twelve on goal difference) and after a match last Tuesday notable for its tensions and controversies, never for its quality, he had the result required to open a way to the finals of 1986. But suddenly the strains that have been mounting mercilessly over the years, strains whose ravages the obsessive in him insisted on belittling, proved too much for a system weakened by that earlier illness and, most crucially, by the desperate car crash of ten years ago.

The pain of his death from a heart attack dug deepest into his wife Jean and into Rae and George, the attractive, strong-minded daughter and son of whom he was so proud. But there were many others in many places who felt last week that they did not have to go down a pit to know what real darkness was.

from the OBSERVER *1985*

Malcolm Allison

BARRY NORMAN

In the long run, said Malcolm Allison, the answer might well lie in psychoanalysis. He waited, with a defensive grin, for the laugh.

Psychoanalysis, I said, not laughing (and indeed it would take a bigger and braver man than I to laugh at Malcolm Allison), for his footballers? Exactly, he said. Brazil had psychiatrists attached to their football squad so why not Manchester City?

After all, there he was with potentially the finest bunch of players in the land, trained to a hair, almost indecently fit, erupting with skill and yet they were pretty damn nearly bottom of the league.

'It's not ability they've lost,' he said. 'It's confidence, and what do you do about that? Ask advice? No. You get plenty of advice offered but you don't go seeking it. If any manager knew the answer he'd win everything every year.'

'There's nothing physically wrong, you see. Players these days are stronger, run faster and jump higher than ever before. But we're not nearly so professional at sorting out the mental side of the game. We don't use psychiatrists. We should, though, and eventually we will. It'll come, I'm sure of that. As a matter of fact I've been thinking about it seriously for a couple of years.'

We eyed each other solemnly across his office. 'Yeah.' he said. 'You can imagine the gags, can't you? "Here, look what old Mal's got there – right bunch of nut cases."'

'It's a matter of convincing the players that a psychiatrist could find out why they're playing badly, why they're not happy in their work. And they aren't happy at the moment: they're bloody miserable. They don't like losing any more than I do.'

Meanwhile, and until the climate is right for the club psychiatrist to be appointed, failure brings other problems in its wake. New rumours spring up every day – Lee's going, Doyle's going. The football gossip columns hint at a berserk and panic-stricken Allison booting his entire squad out of Maine Road. Untrue, he said, all of it.

'I'm a person who makes quick decisions and one of those decisions was that I wouldn't sell any player until I could replace him with a better one and where do I find better players than the mob I've got? God, it's an unbelievable game, football.

'I can tell the exact minute when they're going to start playing badly. They play the first half, they're putting it together, playing great – and then the whistle goes and in the dressing-room everything's gone. It all falls apart – and there's not a thing you can do about it.

'I can talk to them, sure. I do. I talk to them individually, I talk to them in groups. I tell 'em I believe in them – but until they start believing in themselves again they're not going to get the results.'

Wasn't it possible, though, to trace failure back to its source; to pinpoint the moment when things started going wrong? He looked at me with justifiable scorn. Blimey, hadn't he tried that?

Well, then, how about Rodney Marsh? City were top of the league when he joined them: two weeks ago they were practically bottom. Was he perhaps the wrong kind of player for this team?

'No,' said Allison, 'that's nonsense. You can't blame anything on Rodney Marsh. It may be that because he came here with a reputation as an artist, a brilliant ball player, the others felt they ought to show the crowds that they can play a bit, too. That might have upset the rhythm a little but it's hardly Marsh's fault, is it?

'I bought him because he's got more skill than anybody else in English football, he can score goals and he's just got that thing. He affects people – like Bestie, Cassius Clay or Tom Jones. I don't know what it is but he's got it. Besides, I like his originality. He's got the sort of footballing brain that can spot the other team's pattern of play and know just where and how to break it up.'

He prowled about the office in his track suit, a naturally worried but still philosophical man. The situation was serious but not desperate, or desperate but not serious depending on the level of his optimism.

He said: 'Just before the season started I went and looked at the stadium. It was great. The pitch looked great, the stands looked great. The players were confident, the spirit was good. I thought, "Christ, what a season we're going to have."

'I was proud. I looked at all these things and I thought, "It's there. It's all there."' A long, rueful pause, 'And it *is* all there. Losing a few games doesn't change anything really. It just puts you in your place, makes you realise you're not infallible. You see, my players were over-confident. That's what started the whole thing.

'Even when they were getting beat, they were still over-confident, up to a certain time. I remember Arsenal had the same trouble the year after they'd done the double. We went down to Highbury and won and Bertie Mee said to me, "What do I do, Mal?" and I said, "I don't know, Bertie. You just work." That's all we can do here – just work. I always reckon I'm luckier when I work harder.

'But we've had bad patches before – just after we got promoted, then when I got suspended and the team didn't win in twelve matches and again after we won the championship. Anyway, this season's only a quarter of the way through.

'Not that anybody likes the present situation. The players say they can't go into a pub, can't talk to the next-door neighbour. They're ashamed to go into town and it's no consolation that Manchester United are doing just as badly. There's no comfort in that. I mean, I can't go and swop worries with Frank O'Farrell. I can't talk to any managers. All they could advise me on is tactical things and I'm not bothered about them. It's the players' state of mind that causes all the trouble and maybe I haven't worked hard enough on that.

'And yet, in a way, I quite like this situation. I get a certain pleasure out of being down and knowing that I've got to get this right and that right.

'That's what I'm here for. It's what my job's all about.' A helluva job, I said. 'Yeah,' he said. 'Sometimes you think, "I don't need all these pressures; I'd like it a bit easier," and then you think you'd like to go and work at a smaller club, maybe abroad, and have a quieter life.'

He stared wistfully out at the car-park and then he said: 'Ah, but what the hell! If you've made a bit of a name for yourself they'd expect things of you wherever you went. There'd still be pressure. So, finally, I reckon I'm better off where I am.'

from the OBSERVER *1972*

Alf Ramsey

MICHAEL PARKINSON

There were 14,999 other people who will swear to what I am going to tell you now. They and I were present that important day, many years ago, when Alf Ramsey suffered the trauma that changed his life and put the skids under wingers. He was playing right-back for Southampton at the time, an urbane, immaculate footballer who seemed as out of place at Barnsley as a bowler hat in a pawnshop.

In this particular game Johnny Kelly had one of those days when all his genius flowed into his feet. If you have ever seen Matthews or Finney or Georgie Best at their finest then you'll know what I mean. He flicked his hips and Ramsey sat down in wonderment. He waved his foot over the ball like a wand, daring Ramsey to guess what might happen next, and as the full-back anticipated a move outside, Kelly came inside and left him for dead. At one stage he demonstrated his complete mastery by beating Ramsey, waiting for him to recover and then beating him again. Had Kelly been on the Southampton side and doing this to certain of the Barnsley defenders he would have had his impudence rewarded with a bed in the nearest emergency ward. But Ramsey played it clean and endeavoured to look as dignified as any man can when he is having his nose rubbed in the dirt.

The crowd didn't help. They relished the sight of Kelly shredding Ramsey's reputation. This, remember, was in the days when footballers were the victims of individual abuse and not the collective sort they get from today's rehearsed choirs. Thus the comments, though not so loud, were more personal and biting. As Ramsey sat down before Kelly's skill a man near me bellowed:

'Tha' wants to learn how to stand up before tha' plays this game, Ramsey.' And again, as Kelly left Ramsey immobile and helpless as a statue, the same man bawled: 'Ramsey, tha' art about as much use as a chocolate teapot.'

This is as much as any man can be expected to take without consulting the Director of Public Prosecutions. My theory is that as Alf Ramsey sat in that dressing-room in Barnsley, scraping the mud from his boots and his reputation, he first thought of his revenge on wingers. He didn't want just Kelly's scalp, but the destruction of the whole tricky race.

It's not a bad theory, particularly when you consider that Alf Ramsey is where he is today, and Johnny Kelly was last heard of manufacturing a liquid bleach. It's an even stronger theory when you realise that wingers like Kelly are now more rare than five-legged giraffes.

But I have cornered whatever consolation there is left to people who loved the game in the dear, daft days before Mr Ramsey got his paws on it. When I read of the experts trying to explain to themselves just what he is up to, and why, I sit there giggling gently to myself, nursing my memories, thinking fondly of a grey afternoon many seasons ago when a closet winger with bandy legs and baggy shorts made a monkey of a master mind.

from FOOTBALL DAFT *1968*

George Raynor

TONY PAWSON

The *Guinness Book of Records* lists an Englishman as the most successful manager of any national team. He is not Sir Alf Ramsey, but the retired and retiring Yorkshireman, George Raynor. The statistics may have been carefully chosen to give him pride of place, but his record is remarkable. Raynor is no forgotten hero, just one we never recognised. His story tells much of past attitudes to footballers and football management. He took Sweden to an Olympic gold medal in 1948 and a bronze four years later. In the 1950 World Cup when

England were defeated by USA, Sweden came third. With Raynor in charge again they were runners-up to Brazil in Stockholm in 1958. The King of Sweden made him a Knight of the Order of Vasa, Brazil gave him a gold medal, yet English league clubs have given him little but heartache.

He lives now in a bungalow in Armthorpe, close to Doncaster. The light wood panelling is Swedish in style, the room full of silver and glass gifts to remind him of his years of success. Each winter scores of Swedes still come to Armthorpe, making the pilgrimage to a soccer prophet without much honour in his own land.

Raynor was born in 1907, the son of a miner, one of a large family. He was clever enough to win a scholarship to Barnsley Grammar School, but with his father out of work he had to leave to earn money as a butcher's apprentice, then lorry driver. Football was an early passion and he soon turned professional, earning 15s a match. He was to play for seventeen seasons for clubs such as Sheffield United, Mansfield, Rotherham and Bury. £208 a year was his normal wage, though with Bury he reached the magic six, seven, eight – £6 in summer, £7 in the second team, £8 a week in the first. When he was first put up for transfer by Sheffield United he was without pay or work for the summer, unable to draw unemployment money since the Labour Exchange classed footballers as 'seasonal' workers.

During the war Raynor, like so many leading footballers, became a Sergeant Instructor in the Physical Training Corps. It was then that he developed skills as a coach which were confirmed when he trained the Iraqi team for its first successful tour of Arab countries. He had developed his own manual, his own theories on physical fitness, and was determined on a career in coaching.

No English clubs were interested, but the Football Association was more helpful. Stanley Rous gave his name to the Swedes, who had asked assistance in finding a national coach.

Raynor's manager at Aldershot had been one of the game's great thinkers and the player the crowds enjoyed hating, the Irish international Billy McCracken, whose skill with the off-side trap had reduced forward lines to angry shambles.

McCracken's advice was to remember that a manager's job is 60 per cent bluff and be confident that he had enough experience for it. 'But don't pretend you know it all, or you will get no help. You are a nice humble fellow and if you keep that way everyone will confide in you.'

Humility came easily to Raynor after watching Birmingham City play in Stockholm. He was put in the place of honour at the dinner only to be unrecognised by the English players and for their journalists to query persistently how someone of whom they had never heard could be made manager of the Swedish national team.

With the bluff called so early Raynor could justify himself only by his originality, by belief in his methods – and by results. The originality was at once apparent when he was told he could only have the team for brief training periods before matches. 'If they are not to be allowed to come to me I will have to go to them' was the response.

Two weeks at a time he would take over the coaching of the leading clubs, getting to know the players and laying down training routines for them. This was as revolutionary as if Alf Ramsey were to relieve Bill Shankly and then Don Revie shortly before Liverpool and Leeds met in the Cup.

Raynor's personality alone made the unthinkable acceptable. From a firm foundation of knowledge he was able to mould the national team, tell them after they had been beaten by Denmark, 'With the players you have in this country you won't lose to them again in the next ten years.'

His great test came with an international against Switzerland. The Swiss had a new defensive system, the left-back moved into the centre, the wing-halves dropping back to mark the wingers, the centre-half free to roam. They had just held England to a draw, and, when Stanley Matthews and George Hardwick came to Stockholm with an RAF side, Raynor pressed them for the details on which he based his plan. He revived an idea with which Bury had experimented – the G plan or deep-lying centre-forward that the Hungarians were later to exploit so successfully. He pushed Gunnar Gren, a skilled midfield player, into an attacking role beside the right-winger, to exploit the defensive weakness on the left. The press were invited in to see the training and to hear the plan, Raynor staking his reputation on the result. Gren scored four goals, Sweden won 7–2.

Raynor had appreciated that the Swedes were masterly in their control of the ball, but too delicate in keeping possession. He encouraged the skill and covered the weakness with a few strong players like Bertil Nordahl in the key positions.

His training was designed to supplement the tactics. 'You will make our players hungry for the ball like the English – you will keep it from them,' had been his reception. Instead he was soon shown in cartoons with an immense string bag of balls on his back as he emphasised their importance in practice. The quick reaction, the agility and the hardness he built into the Swedish players was usually done under cover of work with the ball.

The better the Swedish results the more he needed his ingenuity, for the Italians bought up the best of the Swedish amateurs, forcing constant change in the national teams.

Raynor himself was finally attracted to Italy, the money to manage Juventus being prudently invested in a house at Skegness. It was the only time he could save from his earnings in the game.

With Juventus and Lazio he achieved results, but was soon disenchanted with Italian football. He sensed that what the goalkeeper was paid often had more influence on matches than the manager's tactics. So, with Jesse Carver, another manager of European reputation, he returned home to Coventry City. There too he found only disillusionment. When Carver went back to Italy, Raynor acted as the team manager. As always he was interested in the development of skilful footballers and that was not always the best prescription for the third division south. Raynor was given no time to test his theories with Harry Warren brought in over him in the usual search for instant success. He had hoped to settle in England but with no other club offering to take him on he accepted the Swedes' importunate requests to prepare them for the World Cup to be staged in their homeland.

Of the British teams only Ireland and Wales reached the quarter-finals, but Raynor's side went smoothly through to the final, destroyed at the last by the Brazilians and the brilliance of Garrincha and Pelé.

Later, England at Wembley were to prove no problem, the tall graceful Simonsson confirming Raynor's confident prediction that Sweden would become the second foreign team to beat us at home. Yet when he left Sweden the best position he could command was a job in the stores at Butlin's camp and to be honorary manager of Skegness Town.

Two final incidents sum up a career of so much talent, so little exploited at home. Alick Jeffery of Doncaster Rovers was briefly the young prodigy of English football, a powerfully built inside forward with an appetite for goals. A broken leg failed to respond to treatment and he was written off as unfit to play again. The insurance of £15,000 was paid for a career prematurely ended. Jeffery's own share was £4,000, soon dissipated in drink and disillusion as he sought vainly to recapture the vanished glamour.

On impulse he wrote to Raynor to ask if he would help him get fit for football again. Raynor's only condition was that Jeffery must work as hard as he would himself. Out of condition, permanently crippled in the medical view, Jeffery was transformed by Raynor's routine of exercises carefully developed over the years. But when Jeffery was declared fit for league football again the authorities had the unrelished problem of explanations to the insurance company, Raynor the criticism, not the congratulations.

In his sixties he was asked by Doncaster, in one of their frequent periods between managers, to help tide them over. He took them to second in their division before declaring his job done and his wish to help with the youth development in the club. This too was a reward that escaped him, but his belief in the value of coaching had won a wider acceptance.

from THE FOOTBALL MANAGERS *1973*

Bill Shankly

TONY PAWSON

Bill Shankly's tactical talks are always positive, based on what Liverpool will do to exploit weakness in the opponents. Only once was he known to pay undue respect to the opposition. As the team gathered round his tactics table one Friday Shankly's admiration for Matt Busby and Manchester United led him to emphasise their abilities. 'Denis Law, now, there's a player. Verra good with his head, and quicksilver on his feet. The man can dance on egg-shells. Watch Bobby Charlton – let him surge through from behind and ye will na' stop his shot. Ye canna' give Best an inch either. He's clever and strong. Ye can hurrt him and hurrt him, but he will keep coming.' There was an anxious silence as Shankly stared at the heavy metal discs on the simulated field, red for Liverpool, white for United. Suddenly his arm sent the white spinning off the table. 'That to Manchester United,' he shouted joyously, 'We'll sweep them off the field.'

It is rare for him to so delay the punch line. One of his ways of building morale is a humorous catalogue of opponents' frailties, deliberately deriding their talent. Having seen them off their coach, he and Albert Shelley, the late trainer, would solemnly recount the depressed looks, limited abilities and unusual antecedents of the visiting team. The routine was designed to amuse, to relax and to build confidence.

Typical of his style was a conversation with Peter Thompson and Roger Hunt, his international forwards, sitting together on the bench before a match. 'Dinna be soft-hearted, Peter. Yon back's so scared after the fool ye made of him last time he's asked to be dropped. He's trembling in the dressing-room. But show him no pity. I'll ask a favour of you, Roger. The goalkeeper's mother is a relation of mine. She's worrit you'll break the puir lad's wrist with your powerful shooting. I've promised her you'll no' hit him, but put the ba' in the corners of the net out of his reach.'

Thompson knew the back had been his master before, Hunt that the goalkeeper's mother had probably never heard of Shankly, but both felt lifted by the familiar patter.

Shankly's ability to enthuse players is obvious enough from the response. Toshack was hardly a worker with Cardiff or Cormack with Notts Forest, but they run themselves breathless for Liverpool. Six scouts from other major clubs rejected Kevin Keegan in his Scunthorpe days as lacking strength and heart. Shankly built this modest, likeable man into the most exciting of players.

Shankly is simple too in his loyalties. In his playing days he was single-minded in his belief in Preston. Tom Finney recalls in the first game he played with Shankly being driven on by shouts of 'Keep fighting. We can do it yet.' They were four goals down with two minutes to play.

After his managerial apprenticeship with Carlisle, Grimsby, Workington and Huddersfield, Shankly has devoted himself to Liverpool with a fervour that came to express a city's feeling. In the final stages of one league championship Arsenal, Derby and Manchester City were all in close competition with Liverpool. Before a critical game between Manchester City and Derby, Shankly rang his old friend Joe Mercer at Manchester: 'I'll be coming to your match with Derby. I hope you both lose.'

There is only one club for Shankly and only one manager who can satisfy Liverpool.

Towns react to certain types of manager, certain styles of football. Liverpool and Shankly are in tune, sharing the same boisterous whole-hearted approach to life, the same passionate feeling which accepts as natural that two fans should ask for their ashes to be scattered in the goalmouth.

Shankly has no sympathy with paperwork, but types all his own letters himself. He has no love of theoretical coaching, but is the epitome of the track-suit manager, passing on his knowledge to his players. His feel for the game and for people is instinctive and practical. Yet his and Liverpool's success stems from a thoroughness of organisation. Shankly was one of the first to have the third and fourth divisions researched in depth when other managers were somewhat scornful of their quality. Before he buys a player he will consider every aspect of his game and his personality. The approach will be oblique, but many people will be sounded out to build up the picture. And if the team has to stay in an hotel Shankly will probably have slept there before to make sure it is not too noisy or too luxurious.

One good team may make a manager's reputation for years. But it is continuity of achievement that proves his powers. While Liverpool were winning the league Championship twice and the Cup once in those three seasons of soaring success in the sixties he was planning the succession.

With few injuries and no failures there was little chance to experiment. No good first-division player would transfer to Liverpool to adorn the reserves. It was then that Shankly built his youth teams and bought from lower divisions. Lloyd was happy to come from Bristol in the hope of taking over in time from Yeats, Clemence to wait until he could replace Lawrence.

That policy and an unsentimental appreciation of the moment great players began to decline has kept Liverpool in the forefront for a decade.

from THE FOOTBALL MANAGERS *1973*

PART 6

The Fans

Viva Valencia

RICHARD BRENTNALL

Dan-Air Flight Number 1770 was preparing for take-off from Gat-
wick. On a cold but bright November Monday, it was now late afternoon as Mick, Derek and myself searched for our seats on the rather
grubby little aeroplane after catching an eyeful of the gorgeous blonde
stewardess framed in the doorway. We were in a particularly light-
hearted mood: buoyant at the outset of a four-day break in the Spanish
sunshine, thrilled at the prospect of the match to be played on Wednesday night – Albion's most glamorous fixture for a very long while –
plus we'd enjoyed a right royal skinful in London's Victoria that lunch
time, when the fine weather had served to put a keener edge still to
our appetite for excitement. Suddenly, seeming almost to fill the plane
with its urgency, there piped up a lone, frantic voice.

'Where's me ticket? Mick! Cor foind me ticket! 'Elp me!!'

Tottering alongside the stewardess, Lamp-post had a look of frozen
horror on his face as he raced through his pockets. No joy. Stepping
backwards for his anxious eyes to dance over the floor, he now paid
this succulent female the supreme compliment of treading on her
delicate toes. He turned to apologise, but bought out only a hiccup:
whereas she, exercising her practised, tolerant smile, calmly extracted
from his lapel pocket some red printed matter which, duly unfurled,
sure enough revealed the name of her employer. Spanish heads at the
front of the plane slowly shook as they re-buried themselves in their
magazines. Lionel had achieved the doubtful distinction of making an
ass of himself before Valencia's residents whilst still in Sussex.

Minutes later, as the plane groaned its path down the runway for
what Lamp-post reckoned was his thirteenth flight, I strained to look
behind where the big oaf was sitting. His eyes were shut upon his
slumped head; but not only was his mouth unfastened, his seat belt
lay dangling by his sides. We were on our way.

When the news had come through that our reward for seeing off
Braga was a pairing with Valencia, I'd had to admit to mixed feelings.
The ideal draw for any fan wanting to follow his team abroad, of

course, is a side who not only come from an attractive part of the Continent but whom you also fancy your chances against. As far as locations go, they don't come much more pleasant than Spain's Mediterranean coast – but nor could the playing opposition have been much tougher. Valencia had a reputation for being a hotbed, so much so that their stadium with its passionate atmosphere is frequently employed as host to the Spanish national side, especially for matches of crucial import; and their highly expensive team boasted some players of rare talent. Two in particular were Mario Kempes, who'd played a goalscoring hero's part in his native Argentina's lifting of the World Cup five months earlier, and Rainer Bonhof, a West German midfielder possessed of lordly skill and a murderous flair for exploiting free-kicks. So despite Albion's own sparkling form at this moment, reflected by only two defeats in fifteen league games and two hurdles safely negotiated in Europe, you might say I was apprehensive of the outcome, and matters weren't helped either by fitness doubts now surrounding Cyrille Regis and Tony Brown. To be perfectly honest, a walloping here wouldn't come as a surprise. But despite that, the glitter of the occasion meant we were all licking our lips in readiness.

A mere two hours after reaching the sky, we found ourselves in the country of orange groves and gypsy guitars, and after walking through the leafy exit of Valencia's airport we hopped onto a bus heading for the neon lights of the city centre, where the night was fully into its swing. There was an air of vitality about this place – and, much cheaper than the official trip, it had cost us just £64 return to get here. Later this night, too, we bedded down for only a couple of quid each. Who wants to fork out the earth for a luxury room when all you really need on a jaunt like this are clean bedsheets and a roof?

And luxury room it certainly wasn't! We found it down one of the rather dingy side-streets around the corner from the railway station. After climbing a spiral staircase for what seemed an eternity, the senor turned the key to disclose a small, dimly lit dormitory comprising a table, three wooden chairs and four single beds, and not even a window. But we had it, and then taking care not to trip over the chamber-pot, let ourselves out on parole for a few hours before returning, well lubricated, for a most welcome kip. First, though, we indulged in an earnest pillow fight followed by an even more earnest sing-song: and at three in the morning, should have refrained. A scruffy little fellow, oily-looking and with at least a two-day stubble, the owner reappeared to demonstrate that if we didn't button it he'd bring in the police. Somewhat strangely, I thought, he was still dressed in his moth-eaten suit and egg-spattered tie. Not wishing to invoke the notorious keenness of the Spanish guardia, though, with their modern-day Inquisition, we did indeed button it and in no time Lionel's rather quaint impression of a dormant fly catcher was accompanied by a decidedly inharmonious chorus of slobbering, snoring and grunting.

It was most unfortunate there was no window, for two reasons. Firstly, the air when we woke up was so rancid that it was almost combustible. Secondly, Lionel had spewed all over his bed. This was pretty ironic since he was only on the trip anyway by courtesy of his friendly Albion-mad doctor, who'd signed him off for a week under the pretence of flu as he'd run out of holidays. It was also unfortunate for Mick, who'd awoken to one of his more zealously playful moods and decided to take a running jump onto Lamp-post's bronzed nakedness. Lionel neatly rolled off his bed allowing Mick to crash-land in his vomit.

We decided we ought to split without further ado, but there remained the task of reviving Derek who yet again was dead to the otherwise hectic world. The first time I'd met Derek had been a rainy day up at Carlisle; we'd walked into a pub prior to the game, and by the door had sat four blokes whom we recognised to be Albion supporters playing cards. Next to them was a pile of coats and jackets, and during the next hour or so quite a few people who came inside assumed that this was an appointed dumping spot for their own. Eventually, with the pile a mile high, this mountain alarmingly began to move and from underneath it, like the silent ghost of Tutankhamun, had emerged a white-faced, bleary-eyed Derek, who'd been sleeping off a marathon drive up the motorway from Tipton. A couple of tugs on his jowls now, a boot in the ribs from Mick, and he was up, wanting breakfast too. After retrieving our passports we set about looking for it, and opted for the station cafeteria where it didn't take Lionel long to remark how funny his chips tasted. It was left to Derek to point out to him, quit crustily, that what he was actually picking at was squid.

Half an hour later as we sauntered around the streets we spotted three shirt-sleeved figures, instantly identifiable, about fifty yards away on the other side of the busy road.

'Len!!' shouted Derek through the whir of the traffic, and amazingly Len heard his cry and waved upon turning round. With Cantello, out for a stroll in the morning sunshine, were Bryan Robson and Ally

Brown, and we crossed over for a few quick words. After courting their envy by describing the opulence of our previous night's sleeping quarters, we posed the inevitable questions. Yes, 'Cyrille should be all right'; but no, Tony Brown didn't have much chance of making it. There was to be a training session at the stadium later, and we said we'd drop in for a look.

Uppermost in our minds was making sure of tickets for the game, and so we decided to visit the ground right now. An attractive city is Valencia, its visual appeal heightened by the numerous fountains adorning its smart plazas. Also numerous are those statues dedicated to the memory of El Cid, the legendary hero of eleventh-century Spain who was the subject for a silver screen epic starring Charlton Heston. As had been the case in Portugal, we had no problems whatsoever in obtaining tickets here, and whilst at the stadium we took a look inside.

The hospitality we encountered was almost overwhelming. Not only were we given several mementoes – magazines, programmes, posters – but we were also presented with a fascinating guided tour of the club offices.

There was unconcealed pride on his face as the man showed us the trophy room. Whilst Valencia can't be bracketed alongside Real Madrid's kingdom or Barcelona's power, they hadn't been short of glory themselves – league champions and Spanish Cup winners four times each, not to mention winning this particular European competition twice in its early days – and this room positively dripped with a plethora of cups and shields, plus colourful pennants collected from meetings with a variety of famous Continental sides over the years.

From the trophy room we moved into the boardroom, immaculately maintained, and it was intriguing to picture in your mind's eye this now vacant chamber to be populated by stout businessmen filling the air with cigar smoke and taking decisions like that sanctioning the engagement of Alfredo Di Stefano, a legend in his own lifetime as a player but who, as a manager, had guided Valencia to their last championship triumph seven years earlier. Or decisions, too, like those leading to the acquisition of costly imports such as the Dutchman, Johnny Rep, of Ajax fame, and Mario Kempes.

The main feature of the president's room itself, meanwhile, was a beautiful model for the proposed enlargement of the stadium: already quite palatial, but which was due to be improved into the form of a magnificent concrete bowl, perfect in its symmetry.

And speaking of the president, we were soon to be reminded of how the world is such a small place. Just over the road from the stadium stands a bar which was to become something of a home from home for us during our stay. The owner, Manuel, was a slightly-built man with spectacles, very friendly, who took great pride in his team, which was evident from the fact that bedecking his walls were photographs of players who'd graced the Valencia side down through the years. As we sat here now, we got talking to a rather fat, effervescent chap who at first seemed a bit too full of himself, knocking back the brandies and talking very loudly and demonstratively. But beneath this extrovert surface he revealed himself to be quite amiable and, later, exceeding generous. His name was Miguel, and so generous was he that he insisted upon driving us back across the city to where he kept his own bar, and giving us not only free drinks for an hour but also a hefty meal of stew and potatoes. Nothing was too much for him. Miguel was obviously crazy about football and took great delight in telling us, in front of his large family, that as a youngster he'd played in the same junior team as one Jose Ramos Costa, now a building millionaire but also none other than the current president of Valencia Club de Futbol! He even showed us a fondly preserved keepsake from those days, the old first-aid box of that team: and it was only then we discovered that those young Spaniards had called themselves . . . Aston Villa. I hope he didn't take our wincing at this as a sign of ill-manners towards himself. He did, though, feel it necessary to say, 'Aston Villa – very famous abroad!' We smiled and resisted the temptation to point out that so was Adolf Hitler.

from JAUNT ACCOUNT

We arra People

JOHN FAIRGRIEVE

They were singing 'Derry's Walls', hundreds of them, and they woke me up. Disbelieving, wondering indeed if this was the final hallucinating for punishment for a long and arduous period of conviviality, I padded, bleary-eyed, scratching, to the window of the hotel and looked out fearfully.

At least, it wasn't my imagination. But it was half-past six in the morning, and it wasn't Glasgow but Nuremberg. That particular street in which stands the Kaiserhof Hotel is not constructed for marching men – though doubtless the disadvantage had been made light of, on previous occasions – and the few locals unlucky enough to be up and about were pressed up against the walls, some ingratiating, some irritated, some awestruck.

A colleague, who had forgotten to put his false teeth in, stuck his head out of an adjoining window and mumbled something I know not what, but I could make a guess. He withdrew, returned a moment later, and said, simply, 'Bastards!'

He was, as I knew for a fact, a dedicated supporter of the Rangers Football Club, and his comment was obviously inspired by the sudden headache that comes with shattered sleep rather than any lack of sympathy with the ideals being expressed in song, four floors below.

Of course, we should not have been surprised. This was 1967, and the occasion was the European Cup Winners Cup final between Rangers and Bayern Munchen. It was inconceivable that Rangers fans should not have followed their team to Nuremberg. A few, a very few, just might have been discouraged had the game been planned for somewhere in the middle of the Gobi, but I would not care to bet heavily on that.

Anyway, here was the advance guard, stepping and pirouetting dantily as the chanting switched to 'The Sash', and I don't suppose there was a raincoat, a suitcase or a traveller's cheque among the lot of them. The only visible items of luggage, so far as I can remember, were duty-free carrier-bags, and the contents of these had had a caning already. They carried on up the street to the railway-station buffet, where a concession would be made to solid nourishment. I went back to bed, and put a coin in the slot that makes the bed vibrate – for some reason, they go in strongly for that sort of thing in Germany – but, far from inducing sleep, a hammering hang-over crept up, and it was keeping time to the beat of 'The Sash'.

Later that day, I took a taxi out to the stadium, the original one, the one that had given Nuremberg a bad name. It wasn't easy to hire a taxi, because the first two or three drivers deliberately misunderstood. I could see their point. They resented me as an intrusive tourist who wouldn't let them forget.

The sky was suitably grey, weeds dotted the vast square that had once been kept like the kitchen of a proud housewife. On the massive balcony and towers where the Leader had urged a nation to enslave a world, the stone was chipped and crumbling. Why had I come to this place? What was I looking for? Who knows? Maybe I was expected to feel something, a hint of evil from a previous age, a bristling of the hair at the back of the neck, as I stood where the torches had flared, where the storm-troopers had shrieked.

Nothing.

And nobody about, nobody . . . except, over there, hunched on one of the giant steps, an old man. I walked across, and he stared. My German is no use, but it didn't matter then.

'English?' he asked.

I nodded. The traditional denial – 'No, Schottische' – suddenly seemed inappropriate.

He waved his arms, in an all-encompassing gesture. 'I am here every morning. Soon, boom, boom, you know?'

I said I didn't know. He said they were going to blow the pillars up, to take all the stone away. I must have looked sympathetic. He spoke German for the first time.

'Ich bin Jude,' he said, and he began to cry.

'It's them,' he said then, jerking his thumb, 'them in the town. They shout like the Nazis . . . they could be shouting "Juden Raus"!'

Walking away, I glanced back at him once, and he was staring again. Then I felt the shiver.

The Rangers fans were reinforced in the afternoon, and, in the narrow streets of Nuremberg, there was more singing and dancing and chanting and swaggering. 'Look at them,' said another colleague who was not a Rangers supporter. 'Bloody animals.'

'Well,' I said, 'they're enjoying themselves. They're not too bad.'

He thought I was joking.

from WE'LL SUPPORT YOU EVERMORE *1976*

Liverpool in the Snow

GEOFFREY GREEN

It was the mid-1960s. Liverpool were due to play Cologne on Merseyside in the second leg of a European Cup-tie. For hours the city was wrapped in the white arms of a blizzard. The snow lay deep everywhere, but for some unaccountable reason the gates of Anfield were opened some half an hour before the night kick-off to let in a shivering 45,000 crowd.

The Cologne players duly came out stripped for a warm-up before the start, kicking about a white polka-dot ball on a frosty white surface. All you could distinguish of the ball itself were those moving dots as if it were a die being rolled on the icing of a Christmas cake. The conditions, of course, were impossible, and the referee called it off before the start, without Liverpool even bothering to take the field.

At some grounds there might well have been trouble, and that Anfield crowd had queued for hours in the snow to get in. Their money had been taken, virtually under false pretences. Yet there is nothing, anywhere, quite to measure up to the Kop at Liverpool. It may contain some villains within a family ranged – some 22,000 strong – behind one goal. But it bursts with original, unpredictable wit and generosity, and when it sings its own adopted battle hymn 'You'll Never Walk Alone', there is about it all the fervour and moving quality of a vast cathedral choir, as it sways and countersways to the music. It sends an endless tingle up the spine.

But in spite of that blank night and the disappointment, there was no explosion. Instead, as the snow still fell in a thick, feathery cloud, there suddenly appeared a dozen or so characters out on the pitch imitating the gyrations of international ice stars one sees on television. And there, too, in the background was one wry wag lampooning the official markings of skating judges as he held aloft the numbered figure plates usually used to convey the half-time scores at other matches. It was a brilliant piece of inspired mime, and but for that the night would have long since passed as a frozen waste into the limbo of forgotten things.

To me that was another small but 'great' moment of football, stemming from unexpected, unexplored depths of the human spirit that makes light of adversity.

from GREAT MOMENTS IN SPORT: SOCCER *1972*

Edwardian Celebrations

JOHN HARDING

With the Cup won, Manchester United were presented with the keys of London by George Robey. The great showman, having dressed the team, now commandeered them and the Cup for a show he was appearing in that evening at the Pavilion Music Hall. Charlie Roberts recalled the chaotic evening. 'When I entered our dressing-room there was the genial George all smiles and as happy as any of us. He asked me if I would take the team up to the Pavilion Music Hall, London, at nine o'clock, and take them on the stage as his guests and bring the Cup with me. I readily consented after all the kindness to us, and it was agreed that we would be at the Pavilion at nine o'clock.

'First we went to the Alhambra Music Hall where we were the guests of the management. I put the Cup in the strongroom there before going to see part of the show. Sandy Turnbull, George Livingstone, Jimmy Bannister and myself subsequently made our way towards the Trocadero restaurant where we had promised to meet some of our friends from Manchester. We found them there sure enough and the order of the evening was merry and bright. I forgot all about the time and my promise to George Robey until Sandy reminded me that it was a quarter to nine. Sandy and I jumped into a hansom and dashed off to the Alhambra for the Cup. We got it out of the strongroom and were lifting it into a hansom when Mr Bentley saw us and said, "Where are you going with the Cup?" I told him of my promise to Robey and then he said, "I think that I had better come along with you two young gentlemen or I can see the Cup being lost in London and another sensation caused."

'With that he joined in. We took the Cup inside and of course left Mr Bentley to pay for the cab. Robey smiled when he saw us struggling in and asked me where all the rest of the team were, as he wanted us to stand for just a minute on the stage in view of the audience with the Cup on the table and, says he, "I'll be ready for you in about five minutes."

'I told him I couldn't possibly get the boys there in that time but that I had four players and officials with me.

'"Well," said Robey. "go and get somebody to make up the team," a request to which I soon complied. I went to the Trocadero which is right opposite the stage door and brought about a dozen of my friends from Manchester, including two or three men of aldermanic proportions. One had a bald head, and another had a silver plate in his side. Robey fixed us up round the table. I stood at one end and Sandy at the other while George Livingstone, Jimmy Bannister, Mr Bentley and Harry Stafford stood at the back, and with my friends all mixed in it was the greatest Cup team you ever saw.

'The cinematograph sheet was down in front of us and then, when we were ready, the notice went on the screen – "The Manchester United Football Team. English Cup Winners".

'The screen then went up and as the Lancashire folk began to cheer I thought I should have fainted and as the crowd were clamouring for a speech from me I was winking at Robey to get the screen down again quick. He gave the desired signal and down it came and then the laugh that I had been bursting to let out came forth in its full strength. It simply was a scream to look at the team I had collected to represent the Cup winners! There was a poultry dealer, a publican, a mantlemaker, a bookmaker, a builder and a greengrocer among them and they enjoyed the experience a treat.'

from FOOTBALL WIZARD *1985*

We're All Going to Italy

BRIAN JAMES

At Rome airport, then at the team's hotel, we ran into the advance guard of the red army of Liverpool fans. Eventually there were to be an astonishing 26,000 of them drawn up like some monstrous legion in the eternal city . . . someone did his sums and worked out that they'd spent £1 million on travel alone, just to get there. Some had left by car or coach straight from Wembley last Saturday; others had had a nightmare three-day journey by train with a five-hour wait at one point with no heat, light or water in the carriage. Their clothes were ruined, their faces looked wrecked, but at the sight of Hughes, or Jones, or Paisley, they broke into instant cheering. And their enthusiasm, like the journey's laughter, only increased my own pessimism.

By nightfall in a hotel so packed with non-residents in red it became a struggle to get a coffee or your room-key, I was convinced Liverpool had thrown away their European Cup chance: they were in the wrong hotel, at the wrong time, had arrived there the wrong way and in the wrong frame of mind.

Travelling with their wives and their rowdy mates seemed a mistake. Staying in the city instead of in the cooler hills outside was surely another. Being so available to the TV crews, radio mikes and reporters' notebooks was a clear error; being in a position to be pestered by fans four-deep wherever they walked seemed a disaster.

Most other British teams, and *every* continental side, would have isolated a team in Liverpool's position as if they had the plague. They would have flown last Sunday to a tranquil pub in a forest somewhere, with security men to ration reporters' access. That would have been the *professional* approach to this game – this was a *package-tour* preparation, for which I was convinced Liverpool players would have to meet the bill.

Listening to coach Joe Fagan in a bedroom corridor on our way to breakfast next morning did not remove all doubts: 'Lose today? Forget it,' he insisted. 'Last Saturday our attitude was all wrong. Going to the match it was just another Cup final. If that sounds daft remember we had been playing games as important as that for weeks . . . seventeen of them in three weeks to be exact. But today's different . . . I've already been round most of the rooms. They're tingling . . . anxious to be at it . . . want to get out there and make them Germans have a bit of it. . . .' He made a punch-up gesture with his fist by way of farewell at the lift.

Nevertheless, the day lasted an age. It was a relief to reach the stadium an hour earlier than necessary, to feel that at last the end was beginning. (Reporters, incidentally, get butterflies too, at these big matches. Like the players they are performers in that what they say, and how they say it, with only seconds to compose their phrase and arguments, will be judged next day by literally millions of readers, and compared by self-elected juries of their professional peers. 'He had a bad European Cup/World Cup,' is a dismissive judgement that a sports journalist can take years to live down.) We spent the time playing Spot The German, for the Olympic Stadium clearly belonged to Liverpool . . . a singing, dancing, flaunting horde that seemed to fill the bowl. The only unit of identifiable Gladbach fans was represented by a small square of green figures high up opposite the main stand – they looked like a patch of moss and were to wither and disappear long before the end.

Someone nearby looked deep into this scene or Hogarthian revelry and said: 'I think foreigners' idea that every Englishman looks like David Niven is destroyed for ever tonight.' It was a nice remark, but wrong. For just then Liverpool's team appeared – and in the next two hours they reincarnated the ideal of the foppishly cool, elegantly-deadly, effortlessly-precise, inately-gracious English Milord – with their football. They stepped straight on to the pitch, slung aside with their track-suit tops all the misery of Saturday, all the distracting bonhomie of the days since, and even their homeland reputation for ploughing through games like some machine.

The stuff they played now was of a different style entirely; from that endless larder of Liverpool resources they reached to a seldom-touched shelf and produced a game-plan that was all about containing, patient, probing attacks pressed home with wit and invention. And when repulsed, they simply went back and built another.

They scored a goal in twenty-seven minutes: Callaghan to Heighway. Heighway forward, and then as Callaghan, Case and Kennedy all made decoy runs as though taking part in some Merseyland morris dance, Heighway through for McDermott to slide past Kneib. It took a rare mistake by Case to give Simonsen an equaliser after an hour ('the noise you heard at that moment which sounded like thunder,' Hughes insisted later, 'was just my jaw dropping.')

It took brilliant saves by Clemence, from Heynkes and Simonsen, to prevent a setback growing into calamity. But Liverpool supremacy was so overwhelming they were merely setting the stage for the final heroics. First Tommy Smith, whose final match before retirement this was to be, came racing to a corner to score with his head. Then Kevin Keegan, whose farewell match before transfer this was to be, completed a ninety-minute job of destruction on the West German captain Vogts – by provoking a penalty. Phil Neal tucked it away . . . 3–1. And finis.

The Kop-in-Exile went predictably beserk behind a barricade of barbed wire and barking police dogs, but the Kop's representative in the team, Joey Jones, festooned himself with caps, scarves, badges and bowler and led his cart-wheeling team-mates in lap after lap of honour. From that helicopter overhead it must have been like looking down into a strange sort of Hades . . . where every mouth was open to sing, shout or laugh.

Below stairs, Bob Paisley, collar and tie askew and sweating buckets, came up to meet the world's press. He looked as bewildered as a man who had stood for election as Peoples' Warden and found when the votes were counted he had become Prime Minister. Yet, though blinded by TV lights, bedevilled by a translation device that bombarded him with his own words in French, German and Italian, he carried it off with a politician's ease.

Then back to the hotel for the party. It would probably be easier to detail every shot of a civil war than to convey a complete picture of this celebration; I can only give glimpses. Like seeing a fan creep into the banqueting room, run to the table to kiss the Cup, and back reverently out, or another supporter who sought out every player in turn and knelt before him, explaining 'Dey's royalty . . . dat's why' . . . or a third Kopite of ferocious mien and stupendously drunk, swaying in front of the Minister of Sport, Denis Howell: 'We are going to have the greatest booze-up ever . . . but don't worry, Mister, we ain't Leeds . . . and we ain't Manchester United . . . we'll behave. Dat's a promise.' (A promise absolutely kept – Italian papers next day praised Liverpool's football *and* lavishly apologised for the harsh things they'd predicted about the supporters.)

At first the fans were kept outside. But Emlyn Hughes (who managed the feat of ending the year as a footballer of fabulous achievement and still a very nice man) kept spotting faces above the policemen's helmets – and making a dash for the door with a fresh bottle of champagne. Eventually, though, the cordon broke . . . the mob burst in, took turns at being pictured with the players, or swigging from the Cup. At one time the huge trophy vanished: 'Never fret.' said a Liverpool official. 'it's outside being trooped around the grounds by the fans. Scared? Listen, if we forget it, it'll turn up at Anfield in two days . . . unmarked and polished like new.'

The party splintered up and was carted to various bedrooms. And around the pool, where Phil Neal got ducked and Keegan got a black eye, and those of us still with a bit to do tried to find a quiet corner to talk and make a few notes, Hughes told me, 'Did I think we'd do it? You want the truth? No. Not after Saturday. I put on the bravest face I could. But deep down I thought we'd left it all behind at

Wembley. But once we started to play . . . I knew nothing could stop us. Now . . . I didn't know it was possible for any man to feel this happy. Only one doubt . . . what the hell do we do for an encore? The treble? No way . . . we are the team of the century . . . and no side will ever get nearer. It can't be done.'

Tommy Smith had this to say: 'I told my missus I'd finish for Liverpool by scoring in the Cup. We both thought I meant at Wembley. But soon as Steve pinged that corner at me I knew this was it. Their keeper is a giant . . . but he looked like a mouse on the line when I headed at him. Even so the ball took ten minutes to hit the net. Who'd have thought me, Tommy Smith, would end up with a Roy of the Rovers stunt like that? Now . . . I'm going to get a gold plate put in me nut . . . to mark the spot. After this, there'll be such a crowd at my testimonial on Friday. I can afford it.'

Next morning around dawn, weary waiters cleared away 385 empty champagne bottles, and tireless players tossed passing reporters into the pool and gardeners prodded bushes and Liverpool fans fell blinking into the sunlight, and every hill in view from the roof of the hotel had little knots of red figures lurching around asking each other, 'What happened to the last coach back to Kirkby?' and it was all over.

from JOURNEY TO WEMBLEY *1977*

The One-legged Footballer

STEPHEN F. KELLY

Personally, I blame the one-legged footballer. But first there was my father.

'I can't find it, Dad,' I wailed down the stairs. I was all of ten.

'It's there, in the drawer in the dressing-table,' he shouted back.

I rummaged again, past greasy combs, strange pinkish balloons and bundles of green trade union cards. But still could not find the missing football programme.

'Dadddd, I can't see it.'

He eventually hoisted his creaky bones up the stairs and, no doubt cursing me under his breath, came to help in the search, immediately pushing the strange balloon to one side. But no, the missing football programme was not there.

'I'm sure it was here,' he said perplexed. 'Ma, have you moved that football programme from my drawer?' he bawled down the stairs. 'I hope you haven't thrown it out.' Funny how men always blame women for moving things they cannot find.

'No,' replied mother also arriving on the scene, though I don't think either of us believed her. We never did find the programme though this same ritual was repeated every other year until I was well into my twenties. The programme in question still escapes my collection. It was Tottenham Hotspur against Tranmere Rovers and my dad, a Tranmere fan, had taken a Hardings coach from Birkenhead one bitterly cold January day in the early 1950s to watch Arthur Rowe's ageing push-and-run team get their cum-uppance. A week earlier at Prenton Park the first-division runners-up had been lucky to escape with a 1–1 draw. It would have been the biggest upset in footballing history, claimed my dad, adding that you know what they say about the Cup: 'You only get one chance'. He was right. Poor Tranmere were crushed 1–9 in the replay.

Perhaps it was the never-ending search around the house for Tottenham against Tranmere that hooked me into collecting football programmes, yet I still blame the one-legged man. Whatever it was, I was gripped by the age of ten. It was 1956 and the European Cup was barely under way. Yet the magic of Europe had already captured my imagination. I wasn't interested in Everton against Blackpool or Arsenal versus West Brom. They were anonymous first-division games. These were the days of the friendly floodlit challenge matches against the Europeans and all I wanted were Honved, Red Banner, Moscow Dynamo, Real Madrid, Bilbao and Juventus.

I had been well and truly captivated by the European dream by the time I came to meet the man with one leg. It was on my first visit to London where we were holidaying at Auntie Lily's, a stout, friendly Yorkshire lass whose husband Uncle Jack was forged in the finest cockney traditions. And in his books no Sunday could possibly be complete without a stroll down Petticoat Lane where he assured us there were bargains galore to be had. Bargains there may have been but it was the hot sarsaparilla and the one-legged man who remain in my memory.

I first spotted him outside a caravan where he was selling a football pools forecasting scheme. Now the thing about these schemes is that if the originator is not rich then they cannot possibly be successful, and judging by his rough coat and muffler his scheme couldn't be too profitable. But what caught my eye was a football programme pinned to a board. England versus Yugoslavia, November 1956, with that familiar aerial view of Wembley Stadium on the front cover along with the name of the chairman and managing director, Sir Arthur J. Elvin MBE. I was mesmerised.

The one-legged man came shuffling over, his ruddy face beaming in the chill wind.

'Do you like football, sonny?' he asked. I nodded. He took the programme from the board and opened it up to the centre pages where a gaggle of legends leapt out at me. Billy Wright, Tom Finney, Stan Matthews, my own hero Johnny Haynes, the elegant Ronnie Clayton and the black cat Vladimir Beara. I must have made the right oohs and ahhs.

'And who's the greatest England player?' he boomed as he towered over me.

'Stanley Matthews, sir.'

'Quite right. Do you collect programmes?' he inquired.

'Yes, but I've only got a couple,' I replied.

'Here you are then, have this,' he said, handing the programme over to me.

'Say "Thank you" Stephen,' said my mother.

'Thank you, sir,' I stammered.

'Now I tell you what,' he said. 'At home I have a very special programme, played before you were born. It was a game I appeared in, at full-back. Would you like it? Yes? Well, give me your address and I'll send it to you.'

My father scrambled in his pockets for some paper, scribbled our address down and we left clutching my new treasure. Uncle Jack reckoned the one-legged man's misfortune was probably the result of a footballing injury caused by a ill-timed tackle on some flying winger like Matthews or Finney.

I thought no more about the one-legged man until a month or so later when through the post popped a large envelope addressed to Master Stephen Kelly. Inside was a pristine copy, albeit just a folded sheet, of Chelsea FC v. Dynamo FC (Moscow, USSR champions), Tuesday November 13th 1945, kick off 2.30 p.m. There were even some welcoming words of Russian on the front cover which I couldn't understand. Inside the programme the name of Chelsea's right-back,

Alex White, had been crossed out and in his place had been scribbled the name Sgt W. Osborne. Was this the one-legged man? There was nothing else in the envelope. No letter, no address. I couldn't even write to thank him. Was Sgt Osborne the one-legged man? I still don't know. In later years I scoured all the statistical books but found no reference to him. According to the records Alex White's place had been taken by Fulham's Joe Bacuzzi although all his other pencilled amendments to the line-up were correct. So, was the one-legged man having me on? Maybe, but who cares. He introduced me to a life-long passion.

Chelsea versus Moscow Dynamo was to go down in history as one of the most magical games ever played in Britain. Coming in the austerity days after the war it drew an unexpected crowd of over 85,000 to Stamford Bridge with at least 11,000 of them sneaking over the fence, free of charge. Some say there were more, as many as 100,000 inside the ground. They swarmed like ants onto the roof of the stands, they spilled onto the dog track and then, when the mysterious Muscovites appeared clutching bouquets of flowers, laugned themselves silly. They didn't laugh for long. Perhaps they had all come to see Tommy Lawton making his debut for Chelsea. If they had they would not be disappointed as he shot them into an early two-goal lead. But the Russians, despite the flowers, were no pansies and in the second half came bouncing back to finally snatch a 3–3 draw.

Everyone agreed they had seen one of the finest football teams in the world. And I had the programme. What's more I still have it, not only the most prized programme in my collection but one of the most valuable of any collection. And I still wonder whatever happened to the one-legged man, as well as that damned Tranmere/Tottenham programme.

from THE FOOTBALLER *1991*

Dreaming of Wembley

J. P. W. MALLALIEU

Every year, about this time, I dream that Huddersfield Town will win the Cup.

I think that is a perfect opening sentence. Those readers who want the class war, or an analysis of *Labour Believes in Britain*, or the inside story of What Really Happened About Insurance, or a forecast of which election the Tories will finally be compelled to fight on policy, turn elsewhere at once on reading it.

Those readers who, without deep roots, happen to follow Bolton Wanderers, Accrington Stanley, the Harlequins or worse, will do the same. So, too, will those who play games but think that watching them is effete.

Which leaves me with those who like sentiment, prejudice, bias, instinct and, here and there, a touch of malice – in other words, who appreciate loyalty. To all such, a Happy New Year.

Every year, about this time, I dream that Huddersfield Town will win the Cup.

Of course, it *might* be Cardiff City. If I were a Cardiff fan, I should remember that great, but somehow sad, moment when in 1927 the Arsenal goalkeeper scooped a stray shot into his own net at Wembley and allowed Cardiff to take the Cup out of England for the first time. I should remember, too, how my club went right down as the South Wales coal, steel and tinplate trade went down, and would see how both trade and team are coming up again.

If I'd stuck to Cardiff in the Thirties, I'd be dreaming about them in the Fifties, even if they have to knock out West Bromwich Albion in the third round.

I would certainly be dreaming about the Spurs if I were a Spurs fan. For no Spurs team is so bad or so unlucky that the roar of White Hart Lane is dulled or turned into jeers. Spurs fans are the aristocrats among fans. They back their team through thick and especially through thin. And now it's thick again, even if they have to play Stoke at Stoke.

Or it might be Blackburn Rovers. Goodness me, there may be Rovers fans who have followed the club since the Football League was begun. They'd be over seventy by now but what a stream of football history would now be ebbing and flowing in their memories! They might even remember 1928 – a year I choose to forget since in that year, the goalkeeper of Huddersfield Town, all-time hot favourites at Wembley, let the ball slip through his hands in the first minute, dived in vain and watched his glittering team troop, beaten and disconsolate, from the field.

But Rovers meet Liverpool – and the only thing I'd know for certain, if I were a Rovers fan, is that my lovely little ground at Ewood Park would overflow.

Maybe I never seriously thought about the Cup before because I supported some little workshop team – a team outside any league that even the Sunday papers would recognise. If so I'd be dreaming of nothing in particular just now, for my team would be out of the Cup already.

Weymouth? Yeovil? Nuneaton? If, like Frank Bowles, the Member for Nuneaton, I could rule Exeter City out of order on their home ground, I might perhaps dream. But if I were a Weymouth fan I would dream only of the nice cheque which would certainly come my club's way after playing Manchester United at Old Trafford. And if I were a Yeovil fan – standing on Chesterfield's bleak terraces – I would dream only of that nice slope I had left at home.

If I were Michael Foot, I'd dream that Plymouth Argyle would beat the Wolves – and, goodness knows, in the Cup any dream can come true.

from SPORTING DAYS *1955*

The Auld Enemy

J. P. W. MALLALIEU

On Friday 17th April 1953, at about 11 p.m., in Piccadilly, a gentleman from Glasgow declined the advice of a gentleman from London. As the gentleman from London was wearing one of those funny helmets, the gentleman from Glasgow spent the night in a cell, and thereafter was decanted before another gentleman from London who wore no helmet but was protected, instead, by two penetrating eyes.

'What,' said the Beak, 'is the charge?' 'Drunk and disorderly,' said a Clerk. 'What,' said the Beak some moments later, nodding his head at the gentleman from Glasgow, 'had he in his pockets?' 'Two pennies and the return half of his ticket to Glasgow,' said the London gentleman who had been wearing his helmet the previous evening. 'Two pennies, the return half of his ticket to Glasgow – and a ticket for the England and Scotland match at Wembley this afternoon.'

The Beak's penetrating eyes bored into the gentleman from Glasgow whose face, whatever colour it might have been at 11 p.m. on Friday 17th April, was by now white. Would it be a lecture? He could not endure it in his shaking state. Would it be a fine? Had anyone ever heard of a 2d fine? Would it be a prison sentence? Then he would miss the match.

The Beak reflected; then, 'One day's imprisonment!'; then, 'But take care that he's out in time to see the match' – and at that, while the Beak rustled the papers of his next case, the gentleman from Glasgow's face suddenly became like the sunrise and the whole police court was suffused with beaming warmth.

Englishmen, on the day, feel strongly about an encounter between England and Scotland whether at rugby or soccer. But their feelings are only strong, not fundamental; they are not expressed, and they exist only on the day. But a Scotsman's feelings on these matters seep down into his being until they become a part of his instinct; they are expressed as steam is expressed through the safety valve of a standing locomotive, and they exist not just for one day but from the moment one match ends until the moment the next match has ended. The fire underneath his boiler is no sooner extinguished than it is rekindled; and if the boiler happens to burst, as I saw it burst last Saturday, well then, there are plenty more boilers where that one came from. The Scotsman turns homeward on the Saturday night. His spirit may deflect him from the homeward line, so that, for example, he finds himself without his train at Crewe, but eventually he gets home; and from that moment he begins to save, as he will save for nothing else, to meet the fare and other expenses incidental to a Wembley trip in two years' time. He must not cheat about this saving. There must be no raiding of his children's boxes, no docking of his wife's money. The savings must really be his own, and, because they are his own, they are his to deal with as he pleases. Once he has paid his fare and got his Wembley ticket, he can blow the whole lot – all but twopence – on the Friday night, and no one will stay his hand. No one? It was a near thing. Not even Jacob, fobbed off with Leah after seven years, could be more downcast than a Scottish football fan fobbed off with a prison cell after two years. But because sportsmen, in England or elsewhere, are sportsmen, the gentleman from Glasgow got his Rachel after all.

I thought of him nearly all that afternoon at Wembley. The tartan bonnets and the red lions of Scotland on their yellow backgrounds so dominated the arena that the greenness of the velvet turf seemed only pale by comparison. The pre-match hum of the 100,000 crowd had a tone which was alien to my ear, and the tunes which were played either by the disabled ex-servicemen without or by the wholly able Marines within were alien too. Wembley that afternoon seemed to be soaked in Scotland. I felt there the demanding eagerness of that two years' expectant abstinence; and, as the game wore on, I felt compassion for those thousands whose new unleashed desires were not, it seemed, about to be fulfilled.

from: SPORTING DAYS 1955

No Ticket

J. P. W. MALLALIEU

For some people – good luck to them – Cup-final day means a trip to London, sightseeing, a couple of beers, and home by the evening train. But for some others it is a social occasion. They don't watch football either. But they must see the final. It is the thing to do. They ought to be prosecuted. So ought the people who let them have the precious tickets.

Because of them, real fans are kept outside, hearing the crowd's roar, but not knowing whether to hope or fear. These fans have followed the team from that last Saturday in August when the crowd sat in shirt-sleeves and the grass was green. They have followed the team through the wet and cold of December until the grass has turned to mud, followed them groaning, followed them protesting, followed them cheering, but always followed them hoping that, this year, the team will have a run in the Cup. Now the spring is here, their team *has* had a run in the Cup, their team is at Wembley, flashing over the velvet turf. But they are outside; and the ticket touts want £6 for a 3s 6d ticket. And all the time there are people inside who don't care which team wins, who don't know the rules and who chatter.

It is an agonising tragedy. Not that the game will be a good one. True, there was Pompey–Wolves in 1939 and Arsenal–Huddersfield in 1930. They were fine. But the usual final is terrible. The tragedy is that the fan is part of the club. Saturday after Saturday he has known the feeling you get on football grounds, that all men are equal, that all men are honest and that, until the game begins, all men are brothers. Right through the season he has given his advice, without charge, to countless referees; he has exhausted his nerves on those long-drawn-out 'eees' and 'oos' and 'ahs' that betoken a close shave, or thrown his whole being into that ecstatic shout that betokens sudden triumph. But now he is outside Wembley, outside the club, outside the deep communal delight of unthinking, wholehearted passionate bias.

And I am inside. Normally, I am only inside when Huddersfield are playing, as they did play five times between the wars – five times between the wars and only once an honest referee. But though it is not Huddersfield today, I still claim a seat by right. Burnley, after all, are a side from Lancashire, which even prejudiced observers admit to be the second-best county. Moreover, is not Alan Brown, the Burnley captain, fresh from playing with Huddersfield Town, where he learned his football? So up the claret and blue.

from SPORTING DAYS *1955*

Brazilian Fever

JOHN MOYNIHAN

The rocky, reverbarated road up to the stadium was compressed by layers of English-mockers. They were so near our bus, the younger ones, you could see down their throats and see the colour of their tongues as the tongues dragged forth abuse. The odd trace of spit splashed against a window, the odd plastic water bag was thrown at our rear.

And so, on such an ominous note of welcome, our bus crawled at last to a parking lot outside the stadium and we descended one by one on to the earthy wastelands surrounding that huge bowl with the circular roof. People were moving very fast in all directions, even though there were still two hours to go before the big match, and pedlars were hovering in the shade of every scraggly tree. The sun was already hot and a pinkish landscape receded away in eerie flatness towards a flatulent blue sky. There was an atmosphere of a duel: one team would win, one lose, it was impossible to imagine a draw. We joined the mobs walking towards the high steps leading to the high-tier boxes: a long procession of Brazilian supporters followed behind a band striding and thumping along: 'BRAZIL – Mexico – BRAZIL – Mexico – *thump, thump, thump.*' The band marched round and round the stadium and the Brazilian crowds massed behind, chanting Pelé's name, and we marched with them, pushed along by hundreds of small boys with their hands out begging for a spare ticket. The beer bars were packed outside our own part of the stadium and we sat down to wait the long hour before going into the stadium for a last half-hour's wait for the match to begin. Fred, Syd, Bill, Harry and many more of the lads you might see drinking outside an East End London public house on a sunny summer's morning were soon hovering over their glasses of oily brew. *'Cevesa!'* roared a barman – 'ENGLEESH DRINK BEFORE YOU LOSE.' The soul of the party was a tall, reedy Brazilian Negro wearing a green boiler-suit with the name of his country glaring from his chest. On his head was an enormous sombrero, and a gargantuan smile never left his face, sometimes expanding as he taunted the supporters in red, white and blue with frenzied gestures of his arms. A resident drummer joined him and thumped out a beat as the Negro bellowed 'BRAZIL – BRAZIL', and Bill and his mob yelled back, 'ENGLAND – ENGLAND'. And now, as we looked for our seats behind the goal, we heard on all sides a murmur of expectancy, willing a great defeat for the present World Champions, a murmur which would soon build into a stunning howl of welcome for Brazil. And above the stadium whirled an hysterical pigeon carrying a green-and-yellow banner. It flew on and on and round and round until exhaustion hurled the bird to the ground.

There was hushed silence as the bird lay in a bundle of feathers near the centre circle, a grey speck on a vivid green sea before rising again, released from its patriotic burden. The cheers, and chants rose again, and the marvel of it, this display of patriotism for what was only after all a football match, a game of footer played with a round ball between twenty-two men, was projected through a great blaze of colour in which the pitch itself almost burnt the eyes, so opulent was the turf under the noonday sun.

from FOOTBALL FEVER *1974*

Brentford Supporters

JOHN MOYNIHAN

When Brentford played Bristol Rovers, in a third-division match at Griffin Park one damp, gusty day in February 1966, I was sitting behind a man with a small, thin moustache hunched up in a fading cavalry twill overcoat. He was a season-ticket holder.

Brentford were at the bottom of the third division. He offered no hint of comfort or loyalty to the sweating struggling side throughout the seventy minutes he watched the game before shambling out of the stadium to be swallowed up in the 'valve, tube and fittings' desert of the Great West Road. During the game I made a note of his remarks.

Brentford played badly that day. Bristol Rovers split their defence apart as easily as shelling a pea pod, with Biggs, a gargantuan centre-forward, scoring three goals which went past Chick Brodie like bullets. The final score was 0–5, a score which lead to a hostile demonstration outside the Brentford offices after the game, but the man with the square moustache had left long before then.

He had sat down on his hard, wooden seat two minutes after the kick-off, watching the game with his left shoulder pointing to the stand on the opposite side of the field. Crossing his legs and occasionally scratching a waxy ear, he watched Brentford make a number of futile attacks on the Rovers goal like a weasel waiting to nip a rabbit's neck. Then the barracking began:

'Come on, idiot, get it right, the goal is the other end, twat, fool, this is football . . .

'You big, gangling fool . . .

'Beautiful pass to Bristol that, terrible innit terrible. Aren't they paid to play this game?

'Well done, pass it to Bristol . . .

'Oh, a good pass for once . . .

'Come on you idiot, come on Block . . .

'Crikey, wake up, clot. Come on, get into him, you idiot, fool, you stupid fool, *wake up* you lot.'

An old man with a severed jaw turned round and whispered: 'Why can't you show some loyalty to the Bees?' He looked pained. And his friend, a fat man with an RAF tie said, 'You're having a go, aren't you?'

Brentford missed an open goal. 'I am so fed up with it. I've got money in this club. I'm so fed up with it.'

'Well done, pass it to Bristol . . .

'They're bottom, do you know that? Do you know why I go on so? I go on because you can't get excited watching it so you must excite other people. Come on the bottom club . . .

'WAKE UP, you wingers, move there you idiot, you twit . . .

'WAKE UP, Block. Don't you know when you're offside? . . .

'YOU HEAP OF RUBBISH. WAKE UP, BLOCK, you idiot. Look, some of them are going already . . .'

Behind the net of Bristol Rovers, a couple wearing crash helmets were no longer watching the game. They were embracing tenderly, their crash helmets touching like two golf balls.

'To think I used to sit here and watch Brentford in the first division. WAKE UP, YOU DEFENDERS' (Rovers missed a chance) – 'It would be nice if we missed one or two . . .'

'Pass it to Bristol, you rotten lot . . .'

Bristol Rovers scored their first goal, Jones moving square across the pitch to send Jarman through with an exquisite pass and Biggs pounding in made Brodie's heart give a berserk twitch.

'Well done, good goal, good goal. They've got you, you twits . . .'

Fifty seconds later Biggs hurtled through on his own and scored with a shot of such power that the ball rebounded back towards the centre circle. 'Well done, a good goal, you see what they're doing to you, you gormless twits . . .'

After half-time he sat farther away from the old man with the severed jaw. Perhaps he did not want to offend him any more, perhaps he felt disturbed by this loyal man who never once uttered a squeak of criticism as his team was reduced from hopeful plodding to sheer mediocrity.

When Mel Scott, the old Chelsea centre-half, and one of the few players having a reasonable game for Brentford, rose up to head a goal of enormous violence against his own side, I waited for the man with the moustache to make further comments. But none came. He had visibly paled, his moustache twitched as if moved by the popping bogs of hell.

He was speechless and then suddenly, as play re-commenced, his voice rose in a hoarse whisper: 'Brentford, I don't love you any more. I don't love you, you gormless twits . . .'

'Why don't they buy George Eastham', shouted a voice down in the Enclosure.

'What, for a farthing?'

The barracker missed the last two Rovers goals, slipping out silently in the rain, looking for verbal support as he made for the gangway. But none came.

The old man with the severed chin watched him with deep hatred.

'What we need is some loyalty around here. It was loyalty which took us up from the third division to the first in the Thirties. What kind of club can this be, with types like that?'

from THE SOCCER SYNDROME *1966*

The Vultures

JOHN MOYNIHAN

Two or three thousand people on the terraces at an English Football Combination or Central League match. The 'Stiffs' as they have been nicknamed, or in more polite terms, reserves, kick about their business in an eerie morgue.

They are watched by small groups of staunch supporters, cliques of mysterious men, who drift in off the streets from seemingly nowhere, and shift workers with no more congenial place to go.

A reserve match is seldom a dignified occasion. I used to go to mid-week reserve games in the Forties and Fifties at Stamford Bridge, White Hart Lane, Griffin Park, Highbury, Loftus Road, Craven Cottage and the Den. Men moved exceedingly slowly on those cold, grey afternoons across the great, empty slabs of terracing. They shuffled to and fro eating peanuts, hanging on crash barriers and howling out their views and grievances. Some spectators preferred to stand on their own against a barrier on the very crest of the terracing, like black, independent shags on a rock, while others massed in a small raucous knot overlooking the half-way line.

These men were often vultures, picking the bones of the older players who had gone over the top, and were wheezing and struggling against the youngsters. These were merciless men in dirty, torn over-coats, mud-stained brothel-creepers and hair drooping over their collars in thick crusts of oil and dandruff. There were sadists, unemployed barrack-room lawyers, and randy labourers on the skive. They were merciless and full of wit, howls of laughter as the home winger went past the balding left-back so that the victim slithered in the mud, his mouth hanging open so that you could see the darkness where his false teeth usually hung.

'Hey, lofty. Put your false teeth back in.'

The visiting centre-half had probably been a noted stopper in the first team, his performances at this ground often proving beyond the means and intelligence of the home team attack. Now he was in the reserves with a paunch, he was a marked man, at least from the terraces. He might be facing a new bustle boy named Bobby Smith, who would soon be going into the Chelsea side at centre-forward and be left dejected on the ground as Smith went past him to shoot aggressively into the top corner of the net.

'GOAL! Get up, big head!'

The new financial deal for footballers has meant that reserve sides are no longer the graveyards that they used to be. Players are often the off-duty members of the first team squad who regard their outings with the second team as mere convenience to recover fitness or form. Clubs have also cut down their playing staff. Chelsea in the early Fifties, for instance, had fifty professionals and many of these players languished from year to year unwanted in reserve football. And there were always the vultures there to pick your bones.

At Griffin Park, Brentford, there used to be a man who would come along for the reserve games with a bazooka on his tongue. Standing there behind one of the goals, he would extract peanuts seemingly from his flybuttons and attack with lust the performances of a young player named Jimmy Hill.

Hill, who later had a distinguished career with Fulham, grew a beard, initiated the splicing of the maximum wage, and then went on to Coventry as a manager, was viewed at this time by this man with almost frenzied hatred. Hill had a prominent chin and the man made fun of it as a matter of course. It was unkind, but there are some unkind anonymous men along the Great West Road.

from: THE SOCCER SYNDROME *1966*

The Loneliness of the
Long Distance Runner

ALAN SILLITOE

Towards the end of the match, when Bristol scored their winning goal, the players could only just be seen, and the ball was a roll of mist being kicked about the field. Advertising boards above the stands, telling of pork pies, ales, whisky, cigarettes and other delights of Saturday night, faded with the afternoon visibility.

They stood in the one-and-threes, Lennox trying to fix his eyes on the ball, to follow each one of its erratic well-kicked movements, but after ten minutes going from blurred player to player he gave it up and turned to look at the spectators massed in the rising stands that reached out in a wide arc on either side and joined dimly way out over the pitch. This proving equally futile he rubbed a clenched hand into his weak eyes and squeezed them tight, as if pain would give them more strength. Useless. All it produced was a mass of grey squares dancing before his open lids, so that when they cleared his sight was no better than before. Such an affliction made him appear more phlegmatic at a football match than Fred and most of the others round about, who spun rattles, waved hats and scarves, opened their throats wide to each fresh vaccillation in the game.

During his temporary blindness the Notts forwards were pecking and weaving around the Bristol goal and a bright slam from one of them gave rise to a false alarm, an indecisive rolling of cheers roofed in by a grey heavy sky. 'What's up?' Lennox asked Fred. 'Who scored? Anybody?'

Fred was a younger man, recently married, done up in his Saturday afternoon best of sports coat, gaberdine trousers and rain-mac, dark hair sleeked back with oil. 'Not in a month of Sundays,' he laughed, 'but they had a bleddy good try, I'll tell you that.'

By the time Lennox had focused his eyes once more on the players the battle had moved to the Notts goal and Bristol were about to score. He saw a player running down the field, hearing in his imagination the thud of boots on damp introdden turf. A knot of adversaries dribbled out in a line and straggled behind him at a trot. Suddenly the man with the ball spurted forward, was seen to be clear of everyone as if, in a second of time that hadn't existed to an spectator or other player, he'd been catapulted into a hallowed untouchable area before the goal-posts. Lennox's heart stopped beating. He peered between two oaken unmovable shoulders that, he thought with anger, had swayed in front purposely to stop him seeing. The renegade centre-forward from the opposing side was seen, like a puppet worked by someone above the low clouds, to bring his legs back, lunge out heavily with his booted foot. 'No,' Lennox had time to say. 'Get on to him you dozy sods. Don't let him get it in.'

From an animal pacing within the prescribed area of his defended posts, the goalkeeper turned into a leaping ape, arms and legs out-stretched, then became a mere stick that swung into a curve – and missed the ball as it sped to one side and lost itself in folds of net behind him.

The lull in the general noise seemed like silence for the mass of people packed about the field. Everyone had settled it in his mind that the match, bad as it was, would be a draw, but now it was clear that Notts, the home team, had lost. A great roar of disappointment and joy, from the thirty thousand spectators who hadn't realised that the star of Bristol City was so close, or who had expected a miracle from their own stars at the last moment, ran up the packed embankments, overflowing into streets outside where groups of people, startled at the sudden noise of an erupting mob, speculated as to which team had scored.

Fred was laughing wildly, jumping up and down, bellowing some-thing between a cheer and a shout of hilarious anger, as if out to get his money's worth on the principle that an adverse goal was better than no goal at all. 'Would you believe it?' he called at Lennox. 'Would you believe it? Ninety-five thousand quid gone up like Scotch mist!'

Hardly knowing what he was doing Lennox pulled out a cigarette, lit it. 'It's no good,' he cursed, 'they've lost. They should have walked away with the game' – adding under his breath that he must get some glasses in order to see things better. His sight was now so bad that the line of each eye crossed and converged some distance in front of him. At the cinema he was forced down to the front row, and he was never the first to recognise a pal on the street. And it spelt ruination for any football match. He could remember being able to pinpoint each player's face, and distinguish every spectator around the field, yet he still persuaded himself that he had no need of glasses and that somehow his sight would begin to improve. A more barbed occurrence connected with such eyes was that people were beginning to call him Cock-eye. At the garage where he worked the men sat down to tea-break the other day, and because he wasn't in the room one of them said: 'Where's owd Cock-eye? 'Is tea'll get cold.'

'What hard lines,' Fred shouted, as if no one yet knew about the goal. 'Would you believe it?' The cheering and booing were beginning to die down.

'That goalie's a bloody fool,' Lennox swore, cap pulled low over his forehead. 'He couldn't even catch a bleeding cold.'

'It was dead lucky,' Fred put in reluctantly, 'they deserved it, I suppose' – simmering down now, the full force of the tragedy seeping through even to his newly-wedded body and soul. 'Christ, I should have stayed at home with my missis. I'd a bin warm there, I know that much. I might even have cut myself a chunk of hearthrug pie if I'd have asked her right!'

The laugh and wink were intended for Lennox, who was still, in the backwater of his personal defeat. 'I suppose that's all you think on these days,' he said wryly.

"Appen I do, but I don't get all that much of it. I can tell you.' It was obvious though that he got enough to keep him in good spirits at a cold and disappointing football match.

'Well,' Lennox pronounced, 'all that'll alter in a bit. You can bet on that.'

'Not if I know it,' Fred said with a broad smile. 'And I reckon it's better after a bad match than if I didn't come to one.'

'You never said a truer word about bad,' Lennox said. He bit his lip with anger. 'Bloody team. They'd even lose at blow football.' A woman behind, swathed in a thick woollen scarf coloured white and black, like the Notts players, who had been screaming herself hoarse in support of the home team all the afternoon was almost in tears at the adverse goal. 'Foul! Foul! Get the dirty lot off the field. Send 'em back to Bristol where they came from. Foul! Foul, I tell yer.'

People all around were stamping feet dead from the cold, having for more than an hour staved off its encroachment into their limbs by the hope of at least one home-team win before Christmas. Lennox could hardly feel his, hadn't the will to help them back to life, especially in face of an added force to the bitter wind, and a goal that had been given away so easily. Movement on the pitch was now desultory, for there were only ten minutes of play left to go. The two teams knotted up towards one goal, then spread out around an invisible ball, and moved down the field again, back to the other with no decisive result. It seemed that both teams had accepted the present score to be the final state of the game, as though all effort had deserted their limbs and lungs.

'They're done for,' Lennox observed to Fred. People began leaving the ground, making a way between those who were determined to see the game out to its bitter end. Right up to the dull warbling blast of the final whistle the hard core of optimists hoped for a miraculous revival in the worn-out players.

'I'm ready when yo' are,' Fred said.

'Suits me.' He threw his cigarette end to the floor and, with a grimace of disappointment and disgust, made his way up the steps. At the highest point he turned a last glance over the field, saw two players running and the rest standing around in deepening mist – nothing doing – so went on down towards the barriers. When they were on the road a great cheer rose behind, as a whistle blew the signal for a mass rush to follow.

from THE LONELINESS OF THE LONG DISTANCE RUNNER *1959*

I Have Dreamed

ALAN SIMPSON

'. . . and as this huge 100,000 crowd at Wembley watch the FA Cup final move into the last five minutes, it's Everton on the attack yet again, it's Mercer to Lawton, Lawton, Lawton a flashing drive and it's there . . . NO! Another fantastic save by young Simpson in the Brentford goal. Will this brilliant youngster ever be beaten? Lawton is shaking his head in disbelief. He's tried everything he knows but Simpson has been absolutely superb today. This incredible fifteen-year-old from Streatham, the youngest goalkeeper ever to play in a Cup final, is surely destined to be one of the greatest keepers the world has ever seen. And as the seconds tick away it's Everton on the attack again . . .'

'*Alan, get out of bed, your breakfast's ready.*'

'*Yes, Mum, coming, Mum.*'

'*One or two eggs?*'

'*Two, please.*'

'. . . we're now into injury time and Brentford are still hanging on to their one goal lead scored by goalkeeper Simpson from the penalty spot, and if the "Bees" win the Cup for the first time it will be due entirely to the masterly performance put up by this young boy today. He has soaked up everything Lawton and his colleagues have thrown at him. And now Everton make what must surely be their last effort to equalise. It's Britton, a square ball to Mercer . . .'

'*Get on with your breakfast, you'll be late for work.*'

'*Yes, Mum.*'

'*And don't be late in tonight.*'

'*No, Mum.*'

'. . . and there it is, the final whistle, Brentford have won the FA Cup for the first time in their history. And as the entire Brentford team hoist young Simpson on to their shoulders and carry him in triumph over to the Royal Box, everybody in this stadium today is asking the same question. How much longer can Frank Swift keep this amazing youngster out of the England team?'

'*Come on, Sonny, fares please, we haven't got all day.*'

'*Oh, sorry. Cannon Street Station, please.*'

'. . . and here is the Sports News. The England team to meet Scotland next month at Hampden Park is as follows: Simpson (Brentford) (captain), Hapgood (Arsenal), Hardwick (Middlesbrough), Britton (Everton), Cullis (Wolverhampton Wanderers), Mercer (Everton), Matthews (Blackpool). . . .'

'*If you don't stop staring into space and get on with your work, Simpson, you can look for another job.*'

'*Yes, sir, sorry, sir.*'

I suppose I spent half of my formative years day-dreaming. Always about football. Actually, I preferred day-dreaming to playing. You meet a much better class of player, and you don't get kicked quite so often. During my long career I played in eight Cup finals for Brentford, won over a hundred and fifty caps for England, including four World Cup tournaments, never let in a single penalty in eight hundred and fifty three first-class games, and had the honour of being the first five hundred pounds a week player in the football league. However, since my retirement as a player, I have had to be content with the four Amateur Cup finals Hampton have won, and of course that thrilling game last season when Manchester United unfortunately knocked them out of the sixth round of the FA Cup in extra time after four replays.

But to be fair to myself, I don't want you to think of me only as a dreamer. I did actually play the game when I was a boy. I was in fact a pretty good goalkeeper. Extremely good in the air but a bit fifties on the ground. Well, let's face it, it's a long way down. The highlight of my real career was when I was playing for Dulwich Hamlet Juniors at the age of sixteen. After the game, I was approached by a Chelsea scout and asked to go to Stamford Bridge for a trial. No, this is straight-up. I'm not day-dreaming now. Unfortunately, I was taken ill a month before the trial and have never kicked a ball since. I wasn't too shattered about it, because I knew deep down that I would never have made a pro. I'll be perfectly honest. I was a coward. I was all right on the flashy stuff. Picking them out of the air, tipping them over the bar, full stretch across the goal and nicking them round the post. But a race between me and the centre-forward for a through ball – forget it! A fifty-fifty ball for me had to be ninety-ten in my favour. And even then I could be talked out of it if he was a bit fierce-looking. I *looked* quite brave, though. I had it down to a fine art. I learnt how to go down at his feet in such a way that it looked good without the aggravation of being kicked. It's all a question of timing. You either go down a fraction too early, so he has plenty of time to go round you, or you go down a fraction late after he's gone. Trick is not to worry whether a goal is scored, just concentrate on not getting hurt. I was never tumbled. I got the reputation of being the unluckiest goalkeeper in Surrey. And the prettiest. Never got marked in seven years. But pro football, that's a different matter. If I had gone to the Bridge, I would have been sussed out in five minutes flat.

But, then again, I wonder . . . Last May I was sitting next to Bill Shankly at the Footballer of the Year Award dinner and . . . what do you mean day-dreaming again? I don't day-dream anymore. I'm too old for that sort of thing. Anyway, I told Bill this story and he said it might have worked out differently. He said that many young goal-keepers start out by not being brave, but as they get older they some-times grow out of it. I wonder? Supposing I hadn't been taken ill? Supposing I had gone for that trial with Chelsea? Supposing . . . Excuse me, I'm just going to tip this vicious twenty-yard drive from Pelé over the bar.

from SPORTSWORLD *1970*

Adventures in Bristol

COLIN WARD

'Go west, young man.' Well I did so one Saturday – to Bristol, which as far as many cockneys are concerned is real bumpkin land inhabited by buffoons who use the phrase 'ooh-aar' in every sentence. In 1976 Bristol City reached the first division and beat Arsenal one-nil at Highbury. Thousands of Bristol fans travelled to Highbury; but the place to teach them a lesson was on their home ground, Ashton Gate.

Paddington Station mid-morning. The Bristol express was stationary, full of expectant Arsenal fans. A few people leaned out of the open windows making banal comments or giving gestures of recognition to other fans. Finally a squeak of brakes being released and the train jerked into movement. By the time the train reached the end of the platform the familiar sound of escaping gas from ring-pull cans could be heard as people started drinking. Word soon spread along the train: 'All in the Bristol end today', and sure enough, when we arrived in Bristol as a group of about two hundred we made our way towards the home supporters' end. We passed row after row of terraced houses exactly the same as any typical north London street, but to some of the group they were inferior simply because they were in Bristol.

'Look at the state of those houses.'

'Yeah, two up two down and an outside shithouse.'

'Every front garden is concrete.'

'Can't afford lawnmovers, can they.'

'I expect they still bath in a tub in front of the fire.'

'Leave it out, running water hasn't reached this far west yet.'

The dialogue reflected the sense of superiority many of the travelling cockneys felt. All that remained was to teach the locals a lesson in terrace manoeuvres.

'We're gonna show these half-wits the new way.'

'One shout of "Arsenal!" and this end will empty.'

'They'll talk about today for a long time.'

Everybody laughed and felt smug; nobody felt threatened. At last the turnstiles: here we go.

Click, click, click is a familiar sound to football fans. It is the sound of the turnstile moving around against the metal ratchet as you go through. It's always reassuring to hear the clicks because you know you have arrived at the main event; but on this day my own heart seemed to be beating as loudly as the turnstile. I was one of the first twenty or so to gain entry, and once through I was confronted by a sea of hesitant faces surveying us for signs that we were cockneys. We had to infiltrate quickly or we were in big trouble. There seemed to be too many people milling around for comfort, and suddenly a shout went up: 'There's Londoners in our end. Do the cockney bastards!'

I heard the sound of fist hitting a face. People who ten seconds earlier had looked hesitant and nervous came forward in a human wave. We backed off and some of our group saw the futility of standing our ground and leapt back over the turnstiles. I couldn't see a way out and just concentrated on covering myself from the shower of blows. The guy next to me got kicked in the face and went down into the gravel. A girl ran up and grabbed his hair, pulling it violently while at the same time spitting at him. She was foaming at the mouth. 'You bastard,' she screamed.

Apart from the girl other people were queueing up to kick him, and the sickening sound of boots hitting his body could be heard repeatedly. It was indiscriminate and nasty: any part of his torso was fair game. One really vicious guy was trying to stamp on his face with the heel of his boot.

'Help me, they're going to kill me,' he pleaded, but no one could do anything. The other Arsenal fans on the other side of the turnstiles made no attempt to come in and help us, although I don't blame them considering the savage beating we were getting. A few pretended to try to come in, but it was only bravado.

I had retreated as far as I could and found myself penned in a corner between a tea hut and a concrete wall. I saw flailing fists and felt blows against my face. I gave up trying to block them and concentrated on curling up into a ball to give my attackers as little target as possible to aim at. Everybody was trying to punch or kick my head, and the sheer weight of numbers and frenzy of the attack saved me, for no one could get a decent blow in and they spent most of their energy kicking each other. I had my arms covering my head and my knees tight up against my chest, and my legs took most of the blows. I managed to glance up through my arms and saw an amazing sight. One Arsenal fan, whose name I later learned was Mick, was making a solitary stand of defiance. He had his back up against a wall and had about twenty-five guys in front of him all trying to give him a punch in the face. Mick would take five or six blows and then give one back, and he had managed to send a couple sprawling on to their backsides.

I thought the nightmare would never end, but the police soon turned up and the Bristol fans scattered, leaving us to pick ourselves up, dust ourselves down and get ejected by the police. Everyone tried to leave with as much dignity as they could muster, but the leers and catcalls rang in our ears.

'Go 'ome, cockneys.'

'You won't try that again.'

'That taught you flash bastards a lesson. You won't come 'ere again and try to take the piss, will you?'

We all walked out of the ground, even including the guy who had taken the severe beating. The police marched us up the other end and as we were shepherded out of the gate a few more home fans charged forward to throw punches at us.

'If it wasn't for the coppers you'd be dead,' sang the Bristol fans as the police escorted us to the opposite end where we had to pay again to gain entry. Some of the fans who hadn't taken a beating cheekily asked for free entry. 'Come on, you're not going to make us pay again, are you?' But the police would have none of it.

After the match the police escorted us to the station and put us on trains back to London. Plenty of us had black eyes, grazes and lumps coming up on our heads, but by Paddington Station Mental Mickey's last stand had given us the self-awarded status of a moral victory. We laughed and joked on the way home, mostly thankful we had survived (even though it is hard to laugh with bruised ribs). To add insult to injury, we had lost the match two–nil.

from STEAMING IN *1989*

Tachini Fashions

COLIN WARD

Travelling to football was always a working-class pastime and this was reflected in the dress code. Flat caps and working clothes gave way to the uniform of the early Seventies: donkey jackets and denim, with compulsory industrial footwear – the famous Doc Marten boot. In the late Seventies the dress code changed again. The designer look set in; Armani, Pringle, Tachini and Lacoste became the hooligans' uniform. Dressed up it was easier to avoid the police, and to get served in pubs. With the massive police presence at some matches the poseurs had free rein to dress up to the nines and pretend they had courage – a bunch of latter-day Tall Erics. I wonder how these guys would have fared ten years earlier.

Sometimes two designer dressers would team up to form a designer duo, and one day this happened in Manchester's Arndale Centre. A duo were walking through past a pub frequented by Manchester City's fans. A group was drinking outside and wolf-whistled the two Chelsea fans as they were walking past. One of the Chelsea fans stopped.

'What are you divs whistling at? I'll give you something to look at.'

With that he dropped his jeans to reveal a pair of Tachini shorts being worn as underpants. He patted them and pointed at the logo.

'See boys, Tachini! One day you'll be wearing these – when you learn about fashion, that is.'

With that he pulled up his trousers, leaving the Mancunians staring open-mouthed.

from STEAMING IN *1989*

Teaching the Turks a Trick or Two

COLIN WELLAND

If soccer is the new religion I've just met the twelve Apostles. There they sat in Ankara Stadium, Turkish pastries wrapped around their faces, hurling healthy abuse at an inept Romanian referee, chatting 'intimately' from stand to pitch with Don and Billy and Norman and swinging with reckless defiance on bank after bank of bloodthirsty Turks. 'Super Leeds,' they cried. 'Super Leeds' – their arms thrown wide in salute – and, passionately, they believed every word.

'Super Leeds' were performing a quiet, ultra-professional suffocating job on a local side all torrid and volatile, full of bounce but with no real football brains. As a policy it was predictable, and to be honest, it was boring. It was also completely inconsequential to the roaring enjoyment of an expeditionary force of twelve Leeds fanatics bent on football and a bloody good time.

Two thousand miles they'd come. Moving with the speed of light infantry – and under the cover of a blue-black sky – they hit the unsuspecting Turkish capital before last Tuesday's dawn . . . and soon even this city, well used to the petulance of old Mother Earth, was shuddering to its very foundations.

Mind you, who'd have guessed? We must have looked quite a respectable lot boarding the plane at Heathrow. A couple of local businessmen and wives, a Yorkshire League ref and son, who won the trip in a newspaper competition (people actually fill them in), a muck-and-brass type company director travelling alone and (here's the crunch) four Bradford publicans who, with a master window cleaner called Big H, provided the party's real firepower. These last five were ready for anything. Inevitably anything wasn't available – but they sure made the most of what was.

On second thoughts perhaps Turkish Airlines should have realised when, during the solemn search for arms, Gilbert (who looked like Charlie Williams and had a voice to match) earnestly requested that the Arab passenger in long flowing robes be given another good do – as he looked like their kid – and he wouldn't trust *him* as far as he could throw him. Surely their suspicions should have been roused when, once airborne, Big H stood proudly and introduced himself to the crowded, sweaty cabin as H. Bower, window cleaner, no job too large or small – as the rest laced the Turkish coffees with duty free Scotch explaining that that's how its done 'in the Gaelic'.

A wiser, more worldly crew would have radioed ahead crying 'Siege'. But then, despite their reputation, they're a kind-hearted lot, the Turks, and fate is often cruel to the kind.

Ankara, although the capital, is by our standards quite an unsophisticated place. Football there is still a game, not a creed. The men are gentle and cling to one another's arms. The women, though no longer veiled, are essentially demure.

Still, we were there to enjoy ourselves, and we set about doing just that. A guide was summoned to show us the sights. An earnest strip of a lad he was, a student, briefed in local ethnological history, eager to trace for us in detail the development of Turkish ceramic art. Give us our due, we gave him a hearing – enjoyed it – but it took a fleeting glimpse of a shapely ballerina flitting across the open doors of the State Ballet rehearsal rooms to really fire our dormant imaginations. In a flash we were in with the chat. 'Dame Margot Fonteyn! Yes! Lovely!' The girls were kind and tolerant and we swept out triumphant to the sun and the mountain air and the spread of our chests.

Ankara was fast becoming our oyster when Leeds flew in and somebody mentioned football and the match. The match! What a fantastic experience that was – not the game, the event. The city, naïvely new to European football, was engagingly enthusiastic. Curious knots of locals clustered about us smiling, clutching our hands. We were proud to be Leedsites, here, miles from anywhere. We patted heads like newly descended gods as exotic sounds and smells crowded our senses.

Suddenly across the compound staggered an unearthly figure. It was hairy, wild-eyed and uttering weird cries, strangely familiar. 'A ticket lads – a ticket?' wailed the creature, his face festooned with mosquito bites. Eight days on the road he'd hitched from Leeds. We pressed him to our bosoms, tended his wounds and gave him a ticket. As he sobbed out his thanks we rebuked him and reminded him that in spite of all he was still British.

And so were we, like it or not. Once inside, Her Majesty's Consul opened his paternal arms and sat us firmly in his private enclosure surrounded by armed troops thoughtfully and insistently provided by the largest standing army in Europe. From what, we asked, were they protecting us? Kindness?

Leeds came, and saw and contained – like benign Victorian grandfathers . . . but this was football à l'Orient, immune from 'civilising' influences. It was a game in which goalkeeper and penalty-taker embrace before the shot, linesmen throw bouquets of flowers to the crowd and bonfires and rockets celebrate a goal.

Afterwards we sat like kings surrounded by adoring Turks who whistled Leeds admiringly through their teeth. Superior beings will scoff at those who travel 2,000 miles to see a game of football. But our lives were enriched by this particular journey.

By necessity I had to leave the following day with half the week still to go. I flew home with the team and their speedily sobering chat of Leicester on Saturday and the points. I left behind the new Gilbert, and Big H and the rest lunching at the Embassy . . . But later that evening, secure in the belief that language barriers just don't exist they'd be swopping yarns over black, sweet Turkish coffee with our new-found Ankaran friends.

I cannot help feeling that this beautiful city will look back with affection not only on the visit of Leeds United but of their twelve supporters.

from the OBSERVER *1972*

Supporting Scotland

GORDON WILLIAMS

Upstairs on a corporation bus, don't ask me what corporation. Lady in fur hat turns and sneers with a sniff: 'Your sort is a disgrace to Scotland.'

Away and boil your head, you frosty-faced old ratbag. I said, awa' an' bile yur heid –

Oh look, Missus, don't mind my pal, he's just been celebrating the big win –

Aye, I was there, Missus, Hampden Park in the rain, Scotland two Inglin nil! Strong men crying, strangers hugging, we'll support ye ever more! Scotlin two Inglin nil, joy joy. Fancy a wee nip, Missus, no everyday your counry smashes the whiteshirted might of the master race, is it? Ach well, never mind her, probably a Third Lanark supporter. She looks a bit like Jimmy Harrower.

Let's get off this bus before you get us arrested.

We are arrested already, arrested development. Don't you sneer at me for being a common s-h-i-t-e, Missus, I got my Highers, don't you worry.

'Pity you didn't do more with your education, then.'

Droppen Sie dead, Bella. Hey, Ian, there's a pub!

All right but I'm just having a couple of lagers to wash out my mouth, mind, I'm not getting involved in another big sesh.

For all I care you can get involved with Jinkie Johnstone in an open boat. What's so great to keep sober about? It's the greatest day of our lives, isn't it? Hey Jimmy, two halfs and two pints a lager. At the gemme wur ye? Oh great, just great. Never thought I'd see the day. Norman Hunter couldnae stand the pace! See that team? They were heroes today. Made ye proud to be Scottish. When the first goal went in I threw a wee fella next tae me up in the air, he turned out to be English wearing a tartan rosette for safety reasons! Nice enough wee bloke though.

from WE'LL SUPPORT YOU EVERMORE *1976*

Sugar Mice and Buzzcocks Albums

NICK HORNBY

Cambridge United v Orient: 4 November 1978

What happened was, Chris Roberts bought a sugar mouse from Jack Reynolds ('The Rock King'), bit its head off, dropped it in the Newmarket Road before he could get started on the body, and it got run over by a car. And that afternoon Cambridge United, who had hitherto been finding life difficult in the Second Division (two wins all season, one home, one away), beat Orient 3–1, and a ritual was born. Before each home game we all of us trooped into the sweet shop, purchased our mice, walked outside, bit the head off as though we were removing the pin from a grenade, and tossed the torsos under the wheels of oncoming cars; Jack Reynolds would stand in the doorway watching us, shaking his head sorrowfully. United, thus protected, remained unbeaten at the Abbey for months.

I know that I am particularly stupid about rituals, and have been ever since I started going to football matches, and I know also that I am not alone. I can remember when I was young having to take with me to Highbury a piece of putty, or blu-tack, or some stupid thing, which I pulled on nervously all afternoon (I was a smoker even before I was old enough to smoke); I can also remember having to buy a programme from the same programme seller, and having to enter the stadium through the same turnstile.

There have been hundreds of similar bits of nonsense, all designed to
guarantee victories for one or other of my two teams. During Arsenal's
protracted and nerve-racking semi-final campaign against Liverpool in
1980, I turned the radio off half-way through the second half of the last
game; Arsenal were winning 1–0, and as Liverpool had equalised in the
last seconds of the previous game, I couldn't bear to hear it through to
the end. I played a Buzzcocks album instead (the *Singles – Going Steady*
compilation album), knowing that side one would take me through to
the final whistle. We won the match, and I insisted that my flatmate,
who worked in a record store, should play the album at twenty past four
on Cup Final afternoon, although it did no good. (I have my suspicions
that he might have forgotten.)

I have tried 'smoking' goals in (Arsenal once scored as three of us
were lighting cigarettes), and eating cheese-and-onion crisps at a
certain point in the first half; I have tried not setting the video for live
games (the team seems to have suffered badly in the past when I have
taped the matches in order to study the performance when I get home);
I have tried lucky socks, and lucky shirts, and lucky hats, and lucky
friends, and have attempted to exclude others who I feel bring with
them nothing but trouble for the team.

Nothing (apart from the sugar mice) has ever been any good. But
what else can we do when we're so *weak*? We invest hours each day,
months each year, years each lifetime in something over which we have
no control; is it any wonder then, that we are reduced to creating
ingenious but bizarre liturgies designed to give us the illusion that we
are powerful after all, just as every other primitive community has done
when faced with a deep and apparently impenetrable mystery?

from FEVER PITCH *1992*

PART 7

The Anguish

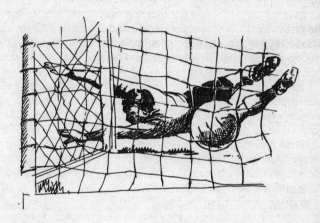

One Campaign Too Many

STEVE ANDERSON

My wife told me about it. I telephoned her after a near-suicidal mission into the northern Saudi desert. I had visited the forward units of the Kuwaiti Army situated just two miles from their own country. Drinking chai with a colonel in his tented headquarters, we could hear American B 52 bombers drumming away at Iraqi artillery positions. I made a hazardous thirty-miles journey alone out of the waterlogged desert plains, and strayed into no-man's land where a sixteen-year-old Egyptian sentry pulled a gun on me, before being reassured by my British passport. It took another six hours to reach base in Dhanran, eastern Saudi Arabia where I telephoned my wife in London to report that I was OK. Everything was well at home too, she said. 'Oh, and by the way,' she added at the end of her report, 'Kenny Dalglish has resigned.'

I tried to keep it in perspective and for a short while I succeeded. Weeks later a colleague, another Liverpudlian, also working on the Gulf story, told me of a similar reaction. 'I was determined not to get upset,' he confessed. 'I told myself to keep it in proportion. It was just football, nothing compared to what was happening in the Gulf. But I couldn't get away from it and by night time it was as if it was the only thing in the world that mattered.'

Memories flooded back – the Wembley debut against Manchester United; a goal in his first game at Anfield, a 2–0 win over Newcastle United; scoring the winner against Bruges in the European Cup final of 1978; his headed goal for Scotland against Wales in the World Cup qualifier; the partnership with Ian Rush; Heysel; the double in 1986; beating Everton in two Cup finals; Hillsborough, when he emerged as a tower of strength in a city that appeared to have suffered one blow too many. It had seemed he would be there forever.

'Pressure' forced him to quit, we began to hear. Even the Saudi Arabian newspapers were reporting it, with a glum-faced Dalglish pictured at the press conference. But wasn't it an artificial pressure when measured against that of General Schwarzkopf, I wondered.

Stormin' Norman was on a fraction of Dalglish's salary, yet was leading 700,000 men into a foreign war. Many lives were at stake and the
future of the 'New World Order' was resting on his shoulders. Tell
Schwarzkopf that all he had to worry about was a league and cup
double and you would have a truly happy man.

Pressure, however, is a relative phenomenon and without doubt it
was being felt by Kenny Dalglish. Pressure from a Liverpool public
sated with success, for instance. I had been watching them for twenty-
five years and had lost count of the number of occasions I had been
to Wembley. I got confused about how many times we had won the
league. When was the last time we had finished outside the top two?
Back in the Seventies, wasn't it? As the seasons passed it was impossible to ignore the complacency that had settled on the Kop Choir.
Once upon a time it was said the Kop was worth a goal start for the
Liverpool team; these days they seldom sang 'You'll Never Walk
Alone' with any enthusiasm, and only seemed happy to cheer when
the goals were flowing in. A friend related to me a story of seeing
Liverpool beat Everton 3–1, a few weeks before the resignation. Leaving the Kop after the game he said that rather than celebrating, Liverpool supporters were complaining that the score should have been 6–
0. Perhaps Dalglish himself had contributed to the problem more than
anyone else. Angry at anything less than victory, he was being
devoured by a monster he helped to create. Success, they never tired
of telling you, breeds success. Football was more important than life
or death, said Bill Shankly; winning, the Liverpool chairman John
Smith once said, was not the only thing at Anfield, it was everything.

But a lust for glory obviously brings its own costs. Try asking
Schwarzkopf to repeat year after year the success he had in the Gulf.
Even a man with his powers of leadership would one day turn to his
President and say it was time for someone else to carry on the fight.
For Kenny Dalglish, in a peer group prematurely old and sick as it
continued its hunt for silverware, it was one campaign too many.

Previously unpublished

The End of a World Cup Dream

IAN ARCHER

From distant corners came the sounds of 'Bonnie Scotland, We'll Support You Evermore, We'll Support You Evermore'. The teams came out, which was great, because we were getting used to this World Cup business and the nerves departed.

There followed a coarse, hard, definitively European game, the extra defenders shutting off space, the wingers unable to beat full backs and the midfield humping up and down like navvies. For long periods, as they say, nothing continued to happen and you didn't quite know whether to be pleased that Scotland were still level instead of behind, or whether to be sad because they had not scored the goal that would carry them onwards. Hughie said at half time, 'They can do it.' There was too long a queue at the Coca-Cola stand.

Dzajic at least is impotent, still not recovered from a car crash. Oblak is in Bremner's pocket. Katalinski dishes it out, but so do some of ours. It becomes very hot all of a sudden as the sun kisses this World Cup for the first time. Much of the chanting and shouting from the terraces is in deference to the occasion rather than because the play on the field warrants high excitement. We get on top for a while, the Yugoslavs hold us and it's pawn to queen five in an orthodox middle game. The minutes pass away, it's almost domino, goodnight Munich and the boys have played great and they did their best and it's not a very good era for Scottish goalscorers and Hughie says it's better than 1954 and 1958 all rolled together and we were never much good at this game and it's absolutely bloody crazy that grown men should behave like this and that he's heard of a boat trip up the Rhine, only 50 marks and should we have a little donner at it on Tuesday.

Yugoslavia go up the park with five minutes left. Dzajic crosses for the first time and Karasi heads past Harvey. The defence is nowhere as it's looking for a goal at the other end. Hughie throws his arms all about me and I can feel hot tears, not three seconds later, all the way through my shirt and on to my shoulders. He stays that way for a long time, sobbing, heaving, muttering 'No, no, no.' I'm getting no sensation at all from my legs.

Behind us there's a man and a woman, not married, never met. He's crying too, snuggling into her and talking as well. 'The last time I cried it was at my father's funeral.' George's head is between his knees. No one's thrown anything yet, I think. There is a deep, bitter, unbelieving silence and our flags have come down. I want home, now, this minute, on one of those time machines that can take me there in a split second.

Scotland go up the park, desperate, chilled, not comprehending. The ball is in Yugoslavia's penalty area, Jordan kicks and slowly it rolls into the net. 'Who scored?' 'Let me see, Hughie.' Does it matter? Have we won, have we lost, just what the hell is that bloody American doing standing in front of me, it's not his game – but is it ours? The referee blows his whistle, they all shake hands and our lot start crying. End Game.

There is still a straw of a chance that Scotland have qualified if Zaire restrict Brazil to two goals in Gelsenkirchen and this statistical fact is passed around the terraces, but soon the electronic scoreboard pings out Brazil 3 Zaire 0 and we've now really no place to go, we've been locked out, unchosen, dismissed, told to geraff this competition. No one wants to throw anything and Hughie is fumbling with his spectacles.

There are a few plastic cups to kick on our way round to the other side of the ground and you would think that you'd want to look round at the other Scots about the place, for we're abroad and there might be someone you know and would like to talk to. But all heads and eyes are down, they are shuffling away and this is a grief too deep for any words.

Showing our passes, we get to see Ormond. Margaret's weeping a few yards away. He's blind with tears that refuse to drop. We're too embarrassed to even shake hands so we just look at each other, long, hard, affectionately. This time I want to cry for it may be all of Scotland that this day is about, but for me, it's this little man, who has endured it, slept it, drunk it, butterflied it for months and *he is* Scotland standing there, small, pawky, unwanted, done in. And maybe he sees this because he smiles.

We all stand about for a long time, waiting for a bus to take us home. Miljanic, in passing, says we 'are good players, but, better, good sports.' Ormond has been into the Yugoslavian dressing-room to congratulate the winners and qualifiers and that deeply impresses this big Stein of a man, who says nothing nicer will happen in the competition. Then we notice a strange movement inside this room towards the window and people are looking out on the most beautiful sight in this dreadful experience.

A group of about 200 Scots has gathered around the team coach, as they do every Saturday at places like Brockville, Dens Park, Cappielow for that, too, is part of our own thing. They start singing slowly, not the supporters' songs but the songs of a people who want to be a nation: 'Flower of Scotland', 'The Road and the Miles to Bonnie Dundee', 'The Star of Rabbie Burns'. When the players come out, smart now and spruce, they cheer, softly. And they end by singing 'We're on our way to Argentina, we shall not be moved.' It is the stuff of legends, the cry of the undefeated. They are singing love songs.

from WE'LL SUPPORT YOU EVERMORE *1976*

Tragedy at Munich

H. E. BATES

Late on a cold February afternoon of this year I was driving home from London when I suddenly saw, under the first lighted street lamps, one of those blue and yellow news placards that are designed so often to shock you into buying a newspaper you don't particularly want and that, nine times out of ten, you would be just as well off without.

'Manchester United in Air Crash', it said. My immediate reaction was, I confess, a mildly cynical one. The announcement seemed to me to belong to precisely the same category as 'Winston Churchill in Car Crash' – the car crash almost invariably turning out to be nothing more than a tender argument between the starting handle of an ancient Austin Seven and the great man's Rolls-Royce somewhere in the region of Parliament Square. I am getting too old, I thought, to be caught by newspaper screamers.

At six o'clock, out of pure curiosity, I turned on my television set. As the news came on, the screen seemed to go black. The normally urbane voice of the announcer seemed to turn into a sledge-hammer. My eyes went deathly cold and I sat listening with a frozen brain to that cruel and shocking list of casualties that was now to give to the despised word Munich an even sadder meaning than it had acquired on a day before the war when a British Prime Minister had come home to London, waving a pitiful piece of paper, and most of us knew that new calamities of war were inevitable.

Roger Byrne, Bill Whelan, Duncan Edwards, Tommy Taylor, David Pegg, Geoff Bent, Mark Jones, Eddie Colman – of Manchester United's flashing young giants hardly one had been out of the cradle at the time of the first Munich disaster. Probably not one of them had kicked a football in that year on the eve of the war when England had sent to Berlin eleven other giants to thrash the team representing Hitler's master-race by six goals to three.

By the time war was over it was inevitable that the heroes of that resounding Berlin victory – men like Tommy Lawton, Raich Carter, Wilf Copping, and Stan Cullis – were on the verge of slipping from the international football scene. A new race of giants had to be found to represent the country that had taught the rest of the world all that was best in the skill and beauty of soccer. And soon, as men like Carter, Drake, Lawton, and Cullis turned their talents to the tutorship of new teams, we began to hear more and more of a man, up in Manchester, who appeared to be dedicated to the apparently revolutionary notion that you can make mature footballers out of boys in their teens.

To me that idea of Matt Busby's never seemed in the least bit extraordinary. There is nothing more true about football than that it is a young man's game. In youth the eyes have a fantastic swiftness, limbs are marvellously supple, with powers of resilience, and recovery unknown later. The clay of young flesh is a beautifully plastic thing that can be trained and shaped under skilled teaching in endless and remarkable ways. Not only in football has the principle of shaping extreme youth proved to be an excellent one. Who, twenty years ago, would have dreamed of swimmers of thirteen and fourteen representing their countries and breaking world records? Today these things are commonplaces.

Gradually, as the Busby principle of teaching was translated into reality, the names of the top students began to emerge. We began to hear of players representing Manchester United in the first division at the age of seventeen. Presently we were to see the greatest of all the Busby prodigies, Duncan Edwards, an appealing giant of a boy, representing England at the age of eighteen, striding the Wembley pitch like a mature colossus, gaining the first of his eighteen international caps, under each of which he increased in stature so much that at twenty-one he was not only a veteran but clearly England's future captain.

If I select Duncan Edwards as the most compelling of all the young Manchester men who will now never play football again it is because he always seemed to me the epitome of all that was best in skill and character in the team that became popularly known – and very foolishly I think – as the 'Busby Babes'. I have always intensely disliked that cheap journalistic label and I have a fancy that most of the players may have done so too. There was certainly nothing of a babe about Edwards. A more mature young man, both in physical strength and artistry, never walked on to that treacherous and difficult turf at Wembley to play for his country.

You could say almost the same of that excellent and cultured back Roger Byrne, who gained thirty-three England caps; of the energetic and enthusiastic Tommy Taylor; and of Pegg, Colman, and Jones, all of whom, like Duncan Edwards, had been schoolboy stars; of Whelan, who also appeared for his native Ireland, and Bent who travelled to Belgrade as a reserve. Footballers, George Bernard Shaw once said, have their brains in their feet, but I have always had a sneaking notion that Matt Busby liked to be sure that his young men had a few brains in their heads too.

But what these young prodigies possessed above all, I think, was class. It is an attribute not easy to define, but when Manchester United were beaten in the 1957 Cup final by an Aston Villa playing very robust but not very good football, it was also pure class that made them, I think, as admirable in defeat as they had so often been in victory. And when they were again and deservedly beaten in the 1958 Cup final it was not merely because they were lacking in the necessary arts and skills. The class was not there.

And how could it possibly have been? Its ashes lay irreparably scattered across a German airfield after the cruellest day in English sporting history. Whether the same degree of class will ever be seen again in the United colours it is too early to tell; but one thing is certain. If it never returns it will not be the fault of Matt Busby, the tutor, happily still with us; or of the young men to whom, so very early in life, he taught the beauties of our national game, and who, having acquired fame in youth, set such an adult example before they were so prematurely and tragically taken from the field.

from THE OFFICIAL FOOTBALL ASSOCIATION YEARBOOK *1958*

The Dark Side of the Game

NEIL DUNCANSON

It's early afternoon as Allan McGraw pulls up outside his house in Gourock, a sleepy Glasgow backwater nestling into the hills overlooking the chill waters of the Clyde estuary. On fine days it's a picturesque view, with nuclear submarines just as likely to glide past his front window as a milk float or a dust truck.

Today the rain is bouncing off the street and Allan eases himself out of the car, walks slowly across the pavement and gingerly negotiates the steep slope to his front door. It's a painful sight, but he makes little of it. After all, he's made it to the house without falling down, something of an achievement when all there is between you and a rapid acquaintance with the ground are two wooden walking sticks and some ageing metal and plastic holding your legs together.

Nothing new there, though. Thousands of people in Britain suffer as he does. But somehow it's much worse for Allan 'Quick Draw' McGraw – certainly to the outside observer.

It doesn't feel right that a man who still holds the British goalscoring record and was once pursued by the nation's premier clubs as the next Jimmy Greaves should have to go through life swallowing dozens of maximum-strength painkillers and every day face the prospect that the only escape from the constant pain is the amputation of both his legs.

Allan McGraw is nothing if not a realist. A modest, affable man, with a dry sense of humour, football is his life and, although he regrets what has happened, he admits he was perhaps a little naive to play on for as long as he did. But back in the 1960s, when the goals were flowing and Morton Football Club were setting Scottish football alight, he thought only of playing. Nothing else mattered. If it meant another injection in those troublesome knees then that was the price of playing the game he loved. Only now is he able to understand the real price.

Today he is manager of Morton, the club he served so well during his playing days, and as he sits stiff-legged at home, contemplating an uncertain future, he has a simple message to any player considering a short-cut around injury.

'I just hope that I would serve as a warning. I'm not complaining, I've done it and that's it. But to any young player who is considering taking injections to play sport, you must know that you are playing with dynamite.' These are not hollow words. His hospital X-rays are an appalling indictment of the medical treatment and advice that McGraw received. The state of his legs would give Barry Sheene nightmares.

Surprisingly, Allan's enthusiasm for the game which has crippled him is undiminished. He loves to work with the young players, enjoys talking football in the cramped little office at Cappielow Park and still thrives on running an unfashionable Glasgow side on a shoestring, knowing that whenever he turns up a promising talent the bigger clubs will snatch it away.

So how did it happen? How did Britain's all-action, record goal poacher turn from the man they called 'the gunboat' to the hobbling shadow of today?

Allan McGraw's professional career began at Morton, after a couple of years in the army, in the early 1960s. He was quick, brave and soon earned a reputation at Cappielow as a finisher of unusual quality. His readiness to go in where it hurt too often left him nursing injuries, but McGraw was proving too valuable to leave out of the team – even when he wasn't fit.

When he first joined the Greenock side, they had just finished the 1960–61 season bottom of the Scottish second division. In the following two seasons they twice rose to claim third place, just missing out on promotion, and the transformation was in no small measure thanks to the goalscoring instincts of McGraw.

But it was the memorable 1963–64 season, arguably Morton's greatest, that earned McGraw lasting fame in Scotland, headlines that compared him with Denis Law and brought him to the attention of big English clubs. Morton simply outclassed the division to win the Championship by 14 clear points, winning 32 of their 36 games, losing just once and scoring 135 goals. If that wasn't enough they performed heroics to reach the Scottish League Cup final, eventually going down 0–5 to Rangers at Hampden Park.

But the real hero of the year was Allan McGraw, who scored 58 league and cup goals, despite nagging knee injuries. It is a tally that remains a British post-war record and an unenviable target for even the most productive scorers of today.

As news of McGraw's exploits spread, Cappielow Park became a frequent watering hole for English scouts. Wolves and Manchester City were keen to take him south and Tommy Docherty, then manager of Chelsea and still trawling for a successor to Jimmy Greaves, offered him a £2,000 signing-on fee and £45 a week for a move to Stamford Bridge – a sizeable increase on the £12 14s his Morton wage packet provided. Docherty offered Morton's manager, Hal Stewart, £25,000 for McGraw's signature. Stewart demanded more; Chelsea refused.

The following year, in the Scottish first division, Morton finished a respectable tenth. McGraw found the tighter defences less amenable to his predatory skills and English interest began to fade. But he continued to play the 'gunboat way' and the injuries kept coming.

He had taken a few bad knocks the season before Morton's glory year, but he'd been given injections to help him train and play. These injections were nearly always cortisone, an anti-inflammatory drug. He had started on a downward spiral of drugs and football that would eventually lead to his present predicament.

Injected into the wrong place or used too often, cortisone can lead to the complete disintegration of tissue, tendons, ligaments and joints. Current medical expertise considers more than one injection of corti-sone in the same area – more than one IN A LIFETIME, that is – to be a danger. In one season McGraw was given injections in his troublesome knees at least every two weeks. To avoid doctors querying the amount he was receiving, he was taken to a variety of hospitals and clinics.

Soon he was unable to train much at all, relying on the drug to enable him to play each Saturday. He was a striker in true Roy of the Rovers mould and has long forgotten the number of times he quite literally climbed off the treatment table to trot out for a game. On one occasion, during an important cup-tie, he was carried off with yet another knee injury and then reappeared minutes before time to knock in the winner.

'Nobody told me that it was all right,' says McGraw, 'because we didn't have a physiotherapist. We had someone who knew a bit about first aid, but it was the doctors at the hospitals that gave me the injections. Nobody told me of the damage it would do. One or two of the older players at the club said I was daft to take so many, but I was young and I thought it wouldn't do me any harm.'

After about a year of injections and playing with them, he found it difficult to train. After every game he needed a few day's rest, and the mobility in his knees began to deteriorate. The club's answer was simply to step up the injections to ensure he could make the starting line-up.

'I really don't think I trained a whole week ever, after that, but it was easy for them to talk me into it. I wanted to play. The thing that I'm angry about now is that nobody told me of the consequences that would happen in later life.'

McGraw has never been sure that Hal Stewart, who is now dead, or anyone else at the club at the time, actually knew of the damage they were doing. All he did know was that after each game the pain in his knees was getting stronger and the amount of time he lost from training was growing.

In 1967 he was transferred from Morton to Hibernian, for a small fee. Now well past his best and beset by injury problems, he still managed to impress the fans at Easter Road. Before a third-round Fairs Cup clash with Leeds in 1968, McGraw was having problems completing any training and his right knee had puffed up like a balloon, but keen to play in such an important game he put on tracksuit bottoms and said nothing about the pain or the injury so he would make the team.

Hibs's physio saw the writing on the wall for McGraw, but he continued to play for another year and a half before he finally admitted defeat and was forced to retire at twenty-eight.

McGraw soon realised his problems were serious and he began to attend hospital regularly. About three years later, working as a storeman in the Glasgow shipyards while coaching Morton's reserves, the lack of mobility was becoming a problem and he had the first of thirteen operations on his legs.

His right knee joint had calcified, and the surgeon performed a bone scrape in the hope that it would help the joint move properly again. It did not.

'The next day the surgeon came in and told me I would never run again. That was a big blow because I had always been a fit person and at that age it was very hard to take.' The surgeon also told McGraw he had the legs of a seventy-year-old and that he would suffer increasing pain for the rest of his life.

Twelve operations later, McGraw has twice undergone replacement of both knees and the joints are a scarred assembly of metal and nylon. He has seen the best surgeons in Los Angeles and in Harley

Street. Quite simply there is nothing more they can do to help him. He takes the strongest painkillers to get through the day and sleep is a problem. The pills are dehydracodine, amputee strength, and he is allowed a maximum of six a day. He rarely takes less than four; any more than six and, as he puts it, he's off with the birds.

It puts a strain on every aspect of life, particularly at home, where his wife Jean and two sons, Allan and Mark, have to be vigilant. Two or three times a day the plastic and metal will lock and the joints have to be manually forced back together. It's a horrible sight to see, but not nearly as horrible as the agony suffered by Allan.

There have been many accidents. He falls quite often and because his knees do not bend the result is usually dramatic. The family joke about the lumps missing from the fireplace at home where Allan literally pitches forward into it. The worst incident happened a couple of years ago when his leg gave way coming down the stairs and his tibia was fractured by the steel pin supporting the plastic knee joint.

The worry now for the doctors is that because he had his second replacement joints fitted so young (he's still only forty-nine), they are unsure how long they will last.

McGraw likes to think he can be a sobering lesson to today's players. He's already had one definite success. His son severed his knee ligaments and was told by doctors never to play contact sports again. Many young men would disregard such advice, but when you see the proof of playing on with serious injury hobbling around your own house, it's hard to ignore.

'I don't want people to feel sorry for me,' says McGraw, 'what's done is done and I've accepted it. But I would like to think that it might help and advise young people: if a doctor or physio says not to play, then don't play. If you finish a football career in your early thirties there's a long part of your life left and you want to lead as full a life as you can. When you're young you think it will never happen to you. I thought that, and it's happened to me.

'I hope I do frighten people who take pain-killing injections because I think they are crazy.'

Understandably Allan prefers not to dwell too much on the future. The family don't much like the talk of amputation, but he admits it is a genuine possibility when the pain becomes too much. 'We try not to think about it, we try to be positive and just hope that medical science can come up with something new.'

To all those who suffer pain and disability, particularly sportsmen and women, Allan McGraw is an inspiration, while for sheer courage, guts and endurance, he's a class apart.

from MOMENTS OF GREATNESS, TOUCHES OF CLASS *1991*

Joe Mercer's Sad Farewell

MAURICE EDELSTON and TERENCE DELANEY

The dead silence of a crowd is rare and disturbing. It carries more emotion than any roar that ever blasted its shock-waves across the green of Wembley or Hampden Park. For a few long minutes of a spring afternoon at Highbury in 1954, you could feel the silence on your skin. On the field the players stood still in threes and fours. On the terraces and in the stands the eyes of every one of 33,000 people followed the only moving figures on the ground, the stretcher-bearers in their dark uniforms who walked steadily along the touchline towards the dressing-room tunnel. On the stretcher, with his broken left leg hastily bound in splints, lay Joe Mercer, Arsenal captain, twenty-two years in football, nearly forty years old. The blankets were drawn to his chin, and his long pale face was screwed up with the pain. As they carried him past the stand, he opened his eyes and rolled his head over towards the crowd. Then he pushed back the blankets, worked one arm free, smiled, and waved goodbye. A few people clapped him, and the clapping spread. Then, as those on the other side of the stadium picked out the bare arm waving against the dark background, the clapping grew, broke to cheers, and Mercer went down and out of sight to an ovation. That was the end of Mercer's career as a player. We all knew it, and there was respect and affection in the applause that followed him off the field.

Something more than his football had earned Mercer this salute. Yet his football was good enough. He won three League Championship medals, one with Everton and two with Arsenal. He captained Arsenal to two Cup finals, and took the cup in one of them. He captained England, and played in twenty-seven internationals. Mercer was a first-class left-half, but he was more than that. He had spirit, courage and determination; he was never half-hearted, never gave up. Above all he had the gift of breathing these qualities into other players. His example drove and shamed them into giving all they had. 'You might be just about ready to drop,' Denis Compton said, 'but you never did – not with Joe behind you.'

Two things about Mercer were unforgettable: his smile and his legs. The smile *was* Joe. It was not a handsome-boy smile, or a big-star smile; there was no affectation in it; it was natural, humorous and warm. It twisted his mouth sideways in his lean face, and the creases of it almost closed his blue close-set eyes. As to his legs, he had to listen to jokes about them from the day he first joined Everton as a boy of sixteen. They were shaped like a pair of brackets, the left rather more bent than the right; he walked with a sagging, plodding motion, and they gave slightly outwards at each step, as if they were made of thick wire. Mercer, captaining a team under pressure, looked like a farmer, with threshing in full swing and rain in the air – striding about with activity all around him, directing, encouraging, jumping in to help or take over, always near the centre of the work. There was no doubt who was the boss.

from MASTERS OF SOCCER *1960*

A Scandal

JOHN HARDING

The match was played on Good Friday 1915, one of the last games to be played before the league suspended its activities until the end of the war. Manchester United had endured a bad season, and were in danger of relegation. They needed a win to stay up. They achieved their objective but the Old Trafford crowd booed and jeered them towards the end of the game and there had been rumours circulating Manchester for days that the game had been 'squared' or fixed. Later it was revealed that bookmakers up and down the country had paid out considerable sums of money to people who had correctly forecast the result, in particular, the score, 2–0.

In the subsequent FA inquiry 'Sandy' Turnbull, old friend and long-time partner of Meredith, plus three other Manchester United players, were suspended from the game for life. Among the four Liverpool players also suspended for life was J. Sheldon – Meredith's one-time apprentice. Centre-forward West later took Hulton Newspapers to court, charging them with libel and thus the whole affair was heard in open court, including an intriguing cross-examination of Billy Meredith.

Meredith's evidence suggested that he knew nothing of the arrangements made before the match. Anderson, Manchester United's centre-forward, felt otherwise. He was asked by Mr Cyril Atkinson KC, for the defence, 'Do you say Meredith was not playing fair?'

Anderson replied, 'I think that they all knew something about it before.'

Meredith denied the allegations. He said that before the match he knew nothing about it being squared but after they had been playing for a bit, he came to the conclusion that something was wrong. He made a statement to Beale, the goalkeeper. At half-time he was practically starved, and after the second goal he got no chance whatever.

He was asked, 'In your opinion, could anyone have played in that game without suspecting there was something wrong?'

'No.'

'Was there any reason for such play at a time like that?'

'No.'

'If you had got the ball were you perfectly fit and ready to go on and take advantage of it?'

'Quite.'

Replying to Mr Atkinson in cross-examination Meredith claimed that he played his hardest whenever he got the ball. He sent word up the line to the captain and at half-time he asked what was the reason for starving him. They said they were doing their best. Meredith said he didn't think so. He would not agree with counsel that play in the first half was exceptionally good.

'Because you were not getting your fair share of the play?'

'No, I have had plenty of the ball when it has been a poor game.'

He continued by asserting that what had gone on during the game was unjustified in terms of footballing strategy and that he had been disgusted with the whole affair.

After three days of futile argument, the judge ruled for the FA and Hulton Newspapers. The rules of natural justice, he decided, need not apply in cases decided upon by the FA, because the latter was a privileged institution, with a duty to prevent dishonesty in the game. As long as the FA acted without malice, then those bound to obey its rules – i.e. clubs and players – must accept its judgements whether they feel they have had a chance to defend themselves or not. The professional footballer, it seemed, was still outside the law; the FA was still his lord and master.

Meredith's part in this shabby business seems to have been a peripheral one. Perhaps he watched the furtive arrangements going on from the corner of the dressing-room and simply turned a blind eye – he had seen it all before, and suffered the consequences. Perhaps he no longer cared what went on among his colleagues. There had been so much unpleasantness between the club and the players prior to this – the FA levy, the squabbles in the dressing-room, the wrangles with the club over his benefit money still outstanding. Perhaps he was content to concentrate on his new public house, the Church Hotel. He was forty years old; the majority of his playing colleagues were half his age.

Meredith never spoke again about the betting ring scandal; he would simply laugh, shift his toothpick from one side of his mouth to the other, and change the subject.

from FOOTBALL WIZARD *1985*

Colin Bell's Knee

BOB HOLMES

'When I used to watch Colin Bell at Bury,' says Malcolm Allison, 'I was aware that other clubs were after him. We wanted to buy him but were waiting for the money to come through. So, when in earshot of the other coaches and scouts, I would say things like: "He can't play, he's no good in the air, he has a hopeless left foot . . .". Until we had the money. Then we bought him.'

City were at home to United in a League Cup local derby on 12 November 1975, and Bell had embarked upon one of his characteristic runs toward the United penalty area after picking up a pass from Dennis Tueart. United's Martin Buchan was the defender charged with cutting him off. He raced across, and Bell saw him coming. 'I had three options,' he says. 'I could shoot. But the pitch was too uneven, and I was too far out. I could carry on but I decided against.

I thought I should check and drag the ball back inside him as he ran past me at speed. But it didn't work as my studs were buried in the pitch, and Buchan caught me. I knew it was bad.'

At first the commentator said: 'He's fallen over the ball.' But then he realised it was serious when a stretcher was called. But no one knew the magnitude until much later. Being 'out for a month' seemed bad enough, but that was before the full extent of the damage was known. Both an artery and a blood vessel had burst, but after a comeback against Leeds in April, clotted blood from the original injury caused a cartilage to splinter. 'That injury was the start of the end of my career,' Bell says.

Bell tried everything to get back: receiving extensive treatment, working out in the gym, running mile after mile. 'I flogged myself to death,' he says. 'But my knee was like a rusty joint; it needed lots of exercises just to get it going.' City seemed to suffer in sympathy with him, and the club's patience was a mark of how much he was revered at Maine Road. Said chairman Peter Swales: 'I consider Colin Bell to be one of the best players of all time and the most finely-tuned athlete I've ever seen. He's irreplaceable.'

Bell eventually returned in the reserves in the 1976–77 season and won a Central League medal, but it was the big time he craved. Countless comeback dates were mentioned, but each one passed with some further setback. Undaunted, Bell carried on, and City waited for him. Eventually, acting manager Tony Book named him as substitute for the Newcastle game. 'The plan was,' says Book, 'to give him a twenty-minute run at the end, but an injury to Paul Power forced my hand and he came on for the second half.'

'Word got around,' says Bell, 'that I was likely to come on and I could hear the crowd roaring when I came into the tunnel. I've never heard anything like it. I had a lump in my throat before I'd even got half-way through the tunnel. It just went on and on, both sets of supporters giving me a standing ovation that never seemed to end. It was a very personal thing, but I'd never expected anything like that. I was stunned and floated six inches above the pitch. I was just over-whelmed.' So were Newcastle as an inspired City suddenly responded to the crowd and to the presence of one of their elder statesmen. Summerbee and Lee had gone, but the sight of the lean, pale figure with the penguin flap of the arms as he delivered a thunderbolt of a shot or a telling pass, had the desired effect. Tueart knocked in a hat-trick and Brian Kidd the other to send the crowd home euphoric.

Bell was to make a further sixteen league appearances that season and played seventeen times in the following campaign. But, slowly and reluctantly, City fans began to realise that it was not the same Colin Bell. With the knee weakening, Bell was told that a further knock could render him a permanent cripple and, however grudgingly, he had to bow to the inevitable. He announced his retirement from football in August 1979. 'I could have played for another four or five years,' he says. 'But at least I had to be thankful I wasn't in my early twenties when it happened. Then I would have been really upset.'

Swales said: 'No words can express the debt which Manchester City and England owe to Colin Bell.' Mike Summerbee declared: 'I'm only sad we never saw his true ability. He could be in the box one second and then back defending the next, before you could say "Jack Robinson".' Franny Lee added: 'He was the most complete inside forward you'd ever see, coming from deep positions and making everything so easy.' Not bad for a player whose left foot was hopeless and who couldn't head the ball.

from THE MATCH OF MY LIFE *1991*

The Funeral of Duncan Edwards

ARTHUR HOPCRAFT

Edwards's funeral took place at St Francis's Church, Dudley, not far from his home. There were at least 5,000 people outside the church. The vicar made it a footballer's service. He said: 'He goes to join the memorable company of Steve Bloomer and Alex James.' Had he lived long enough Edwards would surely have joined the company of England team captains. Instead he left a memory of brilliance and courage and a sense of vast promise he was not allowed to fulfil.

His grave in Dudley cemetery is elaborate. The headstone has an ingrained picture of him in football kit holding a ball above his head for a throw-in. An inscription reads: 'A Day of Memory, sad to recall. Without Farewell, He Left Us All.' There are three flower stands, and one of them is in the shape of a football. It suits the nature of his class and his neighbourhood, and it is attended with great care by his father, a gardener at the cemetery.

His father, Mr Gladstone Edwards, felt he had to explain why he was working at the cemetery. He said: 'People think I came to this job because he's there. But that wasn't the reason. I had to change my work, and I've always liked flowers and gardening. I felt I wanted to be out of doors.' Duncan was his only child.

Neither he nor his wife could hide the depth of their loss. Nor was there any reason why they should try. When I went to see them Duncan Edwards had been dead for nine years, and Mr Edwards, at least, could talk about his son straightforwardly, although all the time with a quiet deliberation. He said that even then there was still a steady trickle of visitors to Duncan's grave. There were days when twenty people would arrive to look at it, like pilgrims. They seldom know that the gardener they stopped to talk to was the player's father. They nearly always said the same thing: that there would never be another Duncan. Mr Edwards added that Friday often brought the most visitors, and they were often lorry drivers with Manchester accents. They had stopped on their long run home from somewhere south. The next day, of course, they would be at Old Trafford to watch the match.

In Mr and Mrs Edwards's small, semi-detached house the front room is kept shaded and spotless. It was in here that Mr Edwards showed me Duncan's photograph album, and also let me open a glass-fronted display cabinet and examine the mementoes of Duncan's life. It contained eighteen of his caps at full international, youth and schoolboy level, to represent the eighteen times that he played in his country's senior team. Each was kept brushed and was filled inside with tissue paper. On top of the cabinet were three framed photographs of Duncan: one taken in uniform when he was in the Army, doing his National Service, another with his fiancée and a third in which he wears a Manchester United shirt. Beside them was a framed £5 note, which was the last present he gave his mother. The tiny room was dominated by a portrait of Edwards in his England shirt, the frame two feet wide by two-and-a-half long. The room was a shrine.

That showcase also had a copy of the order of service which was used on the day that two stained-glass windows were dedicated to Edwards at St Francis's Church. They are close to the font, beside a picture of a gentle Jesus which was given to the church by a mother, in memory of a baby girl. One of the windows has Edwards down on one knee and there is a scroll running across his chest which says: 'God is with us for our Captain.' All the survivors of the Munich crash

were in the church when the windows were dedicated by the Bishop of
Worcester in August 1961. Busby said at the service: 'These windows
should keep the name of Duncan Edwards alive for ever, and shine as
a monument and example to the youth of Dudley and England.'

from: THE FOOTBALL MAN *1971*

Goodbye to the Treble

BRIAN JAMES

But the subsiding motion of the crowd above the tunnel showed at a
glance that the Kop knew what we all knew . . . that the treble was
irreparably broken.

Anything and everything Liverpool did now was merely delaying
the moment when United men could leap in the air and go to collect
their medals . . . the time when Tommy Docherty could dance in
delight for the first time in eight visits to this arena as player and
manager . . . the time when everyone connected with Manchester
United would put on funny hats and run round the ground . . . the
time when the mobs from the Stretford End would go near-demented
as the trophy was trooped past them . . . and the crowd from the
Kop would bit their lips, try to remember their manners and applaud
Buchan and company as best they could.

A Cup final is a drama and it has a script. Losers, too, have lines to
follow. They shake hands with the winners, smile wanly over their
medals, wave to their crowd and walk away to leave the stage for those
rejoicing. And there at the entrance of the tunnel, leaving sunshine
that bears down like a spotlight. cold reality returns. Clemence is first.
He is a big, generally gentle, man . . . he would trample down children
as he covers the next yards, staring sightlessly ahead

Then Keegan. Trotting. A TV hand grabs him around the shoulders
and steers him towards a waiting interviewer-and-camera; he goes
without protest, as though to an execution with no hope of reprieve.
Kennedy manages a wide grin and a joke for photographers. The grin
drops from his face like a shutter two paces further on. Then Case,
head down and muttering. Then Jones, head up, eyes misty.

Smith follows, blazing with anger. He has a fistful of the injured

Phil Thompson's 'civvie clothing'. He is demonstrating the winning goal. 'He'd got my (effing) shirt. Like this. Pulling me out of it! Greenhoff! And that effing ref stood there . . .' His voice fades off down the tunnel.

Hughes is last. He sees you. Knows you, and an innate courtesy makes him pause. But his mind is in neutral. And he tries to say something. and can't. Tries to smile. and doesn't quite manage that either. So he punches you in the side and moves on. Wiping his eyes on a scarf thrown by a fan.

Inside the Liverpool dressing-room there is a silence that screams. Players move about like men under water. Some begin stripping for the bath. Most just sit. It doesn't seem possible that you can have twenty men gazing around a medium-size room and none of them meeting another eye. Yet they manage it.

Since we began this journey we have seen a few losers' dressing-rooms. That was inevitable. part of the shape of the assignment. You start to tell yourself that they were *all* like this – the same bits of bandage about the floor, the same litter of soiled shirts that had seemed such brave uniforms two hours before. But there is a difference. Not because the royal-blue carpet makes this a posher place than Tividale, but because of the scale of what has been lost.

Other sides have lost a game, a chance, a bonus. Liverpool have lost their place in history. One day some side may do the treble. Maybe even a side from Liverpool. But not these men. The disappointment is so intense that hardly anyone – even the press the following day – mentions that Liverpool have also just failed to become the fifth club in history to win the double.

The door opens to admit the FA secretary, Ted Croker. He is flustered and apologetic. There's been a mix-up. The Duchess has given two of Manchester's winners medals to Liverpool losers: Hughes and Heighway indifferently reach up and hand over their blue boxes . . . get red ones in return. Normally such an incident would have brought a tirade of mickey-taking: Mr Croker escapes in silence . . . it's still too early for sarcasm.

Ray Kennedy sighs theatrically. 'One day, perhaps we'll even win a match.' No one smiles. It is still too early for laughs. Bob Paisley starts to talk: 'Well that one's over, but we have still got the big 'un coming on Wednesday . . .' His voice, too, tails off. It's too early for lectures.

More of that appalling silence. What *are* they thinking? Keegan stares across the room . . . looking into the past hour? Or his future?

Then you sense what it is at the core of this mood – self-accusation. All of them have done what they could; but a few have not done what they were capable of. It is this discrepancy that now haunts them.

Terry McDermott suddenly grabs a Muppet; it's Kermit, the green frog. 'What a bloody mascot you turned out. Rubbish, you.' He holds it a minute then boots it explosively across the room. It lies for a while under a bench, being glared at. Then coach Ronnie Moran picks it up, brushes it down and places it in a kit hamper; he knows things said and done now will be regretted later.

Clemence leaps to his feet. 'I know what's got to be done,' he claims. 'Only one thing for it . . . tonight I am going to get SOOOOOOO pissed.' Many funnier things have been said in football. But for some reason this is the ice-breaker . . . gales of laughter. The dressing-room takes a breath, and begins to return to life.

The staff all start talking at once. Paisley, and his coaches Moran and Fagan: 'You were not disgraced' . . . 'Just wasn't our day' . . . 'Got to get our heads up for the *real* one' . . . 'Played worse a dozen times and won.' All the usual clichés. They don't address their remarks to anyone in particular . . . just spray the room, as though their words are disinfectant to destroy any germs of doubt. The players' banter also begins. Clemence and Smith start nagging the scout Ben Bennett about Manchester's second goal . . . 'Seen 'em a dozen times, you have, never mentioned they go for in-off shots did you? That wasn't on the dossier . . . you . . . you're useless.'

Hughes claims he's had news about the team's record 'We Can Do It'. 'It's still No. 1 in the charts. In Peru. But it's dropped to 87 here. How about a follow-up disc . . . 'We Can Nearly Do It?'

Keegan insists he has just discovered some consolation: 'It's still better coming here with Liverpool than with England. That's the first time in two years I've got off that pitch without the crowd singing "What a load of rubbish".'

The players, dressed now, leave to find their womenfolk. Going out they hear the gusts of hysterical laughter from United's dressing-room – just ten paces across the corridor, but light years away in mood. No one begrudges United that . . . they paid their deposit on this pleasure with last year's pain.

I walk around the empty track with Hughes. You can't walk in silence, so you start to speak, 'Emlyn, look . . . I know . . .' and fall quiet. 'Yeah,' he says. 'There are no words, are there? But thanks anyway.'

We go a little way and he begins again: 'I've been here a few times. Great place to win. But it guts the losers. I feel for the lads like Jimmy Case – Christ, what a game *he* had – and Joey Jones and Terry McDermott. That Terry, only young and *twice* he's lost. You feel it most for them. No, that's not right. You feel it most for yourself. Losing here . . . no one will ever get hardened to that.'

from JOURNEY TO WEMBLEY *1977*

Eyewitness at Heysel

STEPHEN F. KELLY

Wednesday 29 May should have been one of the most glorious days in Liverpool Football Club's long and triumphal history. Instead, the dream of winning the European Cup for a fifth time turned into a nightmare.

As we boarded a lunchtime flight from Liverpool's Speke airport that day there was every hope of another European triumph where players and fans would show the watching world that their football and supporters were an example to all. Once in the Belgian capital we were herded from the airport on to coaches bound for the Heysel stadium. Nobody was allowed to escape for even a few hours of free roving around the city. As the coach neared the stadium Liverpool supporters were everywhere, stretching along the roads and packing the pavements cheering each coach as it passed.

By now it was 5.45 p.m. with the temperature still in the high seventies. Outside the ground, the atmosphere was relaxed. Crowds sat on the grassy areas and Juventus fans passed by without any worry. Liverpool fans even swopped rosettes and banners with them. A fellow journalist and I walked towards the Juventus end of the stadium, a little apprehensive at first but desperate to soak in the atmosphere of the big occasion. Certainly there were considerable numbers of police and earlier we had had our first glimpse of the Belgian Riot Police wagons which patrolled the coach park threateningly. But what did surprise us as we ambled lazily around the stadium was the ease with which alcohol could be obtained.

Dozens of market stalls selling hotdogs, hamburgers and cans of lager and beer surrounded the stadium perimeter. It was cheap and there were no queues. With the kick-off still two hours away what better scheme to idle the time away than sit in the sun with some beer and hamburgers and join in the general revelry of singing, chanting and laughter.

At 6.45 p.m. we decided to join the quickly disappearing crowds into the stadium. Equipped with our newly purchased flags we approached the first barrier, a movable steel and wire fence about eight feet high erected by the police around the perimeter of the ground.

At regular points there were small gaps at which we had our tickets checked by the police. As we squeezed through the gap, another policeman snatched the flags from us, ripping the slim bamboo cane out and snapping it over his knee. And yet this display of bravado was not matched by any search for weapons or alcohol.

The tickets, for Liverpool supporters who had opted to stand rather than to sit, were for sectors X and Y and we made straight ahead towards the gate at sector X. As we approached, however, the police were turning fans away, claiming that the sector was full and that they should go to sector Y. This we dutifully did, only to discover that the entrance was a mere door, the size of any ordinary household door with only one policeman taking tickets. Not surprisingly, within a few minutes a substantial crowd had gathered, all impatient to get into the ground and growing angrier by the moment at the slow process. About seven feet to the left of this doorway the stadium wall came out at a right angle and this corner was becoming heavily packed. Some of the more impatient were already shinning up the wall to get in.

'Christ, it's packed inside!' yelled a scally straddling the eight-foot wall. I suddenly had a vision of having travelled hundreds of miles only to be locked out a few feet from the gate and was beginning seriously to contemplate climbing the wall myself when a baton-wielding policeman arrived on the spot and began lashing out at those half-way up the wall. I quickly changed my mind and settled for the push and shove of the crowd.

'Get that fucking policeman off the gate and let's get in,' shouted someone from the back of the mob. The crowd surged forward and sideways so that I suddenly found myself heading for the walled corner and in danger of being trapped and crushed. A young girl next to me was screaming and a father was attempting to pull his son away from the wall and through the gate which he was already half-way into. Tickets were being passed back for anyone without and the policeman, quite sensibly, had given up. There was no choice but to go where the crowd took you.

By this stage and before even being inside the ground it was quite clear that the Heysel stadium was not suitable to hold a major football match. Once inside the ground we could see that the terraces which stretched downwards were packed.

By now I had mislaid my companion in the crush and decided to make my own way down the packed terraces pushing and shoving to gain any distance. Worming my way through the heaving mass it soon became clear that the reason the top part of the terrace was so tightly packed was because most of those lower down were sitting, oblivious to the chaos above them.

As I looked over to my right, some thirty feet away, I could see the flimsy nine-foot-high wire fence separating sector Y from sector Z and consequently the Liverpool and the Juventus supporters. There was no sign of any police near the fence and, for a brief moment, the thought occurred to me that there really was very little separating the two sets of fans.

What happened next is history. We may never know the culprits who smashed down the fence, but whether they were National Front members or drunken Liverpool fans their behaviour was inexcusable.

From our vantage in sector Y we could witness the charge and the painful panic which swept through the terrified Italian fans. We could not tell how serious the incident had been; there were no stretcher-bearers and little sign of medical attention. There seemed simply to be confusion.

But we sensed that the night had turned sour as for the next hour and a quarter we waited for the match to begin, growing impatient as time dragged and legs ached with little sign of anything positive happening. The police continued to act in a bizarre fashion, bringing on horses which paraded up and down for no apparent reason and then bringing in riot-shielded police who faced the Liverpool fans accusingly long after calm had been restored. And when at the other end of the ground, Juventus fans rioted, tearing down the perimeter fence and threatening Liverpool supporters in the stands, the police watched casually. Even when stones, bottles and batons were hurled by them, the police still failed to react.

To add to the confusion we were given no indication of the magnitude of the disaster. Certainly there were some announcements but, on a tannoy system which had much in common with British Rail, they could hardly be heard. Indeed it was not until reading the papers the following day that I discovered that the Liverpool captain had made a personal appeal for calm on the tannoy.

It was only when the game was over and we had returned to our coaches that we discovered the full horror of the evening's catastrophe. Had the crowd known of those deaths it would probably have preferred the game to have been postponed.

As we hurriedly left the ground we had to face similar problems to those we had on entering. This time a larger door about seven foot wide was opened along with two smaller doors either side. But even this was inadequate for the converging thousands now intent upon escaping defeat and the sourness of the night as quickly as possible.

Especially dangerous were the two smaller doors, one of which had been the door through which we had so enthusiastically entered the ground more than four hours previously. As we pushed towards this exit the door which hinged inwards was being closed by the mass of the crowd and then reopened as some of the crowd forced itself finally through the doorway. Suddenly in a moment of panic I found myself being shoved into the space between the opening door and the wall.

We scampered quickly away from the ground towards the coach park and its security with the vivid memory of how Roma supporters had stoned coaches after last year's European Cup final still etched in Liverpool minds. Then we discovered the awful truth.

At first it was not believed but it was soon confirmed, and then came the sickening thought of how we'd sung and danced while the dead lay just a short distance away.

from TRIBUNE *1985*

Hillsborough

STEPHEN F. KELLY

High up in the Kemlyn Road stand sits a woman. It is a Monday afternoon. She is the only occupant of the massive steel and cantilever structure that stretches the length of Anfield, home of Liverpool Football Club. She has not come to watch a football match. She sits staring pitifully into space. Around her the upturned plastic seats glisten in the spring brightness. On the seat next to her lies a bouquet of fresh flowers.

It was my son's first birthday party. Saturday 15 April 1989. An event which demanded my presence. There was never any question of my going to Hillsborough. I stayed at home to supervise the jelly, cream cakes and games as well as the drinks for us older boys. It was just as well. I almost certainly would have been on those terraces at the Leppings Lane end of the ground. On the big occasions, I always preferred to be among the scallies, singing, dancing, cheering rather than sitting anonymously in some stand. At Heysel I had stood, on that ill-fated terrace, at one point within yards of the flimsy fence that would eventually topple the Belgian government and bring shame to Britain.

We listened on the radio. Beardsley struck the crossbar and then confusion. More trouble on the terraces, we thought despondently. I turned the radio off to serve the jelly. Nick looked bemused. His older cousin helped him blow out the candles and we all sang 'Happy Birthday'. It was the last time we were to smile for days.

The radio went back on. Still confusion; nobody certain what was happening but now it looked as if there had been an accident rather than crowd trouble. We returned to the party. Twenty minutes later I stole into the kitchen again. This time it was sounding ominous. Ambulancemen racing across the pitch, chaos everywhere, makeshift stretchers being prepared out of hoardings and behind the goal just a hint of disaster. The news quickly spread around the party yet none of us had any inkling of what was to come. Then the first chilling suggestion of tragedy.

'There are reports of some deaths,' announced a commentator stonily. The afternoon wore on and the figures mounted painfully. 'At least six people are feared dead . . . The death toll has now risen to more than a dozen . . . We have reports of twenty-two dead.' Around me children jostled and shrieked but you can't stop children enjoying themselves. 4.40 p.m. The game should have been finishing. 'Thirty-five are now known to have died'.

People began to leave. Nick, worn out, clung to his blanket. I switched on the television. All afternoon it had been relaying live pictures of the horror. Thankfully I had seen none.

Suddenly it was fifty dead, then almost as quickly sixty. I began to make phone calls. 'Did he go to the game? Was he standing? Have you heard from him?' Then my phone began to ring. 'Did you go? How could it happen?' In between answering calls we watched. Images now trapped in our minds. Faces screwed against wire fences, policemen unheeding to the calls of distress, and those makeshift stretchers. Poor Nick had a rotten birthday party. A day to forget. But we never shall.

Death inevitably brings with it many forms of ritual. From the perfumed smouldering pyres of Varanasi to traditional Mexican villages where villagers pay their respects by laying food, candles and water at the door of the dead. In Liverpool they adopted a ritual of their own. On that Saturday night the scallies sneaked up to Anfield and furtively tied their red scarves to the Shankly Gates. It was their ritual and the dead would have been impressed by it. It was reported on the local radio stations and as Sunday wore on more scarves, hats and flowers were added. By Monday the Shankly Gates had been turned into a shrine, as pile upon pile of flowers, wreaths, scarves and hats hung proudly and sadly from the railings.

Then someone asked if they could lay flowers on the Kop. 'Of course,' said the club and the gates were obligingly thrown open. By the end of the week half a million had filed past the Kop, laid their flowers, wrapped their scarves to the railings, paid their respects. They came from far afield to join in the pilgrimage. The mightiest in the land. Crown Princes, politicians, local dignatories, footballers, supporters, ordinary folk, some who had never even seen a football match, let alone Liverpool. We went with Nick. His first visit to Anfield. It ought to have been to the roar of the crowd. Instead it was in sombre silence. I threw my scarf on the Kop.

Gradually the wreathes spread, extending from the back of the goal to cover the goalmouth, then to hide the penalty area. By the time they closed the gates a week later half the pitch was shrouded in flowers. They said that in the early morning the fragrance and the gentle rustle of cellophane in the Mersey breeze was enough to make any grown man weep.

In Liverpool, that Saturday night, life came to a standstill. The pubs, normally a hubbub of clinking glasses and chattering foursomes, lay deserted, the cinemas empty, the clubs silent, the music switched off. By midnight the death toll was in the nineties. And the next day as the news began to sink in Liverpool turned into a ghost town. Its inhabitants remained indoors, sifting tearfully through their Sunday newspapers, listening to the local radio stations, hoping it was all a nightmare. It was how Manchester must have felt after Munich.

In the evening there was a hurriedly prepared mass at the Catholic cathedral. A white faced Kenny Dalglish clung to his wife; Bruce Grobbelaar, so often the clown of Anfield, his voice now shaking as he bravely read the lesson; John Aldridge shamelessly brushing aside his tears; the other players looking as if they had not slept that night. And outside thousands, listening, praying, sharing their grief. Footballers and fans so often accused of frivolity, now dignified as they mourned. A single choirboy sang 'You'll Never Walk Alone'. And you could hear the nation's tears.

Almost everyone in Liverpool knew of someone who had died. I knew of just one. A young boy, fifteen, who had gone to the game with his elder brother. As they rushed through the open gates they lost each other. Ian's last memory of his brother was seeing him being swept away in the crowd and down 'that dark profound tunnel'. Ian survived, somehow struggling out of the crush, to go in search of his brother. Imagine the guilt he was to feel. What do you say when you meet your parents? The younger brother in his care and he had lost him. He came to my house three days later and sat with glazed eyes, still weeping, a shivering, curled up, frightened teenager. A typical Liverpool scally, cursing and bitter. 'How could the police be so stupid?' he asked again and again. There was no answer. It was impossible to respond. He asked if he could have a copy of my history of Liverpool Football Club. 'But not yet,' he said. 'Soon.' He never did get his copy. He was a diabetic. Six months later they found him in his bed. He was dead. They said he had suffered renal failure. No way, he had died of grief.

Previously unpublished

The Pain of Defeat for England

HUGH McILVANNEY and ARTHUR HOPCRAFT

The men who were left at the Motel Estancia were concerned with their mutual loss rather than recrimination. They were glad of company, their own and that of anyone else who was available. To be alone was to invite a private showing of a horror film in the head. It was better to be out blinking in the sunlight, with other people's voices butting into their thoughts. Their faces had that look of controlled relaxation that comes when men try to keep a distance between what they feel and what they show. Most of the conversation was unnaturally casual, the way it is at funerals. They talked rationally, sometimes lightly, when they must have wanted to scream. All returned to the same unoriginal but acceptable analogy to describe how they felt. It was like being in a nightmare, waiting for the reassurance of waking up. Alan Ball, red stubble glinting on his chin, plunged into the small pool as if that would do it. 'Look at the pace of 'im, look at that *pace*,' he snorted as he splashed across. Later Ball would tell us that he had thrown the medal awarded for competing in the World Cup out of his bedroom window. His father, sitting up to an ungodly hour to telephone from England, had told him before the match, with that wet-eyed sense of drama that goes with the toughness of the family, that he should 'go out and die for England' if he had to. Ball never lacks such willingness but this time it had not been enough and he came back out of the water to join in reconstructing the nightmare. As in all nightmares, the central figures and events were at once familiar and unfamiliar. Bonetti was somehow not Bonetti.

'The Cat didn't look like the Cat out there,' somebody said. 'That first goal were a Weetabix goal,' one of the players added. 'And the second wasn't all that much. But you've got to feel sorry for Peter. He was only told he was in about half an hour before we left for the ground. No wonder he was a bunch of nerves. If he'd had a lot of the ball early on he might have sorted it out but there was hardly anything to do before Beckenbauer stuck that one in. In that sort of situation goalkeepers have no chance to find their feet.'

from WORLD CUP 70 *1970*

Torino's Munich

VITTORIO POZZO

Tragedies, like the one to which Italian football has fallen victim, leave one dazed. It is difficult to write about them, because writing about them seems an irreverence. Unusually painful to recall them, because the last image of the victims, the one which remains in the retina of the eye, is not one of vigorous and exuberant athletes, but of mangled bodies. Almost impossible to comment on them, because heart, mind, and pen refuse.

None of them can have suffered, judging by the condition in which they were found. The tragedy must have been swift, and death instantaneous, for all of them. A flash, a cruel burst of flame, and it was all over. That priest, who was the sole witness of the disaster and who happened to be on the other side of the solid wall of the church, which remained cold and indifferent under the rain, before so many dead bodies, must have had the impression that a thunderbolt had fallen from the sky. In fact it was the team of Torino, the international team of Italy, which fell from the sky in that terrible moment and distintegrated, dissolved into nothing.

In the buttonhole of a piece of a jacket hanging from a tree stump, up there at Superga, was an international team badge – one of those gold ones, with the new design, which I had still been giving out the previous year, telling them to hold them dear and reverence them, for there were little more than two hundred people in Italy who could wear them. Tenacious was the hold that badge exerted, tenacious unto death, when everything else had gone, blown from the players' bodies, shoes first, then watches, jackets, button. Precisely to whom that jacket and that badge belonged, no one knew. To one of the ten players who had worn the blue jersey, and who lay there now, battered to pieces or reduced virtually to pulp.

They made up the finest, strongest team in Italy. A team which had taken years to put together – I knew by heart every detail of the work which had gone towards building it – but which had then given such satisfaction. It had won only four Italian Championships because the war prevented it from winning more. Meanwhile, it had virtually won the fifth. It had had passages of play as shining and resplendent as precious metals. It had won the love and the enthusiasm of the crowds. In its best moments, it had surmounted every obstacle in its way, scoring goals with the facility with which a millionaire gives away thousand lire notes. It had been envied, seduced, at times even spoiled, by popularity, by the ease of its success, by the love of those who wished it too well. It bore a fine name, the name of one of those clubs which passing through joys and griefs, had succeeded in building Italian football out of nothing, a monument of imposing size and of social significance. In its qualities and defects, in its greatness and weakness, it was the genuine image of every human impulse. Gradually it was losing impetus and polish, now and then refusing to give way, with flashes of play which lit up the horizon. Perhaps it was for this reason – so as not to succumb to the common, fatal law of decay – that it preferred to die suddenly, disappear as though struck by lightning, go out with glory.

Now they are no more, these men who, in such numbers, changed the wine-coloured shirt for the blue. The problem of that square centimetre of groin, belonging to the elegant, precise Maroso, object of so much study by the luminaries of the medical profession, is no more. Gone is the question of the hard work Loik was obliged to do, so that he should not get too fat. Gone – because one of the two parties has gone – is the quarrel over the two marriages of Mazzola. All over: pulled muscles, strains, bonuses, arguments and transfers. All that's left is a team which was the strongest in Italy and which, at one blow, one disaster, has become the weakest; empty, shorn of technical means, a team which, if it wants to complete its Championship matches, must take the field – starting with the first match, against Fiorentina, in Turin itself – with the eleven boys who are the only reserves it has left.

Italy's international side is left, too, mutilated, largely empty of content. Ten of its players had from time to time been drawn from this strong, exuberant Torino; there were still six on the last occasion the 'azzurri' were called together. Missing, from this last international team, will be Bacigalupo, the surest and most consistent of our goalkeepers; Ballarin, the full-back whose dedicated life and application had given him international quality; Rigamonti, the born fighter, tough and tenacious as a sentry who refuses to allow his charge to be transgressed; Castigliano, whose class emerged spontaneously during those periods when he kept his body fit; Menti, who improved with the passing of the years; Mazzola who, capricious and effective at the same time, was one of the constructive stalwarts: above all it will miss Maroso, the purest, most classical product of his time, the man who, combining the gifts of a Rosetta and a Caligaris reached in every way the highest level of Italy's glorious football past.

They almost made up a caste, these players who filled our city with their presence and their deeds; a city which looked on them severely when they gave way to caprice, but was always ready to forgive them because it knew their worth, because it wished them well and because it was a little bit proud of them. They should be buried side by side, so that they can remain together in the future as they have lived together, won fame together, and died together. So that they can continue to form a team in the after life, too. So that it will be more natural, simple and human to remember them all, when thinking of the greatest tragedy ever to have stricken football, anywhere in the world, wherever it is played.

from STAMPA SERA *1949*

The Battle of Berne

FERENC PUSKAS

In this ecstasy of happiness and comradeship we returned to the dressing-room. We could still hardly believe our victory and were full of praise for each other's good work, when like an unexpected bomb a soda-water syphon crashed into our midst. Next moment the electric bulb was smashed. More bottles hurtled into the room, and we lay on the floor in the darkness. Then bodies flung themselves upon us. We were completely off our guard, confused and bewildered amidst the babel of grunts, blows, and cries from those who were hurt. It was a remarkable change from the intoxication of victory, and horrifying indeed to be fighting in the dark against an unseen foe; and even worse not being able to see whether the adversary was foe or one's own team-mate.

For ten minutes the fight raged, before it was at last broken up and we were able to check the damage we had suffered. Toth was unconscious and a doctor was trying to bring him round. Another player had a deep gash across his face, another was bleeding from a wound in the head. Everybody had some injury and carried some marks of the brutal, mysterious attack.

What had happened, we discovered, was that the Brazilians, whose dressing-room was opposite ours, had been unable to stand the noise of our rejoicing at our victory. Not unnaturally our excitement irritated them, but to such an extent that they lost their heads. The dressing-room door had been pushed open, somebody had kicked down our outside-right, Toth, and the battle had begun. What the Brazilians hoped to achieve by their unsporting attack, we never knew.

So ended Hungary's match with Brazil. On the football field we had won 4—2. But who had come best out of the 'extra-time' in the dressing-room it was impossible to decide. There had been no referee.

from CAPTAIN OF HUNGARY *1955*

Ibrox Park, 1902

A terrible disaster occurred in Glasgow on Saturday. The international Association football match was being played between teams representing England and Scotland, when one of the stands suddenly collapsed. It was occupied by upwards of 33,000 spectators, of whom many hundreds fell to the ground, about 40ft below. Three were almost immediately killed, and seventeen others received injuries which resulted in death.

During Saturday evening and yesterday the list of injured was very large, and no fewer than 170 persons are at present under treatment in the various city infirmaries. It is feared that several other deaths will take place. In addition to the injured who remain in hospital, eighty persons, after having their wounds dressed there, were able to go to their homes, while a large number of others had their injuries attended to on the field.

By a single vote the Scottish Football Association decided that Saturday's contest should take place at Ibrox. The park was laid out at a cost of upwards of £20,000 two years ago, and was regarded as one of the most perfectly equipped athletic arenas in the country. Accommodation is provided for 86,500 persons.

The crowd began to arrive three hours before the match began, and when the ball was kicked off at half-past 8 o'clock there was not much vacant space within the enclosure. The eastern terrace was densely packed, and late comers who did not wish to pay for covered seats in the grandstand made for the western end of the field. There they rushed up the stairways and went bodily down the terracing, causing a great amount of swaying and unnecessary jostling.

About this time the rain came on heavily, and this had the effect of driving a great many under cover. Hundreds made for the covered enclosure. So congested did the western terracing become that the crowd were forced to leap the iron railing in front, and quickly set about seating themselves round the track. Three mounted policemen who had been doing duty outside appeared on the scene and gradually made some sort of order. The break-in was due not so much to overcrowding on the whole as to the congestion which arose at particular spots. Then something went wrong with the higher portion of the western terracing, and the spectators fought shy of a large area of it, thereby crushing those in front so unbearably that there was nothing left for them but to leap the barricade. As people continued to pour on to the track in thousands, it soon became apparent that only with difficulty would the touchlines be kept clear.

It was at this time that the accident took place. Some of the spectators who were on the western terrace state that they felt the structure tremble, while at least one man left because he felt it swaying.

The tremor or swaying was followed by the cracking and rending of timber, and in a minute there was a yawning gap in the platform 70ft long by 14ft wide. Hundreds of people disappeared from sight through the hole. It was evident that a bad accident had occurred. Play was stopped. Indeed it could not go on, because of a melancholy procession of bearers who crossed the field carrying the dead and dying into the pavilion. After an interval of twenty minutes, play was resumed.

from THE TIMES *1902*

PART 8

The Verse

The Game

Follow the crowds to where the turnstiles click.
The terraces fill. 'Hoompa', blares the brassy band.
Saturday afternoon had come to Ninian Park
and, beyond the goalposts, in the Canton Stand
between black spaces, a hundred matches spark.

Waiting, we recall records, legendary scores:
Fred Keenor, Hardy, in a royal blue shirt.
The very names, sad as the old songs, open doors
before our time where someone else was hurt.
Now, like an injured beast, the great crowd roars.

The coin is spun. Here all is simplified
and we are partisan who cheer the Good,
hiss at passing Evil. Was Lucifer offside?
A wing falls down when cherubs howl for blood.
Demons have agents: the Referee is bribed.

The white ball smacks the crossbar. Stan rose
higher than the others in the smoked brown gloom
to sink on grass in a ballet dancer's pose.
Again, it seems, we hear a familiar tune
not quite identifiable. A distant whistle blows.

Memory of faded games, the discarded years;
talk of Aston Villa, Orient, and the Swans.
Half-time, the band played the same military airs
as when the Bluebirds once were champions.
Round touchlines, the same cripples in their chairs.

Mephistopheles had his joke. The honest team
dribbles ineffectively, no one can be blamed.
Infernal backs tackle, inside forwards scheme,
and if they foul us need we be ashamed?
Heads up! Oh for a Ted Drake, a Dixie Dean.

'Saved' or else, discontents, we are transferred
long decades back, like Faust must pay that fee.
The Night is early. Great phantoms in us stir
as coloured jerseys hover, move diagonally
on the damp turf, and our eidetic visions blur.

God sign our souls! Because the obscure Staff
of Hell rules this world, jugular fans guessed
the result half way through the second half
and those who know the score just seem depressed.
Small boys swarm the field for an autograph.

Silent the Stadium. The crowds have all filed out.
Only the pigeons beneath the roofs remain.
The clean programmes are trampled underfoot,
and natural the dark, appropriate the rain,
whilst, under lamp-posts, threatening newsboys shout.

                                                    Danny Abse

Billy Meredith

He's a darling, he's a duck, is Meredith,
And a mascot, too, for luck, is Meredith,
Though ten casualties we own
Still we don't break down and moan
He can play teams quite alone, can Meredith.

Oh I wish I was you Billy Meredith
I wish I was you, I envy you, indeed I do!
It ain't that you're tricky with your feet,
But it's those centres that you send in
Which Turnbull then heads in,
Oh, I wish I was you,
Indeed I do
Indeed I do . . .

                                                    Anon

Peruvian Nursery Rhyme

Poor poor Peru
If you only knew
What the boys in blue
Are going to do to you:
Too true!
Alan Bold

Kenny Dalglish

In a blinding flash
Of speed Dalglish
Is on the ball:
A player with all
The skills, a stunner,
A glorious match-winner
Who can make midfield space
Before using his pace
To come and score
Then bask in the roar
Of the crowd, arms in the air.
He could play anywhere
For, intensely creative
And imaginative,
His athletic mind seems to know
Exactly where the ball should go
And at the end
Of a buildup, his blend
Of strength, agility,
Natural ability,
Flawless ball-controls
Make unforgettable goals
From a volley, a side-kick,
A graceful leaping headflick:

Subtle, supple, cunning, quick
Dalglish, sheer football magic.

Alan Bold

The Sole Survivor

When the team took to the air
To return home
For a rapturous welcome
The fans followed on
Except for one
Canny Scotsman
Who stayed behind
His mind
Locked on one thought
Behind bars:
If he stayed put
He would have four years
To
Learn the lingo
And be one-up
For the next World Cup
In Spain in 1982.
Now, there's confidence for you!

Alan Bold

The Raconteur

Seeza gless!
Wait'll yi hear: lissen!
We showed thum kless
Oot there, we wur magic,
Just sorta took ower
The place:
Mind you, they're aa
Forinurs,

Dinnae ken much aboot
Anythin'
Hoo's aboot us, eh?
Hoo's afuckinboot us?
See Argentina?
See the burds there?
They're aa left-fitters.
Yi'd think Celtic rooled,
So yi wid.
See me?
A-coulduv pulled
Any numbera burds,
So-a coulduv,
Any number at aa.
Thur aa daft
Aboot Scotland:
Everywhere yi go
Folk ur daft
Aboot Scotland.
Ken kless when they see it.
Ken?
But the burds.
They wur fawin' aboot us,
Followin' us everywhere
Wantin' oor scarves
An' oor flags an' the claes
Oafoor backs.
Me, a-didnae bother
Aboot the burds,
Maist o' them dinnae
Ken a wurd o' English
                                    Alan Bold

The Pride of Scotland

Let Scotland clear the hackers,
The cloggers, the body-attackers,
Out of the World Cup for once and for all;

Take them apart with stamina and skill,
Show them how to play the ball
And not the man,
Prove to them a team can
Win with fierce dignity,
Without inflicting injury,
Without crippling permanently,
Without only malice for method
Let's win with Scottish verve,
With wing magic,
With body swerve,
With slick
Passes that keep us in possession.
Let our obsession
Be with magnificent football,
Not the unprofessional foul
That lesser teams favour.

Alan Bold

Ode to Everton FC

When at thy call my weary feet I turn
The gates of paradise are opened wide
At Goodison I know a man may learn
Rapture more rich than Anfield can provide
In Coulter's skill and Geldard's subtle speed
I see displayed in all its matchless bounty
The power of which the heavens decreed
The fall of Sunderland and Derby County.
The hands of Sagar, Dixie's priceless head
Made smooth the path to Wembley till that day
When Bolton came. Now hopes are fled
And all is sunk in bottomless dismay
And so I watch with heart and temper cool
God's lesser breed of men at Liverpool.

Michael Foot

Football at Slack

Between plunging valleys, on a bareback of hill
Men in bunting colours
Bounced, and their blown ball bounced.

The blown ball jumped, and the merry-coloured men
Spouted like water to head it.
The ball blew away downwind –

The rubbery men bounced after it.
The ball jumped up and out and hung on the wind
Over a gulf of treetops.
Then they all shouted together, and the ball blew back.

Winds from fiery holes in heaven
Piled the hills darkening around them
To awe them. The glare light
Mixed its mad oils and threw glooms.
Then the rain lowered a steel press.

Hair plastered, they all just trod water
To puddle glitter. And their shouts bobbed up
Coming fine and thin, washed and happy

While the humped world sank foundering
And the valleys blued unthinkable
Under depth of Atlantic depression –

But the wingers leapt, they bicycled in air
And the goalie flew horizontal

And once again a golden holocaust
Lifted the cloud's edge, to watch them.

Ted Hughes

Crack

cuts inty thi box
croass cumzthi centre hoff
a right big animull

crack

doon goes Dalgleesh
ref waves play on
nay penahlti

so McNeill complainzty im
oot cumzthi book

tipical
wan mair upfurthi luj.
           Tom Leonard

Yon Night

yonwuz sum night
thi Leeds gemmit Hamdin
a hunnirn thurty four thousan
aw singin
yilnivir wok alone

wee burdnma wurk then
nutsnur a wuz
but she wuzny intristid
yi no thi wey

well there wuzza stonnin
ana wuz thant happy
ana wuz thaht fed up

hoffa mi wuz greetnaboot Celtic
anhoffa mi wuz greetnaboot hur

big wain thata wuz
a kin laffitit noo.

Tom Leonard

'There was that Time . . .'

there was that time charlie tully
took a corner kick
an' you know how he
wus always great at gettin thaem
tae curve in, well charlie takes the corner
and it curved in and fuck me did the wind
no cerry it right intae the net, but they
disputed it, and the linesman hud the
flag up and they goat away wae it and tully
hud tae take it again. an fuck me does he no get
it in the net again. you should've
seen it. it just seemed tae go roon
in a kind o' hauf curcle. above aw their
heids. fuckin keeper didnae know where tae look.
and there was that time john cassidy went into
the toilet and there was no
lightbulb and he just had to fix up with some
water he found in a bucket. and here it was piss.
he didnae discover it until it was actually in
him. he was very sick after that. he goat
very bad jaundice.

Tom McGrath

By the Waters of Liverpool

So many of her sons drowned in the slime of trenches
So many of her daughter torn apart by poverty

So many of her children died in the darkness
So many of her prisoners slowly crushed in slave-ships
Century after red century the Mersey flowed on by –
By the waters of Liverpool we sat down and wept

But slaves and the poor know
better than anyone
How to have a real good time
If you're strong enough to speak
You're strong enough to sing
If you can stand up on your feet
You can stomp out a beat . . .

So we'd been planning how to celebrate
That great red river of Liverpool
As our team rose to a torrent
That would flood the green of Wembley
We'd been planning how to celebrate
The great red dream of Liverpool
For Dalglish held the Cup in his left fist
And the Championship in his right –
By the waters of Liverpool we sat down and wept

Our scarves are weeping on the gates of Anfield
And that great singing ground is a palace of whispers
For the joy of the game, the heart of the game,
Yes the great red heart of the great red game
Is broken and all the red flowers of Liverpool –
By the waters of Liverpool we sat down and wept.

Adrian Mitchell

Ode on the Kop

'Go home you bums' swells up the mighty roar,
The Reds it cheers, the enemy it daunts,
They go to pieces when they hear the taunts,
Ten thousand take it up, and maybe more,
With songs like this their team just has to score.

A new song rises, warm and comforting,
'You'll never walk alone', the Koppites sing.
The anthem then, until the throat is sore.
In three-four time they start to rave and swear,
Then 'easy, easy', husky voices bark.
They sway in time and wave scarves in the air.
Then sing a Christmas hymn as it grows dark.
No other ground has songsters to compare –
Except for Goodison across the park!

Peter Moloney

The Lost Captain

(*Herbert Chapman died on 6 January 1934*)

The last whistle has sounded, the great game is over,
O was ever a field left so silent as this;
The scene a bright hour since, how empty it is;
What desolate splendour the shadows now cover,
The captain has gone. The splendour was his.

He made no farewell, no sign has he given
That for him nevermore shall the big ball roll.
Nor the players he urged on, from his strong heart and soul
Strive again with his skill as they always have striven,
Not again will he hear when the crowd shouts 'Goal!'

But somewhere . . . somewhere his spirit will quicken
With victors and vanquished. For now he has cast
In his lot with the Olympians of old who outlast
This human encounter, this football so stricken
That it seemed for a moment to die as he passed.

Who shall challenge his name, who shall challenge the laurel
We hold out to him through the twilight? His love
Was in beauty of action, and clean limbs that move
With the pride of high combat above the mean quarrel
He led others to share it. And that is enough

Not yet for those others the Full-Time is blowing
The ball will roll on, they will cheer with their throats aflame;
They will think how this steel-minded man in his flame
Had dreamed while he worked, a dream ever glowing,
Of the glory of Greece in an English game.

Thomas Moult

The Death of the Referee

A shroud, a shroud for Spring-Heeled Jack,
The only honest referee,
A crowd to keep the devil back
And sing in tune 'Abide with Me'.

The pit unlocks its cage of doves
To tumble in the dirty air,
And far below the coffin drives
To meet the council and the mayor.

The barges drag through stiff canals,
Milky with clay and black with coal,
And as the varnished coffin falls
The mayor proclaims the grave no goal.

The colours of the local club
Flower to hide the yellow clay,
And all the foundry hammers throb
Their solace of the working day.

At home the silver trophies burn
About the mourning company,
And wishing she could be alone
The widow pours out cups of tea.

For Jack is dead, the man on springs,
Whose whistle trapped the wildest ball,
Whose portrait done in oils now hangs
For ever in the Civic Hall.

Burly with cataracts, the eyes
Are blind at last to local fame
And friends who fail to recognize.
A stranger in the golden frame.

But those who know their loss will make
The winter field his funeral,
And peel their caps to Spring-Heeled Jack
While brass bands play the March in Saul.

Philip Oakes

Limerick

Said a footballer once at Torquay:
'A chance for a goal now I see!'
With a most skilful flick,
He gave a great kick,
And levelled the score in Dundee.

Frank Richards

Easter Road

Green leaf or blade ye'll hardly pass
By *Sweetie Lane* or *Smokey Brae*,
But here's the 'Colour of the Grass'
The Hybees in their Arcady.

A' tools are douned in Redpath Broun
Bliss beiks in every factory,
And here's that bomba'dierin' soun'
O' Hybees in their Arcady.

Above yon emerald gate they cling
And faces flicker, licht as confetti
As play rins tremblin', string to string,
Wi' Hybees in their Arcady.

A busker sings 'The harp that once . . .'
A sky-daft brimstane butterflee
Vaults the high wa' to see this dance
Green Hybees in their Arcady.

Frae Arthur's Seat to Restalrig
The blue's their roof eternally,
There's no a team as jimp and trig
As Hybees in their Arcady.

When racketies like crickets chirr,
The reeds in Lochend wave as bonny
And whisper words that must be myrrh
For Hybees in their Arcady.

Long afore Parkheid saw the Cup
Or Rangers showed sae vauntily,
Never forget it was held up
By Hybees in their Arcady!

Dusk fa's: the air is shrill wi' whistles
Directed at the referee,
Wee Bacchuses clink bags o' bottles
Roond Hybees in their Arcady.

And then like fireflies, matches spurt
Among blue zephyrs o' tobackie:
Triumphant yet owre glaur and durt
The Hybees in their Arcady.

                                        James T R Ritchie

Boyhood

To some, engines, meccano, scientific experiment:
To some, stamps, flowers, the anatomy of insects:
To some, twisting elbows, torturing, sending to undeserved
    Coventry:
To some, soldiers, Waterloo, and miniature Howitzers:

To some, football
In the sadness of an autumn afternoon
Studs and mud the memorable dribble,
Rhododendron at the back of the net
And the steamy dark gathering over bonfires,
The weight of water from the loosened skies.
And fingers too numb to undo laces.

Alan Ross

Stanley Matthews

Not often *con brio*, but *andante, andante* horseless, though jockey-like
   and jaunty
Straddling the touchline, live margin not out of the game, nor quite
   in,
Made by him green and magnetic, stroller
Indifferent as a cat dissembling, rolling
A little as on deck, till the mouse, the ball, slides palely to him,
And shyly almost, with deprecatory cough, he is off.

Head of Perugino, with faint flare
Of the nostrils, as though, Lipizzaner-like, he sniffed at the air,
Finding it good beneath him, he draws
Defenders towards him, the ball a bait
They refuse like a poisoned chocolate, retreating, till he slows his
   gait
To a walk, inviting the tackle, inciting it.

Till, unrefusable, dangling the ball at the instep
He is charged – and stiffening so slowly
It is barely perceptible, he executes with a squirm
Of the hips, a twist more suggestive than apparent, that lazily
   disdainful
   more *toreros* term a Veronica – it's enough.
Only emptiness following him, pursuing some scent
Of his own, he weaves in towards, not away from, fresh tacklers,
Who, turning about to gain time, are by him harried, pursued not
   pursuers.

Now gathers speed, nursing the ball as he cruises,
Eyes judging distance, noting the gaps, the spaces
Vital for colleagues to move to, slowing a trace,
As from Vivaldi to Dibdin, pausing, and leisurely, leisurely, swings
To the left upright his centre, on hips
His hands, observing the goalkeeper spring, heads rising vainly to
    the ball's curve
Just as it's plucked from them; and dispassionately
Back to his mark he trots, whistling through closed lips.

Trim as a yacht, with similar lightness – of keel, of reaction to surface
    – with salt air;
Tanned, this incomparable player, in decline fair to look at, nor in
    decline either,
Improving like wine with age, has come far – born to one, a barber,
    who boxed
Not with such filial magnificence, but well.
'The greatest of all time,' meraviglioso Matthews – Stoke City,
    Blackpool, and England.
Expressionless enchanter, weaving as on strings
    Conceptual patterns to a private music, heard
Only by him, to whose slowly emerging theme
    He rehearses steps, soloist in compulsions of a dream.

                                                        Alan Ross

Football Grounds of the Riviera

Rock-cut, railway flanked, with sea edging its flat
Surface, Monaco hangs top-heavy over dwarfed white posts:
Casinos and aquariums bulge above the crenellated coasts,
Arc-lights strung along the Stadium like cloche hats.
Below, the pitch is smooth as green Casino baize
Whose wheels spin over water pink with haze.
Coated in sunset, the harbour's neat, dark palms,
Like roulette players, keep stiff their salt-drenched arms.

Scrambling over bald, dusty, but flower-scented ground,
Cactus gesticulating, olive-edged, make-shift, and public-owned,

Ventimiglia's forwards fan out round Bordighera's goal,
Jerseys striped like fishes in a noisy shoal.
Mountains bisect the sky with rocky signature
And sea-air modifies the players' temperature.
Mauve waves grow taut and spray the piazza pines,
As fishing boats trail their lamps in golden lines.

Menton at home to Nice, the French League leaders,
Sun only a rind squeezed dry of its heat,
And below us the voices of bathers scratch
At the cellophane air, airing ignorance of the match.
The tide recedes, drawing yachts in gentle retreat.
Outlined against mackerel sky, rack-bound readers
Golden indulgent flesh, absorbed in their books' spilled flush:
The insentient frontier hardens, the coastline in ambush.

Alan Ross

Acknowledgements

Acknowledgements and thanks are due to the following authors and publishers for the use of copyright material: Peter Doherty's *Football in Wartime* from *Spotlight on Football*, published by Art and Educational Publishers Ltd, 1947; *The Footballer* for Stephen Kelly's *Three Liverpool Goalkeepers; The Footballer* also for Stephen Kelly's *The One-legged Footballer*; Stephen Anderson for his original piece *One Campaign Too Many*; *France Football* for Albert Camus's *Football in Algiers*; the BBC for Galton and Simpson's *Hancock's Finest Half Hour*; Sheila Land Associates and Weidenfeld and Nicholson for extracts from Hunter Davies's *The Glory Game*; Mrs Mallalieu for various extracts from J. P. W. Mallalieu's *Sporting Days*, published by Phoenix Sports Books, 1955; Denis Law for his *Leaving the Lira*, published in *Living For Kicks* by the Soccer Book Club, 1964; Tribune Publications for George Orwell's *The Sporting Spirit* and Stephen Kelly's *Eyewitness at Heysel*; the *Sunday Times* for Ivan Sharpe's *A Merseyside Derby*; Macdonald & Jane's Ltd for *Dixie Dean's Sixtieth Goal* from Nick Walsh's *Dixie Dean*, 1977; the Kingswood Press for Bob Holmes's *The World Cup Final 1974*, *Wolves* v *Honved* and *Colin Bell's Knee* from *The Match of My Life*, 1992; Tony Pawson for *Bill Shankly* and *George Raynor* from *The Football Managers*, 1973; the *New Statesman*, now the *New Statesman and Society*, for A. J. Ayer's *Tottenham Hotspur*; Michael Foot for his original piece *Plymouth Argyle* and his *Ode to Everton*; the Naldrett Press for pieces on Bobby Charlton, Tom Finney, Johnny Haynes, Joe Mercer and Len Shackleton from Edelston and Delaney's *Masters of Soccer*, 1960; Headline Book Publishing for the extract from Stephen Kelly's *Dalglish*, 1992; the *Guardian* for pieces by H. D. Davies, Stephen Bierley and Cynthia Bateman; John Harding for *Edwardian Celebrations* and *A Scandal* from *Billy Meredith*, published by Breedon Books, 1985; Queen Anne Press for the extract from Simon Barnes's *Sports Writer's Eye*; Marshall Cavendish for the extracts from Brian James's *Journey To Wembley*; Jonathan Cape for the extract from Dan Kavanagh's *Putting the Boot In*; for the extract from the Estate of J. B. Priestley for *The Good Companions*; the Kingswood Press for Neil Duncanson's *The Dark Side of the Game* and Mike Rowbottom's *The Mind's Eye* from *Moments of Greatness, Touches of Class*, edited by Andrew Longmore, 1991; Dave Hill for *Black or Something* from *Out of His Skin*, published by Faber and Faber, 1989; the Football Association for Terence Delaney's *Boys in the Park* from the *F.A. Yearbook*, 1963; *The Times* for *Ibrox 1902*; Methuen for Harold Pinter's *A Night Out*; the John Arlott Estate for extracts from *Concerning Soccer*, 1950, and *World Cup 66*; the *Sunday Times* for Brian Glanville's piece on Lev Yashin; Harper Collins for extracts from *Saturday Boys* by Brian Glover, Willis Hall and Richard Jobson; the Arnold Bennett Estate for *The Town Hero* from *The Card*; Queen Anne Press for the extract from Frank Keating's *Sport's Writer's Eye*; Pelham Books for the extract from Bryon Butler's *The Giant Killers*; Harper Collins for extracts from Arthur Hopcraft's *The Football Man*; the Kingswood Press for the extract from Brian Clarke's *Docherty*, 1991; the *Observer* for pieces by Danny Blanchflower, Barry Norman, Colin Welland, Arthur Hopcraft and two pieces by Hugh McIlvanney; Wm. Heinemann for the extract from Pete Davies's *All Played Out*; Random House for Roy Hattersley's *A Yorkshire Boyhood*; Wm. Heinemann for the extracts from Eamon Dunphy's *A Strange Kind Of Glory*; the *Independent* for pieces by Ken Jones and Joe Lovejoy; Wm. Heinemann for the extracts from Hugh McIlvanney and Arthur Hopcraft's *World Cup 70*; the Geoffrey Green Estate for various pieces by Geoffrey Green; the *Daily Telegraph* for pieces by Michael Calvin and David Miller; the *Independent on Sunday* for pieces by Guy Hodgson and William Leith; John Moynihan for *The World's Greatest Save*, *Ajax* and *Brazilian Fever* from *Football Fever*, published by Quartet, and for *Tommy Lawton* and *Brentford Fans* from *The Soccer Syndrome*, published by McGibbon and Kee; the Estate of Bernard Joy for *Herbert Chapman* and *David Jack* from *Forward Arsenal* and *Chelsea* from the *Saturday Men*; Random House for Michael Parkinson's *Football Daft*; Pavilion Books for David Miller's *Stanley Matthews*; Mainstream Publishing for the extracts from Hunter Davies's *My Life In Football*; the *Daily Mail* for Ian Wooldridge's *Maradona* and *Burnley Survive*, Guinness Publications for the extract from Brian Glanville's *Champions of Europe*, Ted Hughes for his poem *Football at Slack*, Alan Bold and Alan Ross for their several poems, Alan Sillitoe for an extract from *The Loneliness of the Long Distance Runner* and Victor Gollancz for the extract from Nick Hornby's *Fever Pitch*.

Author Index

Also available from Mandarin

STEPHEN F. KELLY

The Kop
THE END OF AN ERA

'The Kop in its glory is an awesome thing, rising and roaring like a volcano, obliterating rival supporters and teams alike.'

Craig Johnston

'The whole Kop was chanting my name. I felt like a million dollars. It was terrific.'

Phil Thompson

'There was this aura about the Kop. They were the people, they were the fans, they were the heart and soul of Liverpool Football Club.'

Emlyn Hughes

Liverpool's Spion Kop has become a legend wherever soccer is played. No story of Liverpool's phenomenal success could ever be complete without reference to the Kop. More than 25,000 fans used to stand on these terraces, but now the Kop is going to be seated. It will mark the end of an era.

Stephen Kelly has talked not only to the fans but also to the players about what the Kop means to them, to referees, to the police, to the programme sellers as well as to the personalities who have stood on the Kop or played in front of it.

Stephen Kelly's book is a must for everyone who has seen the Kop or heard it in all its flag-waving, chanting glory.

A Selected List of Sport Titles available from Reed Consumer Books

While every effort is made to keep prices low, it is sometimes necessary to increase prices at short notice. Mandarin Paperbacks reserves the right to show new retail prices on covers which may differ from those previously advertised in the text or elsewhere.

The prices shown below were correct at the time of going to press.

☐	7493 1649 7	**The Kop**	Stephen F. Kelly	£5.99
☐	7493 1651 9	**Soccer City**	Shields & Campbell	£5.99
☐	7493 1596 2	**A Game of Two Halves**	Stephen F. Kelly	£6.99
☐	7493 1328 5	**Among the Thugs**	Bill Buford	£4.99
☐	7493 0991 1	**All Played Out**	Pete Davies	£5.99
☐	7493 0499 5	**A Strange Kind of Glory**	Eamon Dunphy	£5.99
☐	7493 0888 5	**Oaksey on Racing**	John Oaksey	£5.99
☐	7493 0293 3	**It's Been a Piece of Cake**	Brian Johnston	£4.99
☐	413 35901 8	**Offiah (hardback)**	David Lawrenson	£12.99

All these books are available at your bookshop or newsagent, or can be ordered direct from the address below. Just tick the titles you want and fill in the form below.

Cash Sales Department, PO Box 5, Rushden, Northants NN10 6YX.
Fax: 0933 410321 : Phone 0933 410511.

Please send cheque, payable to 'Reed Book Services Ltd.', or postal order for purchase price quoted and allow the following for postage and packing:

£1.00 for the first book, 50p for the second; **FREE POSTAGE AND PACKING FOR THREE BOOKS OR MORE PER ORDER.**

NAME (Block letters) ....

ADDRESS ....

....

☐ I enclose my remittance for ....

☐ I wish to pay by Access/Visa Card Number

Expiry Date

Signature ....

Please quote our reference: MAND